Readings in Race and Ethnic Relations

Readings in Race and Ethnic Relations

Edited by
ANTHONY H. RICHMOND

PERGAMON PRESS
Oxford · New York · Toronto
Sydney · Braunschweig

Pergamon Press Ltd., Headington Hill Hall, Oxford

Pergamon Press Inc., Maxwell House, Fairview Park, Elmsford, New York 10523

Pergamon of Canada Ltd., 207 Queen's Quay West, Toronto 1

Pergamon Press (Aust.) Pty. Ltd., 19a Boundary Street, Rushcutters Bay, N.S.W. 2011, Australia

Vieweg & Sohn GmbH, Burgplatz 1, Braunschweig

First edition 1972

Library of Congress Catalog Card No. 78–161451

Printed in Great Britain by A. Wheaton & Co., Exeter

08 016212 6 (flexicover)
08 016213 4 (hard cover)

Contents

Contents

RACE, POLITICS AND CONFLICT

Preface

THIS is one of a series of Readings in Sociology each of which deals with a specific topic in a broad comparative perspective. One of the distinctive features of the series is the inclusion, in each volume, of some articles translated into English from other languages. In preparing this volume the editor wishes to express his indebtedness for the help of Mrs. Margaret Hawkins-Widelock, who undertook an extensive bibliographical search of the English and foreign language literature on race and ethnic relations and provided translated abstracts of many articles which, regretfully, could not all be included in this volume. I should like also to thank my research secretary, Miss Diane Lindgren, for her help in checking bibliographical references and in typing the first drafts of the introduction.

A.H.R.

York University,
Toronto

Acknowledgements

ACKNOWLEDGEMENT is due to the publishers, editors and authors whose material has been reprinted in this volume.
"Ethnic, Caste and Genetic Miscegenation" by F. S. Hulse is reprinted from the *Journal of Bio-Social Science Supplement* No. 1, July 1969, by permission of The Galton Foundation. The American Psychological Association gave permission for us to reproduce "Race *and* Belief: an open and shut case" by D. D. Stein, J. Allyn Piliavin (*née* Hardyck) and M. B. Smith from the *Journal of Personality and Social Psychology*, Vol. 1, No. 4, 1965. "Colonialism and Racism in Algeria" by J. Cohen is reproduced from *Les Temps Modernes*, Vol. ii, No. 119, 1955. "Variations on Black and White" by R. Bastide and F. Raveau is reprinted from *Revue Française de Sociologie* 4 (4), Octobre–Décembre 1963, by kind permission of Editions du Centre National de la Recherche Scientifique. The American Sociological Association gave permission for us to reproduce "Color Gradation and Attitudes among Middle-income Negroes" by H. E. Freeman, J. M. Ross, D. Armor and T. F. Pettigrew from the *American Sociological Review*, Vol. 31, No. 3, June 1966. "Ethnic Differentiation: Ecological Aspects of a Multidimensional Concept" by A. G. Darroch and W. G. Marston from *International Migration Review*, Vol. 4, No. 1, Fall 1969, is reprinted with permission of Center for Migration Studies. Westdeutscher Verlag GMBH Köln und Opladen gave permission for us to reprint "Religion and Urbanization in Africa" by Leo Kuper from *International Yearbook for the Sociology of Religion*, ed. J. Matthews, 1965. "Contrasts in the Community Organization of Chinese and Japanese in North America" by S. M. Lyman is reprinted from the *Canadian Review of Sociology and Anthropology* 5, 2 (1968) by permission of the author and the publisher. "Racial Integration in a Transition Community" by Harvey Molotch is reprinted from *American Sociological Review*, Vol. 34, No. 6, December 1969, by permission of the American Sociological Association. "Stratification and Ethnic Groups" by Stanley Lieberson from *Social Stratification: Theory and Research*, copyright 1970, by the Bobbs-Merrill Company Inc., is reprinted by permission of the publishers. "Distance

Acknowledgements

Mechanisms of Stratification" by P. L. van den Berghe is reprinted from *Sociology and Social Research*, Vol. 44, No. 3, Jan.-Feb. 1960, by permission of SSR, an International Quarterly, University of Southern California. Population Association of America gave permission to reprint "Patterns of Occupational Mobility among Negro Men" by O. D. Duncan from *Demography*, Vol. 5, No. 1, 1968. "Race and Class in Latin America" by Octavio Ianni is reprinted from *Educação e Ciências Sociais*, Vol. 10, No. 9, by permission of Director do Instituto Nacionale de Estudos Pedagógicos (INEP). The American Sociological Association gave permission to reproduce "The Precipitants and Underlying Conditions of Race Riots" by S. Lierberson and A. R. Silverman from the *American Sociological Review*, Vol. 30, No. 6, 1965. *New Society* and *Atlantic Monthly* gave permission to reprint "The Politics of the Police" by S. M. Lipset, published under the title "Why Cops Hate Liberals—and Vice Versa", copyright © 1969, by the Atlantic Monthly Company, Boston, Mass. "Immigrant Involvement in British and Australian Politics" by James Jupp is reprinted from *Race*, Vol. 10, No. 3, January 1969, published for the Institute of Race Relations, London by Oxford University Press © Institute of Race Relations, 1969. "Economic Insecurity and the Political Attitudes of Cuban Workers" by Maurice Zeitlin from the *American Sociological Review*, Vol. 31, No. 1, 1966 is reprinted by permission of the American Sociological Association. (The materials of this article are treated in greater detail in Maurice Zeitlin, *Revolutionary Politics and the Cuban Working Class* (Princeton University Press, 1967; Harper Torchbooks, 1970), Chs. 2 and 3).

Every effort has been made to trace and acknowledge ownership of copyright. The publishers will be glad to make suitable arrangements with any copyright holders whom it has not been possible to contact.

Introduction

ANTHONY H. RICHMOND

THE term "race" is defined differently by biologists and sociologists. To the former a race is a large population which differs from another population in the *frequency distribution* of given hereditary characteristics. Thus it is a purely statistical concept. In practice biologists tend to avoid the term "race" preferring the more precise terms sub-species or gene pool. In sociology a "race" is understood as a category of persons whose social positions are defined in terms of certain physical or other characteristics that are *believed* to be hereditary. In race relations the deterministic and ascriptive basis of role-allocation is crucial. If individuals or groups act on the assumption that genetically determined racial differences exist and govern social behaviour the consequences for society are the same, even if the assumption has no scientific foundation in human biology. Whether or not biologists continue to use the term, the reality of race as a socially defined attribute cannot be denied (Rex 1970).

Some biologists have concluded that the race concept has little or no value in the scientific study of man. They emphasize the wide variety of physical types and the impossibility of drawing hard and fast boundaries between them. As Harrison (1969) pointed out, populations which differ genetically are linked geographically with numerous other populations which exhibit every grade of intermediacy in gene frequency and the variability of morphological traits. Nevertheless, Harrison is reluctant to follow Livingstone (1962) in denying the existence of races altogether. That there are genetic differences within and between large populations is not a controversial issue. Nevertheless, the evolutionary origins of genetic differences between populations remain obscure. Most anthropologists subscribe to a monogenic theory which postulates the origin of the varieties of mankind from a common ancestral stock. Against this view Coon (1962) argued from fossil evidence that five broad physical types may have existed before *Homo sapiens* emerged. He suggested that these types were distributed in various

1

parts of the world and achieved *Homo sapiens* status at different periods of evolutionary time. Other anthropologists have questioned Coon's evidence and his interpretation of it. Washburn (1963), in particular, emphasized that the evolution of races is due to mutation, selection, migration and genetic drift. He argued that it was impossible to understand the process of race formation in isolation from culture, without which the human species as we know it could not survive.

There is a persistent debate among social scientists concerning the relation between heredity and environment in the determination of human abilities, particularly measured intelligence. It is recognized that no tests of intelligence, or other human abilities and personality characteristics, are wholly free from cultural influence. The characteristics measured are *phenotypes*, i.e. they are the product of both genetic and environmental influences. In making comparisons within and between populations it is difficult to partial out the relative importance of genetic and other influences, particularly since they interact upon each other. The mean I.Q. (intelligence quotient) of Negroes in the United States is slightly below the average for the white population. Jensen (1969) argued that the difference could be due to genetic variation. Subsequently, Light and Smith (1969) showed that even if it is assumed that three-quarters of the variance *within* each race is genetic in origin the difference *between* the races could be due to wholly environmental factors. In particular, they showed that the differential distribution of Negroes and Whites by occupational status was sufficient to explain the difference in mean intelligence scores. Using computer-simulated models Light and Smith showed that "A large difference between black and white mean I.Q.s may be explained not by the hypothesis of genetic differences between races, but rather the non-genetic differences in the allocation of blacks and whites to different environments" (Light and Smith, 1969, p. 498).

The probability that most differences in measured ability and behaviour generally between populations socially defined as "races" are due to economic, social and cultural influences is strongly reinforced by evidence of extensive human migration and miscegenation. In an article reproduced in this volume Hulse (1969) points out that in the last few hundred years millions of people have been involved in extensive migration throughout the world. They brought with them not only their genes but their language and culture. The author distinguishes between race, understood as a genetically distinct breeding population, and both "castes" and "ethnic groups". He defined a caste as a "socio-economic group which is set apart rather rigidly from other groups living in the same geographic area". In contrast an ethnic group "is a recognizable socio-cultural unit based upon some form of national or tribal distinction, which lives among other people rather than in its own country". Although castes and ethnic groups may have a tendency towards endogamy, neither is in any sense a genetic group. Apart from specifically racial attributes that may be genetically inherited, ethnic groups pass on from one generation to another distinctive linguistic, religious and other learned cultural characteristics. Shibutani (1965) suggested that an ethnic group consists of people having certain social characteristics in common "which lead them to conceive of themselves as being alike by virtue of their common ancestry, real or fictitious, and who are so regarded by others". When a population is defined socially as a "race", it is because the characteristics they have in common are believed to be genetically determined while, in the case of an ethnic group, it is recognized that the characteristics may have been acquired as part of a cultural heritage.

It is possible to believe in the existence of distinctive races without subscribing to the doctrine of *racism*. The latter implies the belief that races not only differ from each other genetically but that some races are inherently superior to others physically, mentally or in some other ways. Banton (1969) defined racism as "the doctrine that a man's behaviour is determined by stable inherited characteristics, deriving from separate racial stocks which have distinctive attributes and which are usually considered to stand to one another in relations of superiority and inferiority". He distinguishes between "racism" as a doctrine and "racialism" which he considers to be the practical application of racism in social, economic and political policies. Banton went on to suggest that crude racist beliefs are rarely expressed these days by people defending ethnic inequality and discrimination. Instead, they tend to find their rationalizations in the social sciences. Against this view Tajfel (1969a) argued that racism is still widespread and that it serves a clear psychological function for many people. In another paper Tajfel (1969b) explored the cognitive aspects of prejudice and suggested that the common feature of those conditions which give rise to racist ideologies are a conflict of values or a threat to the individual's self-image. Change in the existing relationship between groups imposes on those concerned a need to account for the change in either situational terms or by referring to the characteristics of the groups. In seeking such causal explanations people tend to resolve cognitive dissonance by attributing negative attributes to others.

Belief in inherent racial superiority and inferiority may be a culturally

3

shared belief widespread in certain cultures, as it is among Afrikaners in South Africa. In such a situation the belief is reinforced by the fact that it is shared by other people and has all the attributes of "reality" for those concerned. Elsewhere, racist beliefs may be a matter of opinion about which there may be a good deal of dispute. Innumerable psychological studies have shown that the propensity to accept racist beliefs is character-istic of particular personality types. Adorno (1950) drew attention to the close association between racism, ethnocentrism and authoritarianism. Using a measure of fascist tendencies known as the "F-scale" he and his colleagues showed that early socialization experiences gave rise to a number of different personality traits which combined to form a typical "authoritarian person-ality". Such a person was particularly prone to expressions of anti-Semitism, colour prejudice and hostility towards minority groups.

Christie and Jahoda (1954) criticized the earlier work of Adorno on various methodological and other grounds. In particular, attention was drawn to the possibility of "left-wing" as well as "right-wing" authoritarianism. The original F-scale was evidently a multi-dimensional one and various com-ponents have been recognized including "dogmatism", "alienation", "conventionalism", and "ego-defensiveness". Furthermore, the concept of prejudice needs to be broken down into its cognitive, affective, conative and evaluative elements. Blalock (1967) reviewed the evidence from a number of socio-psychological studies that have been undertaken since the publication of Adorno's work. Blalock pointed out that if, for example, seven dimensions of authoritarianism and three of prejudice are identified, at least twenty-one relationships must be studied, rather than the single one between authori-tarianism and prejudice. It is evident that the psychological components of racial attitudes are highly complex. To these must be added such sociological factors as status inconsistency and the effects of social mobility. The latter was examined by Bettelheim and Janowitz (1964). They considered that intergenerational occupational mobility broke down social controls and created an anomic situation that was associated with a higher incidence of racial prejudice. However, more recent studies by Hodge and Treiman (1966) question this interpretation. The latter considered that the attitudes of socially mobile people were usually mid-way between those of the occupational group of origin and that into which they had moved. They were doubtful whether the experience of social mobility itself generated a need for prejudice as a defensive reaction.

Hoogvelt (1969) showed that people in Britain who wrote letters supporting the anti-immigration views of politician Enoch Powell scored high on measures of ethnocentrism and authoritarianism compared with a control group of students and those who wrote letters criticizing Powell. Other studies in Britain, particularly those of Bagley (1970), show the importance of conservatism and status inconsistency.

To Rokeach (1960) the tendency to reject a person of another race, religion or nationality is not a consequence of ethnic characteristics as such, but because members of other groups are perceived as differing in important beliefs and values. In a study reprinted in this volume Stein, Hardyck and Smith (1965) showed that belief congruence is more important than race in determining how teenagers feel about each other in the United States, only when beliefs are spelled out in considerable detail. Otherwise the subjects reacted in terms of *assumptions* concerning the belief systems of others, and/or the emotional or institutionalized factors governing the situation. There is no doubt that, in practice, there are substantial real or imagined differences in beliefs and values between racial and ethnic groups and that these stereotypes contribute to the persistence of hostility between them.

Stereotypes play an important part in governing race and ethnic relations. They are relatively fixed ideas about the characteristics of other groups that are passed on from one generation to another through the socialization, education, songs, stories and through the media of mass communication. Williams (1964) pointed out some of the functions performed by ethnic stereotypes. They help to maintain systems of group privilege, facilitate in-group consensus and, from a subjective point of view, help to reduce cognitive dissonance, affective ambivalence and incongruity in evaluation. Blumer (1958) suggested that race prejudice could be understood as a "sense of group position". The latter is not reducible to specific feelings of hostility or antipathy but is determined by the historical condition of initial contact, and varies in intensity subsequently. This "sense of group position" not only determines the status relationships between groups but the appropriateness of many kinds of social behaviour in situations of ethnic contact. Most of the psychological studies of racial prejudice and ethnocentrism have concentrated on those subjects who scored very high or very low on an attitude scale. The results have been misleading. As Richmond (1961) suggested, they do not provide an answer to the question "What are the sources of prejudice?" Research of this kind provides the evidence of *who becomes a deviant,* by expressing much greater or much less ethnic prejudice than is typical of the population studied. In other words, undue emphasis upon the psychological correlates of prejudice diverts attention from the historical and cultural factors which make antipathy towards minority groups "normal" in many societies.

Further difficulties arise in relating the attitudes expressed by respondents in a test situation, or in private conversation, with their overt behaviour in situations of racial contact. A knowledge of attitudinal factors alone is not sufficient to provide a basis for prediction. Merton (1949) emphasized the importance of situational determinants. A prejudiced person may refrain from acting in a discriminatory way if there are customary or legal sanctions against such behaviour. By the same token, a person whose personal feelings towards ethnic or racial minorities are sympathetic may be compelled to behave in a discriminatory or hostile way because, as in the Republic of South Africa, law and custom compel him to do so. The number of people prepared to risk fines, imprisonment or social ostracism as a penalty for their liberal attitudes is comparatively small. Linn (1965) has shown experimentally how verbal attitudes may differ from overt behaviour in situations where liberalism is put to the test. Readiness to pose for a photograph with a Negro of the opposite sex was related to whether the photograph was likely to be seen by others in the subject's home town. The pressures to conformity in an illiberal direction were quite evident, notwithstanding the tolerant attitudes expressed by the respondents in the environment of the college.

The relationship between attitudes and behaviour and the influence of particular historical and social conditions is shown very clearly in France. Racial differences appear to be of little consequence in the Bohemian Latin quarter of Paris, but Maucorps, Memmi and Held (1965) showed that prejudice and discrimination against Negroes, Jews and Algerians is widespread in France. More recent studies confirm the extent of racial and ethnic prejudice in France, especially against Negroes and Algerians. Among the historical factors that have influenced French attitudes the colonial situation, particularly in Algeria, has played an important part. An article by Cohen (1955), reprinted in this volume, shows that in Algeria the history of colonialism gave rise to a stereotype of "the Arab" which the white settlers of French origin accepted. This stereotype was reinforced by their everyday contact with Arabs in situations which did not give rise to any basis for mutual understanding or recognition of common interests. The outcome was a violent revolution the ideological basis for which is found in the writings of Frantz Fanon, particularly *L'an V de la révolution algerienne* (1959) and *Les damnés de la terre* (1961).

It is remarkable to note how similar the derogatory beliefs held by the French settlers concerning Arabs were to the beliefs of Whites in the southern United States or in the Republic of South Africa concerning the non-white population of those areas. Often derogatory stereotypes held by a dominant group will come to be accepted by a large proportion of the subordinate group as well, thus affecting their own self-image and sense of identity. Various studies have shown that skin colour is closely related to self-esteem among Negroes in the United States. Freeman *et al.* (1966), in a paper re-printed in this volume, suggest that colour gradation among Negroes in the United States is a status symbol, similar to occupation, which shapes the individual's personal world to a significant degree. Although occupational status was more important than skin colour in determining certain attitudes, anti-white feelings were stronger among dark-skinned Negroes. Among Negro women it was found that the skin colour of the husband was more strongly correlated with attitudes than the wife's own colour.

In recent years there has been a strong reaction among Negroes in the United States against the negative connotation of black skin colour and the other physical characteristics, such as hair texture and style, associated with it. The slogan "Black is beautiful" has been adopted by Negro militants and has had a noticeable effect upon the Negro image projected by the mass media, in advertising, etc., as well as in the actual appearance and behaviour of American Negroes, particularly the younger generation.

If we accept the view that race is a social category defining ascriptively an individual's position in society, it follows that this definition will become at least partially internalized. In a society in which race is an important basis of social classification, racial differences become an integral part of a person's self-image and sense of identity. A dominant group faced with threats to its power and superior status from below may attempt to combat a sense of insecurity by reaffirming the tenets of racism. A subordinate group that has no hope or expectation of improving its lot can maintain a sense of personal worth by attributing inferiority to the system rather than to personal inadequacy. However, ambivalent attitudes may emerge if the system is in the process of change and only limited opportunities for upward mobility are open to members of a subordinate race. In such a context, what Hannerz (1970) calls "the rhetoric of soul" has emerged among American Negroes. He suggests that increasing ambivalence concerning one's life chances is accompanied by doubts about self-worth. The vocabulary of "soul" is a means of idealizing the Negro's own achievements and proclaiming his way

7

of life to be superior. The term is found in connection with music, food, sex and general social relations with others of the same race, particularly in the situation of the black ghetto. Its original religious connotation derives from the importance that the Negro church once had, but those who now call themselves "soul brothers" are not necessarily church goers. Implicit in "soul" ideology is the belief that the way of life of the black man in the ghetto is not only different from that of middle-class Negroes and of Whites, but it is also superior.

Radical leaders of the Negro population in the United States have used the symbolism of "soul" and associated it with "Black Power". In particular, Cleaver (1967) provided an eloquent account of his own tortured response to the humiliation and exploitation experienced by many Negroes in the United States. It is not surprising that white racism has produced a reaction formation in the form of a virulent black racism prepared, if necessary, to overthrow the system by violence. There is a close parallel between the emergence of Black Power in America and the growth of African nationalism. The latter, also, has been concerned with the essence of "negritude" and the emergence of an African personality. This is a direct reaction to colonialism and European domination. It is to be found particularly in the writings of Leopold Senghor (Hymans, 1966).

Because race and colour are so closely related to individual and collective feelings of power or powerlessness there is often a simultaneous preoccupation with the related questions of sex and aggression. This is apparent in the attitudes of dominant and of subordinate groups. White stereotypes of Negro sexuality are commonplace and preoccupation with questions of sexual potency is characteristic of highly authoritarian and ethnocentric personalities. Fantasies of sexual aggression towards white women, symbols of the taboos placed upon the black man, are to be found in the writings of various American Negroes including James Baldwin (Jones, 1966). In the opinion of Bastide and Raveau (1963), whose paper is reprinted in this volume, the study of "psychiatric negritude" throws some light on these phenomena. These authors found that, among African patients in France exhibiting severe neurotic disturbance, the desire for a white woman clearly symbolized aspirations for fuller participation in the white world.

RACE, RELIGION AND URBANIZATION

In the United States the political "problem of the cities" has become synonymous with racial conflict and poverty in the black ghettos. A large-scale movement of Negroes from the south and of immigrants from abroad gave rise to an extremely heterogeneous population in most American cities from the end of the nineteenth century onwards. Wirth (1957) listed certain factors which determined the selection and distribution of urban population into more or less distinct settlements. They included occupation, income, social status, custom, habit, taste, preference, prejudice and the racial and ethnic characteristics of the population concerned. He considered that the simultaneous operation of density and heterogeneity gave rise to the segregation of urban populations into distinct ecological and cultural areas. Frazier (1968) showed that, as a result of selection and segregation following the expansion of the population, the Negro community in Chicago, before World War II, assumed a distinctive spatial pattern. He distinguished seven zones with varying social characteristics. In a similar ecological study of New York's Harlem, Frazier was able to distinguish five distinct zones. He concluded that, where a racial or cultural group is stringently segregated and carries on a more or less independent community life, such local communities may develop the same pattern of zones as the larger urban communities.

European immigrant groups in American cities also exhibited distinctive ecological patterns and marked segregation from each other and the native white and Negro populations. Lieberson (1963b) found persistent and continuing association between measures of residential segregation of an ethnic group and the socio-economic status of the group concerned. Nevertheless, income and occupation alone were not sufficient to explain the segregation of particular ethnic groups. Taeuber and Taeuber (1964) showed that in Chicago, the segregation of Negroes from the native white population was substantially higher than that of foreign-born Whites or native Whites of foreign or mixed parentage. Between 1930 and 1960 improved socio-economic status was accompanied by the *decreasing* residential segregation of white immigrants but an *increasing* segregation of Negroes from the rest of the population. Even when allowance was made for differences in income between Whites and non-Whites, actual residential segregation was eight times higher than chance factors alone would lead one to expect.

Racial discrimination has been the major factor in preventing the dispersion of Negroes. Restrictive covenants, differential criteria for granting mortgages, the policies of real estate firms, and the "flight to the suburbs" of the white population have been influential. In addition, the use of various sanctions, including violence, to deter potential Negro residents in hitherto all-white areas has contributed to the preservation of racial segregation.

9

Among other things, this has made it extremely difficult to enforce school desegregation in accordance with the Supreme Court's injunction, because schools generally serve a local population. Some cities have introduced elaborate systems of transporting children out of their own neighbourhood in order to achieve some degree of racial integration in schools. A distinction is usually made between *de jure* segregation characteristic of the southern states which is embedded in law and reinforced by local traditions, and *de facto* segregation. The latter occurs when patterns of internal geographic mobility result in racially homogeneous neighbourhoods. Edwards and Wirt (1967) reviewed the processes of school desegregation in the north and concluded that the strongest argument in favour of eliminating *de facto* segregation was the benefit it would bring to the educational experience of white as well as Negro children.

Even in those areas in the process of transition, where some degree of geographical propinquity between Whites and Negroes exists, this does not appear to give rise to effective social integration in the community at large. In an article reprinted in this volume Mollotch (1969) shows that in such a transitional community a slight amount of bi-racial interaction occurs in public places but integration is almost entirely absent from informal settings such as church socials, service clubs, taverns, and other recreational situations.

Although European immigrant groups have achieved a greater measure of ecological desegregation than Negroes in the United States, ethnicity and religion continue to be important bases of social differentiation. Fishman (1968) has drawn attention to the continued importance of language loyalty in the United States. The idea that America was an effective "melting pot" for ethnic differences was effectively dispelled by Glazer and Moynihan (1963) in their study of Negroes, Puerto Ricans, Jews, Italians, Irish and other ethnic minorities in New York City. They demonstrated that these groups maintained a distinctive identity and continue to make an impact upon the social and political life of the city. They concluded that "religion and race seem to define the major groups into which American society is evolving as the specifically national aspect of ethnicity declines". They suggested that in large American cities Catholics, Jews, white Protestants and Negroes each constituted a distinctive ethnic group differentiated not only culturally but in terms of social organization. A similar thesis was earlier put forward by Kennedy (1952) who suggested the emergence of a "triple melting pot" based upon religion. Herberg (1955) also regarded the distinctions between Protestant, Catholic and Jew as more important than language or nationality in determining the character of contemporary American society. Rosenthal (1960) described the Jewish community in Chicago as having a high degree of linguistic acculturation and high socio-economic status which were compatible with the persistence of residential segregation and the maintenance of distinctive social organization. He called the process "acculturation without assimilation".

American cities are not unique in the patterns of residential segregation and social organization that they exhibit. In an article reprinted in this volume, Marston and Darroch (1969) show that birth-place, length of residence, mother tongue, religion and socio-economic status all contribute to residential segregation by ethnicity in Metropolitan Toronto. In that city the most conspicuously segregated groups are Jews and Italians, but other smaller minority groups, both white and non-white, are also overrepresented in certain areas. Furthermore, ethnic minorities in Toronto exhibit a high degree of "institutional completeness". That is to say, a wide variety of professional, commercial, welfare and recreational services exists whose clientele are largely confined to a particular ethnic group (Richmond, 1967b). Canada differs from the United States, Britain and Australia in its explicit rejection of monolinguistic and monocultural values and assumptions. The entrenched position of the French-Canadian population in the Province of Quebec ensured that subsequent immigrant minorities were not subjected to the ideology of "Anglo-conformity". Nevertheless, economic pressures have tended to ensure that immigrants, even those resident in Quebec, learn English, although the mother tongue may be retained at home, in church and in informal relations with others of the same nationality. However, the increasing strength of French-Canadian nationalism has resulted in some direct pressure being brought upon immigrants in Quebec to learn French rather than English (Richmond, 1969).

In Britain immigration has given rise to residential segregation which is most marked in the case of non-white populations. Because the proportion of Negroes and Asians in the population is quite small there are no racial ghettos, comparable with those in the United States. Nevertheless, immigrants from Asia and the West Indies are disproportionately found in central city areas where housing conditions are poor. Peach (1968) has shown that West Indian migrants tend to move into those areas that are already losing population. Rose (1969), quoting evidence from the 1966 Census, considered that despite some improvements in the preceding five years West Indian immigrants were the most disadvantaged group with regard to housing.

Although the housing situation for immigrants was most serious in the London and West Midland connurbation, Collison (1967) showed that the residential segregation of non-Whites in Oxford was quite substantial. He found a segregation index of 42 for West Indians, indicating that more than two out of every five West Indians in that city would have to be relocated to achieve a distribution throughout the city proportionate to their numbers.

The situation in South Africa differs from any other country in that residential segregation by race is enforced by law. The Native (Urban Areas) Act of 1923 and the Group Areas Act of 1950 ensure effective residential segregation of Europeans, Africans, Coloured and Asians. Individuals and families may be forcibly relocated to an area designated for their particular racial group. However, the ecological distribution of non-white residents in South African cities is almost the reverse of that in American cities. Instead of centrally located ghettos there are vast sprawling African suburbs, typically stretching 15 to 25 miles from the centre of the city, housing industrial, commercial and domestic workers essential to the maintenance of the urban industrial economy. Nevertheless, under South African law, African workers have only temporary status in the towns. Although only 13 per cent of the total land area of South Africa is allocated as African "reserves" or potential "Bantustans", these are the only areas in which Africans may own land and are regarded as the place of permanent residence. This is irrespective of how long the person concerned may have actually lived in an African "location" or township close to the white-controlled mines or other industrial enterprises (Brookes, 1968).

The most intense antipathy towards non-Whites in South Africa is expressed by the Afrikaners of Dutch descent. Their attitudes are closely bound up with their own experiences as a persecuted minority under British rule. The strong Calvinistic element in the Dutch Reformed Church led to a reinforcement of their self-definition as a "chosen people". The Afrikaner population itself has experienced rapid urbanization in the last 50 years but this does not appear to have diminished their ethnocentrism. Lever and Wagner (1969) suggested that the most conspicuous feature of Afrikaans-speaking South Africans was the homogeneity of their racial attitudes, irrespective of whether they were living in rural or urban areas. They concluded that urbanization itself would not lead to more tolerant attitudes towards Africans or to any disenchantment with the policies of *apartheid* in the future.

Social organization

In an article reprinted in this volume Kuper (1965) has stated that when different racial and religious groups are drawn together in a single society, as in a colonial situation, new social structures and standards emerge which regulate the relationships between them. Traditional religious beliefs and practises undergo substantial modification in the process of urbanization, but these changes must be understood in the context of race and culture contact. Kuper argues that "African urban religions must be seen in part as a form of race relations". Furthermore, he indicates that differences of race and class combine to promote extreme social cleavage which may lead to political conflict.

In the African context it has been shown that, in the early stages of urbanization, migrants may not entirely sever relationships with the tribal community and territory of origin (Mayer, 1963). They may move backwards and forwards between the city and the tribal home although, with increasing adaptation to urban life, ties with the former place of residence may become attenuated. This does not mean that racial and ethnic affiliation cease to be of significance in the city. On the contrary, Rouch (1954) suggests that the processes of urbanization and industrialization may strengthen tribal cohesion and pride in race. However, Little (1965) considered that tribalism in towns takes on a different meaning for the migrant. Voluntary associations of various kinds assist the adaptation of the migrant to city life and the redefinition of tribal affiliation. These associations also perform important new functions in the rapidly changing conditions of urban life. A person may belong to a friendly society, a tribal association, a recreational group and be involved in an extensive network of social relations with others at the same work place or living in the same area. In this situation, voluntary organizations exhibit a variety of aims and greater specialization than is characteristic of the kin-based associations of the traditional tribal community. The associations perform a socializing function preparing the individual for the new roles he will play in the urban social structure. New status hierarchies are established and the associations may also be the basis upon which political leadership and new interest groups emerge sometimes leading to the affiliation of smaller associations into larger political organizations, expressing the nationalistic aspirations of the people concerned. In this respect, Little shows that voluntary associations perform important adaptive and integrative functions for migrants with various ethnic backgrounds.

The ways in which ethnic groups adapt to each other, and to the processes

13

of urbanization and industrialization that have brought them together, will depend not only upon the conditions in the receiving area but also on the social organization and values of the migrants themselves. Nagata (1969) showed that, among Greek immigrants in Toronto, there were marked differences in economic and social status that reflected generation and length of residence. She described the position of recently arrived working-class Greek immigrants as one of "precarious marginality in which two social networks must be managed and a narrow course steered between the demands of two cultures". She rejected the view that there was a unilinear process of change away from Greek customs to complete absorption into Canadian society. The evidence suggested that, once established in the host society, the economically successful Greek immigrant and his children can afford to reassert Greek interests, support the Greek Church, encourage his children to learn the Greek language and promote a sense of Greek identity within the wider Canadian context, with less constraint than the more recently arrived immigrant. In this situation, Nagata emphasized the importance of the Greek Orthodox Church as a culture-preserving institution. She noted that the Church received its strongest support from the second-generation Greek immigrants in Toronto.

In an article reproduced in this volume, Lyman (1968) stresses the need to consider differences between ethnic groups in their adaptation to similar conditions in the receiving society. In comparing the Chinese and Japanese in North America, he notes particularly the importance of demographic variables, cultural values and social organization. Whereas the Chinese in the United States and Canada maintained conspicuously separate communities, the Japanese acculturated and dispersed more rapidly. Chinese communities in other parts of the world have also retained a higher degree of autonomy than other Asian migrants. Although Chinese emigration to other parts of Asia, Europe and North America began in the middle of the nineteenth century, they and their descendants have not fully adopted the way of life of the countries in which they have settled. In contrast, the rapid acculturation of the Japanese has been very marked wherever they have settled. Lyman traces these differences to historical circumstances of emigration, the demographic structure of the migrating populations, the occupational characteristics of migrants in the receiving society and the different bases for social solidarity and community power. He concludes by criticizing Park (1926) whose original formulation of the "race relations cycle" led him to believe that a process of social and cultural assimilation followed inevitably from initial stages of competition, conflict and accommodation between racial and ethnic groups.

Other writers have criticized the view that assimilation is the inevitable outcome of contact between racial and ethnic groups. Lieberson (1961) made an important distinction between the consequences of contact between a superordinate migrant group that establishes a dominant position over an indigenous majority in a receiving society and the situation where the migrant group is a subordinate minority. He concluded that subordinate migrants were more rapidly assimilated than subordinate indigenous populations. Eisenstadt (1954), after examining the position of immigrants in Israel and reviewing the evidence from other societies, concluded that, under certain conditions, a stable pluralistic form of integration was more usual than complete assimilation. When the expectations of the host society and of the migrants are "balanced" or complementary (particularly with regard to social status and power) the stage which Park regarded as a temporary form of *accommodation* to competition and conflict, could become a more or less permanent equilibrium. More recently, Richmond (1969) suggested that, in post-industrial societies undergoing rapid technological change, migrants with high educational and occupational qualifications may be agents for the active mobilization of the material and human resources of the receiving society. Far from "assimilating" to the social and cultural conditions of that society, they form a migratory élite who do not necessarily establish a permanent residence in any one locality. He coined the term "transilient" to describe this type of migrant. In this context the racial or ethnic characteristics of the transilient migrant are less important than his education and technological skill. Gardiner (1967) suggested that, since non-white countries have now joined the ranks of nuclear powers, certain inexorable and irreversible processes of change had been set in motion, in which race and colour were not decisive agents. He noted a trend towards universalism which was most marked in institutions of higher education and scientific research. Against this view, it could be argued that the world as a whole is becoming increasingly stratified into the economically privileged and the economically deprived. This distinction is highly correlated with the broad classification of the world's population into "white" and "non-white" categories.

RACE AND ETHNIC STRATIFICATION

Shibutani (1965) pointed out that all systems of ethnic stratification involve the division of the population into categories in terms of their presumed ancestry and the hierarchical ordering of these categories in the social structure. Nevertheless, systems of ethnic stratification vary in the degree of specialization and the number of gradations. The social distance maintained between the strata also varies as does the extent to which the groups in contact actually differ from one another physically and culturally. Groups involved in a stratified social system exhibit varying degrees of ethnic consciousness and solidarity. Some systems are more formally institutionalized than others. In stable situations there may be a measure of consensus among members of different ethnic groups, at all levels in the ethnic hierarchy, concerning the appropriateness of the system and the legitimacy of the allocation of economic rewards, social status or political power. However, systems of ethnic stratification undergoing change rarely exhibit consensus on these questions. One of the most important dimensions of ethnic stratification is the degree of social mobility permitted to the members. In most systems of ethnic stratification, acculturation and economic success are not sufficient to guarantee admission to a dominant ethnic stratum.

One of the most rigid systems of ethnic stratification is the Hindu caste system. Béteille (1967) suggested that the organization of Indian society on the basis of birth-status groups and the acceptance of a hierarchical order ascribed by birth have given a distinctive character to the absorption of alien ethnic elements and to the place they acquired in the Indian social system. The unit of absorption appears to have been the community rather than the individual. Hindu society appears to have grown by adding new segments exhibiting a large measure of autonomy and separate identity. Ecological, genetic, linguistic and other cultural factors contributed to the maintenance of this autonomy. Traditionally there was a close association between caste and economic or political power. Conflict between castes was often over land ownership. Caste and occupation have been traditionally associated in an elaborate hierarchy, also involving ideas of purity and pollution.

Opinions differ concerning the applicability of the concept of "caste" to social systems other than those of the Hindu. Many sociologists have used the term in a broad sense to mean a rigid system of ethnic stratification exhibiting endogamy and a permanently ascribed social position based on race or colour. Thus, MacCrone (1937) described the South African system of race relations in terms of caste and the same terminology has been used in the United States by Myrdal (1944) and other writers. Van den Berghe (1967) considers that caste-like relations are typical of paternalistic systems that are most frequently found in complex but pre-industrial societies. Paternalistic systems are based at least partly on the consent of the sub-ordinated group who accept the legitimacy of the system although its stability may also depend on coercion. He contrasts this with the competitive type of race relations in which *class* differences become more salient than caste. In urban industrial societies, racial membership remains ascribed but there is more geographical and social mobility. In an article reprinted in this volume, van den Berghe (1960) points out that, in this situation, physical segregation tends to replace social distance as a means of social control. He suggests that social distance and spatial distance tend to vary in inverse relation to each other during the transition of multi-racial societies from paternalism to competition.

It might be expected that industrialization would itself be a sufficiently powerful force to break down racial and ethnic barriers and to promote effective economic and social integration on a basis of *achieved* rather than *ascribed* characteristics. Economic rationality alone might be sufficient to ensure that allocation to social and occupational roles would be on the basis of ability and qualification rather than race. Blumer (1965) has shown that this is not necessarily the case. Systems of racial stratification that were institutionalized at one stage of economic development tend to persist despite the pressures of modernization and industrialization. However, the emergence of new social classes, as a consequence of industrialization, may depend upon the nature of the preceding structural arrangements and the dominant ideology which may differ from one society to another.

Banton (1967) related the ideological aspects of racism to a Marxist interpretation which emphasizes economic determinants. According to the Marxian interpretation racist ideologies are a response to the requirements of capitalism and imperialism. Beliefs and attitudes towards minority groups are epiphenomena wholly determined by the economic organization of society and the exploitation of labour. The deliberate propagation of racist attitudes and the encouragement of ethnic prejudice divides workers against themselves and facilitates the maintenance of a dominant economic class. In an article reprinted in this volume Ianni (1962) examines the relation between race and class in Latin American countries using a Marxist interpretation. He examines the situation of Negroes and Mulattoes in Brazil and other parts of Latin America. Their position in the emerging industrial society was affected by their former slave status and by the various European immigrant groups who were also allocated to a separate and socially inferior category. The

17

position of the native Indian in South America differed as it was governed largely by a conflict over the use of land. However, the single common denominator in all these cases was the importance of economic factors in maintaining a relationship of domination–subordination.

Various writers have drawn attention to significant differences between the pattern of race and ethnic relations in South and Central America, compared with the United States. Pitt-Rivers (1967) pointed out that "segregation" as it is found in the United States does not exist in Latin America. Intermarriage is not regarded with horror. Colour is a matter of degree and not the basis of a rigid division between black and white. Skin colour is merely one of the factors which contribute to a person's social position and self-image. A person considered a Negro in the United States might be classified as *moreno* in Mexico, *canela* in Panama and white in Colombia. Colour tends to be an indicator of class rather than of caste in these countries. However, there are marked degrees of social differentiation that are based upon physical characteristics. Pitt-Rivers suggests that the status of ethnic groups in modern Latin America vary in number from a simple dichotomy between *Indian* and *mestizo* in northern Mexico to a more complex four-fold classification in Peru. He suggests that "if the concept of 'social race' teaches us to think about race in terms of social structure, we should also have a concept of 'ethnic class' to remind us that class systems no longer function in the same way once class has phenotypical associations. Processes of selection come into operation that cannot exist in a homogeneous population however it is stratified" (Pitt-Rivers, 1967, p. 555).

There is no doubt that, notwithstanding the extensive urbanization and industrialization of Negroes in the United States, they have not had equal opportunities for obtaining education. Even when they are well educated Negroes still experience discrimination in the occupational system. The quality of education obtained in ghetto schools in the cities and by Negroes in the rural south is poor by comparison with that enjoyed by the white population. Despite federal and state legislation governing fair employment practices, discrimination continues to limit occupational opportunities of Negroes, irrespective of their qualifications. In an article reprinted in this volume, Duncan (1968) shows the extent to which Negroes have been limited in their intergenerational mobility and in intragenerational mobility. In 1962 the majority of Negro males were in lower manual occupations. Negroes who originated at the lower levels in the occupational system were likely to remain there while white men were likely to move up compared with their fathers. Negroes who originated at the higher levels were likely to move down while white men were more likely to remain in a higher position.

Blau and Duncan (1967) examined the comparative social mobility of Whites and non-Whites in the United States. (The non-white category contained a small proportion of persons who were not Negroes but the conclusions apply primarily to Negroes.) They found that even when the occupational status of the fathers of non-white males, the lower education and first occupation of non-Whites were taken into account, the occupational achievement of Whites was still superior. The average difference in ultimate occupational status when social origins, career beginnings and education were held constant remained more than nine points in favour of Whites. Non-Whites were handicapped by having poor appearance, less education and inferior earlier career experience than Whites. However, even if these effects were statistically controlled, there was a residual discrepancy that could only be explained by direct discrimination against non-Whites. They found that non-Whites were more likely to be downwardly mobile, and less likely to be upwardly mobile than Whites. More highly educated non-Whites suffered more from occupational discrimination than the less educated. The same amount of educational investment yielded considerably less return in the form of superior occupational status or mobility to non-Whites than to Whites. An analysis of age differences suggested that opportunities for non-Whites in the north had improved in recent decades, but no such trend was evident in the south.

Immigrants moving to a new country may also be handicapped in their occupational achievement and social mobility. They may also experience discrimination, but language problems, lack of experience of the conditions prevailing in their particular trade or profession and the state of the job market at the time of arrival may also cause downward mobility after migration. Richmond (1967) found that, in 1961, 44 per cent of post-war immigrants in Canada had experienced downward mobility when the occupation abroad and the first occupation in Canada were compared. There were differences between immigrants from Britain and other countries. A third of the former, compared with almost half of the latter, had been downwardly mobile. A higher proportion of the British immigrants subsequently recovered or improved upon their occupational status before migration. English-speaking immigrants from Britain, Commonwealth countries and the United States tended to have higher education and occupational status before migration than the non-English-speaking immigrants in Canada. As a consequence they increased the association between ethnicity and occupational status in Canada.

Porter (1965) described what he called a "vertical mosaic" in Canada. Native Indians and Eskimoes together with Negroes in Canada had the lowest occupational status, but French-Canadians (who made up approximately 29 per cent of the population) were also disproportionately represented at the lower levels in the occupational system. Persons of British and Jewish origin tended to be overrepresented at the higher levels. Porter concluded that there was a white-Anglo-Saxon–Protestant establishment in Canada that tended to dominate the economic and political system. Canada's professed tolerance of ethnic diversity was a means of maintaining the existing power and status system. Unfortunately, in his examination of the patterns of occupational stratification and social mobility he did not control for parental origin, education and first job, as Blau and Duncan did in their study of the American occupational structure. However, there is little doubt that inequalities in the distribution of power and status in any ethnically plural society will create or exacerbate conflict.

RACE, POLITICS AND CONFLICT

Although examples of racial and ethnic groups living and working together in comparative harmony can be found, the fact that "race" is a social category and a basis of differentiation within a society means that there are potential differences of interest between racial groups which may become the basis of overt conflict. Coser (1956) distinguished between realistic and non-realistic conflict. The former arises out of objectively definable differences of interest and sources of frustration. The latter are the consequence of displaced hostility and the need for tension release. Distinctions must be made between realistic conflicts arising from consensus leading to *competition*, in contrast with dissensus which leads to *oppositon*. Inconsistent values or structural arrangements (nonsensus) give rise to *contradiction* and the reaction of subordinates to the exercise of power leads to *rebellion*. Conflicts between racial and ethnic groups frequently contain elements of all these forms of conflict which, when combined, may lead to revolution.

Rex and Moore (1967) singled out competition between coloured immigrants and the native population in Britain for scarce resources, particularly jobs and housing, as the main source of conflict between them. They minimized the importance of racial prejudice and non-realistic conflicts arising from psychological factors. However, Richmond (1970) showed that subjective orientations, including racist attitudes, were more important determinants of attitudes and behaviour towards coloured immigrants than the housing class to which the white resident belonged. In an earlier study, Richmond (1950) drew attention to the relation between economic insecurity, stereotype formation and manifestations of racial prejudice and conflict. Racial disturbances in Liverpool, England, in 1948, were closely related to the experiences of unemployment and economic insecurity of both white and coloured workers. In a later study by Richmond (1960) it was shown that the race riots, which broke out in London and Nottingham in 1958, were partly the consequence of a sudden rise in juvenile unemployment in those cities.

In an article reprinted in this volume, Zeitlin (1966) examines the relation between economic insecurity and the political attitudes of Cuban workers. He shows that, among Negroes and Whites, those who experienced the most pre-revolutionary unemployment were more likely to support the revolution. Those who were in secure employment both before and after the revolution were less likely to support the new political régime than those who were employed more regularly since the revolution. Even when pre-revolutionary employment status and subsequent change in employment status were controlled, Negroes were more likely than Whites to support the revolution. However, Negroes experiencing pre-revolutionary unemployment were not necessarily more pro-communist before the revolution. Zeitlin attributes this to the inferior racial status of Negroes before the revolution which meant they were less likely to see the situation in class terms. Subsequently, the combination of racial membership and pre-revolutionary unemployment combined to make them more favourable towards the revolution than Whites.

Conflict and tension between racial and ethnic groups may persist for long periods without necessarily giving rise to violence. It is necessary to distinguish between the underlying and precipitating causes of race riots and other forms of violent conflict. Grimshaw (1960) drew attention to differences between the riots which occurred in American cities before and after World War II. Ecological factors appeared to be important in this respect particularly those relating to population growth and movement. The earlier riots were largely attacks by Whites upon Negroes. More recent racial disturbances in the United States seem to be attacks by Negroes upon white property and symbols of authority. In an article reprinted in this volume Lieberson and Silverman (1965) examine the factors associated with race riots in America between 1913 and 1963. Precipitating causes included rape, murder, assault and police brutality. Contrary to hypothesis, demographic and housing characteristics were not significantly associated with race riots. They found no evidence that riots were due to communist influence, hoodlums or rabble rousers. Riots were most likely to occur in communities where institutional malfunctioning, cross-pressures or other inadequacies meant that there was no effective machinery for dealing with legitimate grievances.

Campbell and Schuman (1968) undertook a study of racial attitudes towards violence on behalf of the U.S. Advisory Commission on Civil Disorders. They found that advocacy of violence was several times more likely among males between 16 and 19 years than among women or older men. Surprisingly, education did not appear to be a significant influence. However, there is some reason to suppose that status inconsistency may be more important than actual levels of education or occupational status. In other words, when an above average education does not enable a person to obtain a commensurate income or occupational status there will be a predisposition to condone or engage in violence. Campbell and Schuman point out that most *interracial* violence in American history has been directed towards Negroes by Whites, rather than the reverse. They showed that about one in five white male teenagers said that "Whites should do some rioting". This was approximately the same proportion as for black male teenagers. They concluded that "what at first might have been taken as a racial phenomenon somehow peculiar to young Negro males seems now to be explicable more easily in terms of a conception of teenage masculine daring that has little to do with race".

The U.S. National Advisory Commission on Civil Disorders (1967) considered that the incidence of physical abuse or harassment of Negroes by white police was probably exaggerated. However, the belief that police brutality and harassment occurred frequently in Negro neighbourhoods was one of the major reasons for intense Negro resentment against the police. In an article reprinted in this volume Lipset (1969) examines some of the factors which make the police in the United States unsympathetic towards Negroes and conservative in their attitude towards the use of force and the maintenance of law and order. He considered that here also status inconsistency may be a contributory factor in determining police attitudes and behaviour. In some cases radical extremists deliberately provoked the police into a violent reaction and this may have exacerbated the right wing and authoritarian predispositions of many police. Banton (1964) drew attention to some of the role conflicts experienced by police which can be particularly acute in a situation of inter-ethnic conflict.

A systematic study of the relation between ethnic minorities and the police was undertaken by Bayley and Mendelsohn (1969) in the city of Denver, Colorado. They found a good deal of mutual suspicion between the police on the one hand and Negroes and other minority groups on the other. From the point of view of the minorities the police stood for power and authority and were visible signs of majority domination. Police in their turn were suspicious of the ethnic minorities and were apprehensive of the hostility which they believed existed in minority neighbourhoods. Although the police shared the fundamental attitudes of the majority group their expectations were not primarily the result of prejudice. The police felt cynical and sometimes angry because they were asked to maintain law and order in tense situations, not of their own making. The authors concluded that removing prejudiced policemen would no more improve police-minority relations than seeking "outside agitators" would eliminate urban riots. Similar problems in the relations between police and ethnic minorities undoubtedly exist in many countries. For example, Lambert (1970) examined the relations between police and immigrants in Britain and concluded that the policeman, like most white people, has little understanding of the immigrant community or of race relations but that individual officers and the police service must relate to coloured citizens in ways which enable the traditional public service role of the police to be effectively performed.

When racial and ethnic minorities, whether immigrant or native-born, are effectively integrated in the political system and feel that their legitimate needs can be met through normal democratic processes and institutional channels there is less likelihood of overt conflict and violence. If a minority group feels politically alienated, it is more likely to engage in anti-social behaviour and respond to totalitarian appeals either from the radical left or the radical right. Exponents of "black power" in the United States, such as Stokely Carmichael, through organizations such as S.N.C.C., have endeavoured to win political power for impoverished southern blacks and establish an independent party. Where Negroes are in a majority they seek to control local government and where they are a minority they seek proper representation and sharing of control. An ultimate aim is creation of a national "Black Panther Party" which will ensure the election of representatives who will speak to the needs of the black population (Carmichael and Hamilton, 1967).

In an article reprinted in this volume, Jupp (1969) suggests that the political institutions of America are incapable of satisfying the Negro population. He examines the situation of immigrants and ethnic minorities in America, Britain and Australia and finds important differences between them. He suggests that "provided that all constitutional channels are kept open and that discrimination is progressively reduced by legislation and example, there is little reason to suppose that Britain or Australia will produce a militant radical generation of immigrant origin". However, he expresses some doubt whether, in fact, Britain will succeed in reducing discrimination or increasing the political integration of first- and second-generation immigrants. This suggests that the situation in Britain could become polarized, with white racists and black radicals in open conflict.

Potentially the most serious outbreaks of violent conflict between races is likely to occur in southern Africa (especially the Republic of South Africa and Rhodesia). Gluckman (1955) showed that, despite the evidence of racial discrimination and segregation in South Africa, the colour bar generated some cross-cutting ties which contributed to the cohesion of the society and reduced the probability of overt conflict. A multi-racial society, or one in which there are a number of ethnic minorities, is subject to both centrifugal and centripetal pressures. However, when differences of race, language, class, religion and political power are superimposed on each other, opportunities for co-operative relationships and loyalties which transcend racial boundaries are substantially reduced. Under these conditions, what Gluckman has called the "bonds of the colour bar" will be severed. The probability of violent conflict in South Africa has undoubtedly increased since Gluckman made his observations. Legum (1967) has pointed out that the South African political system demands increasing coercion in defence of white supremacy and this progressively isolates the Republic from the international community. The ideology of the nationalist party in South Africa pursuing a policy of *apartheid* is that total control over the sources of power must be retained by the white minority and that this objective justifies any coercive means necessary to secure it. Not only has the non-white majority been stripped of all effective political representation, but repressive legislation has been enacted which ensures that even the mildest criticism or protest against the regime by black or white liberals is severely penalized. Until 1960 the African National Congress advocated only non-violent methods of opposition. In the face of increasing coercion by the government violent opposition is now regarded as necessary by many who formerly hoped to achieve their aspirations peacefully. Other African and communist countries are now believed to be training guerrillas who will engage in an armed liberation struggle. There is no doubt that the other African states are committed to the destruction of white supremacy; but it is unlikely that they will be able to pursue this goal so long as their own economic position is so much weaker than that of South Africa. Legum considers that a transfer of power from the white minority to the black majority in South Africa will only result from the application of force, either inside the Republic or by such agencies as the Organization of African Unity, communist countries in support of national liberation movements, or the United Nations. However, he thinks it unlikely that the United Nations or Western powers will become directly involved unless and until they feel their own interests are threatened. The unwillingness of the white minority in South Africa to sacrifice immediate economic interests for longer-term survival may sow the seeds of a race war on a global scale.

Counter-ideologies, developed by and on behalf of oppressed minorities, which glorify violence and civil war as a means of collective catharsis and liberation, have tremendous appeal to young people of all races everywhere today. The fact that the ideologies which sustain oppression and those which seek to destroy it are not held exclusively by any one racial group may be the one hopeful sign for race relations in the future.

BIBLIOGRAPHY

ADORNO, T. W., FRENKEL-BRUNSWICK, ELSE, LEVINSON, D. J. and NEVITT SANFORD, R. (1950) *The Authoritarian Personality*. New York: Harper. American Jewish Committee, Studies in Prejudice.

BAGLEY, CHRISTOPHER (1970) *Social Structure and Prejudice in Five English Boroughs*. London: Institute of Race Relations, Special Series.

BANTON, MICHAEL (1964) *The Policeman in the Community*. London: Tavistock Publications.

BANTON, MICHAEL (1967) *Race Relations*. London: Tavistock Publications.

BANTON, MICHAEL (1969) What do we mean by racism? *New Society* 13 (341), 551–4.

BASTIDE, ROGER and RAVEAU, FRANÇOIS (1963) Variations on black and white. *Revue Française de Sociologie* 4, 387–94.

BAYLEY, D. H. and MENDELSOHN, HAROLD (1968) *Minorities and the Police*. New York: The Free Press.

BETEILLE, ANDRÉ (1967) Race and descent as social categories in India. *Daedalus* (Spring), pp. 444–63.

A. H. Richmond

BETTELHEIM, BRUNO and JANOWITZ, MORRIS (1964) *Social Change and Prejudice, Including Dynamics of Prejudice.* New York: The Free Press.

BLALOCK, H. (1967) *Toward a Theory of Minority Group Relations.* New York: Wiley.

BLAU, PETER and DUNCAN, O. D. (1967) *The American Occupational Structure.* New York: Wiley.

BLUMER, HERBERT (1958) Race prejudice as a sense of group position. *Pacific Sociological Review* 1 (1), 3–7.

BLUMER, HERBERT (1965) Industrialisation and race relations in GUY HUNTER (ed.), *Industrialisation and Race Relations: A Symposium.* London: Oxford University Press, pp. 220–53.

BROOKES, EDGAR HARRY (1968) *Apartheid.* London: Routledge & Kegan Paul.

CAMPBELL, ANGUS and SCHUMAN, HOWARD (1968) *Racial Attitudes in Fifteen American Cities.* A Preliminary Report Prepared for the National Advisory Commission on Civil Disorders. Ann Arbor: Institute for Social Research, The University of Michigan.

CARMICHAEL, STOKELY and HAMILTON, CHARLES V. (1967) *Black Power: The Politics of Liberation in America.* New York: Vintage Books (Random House).

CARMICHAEL, STOKELY (1968) Power and racism, in F. B. BARBOUR (ed.), *The Black Power Revolt: A Collection of Essays.* Boston: P. Sargent, pp. 63–76.

CHRISTIE, R. and JAHODA, M. (eds.) (1954) *Studies in the Scope and Method of "The Authoritarian Personality"; continuities in social research.* Glencoe: The Free Press.

CLEAVER, ELDRIDGE (1967) *Soul on Ice.* New York: McGraw-Hill.

CLEAVER, ELDRIDGE (1969) *Post-Prison Writings and Speeches.* New York: Random House.

COHEN, JEAN (1955) Colonialism and racism in Algeria. *Les Temps Modernes,* 11 (119), 580–90.

COLLISON, PETER (1967) Immigrants and residence. *Sociology* 1 (3), 277–92.

COON, C. S. (1962) *The Origins of Races.* New York: Knopf.

COSER, L. (1956) *The Functions of Social Conflict.* Glencoe, Illinois: The Free Press.

DARROCH, A. GORDON and MARSTON, WILFRED G. (1969) Ethnic differentiation: ecological aspects of a multidimensional concept. *International Migration Review* 4 (1), 71–95.

DUNCAN, OTIS DUDLEY (1968) Patterns of occupational mobility among Negro men. *Demography* 5 (1), 11–22.

EDWARDS, T. B. and WIRT, F. M. (1967) *School Desegregation in the North.* San Francisco: Chandler Publishing Co.

EISENSTADT, S. N. (1954) *The Absorption of Immigrants.* London: Routledge & Kegan Paul.

FANON, FRANTZ (1959) *L'an V de la révolution algerienne.* Paris: Maspero.

FANON, FRANTZ (1961) *Les damnés de la terre.* Paris: Maspero.

FISHMAN, JOSHUA A. (1966) *Language Loyalty in the United States.* The Hague: Mouton.

FRAZIER, E. F. (1968) *E. Franklin Frazier: On Race Relations.* (Edited with an Introduction by G. F. EDWARDS.) Chicago: Univerity of Chicago Press.

FREEMAN, H. E., ROSS, J. M., ARMOR, D. and PETTIGREW, T. F. (1966) Color gradation and attitudes among middle-income Negroes. *American Sociological Review* 31 (3), 365–74.

GARDINER, ROBERT K. A. (1967) Race and color in international relations. *Daedalus* (Spring), 296–311.

GARDNER, R. C., WONNACOTT, E. JOY and TAYLOR, D. M. (1968) Ethnic stereotypes: a factor analytic investigation. *Canadian Journal of Psychology* **22** (1), 35–44.

GLAZER, NATHAN and MOYNIHAN, DANIEL PATRICK (1963) *Beyond the Melting Pot: The Negroes, Puerto Ricans, Jews, Italians, and Irish of New York City.* Cambridge, Mass.: The MIT Press and Harvard University Press.

GLUCKMAN, MAX (1955) The bonds in the colour-bar, in MAX GLUCKMAN, *Custom and Conflict in Africa.* Oxford: Basil Blackwell, pp. 137–65.

GRIMSHAW, A. D. (1960) Urban racial violence in the United States: changing ecological considerations. *American Journal of Sociology* **66** (2), 109–19.

HANNERZ, ULF (1970) *Soulside—Enquiries into Ghetto Culture and Community.* New York: Columbia University Press.

HARRISON, G. AINSWORTH (1969) The Galton Lecture 1968: the race concept in human biology. *Journal of Biosocial Science,* Supplement No. 1 (July) pp, 129–42.

HERBERG, WILL (1955) *Protestant–Catholic–Jew: An Essay in American Religious Sociology.* New York: Doubleday (Anchor).

HODGE, R. and TREIMAN, D. (1966) Occupational mobility and attitude toward Negroes. *American Sociological Review* **31** (1), 93–102.

HOOGVELT, A. M. M. (1969) Ethnocentrism, authoritarianism and Powellism. *Race* **11** (1), 1–12.

HULSE, F. S. (1969) Ethnic, caste and genetic miscegenation. *Journal of Biosocial Science,* Supplement No. 1 (July), 31–41.

HYMANS, J. L. (1966) French influences on Leopold Senghor's theory of regrude, 1928–1948, *Race* **7** (4), 365–70.

IANNI, O. (1962) Race and class. *Educacao e Ciencias Sociais* **10** (9), 88–111.

JENSEN, ARTHUR R. (1969) How much can we boost I.Q. and scholastic achievement? *Harvard Educational Review* **39** (1), 1–123.

JONES, BEAU FLY (1966) James Baldwin: the struggle for identity. *The British Journal o Sociology* **17** (2), 107–21.

JUPP, JAMES (1969) Immigrant involvement in British and Australian politics. *Race* **10** (3), 324–40.

KENNEDY, RUBY JO (1952) Single or triple melting pot? Intermarriage in New Haven, 1870–1950. *American Journal of Sociology* **58** (1), 56–59.

KUPER, LEO (1965) Religion and urbanization in Africa, in J. MATTHES (ed.), *International Yearbook for the Sociology of Religion.* Koln: Westdeutscher Verlag, pp. 213–30.

LAMBERT, JOHN R. (1970) *Crime Police and Race Relations.* London: Oxford University Press for the Institute of Race Relations.

LEGUM, COLIN (1967) Color and power in the South African situation. *Daedalus* (Spring), pp. 483–95.

LEVER, H. and WAGNER, O. J. M. (1969) Urbanization and the Afrikaner. *Race* **11** (2), 183–8.

LIGHT, RICHARD J. and SMITH, PAUL V. (1969) Social allocation models of intelligence. *Harvard Educational Review* **39** (3), 484–510.

27

A. H. Richmond

LIEBERSON, S. (1961) A societal theory of race and ethnic relations. *American Sociological Review* **26** (6), 902–10.

LIEBERSON, S. (1963a) The old–new distinction and immigrants in Australia. *American Journal of Sociology* **28** (4), 550–65.

LIEBERSON, S. (1963b) *Ethnic Patterns in American Cities*. New York: The Free Press.

LIEBERSON, STANLEY and SILVERMAN, ARNOLD R. (1965) The precipitants and underlying conditions of race riots. *American Sociological Review* **30** (6), 887–98.

LIEBERSON, STANLEY (1970) Stratification and ethnic groups. *Sociological Inquiry* **40,** 2.

LINN, LAWRENCE S. (1965) Verbal attitudes and overt behaviour: a study of racial discrimination. *Social Forces* **43** (3), 353–64.

LIPSET, SEYMOUR MARTIN (1969) The politics of the police. *New Society* **6** (March), 355–8.

LITTLE, K. L. (1965) *West African Urbanization: A Study of Voluntary Associations in Social Change*. London: Cambridge University Press.

LIVINGSTONE, F. B. (1962) On the non-existence of human races. *Current Anthropology* **3,** 279.

LYMAN, STANDFORD M. (1968) Contrasts in the community organization of Chinese and Japanese in North America. *The Canadian Review of Sociology and Anthropology* **5** (2), 51–67.

MACCRONE, I. D. (1937) *Race Attitudes in South Africa*. Johannesburg: Witwatersrand University Press.

MAUCORPS, P. H., MEMMI, A. and HELD, J.-F. (1965) *Les Français et le racisme*, Paris: Payot.

MAYER, P. (1963) *Townsmen or Tribesmen? Conservation in the Process of Urbanization in a South African City*. Capetown: Oxford University Press.

MERTON, ROBERT K. (1949) Discrimination and the American creed, in R. M. MACIVER (ed.), *Discrimination and National Welfare*. New York: Harper, pp. 99–126.

MOLOTCH, HARVEY (1969) Racial integration in a transition community. *American Sociological Review* **34** (6), 878–93.

MYRDAL, GUNNAR (1944) *An American Dilemma: The Negro Problem and Modern Democracy*. New York: Harper.

NAGATA, J. A. (1969) Adaptation and integration of Greek working class immigrants in the City of Toronto, Canada: a situational approach. *International Migraiton Review* **4** (1), 44–69.

PARK, R. E. (1926) Our racial frontier on the Pacific. *Survey Graphic* **61** (3), 196.

PEACH, CERI (1968) *West Indian Migration to Britain: A Social Geography*. London: Oxford University Press for the Institute of Race Relations.

PITT-RIVERS, JULIAN (1967) Race, color, and class in Central America and the Andes. *Daedalus* (Spring), 542–59.

PORTER, JOHN (1965) *The Vertical Mosaic*. Toronto: University of Toronto Press.

REX, JOHN and MOORE, ROBERT (1967) *Race, Community and Conflict: A Study of Sparkbrook*. London: Oxford University Press.

REX, JOHN (1970) *Race Relations in Sociological Theory*. London: Weidenfeld, and Nicolson.

RICHMOND, A. H. (1950) Economic insecurity and stereotypes as factors in colour prejudice. *The Sociological Review* **42** (8), 147–70.

RICHMOND, A. H. (1960) Applied social science and public policy concerning racial relations in Britain. *Race* **1** (May), 14–26.

RICHMOND, A. H. (1961) Sociological and psychological explanations of racial prejudice: some light on the controversy from recent researches in Britain. *Pacific Sociological Review* **4** (2), 63–68.

RICHMOND, A. H. (1967) *Post-War Immigrants in Canada.* Toronto: University of Toronto Press.

RICHMOND, A. H. (1969) Sociology of migration in industrial and post-industrial societies, in J. JACKSON (ed.), *Sociological Studies II: Migration.* Cambridge: Cambridge University Press, pp. 238–81.

RICHMOND, A. H. (1970) Housing and racial attitudes in Bristol. *Race* **12** (1), 49–58.

ROKEACH, MILTON (1960) *The Open and Closed Mind.* New York: Basic Books.

ROSE, E. J. B. in association with NICHOLAS DEAKIN and others (1969) *Colour and Citizenship: A Report on British Race Relations.* London: Oxford University Press for the Institute of Race Relations.

ROSENTHAL, E. (1960) Acculturation without assimilation: the Jewish community of Chicago. *American Journal of Sociology* **66** (3).

ROUCH, JEAN (1954) "Migration in the Gold Coast" (English translation). Accra. Cited in K. L. LITTLE, *West African Urbanization: A Study of Voluntary Associations in Social Change.* London: Cambridge University Press (1965), p. 144.

SHIBUTANI, T. and KWAN, K. M. (1965) *Ethnic Stratification: A Comparative Approach.* New York: Macmillan.

STEIN, DAVID D., HARDYCK, JANE ALLYN and BREWSTER SMITH, M. (1965) Race and belief: an open and shut case. *Journal of Personality and Social Psychology* **1** (4), 281–9.

TAEUBER, KARL E. and TAEUBER, A. F. (1964) The Negro as an immigrant group: recent trends in racial and ethnic segregation in Chicago. *The American Journal of Sociology* **69** (4), 374–82.

TAEUBER, KARL E. and TAEUBER, A. F. (1965) *Negroes in Cities: Residential Segregation and Neighbourhood Change.* Chicago: Aldine Publishing Co.

TAJFEL, H. (1969a) Racism. Letter in *New Society* **13** (348), 852.

TAJFEL, H. (1969b) Cognitive aspects of prejudice. *Journal of Biosocial Science*, Supplement No. 1 (July), pp. 173–91.

UNITED STATES NATIONAL ADVISORY COMMISSION ON CIVIL DISORDERS (1967) Report of the U.S. National Advisory Commission on Civil Disorders. New York: Bantam Books.

VAN DEN BERGHE, PIERRE L. (1960) Distance mechanisms of stratification. *Sociology and Social Research* **44** (3), 155–64.

WASHBURN, S. L. (1963) *Classification and Human Evolution.* Chicago: Aldine Publishing Co.

WILLIAMS, ROBIN, M. (1964) *Strangers Next Door: Ethnic Relations in American Communities.* New Jersey: Prentice-Hall.

WIRTH, L. (1957) Urbanism as a way of life, in A. J. REISS and PAUL K. HATT (eds.), *Cities and Society.* Glencoe, Illinois: The Free Press, pp. 46–63.

ZEITLIN, MAURICE (1966) Economic insecurity and the political attitudes of Cuban workers. *American Sociological Review* **31** (1), 35–51.

ZUBAIDA, SUMI (editor) (1970) *Race and Racialism.* London: Tavistock.

Race, Racism and Identity

Ethnic, Caste and Genetic Miscegenation

F. S. Hulse

It was with some diffidence that I agreed to deal with the topic of miscegenation: a topic which is so complex, so ill-understood, so charged with emotion. Yet miscegenation is of obvious interest to all who concern themselves with human biology, human society and the future of humanity. It is a topic worthy of study, and a topic which needs to be discussed frankly if myths are to be dispelled, confusion to be reduced, and problems resolved. For miscegenation has been a continuous process since the earliest times: it is nothing new. As my own guru, Professor E. A. Hooton, was fond of saying. "When peoples meet they sometimes fight, but they always mate."

Human social organization, after all, evolved out of primate social organization; and though it is fatuous for us to think of ourselves as nothing but Naked Apes, we share many aspects of our social and sexual behaviour with our quadrumanous cousins. We are continuously social, for instance, disliking solitude, and upset at being excluded from groups. Yet, more often than not, social groups tend to retain their identity by practising exclusion. Even among the lemurs of Madagascar we find these traits exemplified. Allison Jolly (1966) reports the case of a lone, and no doubt forlorn, individual of the species *Lemur macaco* who joined a troop of *Lemur catta*, since he had no closer kinsfolk in the neighbourhood. He was tolerated, but females cuffed him when he tried to groom them. Juveniles, however, who had known him all their lives, accepted his advances in a much more friendly way. Traditions may be hard to break down, but habituation often works wonders.

Much of the confusion which is apparent in studies of miscegenation or race-mixture is terminological. This does not mean that the use of proper

33

terms in the proper context will be all that is needed to remove misunderstanding. But it is a required first step towards understanding. Like the word inheritance and like the word race, we have here a blurring of the distinctions between concepts, or even material objects, which sometimes share something in common but which, in fact, belong in different realms of discourse. The manner in which we inherit property differs from the manner in which we inherit facial expressions or food habits, and the way in which we inherit any of the above differs from the way in which we inherit skin colour, blood-type or the ability to stand and stride erect. We may inherit property from a rich uncle or even an older brother. This is a legal matter, and purely cultural. We may inherit facial expressions from those, older than we, among whom we grew up. These are likely to be our parents, but others of their generation may be influential too. Such inheritance, although transmitted unwittingly, is purely cultural too. It is from our parents alone, our biological parents, that we inherit whatever blood-types we possess. The mode of inheritance involves the genes alone, and involves both, not just one, of our parents. This is a vital distinction which is very obvious, but which seems to be constantly forgotten.

The term race, also, has been used in many ways. People commonly appear to suppose that they are dealing with biological inheritance when they use this word, and they are certainly thinking in terms of inheritance. But it is all too easy, and frequently it is convenient, too, for its users to avoid distinguishing between cultural inheritance and genetic inheritance. Traits which are glaringly cultural in origin and modes of transmission have been recklessly attributed to race. Traits which are demonstrably plastic, and subject to environmental modification, have been listed by reputable scholars as racial characteristics. To complicate matters still more, we often find that a feature—stature is a good example—may have a strong genetic component, yet be subject to considerable variation for environmental reasons.

Furthermore, doubtless in relation to the in-group exclusiveness which is so common a feature of primate social organization, the concept of the racial type became common in earlier anthropological thought. Somehow it came to be supposed that once upon a time all races were pure—which was taken to be a virtue—and that in this virginal state all the members of the race resembled one another very closely. In fact, of course, only by parthenogenesis could such a situation be produced. In a bisexual species such as ours, variety is inevitable—which leads one to suspect that variety is beneficial, too. This is indeed the case, as geneticists and evolutionists have demonstrated. Nor is there any evidence in the record of the past that early man was less varied than man is today.

In any discussion of the biosocial aspects of miscegenation or race mixture it is important to keep these facts in mind, for they help to explain why so many mistakes have been made in the interpretation of the results of this sort of outbreeding. The term miscegenation has been used in at least three quite distinct ways, and applied to at least three totally distinct processes. Sometimes it is used in reference to matings between members of different castes; sometimes with reference to mating between members of different ethnic groups; and sometimes in reference to mating between members of genetically distinct breeding populations. This is very natural, although it is unfortunate, because these three sorts of human groupings are very likely to overlap in their composition. It is very unfortunate, although it is natural, because this overlapping makes it possible to claim that the results of one sort of mixture are really due to another sort of mixture. Since explanations of this sort are often emotionally comforting, they have been readily accepted and form part of the common folklore.

A caste is a socio-economic group which is set apart rather rigidly from other groups living in the same geographic area. Ritual sanctions are applied to enforce the separation. Often the members of a caste are engaged in specified occupations, or their ancestors were. As a rule, different castes within a society are hierarchically arranged; at least some are regarded as better than others. As a rule, matings between members of different castes are forbidden by custom or even by law; although in some cases females may marry males of a higher caste, and in some, males may take lower caste females for their pleasure. Sanctions against a male who attempts to mate upward are frequently ferocious. Consequently gene flow between different castes tends to be minimized. Yet different castes need not be genetically distinguishable. The Eta of Japan have been called "Japan's Invisible Race" (De Vos and Wagatsuma, 1966) since, despite segregation, there is no way to spot a member of this group by physical appearance. The keymarks of caste are rank and rigidity.

An ethnic group is a recognizable socio-cultural unit based upon some form of national or tribal distinction, which lives among other people rather than in its own country. The unity is one of sentiment and tradition, and need not involve economic factors nor hierarchical status. Both its own members and their neighbours recognize the existence of an ethnic group.

35

Yet it is not rigid, nor even necessarily stable. In a New England town (Warner, 1963) only the members of old families of eighteenth-century vintage are thought of as Yankees. In New York and further west all New Englanders are thought of as Yankees. In the ex-Confederate States all northerners are thought of as Yankees. In Europe all people from the United States are thought of as Yankees. Nor need an ethnic group be in any sense a genetic group. In Hawaii the Portuguese comprise an ethnic group of whom some members are from the Cape Verde Islands and obviously dark, while others are from the Azores and obviously light. Neither physical appearance nor allele frequencies are useful criteria for distinguishing the Yankees from the Irish at Newburyport. But all the neighbours know who belongs to which group.

A genetically distinct breeding population is an entity of a thoroughly different sort, since it may be characterized in biological terms. Castes and ethnic groups are found only in the human species, but breeding populations exist in most if not all bisexual animal species. The barriers between castes and ethnic groups are the result of human culture and human imagination. The barriers between breeding populations may be oceans, mountains, deserts, climatic zones as well. As I mentioned earlier, primates in general, not just human primates, tend to live in social groups. Indeed, breeding may be almost entirely restricted to a given social group, as Washburn and Devore (1961) found it to be in the baboon troops which they studied. Society often determines the composition of a breeding population, but it is less able to determine its genetic characteristics. In many cases, at least within the human species, social regulations may be effective in causing genetic distinctions to be retained, but it is far more doubtful that social regulations caused them to originate.

The genetic characteristics of a population have, as a rule, evolved in response to environmental stress. They presumably reflect adaptive requirements; and adaptation is to the ecology as a whole, not simply to the social aspects of the ecology. Consequently we find that human breeding populations whose ancestors lived for thousands of generations in different parts of the globe have evolved varied peculiarities. Depigmentation is most frequent among North-west Europeans, blood-type B among Eastern Asians, steatopygia among Bushmen and Hottentots, blood-type R_2 among American Indians, and so on. Breeding populations which are genetically distinct from each other have come, in almost all cases, from different parts of the world. It is reasonable to suppose that they would have evolved no matter what form of social organization might have existed among them.

In the course of human history, however, migrations have become extensive, and during the last few hundred years millions of people have travelled thousands of miles to a new home. Consequently we find individuals, families and entire genetic isolates now living at a great distance from their ancestral area and among others who came from an entirely different place. In many instances they have brought with them not only their genes but many or most aspects of their parental culture. Thus we find a great many genetic isolates, or at least somewhat distinctive breeding populations, which are also ethnic groups. The Italian Swiss whom I studied both in Ticino and California are an example of this sort. So are the group in Hawaii known as Haoles: those of European ancestry. So are the Indians of South Africa and of Trinidad and Guyana. As time goes on, ethnic distinctions may break down and genetic distinctions vanish. They tend to be mutally dependent, but it must never be forgotten that their origins are different.

Also, in the course of history, conquests have been made, ruling aristocracies of foreigners have been imposed upon local populations, and captives transported into slavery in distant lands. More or less rigidly stratified castes have originated from these activities, as well as from other historic causes, such as the degradation of certain occupations. Thus castes may be, but need not be, genetically distinct breeding populations just as they may be, but need not be, ethnic groups as well. The Eta of Japan appear to be a caste with neither ethnic nor genetic distinctions. Many castes in India have different gene frequencies but do not differ ethnically. Many of the Ashkenazic Jews of Europe resembled their Gentile neighbours in allele frequencies much more closely than in ethnic characteristics. The Coloured population of the United States resemble their Caucasian neighbours much more closely in ethnic characteristics than in allele frequencies. The French colonists in Algeria differed from their Berber neighbours ethnically and genetically as well as in being the dominant caste.

All possible combinations of caste, ethnic group and race can be found. It is really not surprising that the term miscegenation has been used in such a loose way, nor that its results have been so frequently misinterpreted. There can be no question but that, when forbidden matings occur, the offspring can be made to suffer, and may be so badly mistreated that they learn undesirable forms of behaviour. Furthermore, scholars and scientists are no

37

more free of prejudice than are other people. Davenport and Steggerda (1929) wrote of anatomical disharmonies among mulattoes in Jamaica: long legs inherited from the African, and short arms from the European ancestors. Interestingly enough, they were quite unable to find instances of this: arms and legs can be measured precisely. They also claim mental disharmonies: although the mulattoes to whom they gave intelligence tests did not do badly, they allege that many of them "were muddled and wuzzle-headed". What this means, if anything, is obscure. It is not something which can be measured precisely. Mjøen (1921) found Lapp–Norwegian hybrids to suffer from "want of balance" and "unwillingness to work"— characteristics which are certainly not subject to measurement of any sort.

It has also been alleged that the offspring of miscegenation are less fertile than members of "pure" races. In view of the continuing population explosion, one might wish that this were true: it would be a great advantage to the future of the species. But there is no shred of evidence to support this notion. Fischer (1913), in his classic study of the Rehobother Bastards, found 7·7 children per family among them more than a century after the group originated. Shapiro (1929, 1936) found that the descendants of mutineers of the *Bounty* multiplied at an equally rapid rate. Other investigators report similar findings in similar circumstances. To be sure, if they dwell in places where they are despised outcasts, hybrids may lack the opportunity and the incentive to rear large families. If they are striving to better their position in life, or that of their children, the same thing is true. Family size, among human beings, is not a measure of fertility, and has little to do with biological abilities; since our ancestors attained cortical control of their sexual impulses, it has been determined by socio-cultural factors.

It has also been alleged that miscegenation brings out the worst character-istics of the two ancestral stocks which are hybridizing. What, if anything, does this statement mean? It certainly is not a statement concerning genetics or any other aspect of biology. In a cultural context, it is understandable, whether it be true or false. When two societies are in close contact, indi-viduals who have some understanding of the culture of both have an advantage which they may exploit. This often proves disconcerting to their neighbours who are less empathetic or less alert. At the same time, an individual of mixed ancestry is commonly at a social disadvantage to start with, and needs to take every advantage to get along. Thus, those who are prejudiced against him from the beginning can easily condemn him for playing the game according to two sets of rules. If, on the other hand, the hybrid becomes discouraged with his lot, it is just as easy to condemn him for not playing the game at all, but in both cases behaviour which is condemned is culturally, not genetically determined. Furthermore, such evidence as has been advanced in support of this statement is purely anecdotal, and totally lacking in scientific value.

In summary, we can say with complete confidence that all statements alleging disadvantageous effects from miscegenation refer either to caste or to ethnic miscegenation. Most of them concern caste miscegenation, and simply reflect the speakers' prejudices in regard to status. There is no indication that genetics is concerned in any way. The essential mistake made by those who assert disadvantageous effects has been a total disregard of cultural factors; an assumption that all human behaviour is genetically determined.

There are, of course, scientists, scholars and publicists who assert that miscegenation is beneficial rather than unfortunate. The high birth rates noted earlier have been taken to indicate hybrid vigour, for instance, and Shapiro (1929) goes on to proclaim that the Pitcairn Islanders created a social structure superior to that of either Tahiti or England. Rodenwaldt (1927) praised the vigour of the "Mestizen auf Kisar" whom he studied, and Williams (1931) wrote of the vitality of the Maya–Spanish crosses in Yucatan. Many historically minded scholars have noted cultural efflorescence after two groups of people merge, and have attributed this to the beneficial effects of introducing "new blood" into the population. Certainly cultural interchange can have a stimulating effect, but this is true whether genes are exchanged or not. The Japanese, whose island country has taken in a smaller proportion of immigrants during the last fifteen hundred years than any other nation I know of, have been as stimulated by culture contact as any people in the world.

Hybrid vigour, or heterosis, which has already been mentioned, has been claimed as one of the chief virtues resulting from miscegenation, but this is almost certainly due to a misunderstanding. Mendel (1866) noted that, in the F_1 generation of some of his hybrid peas, the plants grew extra large. As a phenomenon of the first filial generation after crossing of two genetically distinct strains, many later investigators have noted such hybrid vigour as well. Biologically, however, this is evanescent. Later generations, if inbred, do not continue to manifest this characteristic. If indeed extra vigour is noted among such groups as those studied by Shapiro and Fischer, it can scarcely be termed hybrid vigour and, in any case, Trevor (1953) in reviewing a number of studies of miscegenation, was unable to confirm its existence in any of them. As Penrose (1955) has pointed out, the classic studies of race mixture have described cases of hybridization between groups neither of which were in fact genetically pure strains like Mendel's peas.

Another, but possibly related, advantage attributed to miscegenation is the lessened frequency of appearance in the phenotype of harmful recessives. This is a reasonable expectation, in accordance with genetic knowledge and theory. One has to remember, however, that not all genetic recessives can be described as harmful, nor are all deleterious alleles recessive. Let us consider the case of blue eyes, which are found among about half of north-western Europeans, so that the allele frequency may be calculated at about 70%, but not at all among aboriginal North American Indians. A good deal of miscegenation has taken place between these two groups during the last few hundred years, and it has been genetic as well as ethnic miscegenation. The allele frequencies in a population of hybrids would then be about 35% and, if they mated only with one another, the phenotype frequency of blue eyes would be one in eight. Is this advantageous, disadvantageous or simply irrelevant except aesthetically? We would expect the allele frequency for Rh negatives to be halved in such a mixed group, too, so that the phenotypic incidence would drop to one quarter of that found in West European populations. This might be considered advantageous from the European point of view, but an American Indian might become indignant at the introduction of a new hazard into his population.

In the malarial regions of Africa, a mulatto population would, at first, have a lower frequency of sickle cell alleles, and consequently a lower incidence of heterozygotes useful as a buffer against malaria, than a Negro population long resident in the area. But natural selection might remedy this misfortune within a few generations. In the United States or England, on the other hand, since malaria is a minor hazard in these countries at the present time, the allele for HBs is properly considered deleterious. Whether a certain genetic factor is harmful or not depends upon the environmental stresses to which a population is subject. It is rash and prejudicial to consider it a matter of absolute good or bad. We may conclude, however, that extensive outbreeding, whether or not it involves caste or ethnic miscegenation, does serve to retain recessives in the gene-pool, and this is good insurance against possible environmental changes in the future. What we deplore now may serve a useful function for later generations.

Heterozygote advantage, which seems to have been pretty well demonstrated in the case of the sickle-cell locus (Allison, 1954) has been another of the arguments advanced in favour of miscegenation. There may well be many cases in which heterozygotes do enjoy an advantage of some sort. At any rate it is difficult to explain the numerous cases of balanced polymorphism in any other way; and the excess of the phenotype MN over expectation in so many family studies supports this opinion too. But, in fact, genetic polymorphism is so common at so many loci within each caste or ethnic group which has been studied, that intermarriage between members of different social groups is not required to ensure its continuance. Even in so small and inbred a genetic isolate as the Samaritans, Bonné (1966) reports astonishing variety which can only be due to polymorphism.

Studies of miscegenation, as distinct from polemics, date at least as far back as Boas's (1894) publication, "The half blood Indian". As our understanding of the mechanisms of biological inheritance, and of the relationships between genetics and environment have improved, investigators have turned more and more to the analysis of special problems rather than all-embracing population surveys. This has permitted more precise analysis of the particular problem chosen, but has sometimes resulted in a neglect of factors which are relevant to the dynamics of miscegenation. Stuckert (1958) published a provocative paper on "African ancestry of the White American population" which neglected to take into account the fact that most of the American Coloured were concentrated in a relatively small area within the United States, the fact that about 40% of American Whites are of quite recent European extraction, the fact that sanctions against Coloured males mating with White females have been of the utmost ferocity, and the fact that "passing" as White has been exceedingly difficult. In any study of genetic miscegenation, both cultural and geographical circumstances have to be considered.

The study of the people of Martinique by Benoist (1963) does exactly this. Climate, topography, diet, demography, the history of the various ethnic and genetic groups which came to live on this island are all considered in relationship to the biological characteristics of its present inhabitants. Consequently the conclusions presented by the investigator are scientifically meaningful. It is doubtful whether a much more numerous group, or a group not dwelling on an island, could have been so thoroughly studied.

Both Glass (1955) and Roberts (1955) made careful estimates of the ancestry of the American Coloured, which seem to dispose quite effectively of the myth that American Indians contributed, in a significant degree, to their ancestry, at least in the United States. This seems a very probable conclusion in view of the relative numbers of Africans and American Indians who were in geographical propinquity. However, we know almost nothing about the aboriginal allele frequencies of South-eastern United States Indians, which may or may not have approximated those of the Indians still living in the western states. Nor was selection during the course of the last few generations taken into account in either of these studies, as it was in a later study (1963) by Workman, Blumberg and Cooper of a county in Georgia. If, as most human biologists now suppose, selection is still continuing to alter allele-frequencies within the human species, recently mixed populations are not exempt from this process.

Indeed, selection in such populations probably has some unique aspects. Mating is never at random in the human species, and among those who mate across the barriers of caste or ethnic group it is clearly less random than among those who mate within their own social group. Slave-owners have been more likely to mate with slaves than have members of the slave-owner's stock who do not own slaves. Wandering fur traders were more likely to mate with American Indians than were their kinsmen who remained at home. Sailors whose ships took them to the South Seas were almost the only Europeans to mate with Polynesians. We have very little information on the physical, let alone the genetic, characteristics of those particular European males who were the ancestors of the hybrid groups which have been analysed in the classic studies of race-mixture. Nor do we know much about their consorts. We can imagine that slave-owners picked the girls who pleased them most, and Henriques (1953) presents convincing evidence that social preference has, at least in Jamaica, led to an increase in the frequency of alleles for lighter pigmentation. In studies of the Hoopa (Hulse, 1960) and Quinault (Hulse and Firestone, 1963) it appeared that Indians of tribally mixed ancestry were those most likely to mate with non-Indians. If selected groups from the general population are those who miscegenate, we cannot be at all sure that they are genetically representative of their ancestral groups.

Furthermore, since, in cases of ethnic miscegenation, at least one of the participating groups must have come from another region, they may be subject, and their offspring may be subject, to unfamiliar selective stresses which would result in shifts in allele-frequencies whether or not race-mixture took place. This was found in the Georgia study (1963) cited above; the incidence of HbS among the Coloured had declined much more than it would have if hybridization with North Europeans alone had been responsible. When we are dealing with populations which have resulted from miscegenation several centuries ago it becomes very difficult to estimate the relative proportions of alleles contributed by each of the ancestral stocks concerned. Pollitzer (1958) in a beautifully designed study of "The Negroes of Charleston, South Carolina" compared this population with West Africans, American Whites and the larger group of American Coloured for serological and morphological traits. He found that in blood-type frequencies both the Charleston Negroes and the United States Coloured as a whole resemble West Africans more closely than they do in morphology. Manuila (1956) noted a higher incidence of blood-type B in those parts of Eastern Europe overrun by the Mongols than in neighbouring areas, yet the inhabitants do not look in the least Mongoloid. It seems to me quite possible that social selection has been operative in both these cases, inasmuch as humans have not yet developed such prejudices about blood types as they have about external anatomical features. Further studies are needed, of course, to confirm or deny this guess of mine.

Harrison and Owen (1964) in Liverpool studied the skin colour of a group of mixed European–West African ancestry and many of their European and West African parents. Since there is no overlapping at all in the degree of pigmentation of the unexposed skin in West Africans and North Europeans, a study of this sort is most suitable to determine the number of loci involved in the inheritance of skin colour. Much more precise genetic analyses can be made in a situation such as this: here we see the essential difference between cultural and genetic inheritance. Cultural characteristics are transmitted from one generation to the next at large, genetic characteristics only from biological parents to their own personal offspring. Thus it was possible in the Liverpool study to compare children with their own parents and reach conclusions concerning the number of loci involved in the determination of pigmentation. Only by a study of genetic miscegenation conducted in this manner can this sort of information be uncovered. Caste and ethnic factors are eliminated, and selection can scarcely have had time to operate in the course of two generations.

Although most people would not regard the breakdown of localized genetic isolates all of which are within a single ethnic group or caste as miscegenation, from a genetic point of view it cannot be regarded as anything else. Studies of the result of the breakdown of such isolates have the advantage that effects from mixing cultures cannot be confused with the results of

43

mixing gene-pools, because cultural mixture is not taking place. A few years ago, in a study of the Italian Swiss of the Canton Ticino (Hulse, 1957) I was astonished to find that the sons of men who had married girls from another village were taller than were the sons of men who had married fellow villagers. Later, Damon (1965) noted the same sort of evidence for heterosis in a sample of south Italians. Further study, including analysis of diet, sibship size, and age effects was undertaken: none of these factors served to explain the observed differences. Finally (Hulse, 1968), a series of father–son comparisons indicated that the differences were greatest in the first filial generation of village outbreeding, which adds the best sort of support to the hypothesis that hybrid vigour is responsible for the observed effect.

During the present and the coming generation, it seems to me that the best place in the world to study genetic miscegenation will be Israel. Into this state, populations of Jews from many different parts of the world have just been gathered together. Many of these populations have been highly inbred for centuries, and they differ from one another in a great number of sets of allele-frequencies. They are just beginning to interbreed with one another. Parental, as well as first and second filial generations will all be available for study during the next two or three decades. Ethnic and even caste-like differences exist, but are minimized and can readily be factored out by careful analysis. The cultural atmosphere of the nation favours scientific research, and its compact size makes field work easy. It can therefore be hoped that many important discoveries concerning the consequences of miscegenation will be made by physical anthropologists and human geneticists working in unison in the natural laboratory of Israel.

REFERENCES

ALLISON, A. C. (1954) The distribution of the sickle cell trait in East Africa and elsewhere, and its apparent relationship to the incidence of subtertian malaria. *Tran. R. Soc. trop. Med. Hyg.* **48**, 312.

BENOIST, J. (1963) Les Martiniquais. Anthropologie d'une population métissée. *Bull. Mem. Soc. Anthrop. Paris*, **4**, 241.

BOAS, F. (1894) The half blood Indian. *Pop. Sci. Monthly*, **14**, 761.

BONNÉ, B. (1966) Genes and phenotypes of the Samaritan isolate. *Am. J. phys. Anthrop.* N.S. **24**, 1.

DAMON, A. (1965) Stature increase among Italian-Americans: environmental, genetic or both? *Am. J. phys. Anthrop.* N.S. **23**, 401.

DAVENPORT, C. B. and STEGGERDA, M. (1929) *Race Crossing in Jamaica*. Carnegie Institution, Washington.

DE VOS, G. and WAGATSUMA, H. (1966) *Japan's Invisible Race*. University of California Press, Berkeley.

FISCHER, E. (1913) *Die Rehobother Bastards und das Bastardierungsproblem beim Menschen*. Gustav Fischer, Jena.

GLASS, B. (1955) On the unlikelihood of significant admixture of genes from the North American Indians in the present composition of the Negroes of the United States. *Am. J. hum. Genet.* **7**, 361.

HARRISON, G. A. and OWEN, J. J. T. (1964) Studies on the inheritance of human skin colour. *Ann. hum. Genet.* **28**, 27.

HENRIQUES, F. M. (1953) *Family and Colour in Jamaica*. Eyre & Spottiswoode, London.

HULSE, F. S. (1957) Exogamie et heterosis. *Arch. suisses Anthrop. gén.* **22**, 104.

HULSE, F. S. (1960) Ripples on a gene-pool: the shifting frequencies of blood-type alleles among the Indians of the Hoopa Reservation. *Am. J. phys. Anthrop.* N.S. **18**, 141.

HULSE, F. S. (1968) Migration and cultural selection in human genetics. *Anthropologist*. (In press.)

HULSE, F. A. and FIRESTONE, M. M. (1963) Blood-type frequencies among the Indians of the Quinault Reservation. *Proc. II Int. Congr. hum. Genet.* **2**, 845.

JOLLY, A. B. (1966) *Lemur Behavior*. University of Chicago Press.

MANUILA, A. (1956) Distribution of ABO genes in Eastern Europe. *Am. J. phys. Anthrop.* N.S. **14**, 577.

MENDEL, G. (1866) Experiments in plant hybridization. *Proc. Natur. Hist. Soc. Brünn.* (English translation: Harvard University Press, 1948.)

MJØEN, J. A. (1921) Harmonic and disharmonic race crossings. *Eugenics in Race and State*, **2**, 41.

PENROSE, L. S. (1955) Evidence of heterosis in man. *Proc. R. Soc.* B, **140**, 203.

POLLITZER, W. S. (1958) The Negroes of Charleston (S.C.): a study of hemoglobin types, serology and morphology. *Am. J. phys. Anthrop.* N.S. **16**, 241.

ROBERTS, D. F. (1955) The dynamics of racial intermixture in the American Negro—some anthropological considerations, *Am. J. hum. Genet.* **7**, 361.

RODENWALDT, E. (1927) *Die Mestizen auf Kisar*. Gustav Fischer, Jena.

SHAPIRO, H. L. (1929) Descendants of Mutineers of the Bounty. *Mem. Bernice P. Bishop Mus.* **9**.

SHAPIRO, H. L. (1936) *Heritage of the Bounty*. Simon & Schuster, New York.

STUCKERT, R. P. (1958) African ancestry of the White American population. *Ohio J. Sci.* **58**, 155.

TREVOR, J. C. (1953) Race crossing in Man: the analysis of metrical characters. *Eugen. Lab. Mem.* **36**.

WARNER, W. L. (1963) *Yankee City* (abridged edn.). Yale University Press, New Haven.

WASHBURN, S. L. and DEVORE, I. (1961) Social behavior of baboons and early man. In: *The Social Life of Early Man. Viking Fund Pub. Anthrop.* **31**.

WILLIAMS, G. D. (1931) *Maya-Spanish crosses in Yucatan. Paper of Peabody Museum*, **13**. Harvard University Press, Cambridge, Mass.

WORKMAN, P. L., BLUMBERG, B.S. and COOPER, A. J. (1963) Selection, gene migration and polymorphic stability in a U.S. White and Negro population. *Am. J. hum. Genet.* **15**, 429.

Race *and* Belief: an open and shut case[1]

DAVID D. STEIN, JANE ALLYN HARDYCK AND M. BREWSTER SMITH

ONE of the many ideas presented in *The Open and Closed Mind* (Rokeach, 1960) is that prejudice may be in large part the result of perceived dissimilarity of belief systems. That is, Rokeach, Smith, and Evans (1960) contend that the prejudiced person does not reject a person of another race, religion, or nationality because of his ethnic membership *per se*, but rather because he perceives that the other differs from him in important beliefs and values. He reports two studies in which subjects were asked to rate pairs of stimulus individuals on a 9-point scale, defined at the ends by the statements "I *can't* see myself being friends with such a person" and "I can *very easily* see myself being friends with such a person". In one experiment, the stimulus individuals were white or Negro; in the other they were Jewish or gentile. Racial and religious attitudes and general beliefs of the stimulus individuals were also varied. In this situation, it was found that the friendship preferences expressed were determined primarily on the basis of congruence in beliefs rather than on racial or religious grounds.

Triandis (1961) took issue with this position, stating that: "People do not exclude other people from their neighbourhood, for instance, because the other people have different belief systems, but they do exclude them because they are Negroes" (p. 186). He has reported results contrary to Rokeach's contention regarding the primacy of belief congruence over race as a determinant of prejudice. Since he objected to Rokeach's use of the single criterion of friendship as the measure of prejudice, he employed a social distance scale of 15 items. For his manipulation of belief congruence, he used "same philosophy" or "different philosophy" as determined by the subjects' most and least preferred of Morris' (1956) "13 ways to live". Stimulus individuals in the study were varied in race, religion, and occupational status

[1]This paper may be identified as Publication A-26 of the Survey Research Center University of California, Berkeley.

46

as well as in philosophy. He obtained a "race effect" that accounted for about four times as much variance, in terms of the percentage of the total sum of squares, as any of the other three effects singly, although all four main effects were highly significant.

Rokeach (1961) replied with the objection that the long and involved passages of Morris' "ways to live" could not be equated with belief systems as he defined them; the "ways to live" were too vague and were not salient to the subjects. He concluded that the results of Triandis' study were therefore irrelevant to the point at issue. In a more recent study, Byrne and Wong (1962) essentially supported Rokeach's position, employing personal feelings of friendliness and willingness to work together in an experiment as dependent variables.

The present study was designed with the intent of reconciling these disparate findings. It seemed reasonable to assume that there might be some truth in each position, and that the large differences between the results obtained by Rokeach *et al.* and by Byrne and Wong, on the one hand, and by Triandis, on the other, followed primarily from the methods used.

In the design of the present study, our first concern was that of making our "stimulus individuals" appear real to our subjects. In Rokeach's studies, pairs of individuals, described in very sketchy fashion, were presented in such a way that it was rather obvious to the subject that a choice was to be made between race and belief. In Triandis' study, there was less of a suggestion of choice, but the descriptions were equally sketchy and the measure of belief was, indeed, very vague. Our intent has been, following an improved procedure devised by Byrne (1961), to present to our subjects, as nearly as is possible on paper, realistic stimulus individuals. In this study, as in Byrne and Wong (1962), stimulus individuals were varied in race and in the similarity of their beliefs to those previously expressed by the subjects. This procedure makes it possible to elicit absolute rather than comparative judgments so as to minimize selfconsciously ideological responses. As our dependent variables, we employed both a measure of friendly feelings and a social distance scale, on which responses to each individual item could be separately analyzed.

METHOD

The sample consisted of 23 male and 21 female white teen-agers in two ninth grade classes of a California high school. The subjects, all of whom

47

On this page and the one facing it are the answers given by TEEN-AGER I. After you have looked over the answers and have a good picture of what you think this person is like, turn the page and answer the questions about how you feel toward this person.

Every teen-ager has his own ideas about how his fellow students ought to be. We would like you to tell us, for each of the items on the list below, whether or not you think teen-agers in general ought to be like that, and how strongly you feel about it.

"Do you think teen-agers in general *ought* to ...."

	Strongly feel they should	Feel they should	Don't care	Feel they shouldn't	Strongly feel they shouldn't
1. Try to please their parents by the things they do.	**	*—	0	—	—
2. Have school spirit; know what's going on in school and take part in activities.	**—	*	0̲		
3. Be able to express their feelings freely and "let themselves go."	**	*	0		
4. Try to get average grades, not go "all out" for "A's".	**—	*—	0		
5. Be intelligent, be able to think clearly about things.	**	*	0		
6. Be well groomed, keep themselves neat and attractive.	**—	*—	0		
7. Have good taste in clothes.	**—	*	0		
8. Be concerned about other people, *not* be self-centered.	**—	*—	0		
9. Be modest, *not* try to draw attention to themselves.	**—	*	0		
10. Be good at athletics.	**	*—	0		
11. Be sincerely religious.	**	*	0̲		

12. Have respect for other students' wishes and beliefs; *not* be bossy.
13. Let everybody have his fair say in running things in the school.
14. Be honest and trustworthy.
15. Be generally friendly and sociable, mix with different kinds of students.
16. Treat other students as equals, *not* be conceited or snobbish.
17. Be quiet and well behaved in school, *not* get into fights.
18. Follow all the rules and laws that have been made by those in authority.
19. Stay in groups where they are welcome, *not* be "social climbers".
20. Live up to strict moral standards.
21. Be good at expressing their opinions.
22. Be good at dancing.
23. Be able to stick to hard problems, try to do well in school work.
24. Go along with what most other students do and stand for, *not* be too different.
25. Stand on their own feet, work for things, not seek special favors.

FIG. 1. Example of information concerning values provided to describe a "stimulus teen-ager". (Underlined responses reflect the subject's own responses from the pretest questionnaire.)

49

D. D. *Stein, J. A. Hardyck, and M. B. Smith*

TEEN-AGER I

1. Sex ___M___ Grade ___9___

2. What program are you taking in school? (If undecided, mark the program you think you will take.)

   0 _____ Vocational
   1 _____ Commercial
   2 _____ College preparatory
   3 __×__ General
   4 _____ Other _____ (write in)

3. Last year, what kind of grades did you get?

   0 _____ about an A average
   1 _____ between an A & B average
   2 __×__ about a B average
   3 _____ between a B & C average
   4 _____ about a C average
   5 _____ between a C & D average
   6 _____ about a D average
   7 _____ below a D average

4. What is your race?

   0 __×__ white
   1 _____ Negro
   2 _____ Oriental
   3 _____ other (What? _____)

Fig. 2. Example of information, other than values, provided to describe a white–like or white–unlike stimulus teen-ager.

were 14 years of age, came mainly from working class homes in a non-metropolitan industrial community. They participated in the study during their advisory periods.[2]

At the beginning of the period, the experimenter introduced himself as "a research worker from the University of California" and handed out a mimeographed booklet to each student, by name. The instructions were printed on the front page of the booklet and read as follows:

> As you remember, a few months ago we asked you to answer some questions concerning your interests and attitudes about yourself, your friends, and certain groups of teen-agers. You may also recall that there were some questions asking you to give first impressions about people when you knew only a few things about them, such as the person's religion or type of job. We are very much interested in how people form these impressions.
>
> In fact, we would like to know how you would feel about some teenagers who took the same questionnaires as you did, but in other parts of the country. Therefore, we have taken some of the answers and presented them on the following pages.
>
> We want you to look at the descriptions of *four* teenage boys (girls) and then answer some questions about how you feel toward them. The four teen-agers will be called: TEEN-AGER I, II, III, and IV. If you have any questions, please raise your hand and the research worker will help you. Be sure to read everything carefully.[3]

As the instructions indicate, 2 months prior to this study the students had filled out the pretest version of a questionnaire being developed for a large-scale study of teen-age attitudes towards minority groups.[4] A value scale on the pretest questionnaire had asked the students, "Do you think teen-agers in general *ought* to . . ." about each of 25 items. Five response alternatives were provided, ranging from "Strongly feel they should" to "Strongly feel they shouldn't". The students' own responses to these items on the pretest provided the basis for the manipulation of belief congruence in the present study (Fig. 1).

[2]We would like to thank Wayne Henderson, his teaching staff, and the students at Pacifica High School, Pittsburg, California, for their cooperation in this research, and Herbert Weissman who served as experimenter in one classroom.

[3]Male subjects answered questions about boys; female subjects answered questions about girls. Wording throughout the questionnaire was adapted to the sex of the subject.

[4]This study of teen-age attitudes is a part of a 5-year program of research on various aspects of anti-Semitism being conducted at the Survey Research Center of the University of California under the general direction of Charles Y. Glock. The research is supported by a grant to the Survey Research Center from the Anti-Defamation League of B'nai B'rith. We gratefully acknowledge our indebtedness to the Anti-Defamation League, but this organization is not to be held responsible for our interpretations.

D. D. Stein, J. A. Hardyck, and M. B. Smith

For each of the subjects, two "stimulus teen-agers" were constructed who were like him in values, and two were constructed who were unlike him, following a procedure similar to that used by Byrne (1961). One "like" stimulus teen-ager was made up whose responses were identical with those given by the subject. In order to avoid raising the suspicions of the subjects, the other "like" teen-ager was made to differ slightly from the first by moving the responses to six items, chosen at random, one step on the 5-point scale.[5] Each "unlike" teen-ager was created by choosing at random three of the items the subject had answered "Strongly feel they should" and changing them to "feel they shouldn't". Three more modest alterations were made as well, depending on the subject's original pretest response pattern.[6]

Besides the information on how the stimulus teen-agers had "answered" the value items, the subjects were given the sex, grade and program in school, last year's grades, and race of the teen-ager (Figure 2). For half the subjects, this additional information preceded that on values throughout the booklet, and for the other half, the value scale information was presented first. The sex and grade in school were always the same as that of the subject, the program in school was college preparatory, and grades were "about a B average". Only race was varied. Thus, by combining like and unlike responses on the value scale with "Negro" and "white", four stimulus teen-agers were created. These will be referred to as white-like, white-unlike, Negro-like, and Negro-unlike. These four were presented in eight different orders, the only restriction on ordering being that like and unlike teen-agers were alternated.

As the subject opened his booklet, he was confronted with the description of one of the four stimulus teen-agers, called Teenager I. The subject read this first description, at his own speed, and then turned to the next pair of pages and answered three questions. One of these served as a check on the manipulation of belief congruence, and the other two were measures of friendliness and social distance towards the stimulus teen-ager. The questions will be discussed in more detail under Results. The subject then went on to

[5] A check of responses to the question, "How much like you is this teen-ager?" showed that responses to an "exact-like" stimulus teen-ager differed somewhat from those to a "modified-like" teen-ager ($t = 1.76$, $p < .05$, one-tailed test). Since half of the white-like stimulus teen-agers were "exact like" and half of each were "modified like", this difference cannot have affected our results.

[6] A pilot study revealed that more drastic changes than the ones finally used made the stimulus teen-agers appear unreal. Details of procedure for constructing the stimulus teen-agers may be had by writing to the first author listed.

52

read the description of Teenagers II, III, and IV and in turn to answer the questions about them. When he had finished, usually in 20–25 minutes, he turned over his booklet and waited for the rest of the class to complete their booklets.

RESULTS AND DISCUSSION

Check on the Manipulation of Belief Congruence

One question answered by the subjects about each of the four stimulus teen-agers was the following:

How much like you would you say Teen-ager X is?

0———as much like me as any teen-ager I can think of
1———very much like me
2———a little like me
3———a little unlike me
4———very much unlike me
5———as much unlike me as any teen-ager I can think oι

The subjects' responses to this question served as a check on the manipulation of similarity between the subject and the stimulus teen-agers. Mean responses to this question, for each of the four stimulus teen-agers, may be found in Table 1. It is clear that the white-like (1.63) and Negro-like (1.91) teen-agers are seen as more like the subjects than are the white-unlike (2.76) and Negro-unlike (3.27) teen-agers. The mean of responses to both like teen-agers combined (3.56) differs from the mean of responses to both unlike teen-agers (6.05) at well beyond the .001 level ($t=6.99$). All individual like-unlike comparisons also yield t values significant at beyond the .001 level (p values reported henceforth are all two-tailed). From these data we may conclude that the manipulation of similarity or dissimilarity between the subjects and the stimulus teen-agers has been successful.

"Friendliness" Question

The first question the subject answered about each stimulus teen-ager was the following:
If you met this teenager for the first time, what would your immediate reaction be?

I think I would feel:

0___quite friendly
1___a little friendly
2___nothing either way
3___a little unfriendly
4___quite unfriendly

This question was intended to be a nearly pure measure of "affect"; that is, a measure of the subject's overall reaction to each stimulus teen-ager. The mean responses with respect to each of the teen-agers are given in Row 1 of Table 1. Subjects would feel most friendly towards the white-like teen-ager (.59), followed by the Negro-like (.83), white-unlike (1.69), and Negro-unlike (1.86) teen-agers. An analysis of variance[7] using McNemar's (1955, p. 330) Case XIV mixed model reveals that belief congruence accounts for a much larger part of the variance of responses than does race, although the effects for both race and belief are significant. (F for the belief effect $= 37.72$, $p < .001$; F for the race effect $= 5.21$, $p < .05$). This result, of course, is consistent with Rokeach's theory.

This question was also asked, in a somewhat different format, on the "pretest" questionnaire mentioned earlier. At that time subjects were asked to respond to a list of many different individuals, of which one was "A Negro teen-ager". Of the subjects in the present experiment, 35 answered this item on the pretest. An interesting finding emerges when we compare responses to "A Negro teen-ager", with no other information, with responses to Negro-like and Negro-unlike in the present study.

A rather obvious expectation is that the mean of responses to "A Negro teen-ager" should fall between the means for Negro-like and Negro-unlike. This is the case. Means for those subjects present on both occasions ($N = 35$) are given in Table 2. (They are .91, 1.34, and 1.80 for Negro-like, Negro teen-ager, and Negro-unlike, respectively.) Subjects feel significantly more friendly towards the Negro-like teen-ager than towards the Negro teen-ager ($t = 2.08$, $p < .05$) and significantly more friendly towards the Negro teen-ager than towards the Negro-unlike teen-ager ($t = 2.88$, $p < .01$).

One should also expect that subjects' responses to the Negro teen-ager should correlate moderately both with responses to Negro-like and Negro-unlike. This should be the case unless, for some reason, subjects have an expectation that Negro teen-agers in general are either like them or unlike

[7]All analyses of variance reported follow this model.

TABLE 1. MEAN RESPONSE TO STIMULUS TEEN-AGERS

Question	N	Stimulus teen-ager			
		White-like	White-unlike	Negro-like	Negro-unlike
1. "How friendly"[a]	42	.59	1.69	.83	1.86
2. Social distance scale total score[b]	44	9.84	5.90	7.81	5.54
2A. Individual items on social distance scale[c]					
Invite home to dinner	44	.82	.36	.39	.20
Go to party to which this person was invited	44	1.00	.80	.93	.70
Go to same school	44	1.00	.91	1.00	.91
Have as member of social group	44	.91	.32	.82	.48
Have as speaking acquaintance	44	.91	.59	.91	.59
Live in same apartment house with this person and his (her) family	44	.89	.45	.43	.27
Eat lunch at school with	44	.93	.57	.84	.57
Sit next to in class	44	.98	.70	.93	.73
Close personal friend	44	.80	.27	.59	.32
Work on committee with	44	.93	.68	.91	.73
Date my sister (brother)	44	.68	.25	.09	.05
3. "How much like you?"[a]	43	1.63	2.76	1.91	3.27

[a]For these questions, a low score signifies greater friendliness and perceived similarity, respectively.
[b]Scoring: 1 for "yes", 0 for "no"; 11 points possible.
[c]Scores run from 0 to 1. A mean of 1.0 signifies endorsement of the item by everyone.

TABLE 2. ANALYSIS OF RESPONSES ON THE "FRIENDLINESS" SCALE TOWARDS VARIOUS STIMULUS TEEN-AGERS ($N=35$)

Stimulus teen-ager	M^a	a^2	Comparison	Correlation	t between means	t between variances
Negro-like	.91	.48	Negro-like versus Negro teen-ager	.15	2.08*	2.31*
Negro teen-ager[b]	1.34	.99	Negro teen-ager versus Negro-unlike	.62***	2.88**	<1
Negro-unlike	1.80	1.13	Negro-like versus Negro-unlike	.29	4.68***	3.01**

[a] A low score indicates greater friendliness towards the stimulus teen-ager.
[b] From pretest questionnaire.
*$p < .05$.
**$p < .01$.
***$p < .001$.

them. Again referring to Table 2, we note that the correlation between Negro-like and Negro teen-ager is .15 and the correlation between Negro-like and Negro-unlike is .29. Neither of these correlations is large enough to be considered significantly different from zero. (The *CR* for the correlation of .29 reaches the .09 level of significance.) The correlation between Negro teen-ager and Negro-unlike, however, is .62, significant at beyond the .001 level, and also significantly different from the other two correlations, at the .01 and .05 levels, respectively.

These differences would seem to demonstrate an important point: namely, when our white subjects are given no information at all about a Negro teen-ager, they apparently assume that he is different from them in values and react towards him accordingly. It should be noted here, referring again to Table 2, that the variance of responses to the Negro-like teen-ager is significantly smaller than the variance of the other two distributions. Some caution must be exercised in the interpretation of the differences between the correlations for this reason. Our data from the question "How much like you would you say Teenager X is?" add further information, however. On that question, the subjects perceived the Negro stimulus teen-agers to be significantly less like them than were the white teen-agers, even when given the same information about both. The mean of responses to Negro-like and Negro-unlike teen-agers combined was 5.33, while the mean for like and unlike white teen-agers was 4.44 (*t* for this difference is 3.29, $p < .01$). That is, with belief similarity held constant, the subjects perceived that the white stimulus teen-agers were more like them, given *identical* information about the whites and Negroes. These results parallel findings reported by Byrne and Wong (1962, p. 247, Table 1), in which white subjects attributed greater similarity of attitudes to unknown whites than to unknown Negroes. Our data further indicate the expectation held by the subjects that a Negro teen-ager, simply by virtue of his being a Negro, will be different from them. It seems likely that their propensity to react negatively towards the Negro is based on this expectation, or, equally compatible with the obtained relationship, for persons sharing the anti-Negro prejudices endemic in American society, the sheer fact that a person is Negro marks him as significantly "different", however similar he may be in other respects.

Social Distance Scale

Our major measure of reactions to the four stimulus teen-agers was the following "teen-age social distance scale":

57

Everyone has his own preferences about the people he wants to associate with. There are probably some people with whom you would be willing to be very good friends, and others whom you would just as soon not ever be with. We would like you to tell us how close a relationship you think you would be willing to have with TEEN-AGER X. Check the blank under "yes" for each statement you agree with, and the blank under "no" for each statement you disagree with for TEEN-AGER X. Guess if you aren't really sure.

I think I would be willing:

Yes No
— — to invite this person home to dinner
— — to go to a party to which this person was invited
— — to go to the same school with this person
— — to have this person as a member of my social group or club
— — to have this person as one of my speaking acquaintances
— — to live in the same apartment house with this person and his family
— — to eat lunch with this person in school
— — to sit next to this person in class
— — to have this person as a close personal friend
— — to work on a committee at school with this person
— — to have this person date my sister (brother)

This social distance scale, which was devised for the pretest questionnaire, was patterned after that of Triandis. Items were changed, omitted, and added to make the scale suitable for teen-age subjects; for example, no negative items were used, on the assumption that they would not discriminate between the subjects. Total scores on the scale were obtained by simply summing responses to the 11 items, each scored "1" for "yes" and "0" for "no".

TABLE 3. ANALYSIS OF VARIANCE OF TOTAL SOCIAL DISTANCE
SCALE SCORES

Source	SS	df	F
Individuals (A)	528.11	43	—
Race (B)	62.64	1	7.20*
Belief (C)	423.46	1	48.51**
A × B	374.11	43	< 1
A × C	375.29	43	< 1
B × C	30.28	1	< 1
A × B × C	9225.11	43	—
		175	

*p < .02.   **p < .001.

TABLE 4. SOCIAL DISTANCE SCALE ITEM COMPARISONS WITH
RESPECT TO BELIEF AND RACE ($N = 44$)

Items in social distance scale	t for belief[a]	t for race[b]
1. Invite home to dinner	4.57★★	5.00★★
2. Go to party to which this person was invited	4.30★★	2.00
3. Go to same school	2.57★	< 1
4. Have as member of social group	7.75★★	< 1
5. Have as speaking acquaintance	4.92★★	< 1
6. Live in same apartment house	5.36★★	4.92★★
7. Eat lunch at school with	4.92★★	< 1
8. Sit next to in class	4.00★★	< 1
9. Close personal friend	6.15★★	1.23
10. Work on committee with	3.75★★	< 1
11. Date my sister (brother)	4.80★★	6.67★★

[a]Based on the difference in mean response to like and unlike stimulus teen-agers, regardless of race: (white-like + Negro-like) − (white-unlike + Negro-unlike).

[b]Based on the difference in mean response to white and Negro stimulus teen-agers, regardless of whether like or unlike: (white-like + white-unlike) − (Negro-like + Negro-unlike).

★$p < .02$.

★★$p < .001$.

Responses to the social distance scale were analyzed in two ways. First, an analysis of variance of the total scores was computed; results are presented in Table 3. As in the analysis of the "friendliness" question, belief accounts for by far the largest amount of the variance, although effects for both race and belief are highly significant. (F for race = 7.20, $p < .02$; F for belief = 48.51, $p < .001$.) Then, t tests for both race and belief effects were calculated for each of the 11 items. That is, each subject's responses to the two Negro stimulus teen-agers were combined, and his responses to the two white stimulus teen-agers were combined. The t between the means of these scores evaluates the race effect. The belief effect was tested similarly, by combining responses to the two like teen-agers and comparing the mean of these scores with the mean of the summed responses to the two unlike teen-agers.

D. D. Stein, J. A. Hardyck, and M. B. Smith

The *t*-test analysis, presented in Table 4, adds more specific information concerning the areas in which race and belief effects are strongest. It is clear that belief has a very strong effect on all 11 items. All but one of the differences between responses to like and unlike teen-agers are significant at beyond the .001 level; the difference on the item concerning "Go to the same school" is significant at the .02 level. The race effect, however, appears to be specific to three items: "Invite him home to dinner", "Live in the same apartment house", and "Have him date my sister (brother)". These 3 items on which the race effect is significant at beyond the .001 level seem to be "sensitive areas", ones in which there is widespread resistance, in American society, to Negro-white contacts. Rokeach (Rokeach *et al.*, 1960) has stated that his theory applies "insofar as psychological processes are involved . . . (p. 135)". As an example of institutionalized racial prejudice outside the framework of his theory he later states "the southern white bigot would not want his daughter to marry the 'good' Negro any more than the 'bad' one (p. 165)". In Rokeach's sense, the present "sensitive" items would seem to fall in the latter category. Clearly, an empirical definition of institutional prejudice in terms of an obtained "race effect" would be circular and meaningless. For purposes of future research, we would suggest two criteria for situations that may be expected to produce a "race effect": intimacy of contact and presence of others—in this case parents—who are the enforcers of social norms. At present, all we can state from our empirical finding is that a belief effect is strong on all the items, whereas a race effect occurs on items that appear to involve publicly visible relationships that are "sensitive" or controversial by prevailing cultural standards.

TABLE 5. ANALYSIS OF VARIANCE OF TOTAL SOCIAL DISTANCE
SCALE SCORES, PRETEST DATA

Source	SS	df	F
Individuals (A)	408.77	36	—
Race (B)	283.95	1	45.50*
Status (C)	134.33	1	28.52*
A × B	224.80	36	< 1
A × C	169.42	36	< 1
B × C	10.28	1	< 1
A × B × C	8695.45	36	—

*$p < .001$.

One further set of data is available, from the pretest, which provides an important comparison with the results of the social distance scale in the present study. On the pretest, subjects were asked to respond, on the same "teen-ager social distance scale," to stimulus teen-agers who resembled quite closely the stimulus individuals used by Triandis. "Same or different philosophy" and "same or different religion" which he used as variables were omitted. Our stimulus teen-agers were all stated to be Christians, and varied only in race, white versus Negro, and in status. For the status variable, program in school and grades were varied. The teen-agers were thus described as either "in the college preparatory program getting Bs" or "in the vocational program getting failing grades". Again, there were four stimulus teen-agers: white, low status; white, high status; Negro, low status; and Negro, high status.

The results of the analysis of variance of total scores on the social distance scale, in response to these four stimulus teen-agers, are given in Table 5. In this case, there is a very large race effect ($F = 45.50$, $p < .001$), about twice as large as a smaller, but still highly significant status effect ($F = 28.52$, $p < .001$), in terms of percentage of variance explained. These results, obtained on 37 of the 44 subjects used in the later study, resemble quite closely those obtained by Triandis. When belief is not a variable, as in these data, or when the belief effect is weakened by the ambiguity of the information provided, as in Triandis' data, both race and status account for appreciable portions of the variance, with race being by far the more important variable.

The explanation for all of these data, it would seem, is to be found in a very simple fact. Individuals make judgments about others on the basis of all the relevant information they possess. If little information is provided, and a judgment is demanded, it is made on the basis of inferences from past experiences or information obtained from others. That first impressions are seldom accurate is due to the fact that very little information is available, and the person must be judged on the basis of some known group membership. The correlations presented earlier, between responses to Negro-like, Negro teen-ager, and Negro-unlike, seem to indicate that the inference made by most subjects about a Negro teen-ager, in the absence of other information, is that he is *unlike* them.

If the foregoing interpretation is correct, the very large race effects obtained by Triandis and also demonstrated in the pretest data are easily accounted for. The subjects are forced to guess at the belief systems of the stimulus individuals, and their guess is that the Negro is unlike them. Our subjects in this situation respond with a very large "race effect". When essentially the same subjects were provided, in the later study, with actual information about the belief systems of the stimulus individuals, they no longer had to guess, and they responded primarily, though not exclusively, in terms of the information about belief congruence with which they had been provided.

CONCLUSION

The data presented strongly support Rokeach's theory that the variable of belief congruence accounts for a major portion of the variance in prejudice, if it does not tell the "whole truth" about it. The teen-age subjects in this study, when given extensive information concerning the belief systems of stimulus teen-agers, react primarily in terms of similarity of beliefs and only very secondarily in terms of race. This was the case in an analysis of total scores on a social distance scale, and in an analysis of "friendliness" responses. Strong "race effects" were obtained on "sensitive" items on the social distance scale, perhaps reflecting institutionalized areas of prejudice, and on total social distance scores when information concerning belief systems was not provided.[8]

Not only do our results support Rokeach's contention regarding the primacy of belief congruence, but they also account for the discrepancy between the findings reported by Rokeach *et al.* (1960) and by Byrne and Wong (1962), on the one hand, and those reported by Triandis (1961), on the other. When subjects are forced to evaluate stimulus individuals in terms of their beliefs, then belief congruence is more important than race. But when the belief component is not provided, spelled out in considerable detail, subjects will react in racial terms on the basis of assumptions concerning the belief systems of others, and of emotional or institutionalized factors. The practical implications of these results are obvious. If people of different races encounter one another under conditions favoring the perception of belief congruence (as, for example, in equal-status contacts), then racial prejudice should be substantially reduced.

[8]Current research by one of the authors (DDS) replicates these findings for white ninth grade subjects in an Eastern school system in which there were substantial numbers of Negro students.

REFERENCES

BYRNE, D. (1961) Interpersonal attraction and attitude similarity. *Journal of Abnormal and Social Psychology* **62,** 713–15.

BYRNE, D. and WONG, T. J. (1962) Racial prejudice, interpersonal attraction, and assumed dissimilarity of attitudes. *Journal of Abnormal and Social Psychology* **65,** 246–53.

McNEMAR, Q. (1955) *Psychological Statistics*. New York: Wiley.

MORRIS, C. (1956) *Varieties of Human Value*. Chicago: Univer. Chicago Press.

ROKEACH, M. (Ed.) (1960) *The Open and the Closed Mind*. New York: Basic Books.

ROKEACH, M. (1961) Belief versus race as determinants of social distance: Comment on Triandis' paper. *Journal of Abnormal and Social Psychology*, **62,** 187–8.

ROKEACH, M., SMITH, PATRICIA W. and EVANS, R. I. (1960) Two kinds of prejudice or one? In M. Rokeach (Ed.), *The Open and Closed Mind*. New York: Basic Books, pp. 132–68.

TRIANDIS, H. C. (1961) A note on Rokeach's theory of prejudice. *Journal of Abnormal and Social Psychology* **62,** 184–6.

Colonialism and Racism in Algeria (*circa,* 1955)

JEAN COHEN

COLONIALISM is primarily a question of economics entailing the ruthless, methodical exploitation of native peoples. In Algeria the majority of native workers have no opportunity to improve their lot; there are no trade unions, no family allowances, no workers' canteens, no housing estates. Wages are determined by the minimum necessary to sustain a worker's production. In Europe, however, conditions are less severe and the worker has been success-ful in obtaining some small fringe benefits, such as radio sets, bicycles and perhaps even curtains for his windows. But in Algeria, the worker owns only four mud walls, a sheepskin on the floor and just enough bread and figs to keep himself alive and to work a ten-hour day. Shanty towns, cave dwellings, undernourishment, dirt and illiteracy and universal exploitation are the most flagrant and, no doubt, best known aspects of colonialism.

But colonialism has also another aspect, less obvious, less tangible and more difficult to define. Because it is both psychological and commonplace, it cannot be described with documents or statistics. In order to make this understood—or rather to get the feeling of it—one must compile anecdotes, analyse everyday expressions, and amass trivial details and little signs. Each in itself may be insignificant, but in the aggregate may constitute a very important side of colonialism and amount to a form of "spiritual murder".

"Spiritual murder?" Any colonist accused of such a crime would be astonished and incapable of understanding what was implied by the term. He believes in the land and its productivity, in the government and in American automobiles. "Spiritual murder" suggests hatred and cruelty. But temperamentally the Algerian colonist is neither cruel nor filled with hatred; on the contrary he is a well disposed, good-natured fellow, who enjoys a good laugh and an easy life. Has he ever deliberately harmed the natives? On the contrary; he has neither tried to drive them out, nor to destroy them. Compared with the genocide practiced by the Anglo-Saxons in America,

64

the Algerian colonist[1] has every right to be proud of his record; he has respected the customs of the natives, their religion and their poverty. For what can he be blamed? With no knowledge of the past, he believes implicitly that the natives have always been as he finds them. He is quite oblivious of the fact that a shanty town is not what the Muslim really prefers in the way of urbanization; nor does he realize that poverty, illiteracy and unemployment are the consequences of his own works. Moreover, he is totally unaware of his greatest crime—the creation of a stereotyped image of the native Algerian, a complete fabrication which, although counterfeit, passes as legal currency. A stereotype is not necessarily something to be despised, but on the other hand it can be the worst form of oppression ever invented. Woe betide the man who finds himself cast in a false image by those whose path he crosses. It is no use fighting against it; such a stereotype is stronger than reality. If it endures at all, it eventually becomes true.

In North Africa colonialism has created a stereotype to which the name "Arab" has been given. What is an Arab? The descendant of the famous conquerors of the Middle Ages? Not at all; he is merely that strange creature clad in a tattered *djellabah* and filthy head cloth. His wife is swathed in a white robe and his children go barefoot. There is no mistaking him. Everything about him, both physical and moral, testify to his essentially "Arab" qualities. He can neither read nor write; he speaks pidgin French (*sabir*), believes in Mahomet, sleeps on the floor, eats *couscous* and never washes. Not only is he dirty, but he is also a liar, a thief, lazy and aggressive. It is unwise to pick a quarrel with him for he is as good as anyone with a knife. Don't entrust him with any difficult work, since he has neither the inclination nor the ability to carry it out; he would only make "an Arab's job of it"—an expression which has passed into current usage. By all means give him some thankless task, because then you need only pay him a pittance. You need not be ashamed, because he needs nothing.

How did this image originate? The answer is not difficult to find; it is the result of colonialism itself.

[1]For the sake of accuracy, one must make a distinction between colonists and European city dwellers. Their reactions are not exactly similar. The general attitude towards the native population has been dictated by the colonists who are responsible for the creation of the "arab" image; the city dwellers have only contributed minor variations. It must also be remembered that no opinions on human behaviour can ever be 100 per cent true. The reader would therefore be well advised to add a mental reservation, such as "in most cases" or "nearly always" when reading the opinions expressed in this article.

J. Cohen

In the non-colonial world there are two classes of society—the proletariat and the bourgeoisie. The proletariat are not so well dressed as the bourgeoisie; their speech is coarser and their hands are roughened by toil. But there the difference ends. Bourgeois and proletarian both have the same physical characteristics, they both speak the same language and both like the same things, and both believe (or disbelieve) in the same god. They have similar names and are sometimes even cousins. The middle classes have recognized that the proletariat should enjoy the same legal and political rights as themselves, and, furthermore, when it comes to the question of patriotism, they are united. A working man is a working man by accident. There is nothing that justifies his condition. It is incidental and is not due to any essential quality in his make-up; thus he is always a reproach to the middle classes and remains a constant cause of an uneasy conscience.

In North Africa there are also two social classes—the bourgeoisie and the proletariat, but these are also two peoples, two separate "races": "Europeans" and "Arabs". The Europeans constitute the bourgeoisie, the Arabs the proletariat.[2] The Arabs therefore belong, at one and the same time, to a specific social stratum and a specific race. Because of their race, or to be more exact, because they are brown skinned, they wear the *djellabah* and worship Allah, and because of their social class, they sleep on the ground and wear rags. But during 120 years of colonialism there has always been confusion in the minds of Europeans who have never been able to distinguish between race and class, "Arabs" and misery. A race of proletarians; what a paradoxical concept; but this is the basis of colonialism.

In addition to this aspect we must add a second; the colonial system has barred the coloured people from the road to history. This road was cut off abruptly in the middle of the nineteenth century with the introduction of industry, compulsory schooling, cheap books and the press. In Algeria, after 1830, the Arabic language has scarcely ever been used in writing. Although it possesses the same system of graphic signs once used by the great North African Arab historian Ibn-Khaldoun (1332–1406), there are now practically no books or newspapers printed in the language. Arabic in Algeria, therefore, has become one of those non-written languages like

[2]This is not quite exact. A certain proportion of the workers in the towns are European. But they are, by comparison with the natives, an upper working class, better paid, better thought of, and who, until recently, showed the same colonialist reaction. Since 1945, however, the situation has evolved favourably in the sense that there is a growing solidarity with the native workers.

Polynesian or low-Breton. Since 1830, the native Algerian has read nothing, unless he knows French. But who is there to teach him? Four-fifths of Algerian children do not attend school. To economic subordination is then added historical regression. Between them, these two factors that have made the native Algerian a mediaeval relic, which the colonists like to regard as the "real" native, the "eternal Arab" as created by God.

In this way the stereotype has become objective. The colonist need no longer have a bad conscience; exploitation can be regarded as justifiable from a metaphysical standpoint. In Europe it is no longer possible for the middle classes honestly to believe that the proletariat is in any way essentially different to themselves; they are too much alike. In Algeria, however, the difference is manifestly obvious, it can be seen, heard and felt. This difference between human beings explains and justifies the differences within society. Since the Arab needs nothing, why raise his wages? Since he likes sleeping on the ground, why build him a house? What use is there looking after him? "*Ces gens-la, ça ne crève pas.*" And of what use is it to respect his liberty? To a delegation asking that some Muslim children, held on remand after a demonstration, should be released, the judge replied; "What's the good? They are better off here than at home!" The worst of it is, he was quite right.

Thus the Arab has lost the dignity of manhood. This is not just a metaphor, but a living truth. A man is someone who produces in me a certain specific inner reaction, someone for whom I have at the least some social consideration. If I don't know him, I address him as "Monsieur" and say "Vous". If he were in difficulties, I would come to his help, or maybe find excuses for not doing so. If I saw two men fighting, I would separate them, or alternatively turn away in order not to become involved. But with an Arab, things are different. An Arab is someone of no consequence whatsoever, who is addressed with the familiar "tu", who is bullied by the police, and with whom gaolers have no patience. An Arab is the fellow you call to carry the bags or wash the car. At the sight of him, the shop assistant instinctively becomes more wary, the unaccompanied woman hastens her steps. If he is wounded or ill, he does not arouse the normal reflexes of compassion and pity. No decent woman in Europe could bear to see a 5-year-old child sleeping on a pavement; in Algeria it is not only tolerated because it is such a frequent sight, but what is more serious, because it is so *normal*. An Arab would never "hitch-hike". He would hesitate to ask for a light; he doesn't ask for credit in shops, or if he does, he thinks it necessary to leave a deposit to secure the loan. He knows that in the eyes of Europeans

67

he is not a man and behaves accordingly; hence he is undemanding and hesitates to complain or to protest. But when he does, it often takes an explosive form, because he knows that a simple demand would be disregarded. In consequence it is said that he is quarrelsome and vindictive, but what this overlooks is that he is compelled to take justice into his own hands.

The language used by Europeans testifies to the fact that the Arab is not regarded as a man. One day, a European was giving evidence in court. "Are there any other witnesses?" asked the judge. "Yes, five: two men and three Arabs." This expression is revealing; the Arab is not a man, he is merely an Arab. If you are told that someone wishes to see you, you may be sure that the "someone" is a European; had he been a native, the fact would be specified. The Arab is denied the dignity of being an anonymous "someone"; he is excluded from the social hierarchy altogether. Here is another very telling phrase heard recently: "It was an Arab, but he was dressed as a person." A typical remark! Native costume is enough to designate him, enough to depersonalize him. This is why many Muslims who wish to avoid being treated as "Arabs" dress in European fashion. But, not daring to substitute the national head-dress for a European hat (which is regarded by their co-religionists as shameful) they go bare-headed summer and winter, come rain, come shine.

Excluded from society, the Arab is also deprived of all individuality: each man is called "Mahomet", each woman, "Fatima". A single name, because they are all of a kind.

The Arab has therefore lost, one by one, all the attributes of a man, and this is why he does not count, or only counts for half. "Has such and such a doctor got a large practice?" "Yes, but his patients are all Arabs."

An element of hate, contempt and indifference is present in the actual complex of colonial racism. But hate is not the dominant feature, except when the native "shows his teeth". When times are peaceful, the Arab is not regarded as an evildoer who must be destroyed. There is no *passionate* anti-Arab sentiment, equivalent to the extreme anti-Semitism. Contempt is a more marked feature, but it is not an essential element if, by contempt, a feeling of superiority is implied. The colonist does not consider himself superior, for the very good reason that he never gives the matter any thought. I mean that he does not regard himself as one of a chosen people, with a superior culture which gives him the right to stand in judgment over others like the race-conscious Germans. In his own eyes the colonist is just an ordinary civilized human being; in short, just a plain ordinary fellow. The

Arab, on the other hand, is an outsider. He dresses differently from everyone else; he does not react in the expected way; he does not think like a normal person. He is not really a man. That is why the basis of colonial racism is one of exclusion and negation. You don't hate the Arab, you just ignore him. You don't want to know him. There is no single aspect of Algerian colonial life which is not affected by this negative attitude. An American journalist visiting North Africa once stated: "In this country there are no signs of racial segregation." True, in Algeria he did not see notices such as he was accustomed to see in his own country, bearing the legend "Forbidden" or "Reserved". Such a form of public segregation does not exist here, but this is only because it is not needed. There is no notice on the door of the Ritz forbidding a working man to come in for a cup of tea. Such a notice would be pointless. It is the same in Algeria. Third-class railway coaches are not officially reserved for natives but it is here they go all the same. It is true that if an Arab is rash enough to travel first class he will have the privilege of having the compartment to himself, except if the train is full. The Arabs have their own quarter, their own cafés and cinemas where no European ever goes. Segregation started as a one-way affair, and still remains so. A servant is willing to go to his master's house but the master would never go to return the compliment. The natives even have their own doctors and lawyers. Not by choice but one clientèle drives out another and specialization happens of its own accord. Apart fron official ceremonies, Arabs and Europeans hardly ever entertain each other. Friendships between colonists and natives are extremely rare, sexual relations almost nil, and mixed marriages are non-existent. European children do not play with "little Arabs". They are not forbidden to do so, but from their cradles they have been told that if they are naughty the "Arab" will come to fetch them. One does not play with the children of a werewolf.

If this negative attitude is evident on the ordinary day-to-day level, it operates even more radically on the cultural level. The curse which weighs on the Arab also affects his language, his art, his past and his life. The French colonist usually speaks Arabic, but this is from necessity. He neither tries very hard nor pretends to speak it well. Arabic classes in the *lycées* have half a dozen pupils, while English classes are filled to overflowing. Arab music —that's to say Andalusian music—is regarded as barbaric. Egyptian films have a strictly native audience and are shown in special cinemas. When the colonist builds a villa for himself, it is nearly always inspired by a Swiss chalêt or a Greek temple, never by Moorish architecture, however elegant and suitable for the climate it may be. Of all that constitutes the soul and taste of Islam, the colonist has availed himself of nothing, with the exception of *couscous*. Even certain colours, certain shapes, beautiful in themselves, are not acceptable because they have a "Moorish flavour".

Muslims in North Africa lead their own lives and conduct their own dialogues over the heads of the Europeans. They initiate and disband parties, constitute their own religious or philosophical movements, of which no echo ever reaches the ears of the colonists with whom they rub shoulders. To give a single example: not one European in a thousand has ever heard the name of Sheikh Brahimi in his own home town. But this theologian from Tlemçen is read throughout the whole of Islam and is received in Pakistan with the honours due to a sovereign. Just experiment yourself. Pick any European in Algeria and ask him who are the Oulemas? He won't know. Ask him what are the Algerian parties? He confuses one with the other. What is the historical background of Algeria? He knows nothing of it. What difference is there between "Berbers" and "Arabs"? He cannot decide. I myself have astonished my fellow citizens by telling them that one of the principal demands made by the native population is the separation of Church and State. "What!" they exclaim, "Aren't they separate in Algeria?" The answer is "no"; in Algeria, the government appoints and pays the salaries of the numerous *muftis* and *imams*.

This negative attitude is also to be found in the literary world. North Africa has several very good French writers. However, most of them don't seem to be aware of the existence of a native way of life. But it would be unfair to criticize them for this omission. A genuine author, unless he wishes to write so-called "edifying literature", should confine himself to writing about what he himself has experienced and felt. How can an author, born and bred in strictly European surroundings, live and experience the problems that beset the Arab community? Between Algeria and France there are only a thousand kilometres of sea; between the European and native quarters of a city, colonialism has created a void of astronomic proportions.

When the first colonists arrived in Algeria they had intention of settling there and putting down roots. They disembarked there, with the intention of devoting ten years of their lives to making money and then returning home. But the land was fertile, there was an abundance of cheap labour and the climate was temperate. They stayed on and had children. Today the great majority of the French in Algeria have fathers and grandfathers who were born in the country. Thus they feel at home here and intend to remain so.

It is this that gives the Algerian problem its peculiar character, for there are people who wish to remain both Algerian and French, but who are, at the same time, opposed to giving the Algerian people equality with the French. They refuse to allow equality for calculated economic reasons and also from the dictates of their hearts. Algeria is their country, but not their motherland; it remains a colony. The colonist has inherited, from his grandfather's time, the conviction that he is there to make money not to create a new country. Of what use would it be to build museums, libraries, or to preserve natural beauties, open up parks and seaside resorts? Would this produce more crops to the acre? There is nothing so sad or so ugly as an Algerian village in the colonized zones. But the colonist could not care less. When he wants security, green pastures or picturesque scenery, all he has to do is take the aeroplane or the boat to France. When he returns from his annual holiday in a French holiday resort, he always looks with disdain at his poor, miserable, abandoned and ruined Algerian country, whose natural beauties are slowly disappearing under the ugly domination of colonialism.

The true motherland remains metropolitan France. It is to France that the colonist looks. France exports machinery and finished products, France provides ideas, books and teachers, France sets the fashion and dictates good taste. In crossing the sea, cultural ideas become several years out of date and are often debased. But what does that matter? Everything coming from France has an enhanced value; in return, the colonist is ashamed of being an Algerian; the word Algerian even has a pejorative implication. To say "it's real Algerian" is far from complimentary. The "French from France" enjoy a position of prestige in Algeria, similar to that of a Parisian in the provinces. This is what Algeria is. It is a *sous-province*, with petty social coteries and ridiculous provincial snobberies. Land of "notables", where colonists, who are merchants or civil servants, are treated as princes. The local press devotes whole columns to their obituaries, marriages, receptions and the honours conferred on them. A *prefect* (or local commissioner) is treated like a king. His retirement is regarded as a major event. Every time he opens his mouth, the local press devotes a whole page to reporting "the noble words" of this representative of France "which have brought comfort to the afflicted peoples of the Plateau". As for the Governor, he is no less than God himself.

Algeria is divided into three French *departements*. However, this is legal casuistry. Algeria is not a *departement* but a colony. Its role is to furnish primary products and raw materials. Quantity is more important than quality. This is true in the economic sphere as well as on a cultural level. The Algerian wine producer is not concerned with producing a vintage *cru* any more than he is interested in creating literature or art. The role of a colony is never, and never has been, to promote any form of culture. But is any authentic culture possible without real links with a people and their past? But colonialism has debased the people and nullified their history. With its millions of untilled acres, Algeria suddenly appeared on the map one fine day in 1830. There was no time to cultivate both the land and the spirit.

Create an Algerian community? But what with? With Arabs? How absurd! If it were suggested to a colonist that careers and civil service jobs should be open to native Algerians, such an idea would be met with utter incredulity. The stereotype of the Arab which he has created is so firmly implanted in his mind, that the very thought of a judge or a mayor dressed in a burnous seems to him not only absurd, but almost comic. In any case, he could not possibly believe an Arab competent to undertake such work. As we have already pointed out, an Arab is essentially a pauper, lazy by nature, dirty by preference and an ignoramus by vocation. "Listen, I'll give you an example . . ." An example? There are hundreds of them. Some are true; nor should we be surprised. For ever since Algeria was colonized, colonialism has formed its own image of the native. Never having had the experience of school discipline, having gone barefoot from father to son, always uncertain of where to find his next meal, it is only natural that the native worker has developed an unstable mentality and that he is irresponsible and rebellious. Without any education, without a trade, with no professional ties, he wanders about the country, taking the first thing offered, happy that another day has been taken care of. He is what others have made him; he is always the victim of unjust complaints. The colonist is like a father who constantly grumbles at his own children.

The settler has never conceived any relationship possible other than that of colonist and colonized. Any other sort of relationship seems unthinkable to him. When he hears about native claims to equal rights and free elections he believes that they either want his death or his expulsion—a question of "suitcase or coffin". He feels rightly indignant. "Why do they want to drive us out? After all, we made this country." Trying to explain to him that not for a moment is there any question of expulsion is like banging your head against a brick wall. He is and always has been a colonist. If he can't continue to be one, then he'll go. Besides, being more conscious of colonial oppression than he cares to admit, he cannot imagine the natives wishing for anything other than the expulsion of their oppressors. Confront him with Bourguiba's statement: "If the French try to leave, we will force them to stay" and he will merely shake his head and say, "really, how naïve can you be". Perhaps if he is in a more confiding mood, he will wink and say, "well, what would you do in their shoes?" It is no use telling him that the country needs a nucleus of experienced people and cannot survive without the European population; or that racialism is not essential to the health of the vineyard, that Algeria does not have to be a colony and that the colonist could perfectly well continue to live and prosper there, even if it were to become a democratic country like any other, even, for that matter, like France. He won't believe you, because he does not want to. Of the two roles he plays here—as head of some commercial enterprise and as feudal lord, the second is the only one that he recognizes. If he had to abandon that and assume only the role and privileges that devolve on the head of a business under the capitalist system, he would not recognize himself. No, it were better to return to France, where he has prudently invested his capital in land or real estate. True, it would be a wrench for him to leave; for after all, this country is his, but only in a possessive sense. His departure, however, would not mean real exile because, here, whatever he may say, he has never really felt at home. But this is only natural, for he regards the eight million natives as so many strangers, and after all, one can only feel at home among ones own kind.

Colonialism presents immense economic, social and political problems, the most important of which is political. Some say that the social problem should take priority over political ones. But this is wrong because politics condition the social order and, above all, condition human nature. In this instance the native is not alone in wanting to be treated like a man. The French colonist has never seen any answer to this problem other than assimilation, by which he means "westernization". The reason is obvious, for in the eyes of a colonist "human" is synonymous with "Western". If the Arabs really want to be men let them dress in European fashion and speak French. The nature of this argument is well known; the master identifies himself with people in general, but does not admit the slave is a person. But the colonist forgets, when arguing in this way, that it is he who really rejects the idea of assimilation. He is constantly placing obstacles in the way, for example he nearly rose in revolt when the Blum–Violette plan proposed to give French nationality to some 50,000 native Algerians who were recipients of decorations or certificates of education. Would assimilation have been

73

viable had the colonists agreed to this plan? No one knows but some think so. Until recently the Berbers were still only partially Islamic and had no particular nationalistic ideals. Ten thousand teachers in Algeria might have been enough to make ten million more Frenchmen. Such a thing was then possible, but today it is too late. Islam and the concept of nationalism have won the hearts and minds of the vast majority of the native population. This is the inevitable result of the negative attitude of the colonists. This is a normal reaction and applies on a social as well as an individual level. An individual who sees himself threatened by those around him reacts in one of two ways. He either tries to efface himself and lose himself in the crowd (which was the attitude adopted by the Jewish minority in Algeria), or alternatively he draws attention to himself and deliberately enhances his own individual characteristics. This was the reaction of the majority of native Algerians. The rapidly growing strength of Islam[3] has no other meaning than a reaffirmation of the self and the awakening of a national conscience is no more than a negation of a negation.

[3]This Islamic sentiment must not be overlooked by all those Algerians who acknowledge the charge of being "theocratists" as opposed to being Muslim nationalists. Inversely, Muslims should not forget that Islam retains its own religious content which supersedes that of nationalism.

Variations on Black and White

ROGER BASTIDE and FRANÇOIS RAVEAU

ETHNOPSYCHIATRY is divided between two schools of thought. According to the organicist thesis, every race has its own pathology specific to its constitution—"Negroes never have paranoia", "There are no black schizophrenics". According to the thesis of cultural anthropology, mental illness is determined by the cultural environment of those affected, and in this case illnesses, which are essentially the same throughout the human race, merely assume different cultural forms according to the civilization in which they occur. Of course, the situation grows more complicated when civilizations change under the impact of mutual contact and interpenetration, as is happening in present-day Africa.

Of particular interest in the light it sheds on this controversy is the colour problem. Skin colour is an organic and genetic trait which can generate specific pathological behaviour: one might even use in this context the well-known expression "psychiatric negritude". But this pathological behaviour arises as a reaction to a white environment; in other words, it is not colour as pigmentation which acts as a factor in mental illness, but colour as a representation, or better, a symbol. If we were to replace the colour problem (black—white) by the problem of height (tall—short) or even by a social index (country dweller—city dweller), we should not really be changing the problem, for in each case a difference is involved, and it is the realization of this difference which provides the driving force for neurosis or success. This last observation may appear to set narrow limits to our subject, but this is not the case: although differences in height and physical appearance do play a part in certain psychoses and neuroses which are erotic in origin, they have not assumed anything like the importance of colour differences in our civilizations. The field of colour differences is far richer in symbolism and presents far more variations for various cultures and societies.

The theme of colour in psychoses and neuroses is therefore a fitting

75

subject for study, and it will be seen that important theoretical and practical conclusions may be derived from our observations. One of the authors of this article had his attention drawn to the problem in the course of a social psychiatry survey in Brazil. He was struck initially by the role played by colour in the dreams of Blacks and Mulattos; it symbolized rejection in the case of the Blacks, and in the case of the Mulattos, the Whites' reaction to their wish for social ascendancy. For example, a Mulatto of the coloured lower middle class dreamed that on retiring for the night he put his yellow slippers near his bed, but when he got up next morning he found that while he had been asleep his yellow slippers had been taken away, and black ones put in their place. The same symbolism is apparent in the manias of the mentally sick: psychiatric wards contain inventors of cunning machines designed to turn very dark-skinned Negroes white, or, by a compensatory reaction, Messiahs who in spite of or because of their black skin, have been entrusted by God with the mission of saving white humanity. This is because Brazil is a multiracial class society, and not a caste society; unlike the United States, prejudices there are not related to origin but to appearance, and consequently the lighter the colour of one's skin, the higher one can rise in society. Thus colour becomes a symbol of social status, placing one within the class system, and it is around this symbolic meaning that the images of dreams and manias crystallize out. Starting from these few observations, it was tempting to investigate what happens in other social situations, in the totally different world of the Africans who come to live for a short time in the world of the Whites, to prepare themselves for their future task as directors or ruling élite.

The sociological situation of the African in France is completely different from that of the Black man in America. It is evident that in both cases, the problem of the relationship between colour and mental illness presents itself only when the sufferer is placed in a situation which makes him conscious of his blackness. In Africa, the African does not have this awareness, but on his arrival in France he is made to feel his difference, his "Negritude", just as the Afro-American does. Nevertheless, this awareness does not take the same form in both cases, because the symbolic meaning of colour is not the same. This is easily ascertained if one looks through the case-histories of Blacks confined with psychoses in the mental hospitals of Paris. Persecution mania related to alleged hostility of the white environment is found much more frequently in Black West Indians than in Africans, who show above all attacks of anxiety related to hospitalization in a general health service. This is because the West Indian carries with him a particular colour symbolism which is not unlike the Brazilian symbolism, while the African has no such conception. For persecution mania to appear in the African, certain special conditions have to be satisfied. One student had exhibited slight adaptation difficulties during his first academic year in France, but had none the less done brilliantly in his studies; however, after three weeks in the provinces he had developed a persecution mania, accompanied by deep anxiety, and had to be interned for treatment in a specialized institution. "Because he was black, people were hostile"; "People were laughing at him behind his back"; "Because he was an African, they were all pretending to be nice, but because he was Black they rejected him". A close study of this subject carried out by one of us showed that the patient's adaptation threshold, which was adequate for Paris, where he lived surrounded by African friends, was insufficient for the provinces, where he stood alone confronted by the curiosity of the Whites, and had to come to terms with the situations of his new environment alone. Then he very rapidly built up this mania containing persecution themes and putting an interpretation upon his skin colour; he himself asked to be treated, so that he could "live like a White among the Whites". Here, therefore, colour only appears as a symbol of "difference", and not as a symbol of inferior "social status". In order for the patient to become aware of this difference as a hostility factor, certain conditions have to be satisfied—conditions which define a threshold of adaptation to the white world. When the West Indian sees his blackness as more than a difference in colour, he is thinking of it as it is regarded in the West Indies, in the light of ideologies of superiority—inferiority. In the field of neuroses, we also find differences between West Indians and Africans. We are not, of course, denying the existence of colour prejudice, which is often present in a hypocritical or concealed form; nevertheless, Black people in Brazil misrepresent their own failures to themselves by introducing racial discrimination as a rationalization of their own lack of effort. Similarly, compensatory aggression in West Indians makes use of colour as an outlet. Black West Indians living in France tend to see a restriction which is applicable to everyone, as being a measure of discrimination directed solely at themselves. Nobody wants me because I am Black. On the other hand, this attitude is hardly ever found in Africans, so that we must look elsewhere for the meaning and symbolism of colour for the African.

In most of the cases we examined, if not all, the problems and difficulties which crystallized out around the concept of colour were difficulties of

77

adaptation either to French society (human relations) or to French culture (study programmes). From case to case, there were subtle variations on the theme of colour: it would cause or foster psychopathological disturbances, or be introduced later as a rationalization of failure, or serve as an explanation for troubles of a different kind after the event, while also increasing them. Sometimes the colour white symbolized the hostility of the outside world, or the wickedness of men, while black stood for a refuge, and the lost paradise of childhood. Sometimes the patient would turn against his blackness, which was considered as responsible for his failure, and Western and Christian symbols would be adopted which identified whiteness with purity, and blackness with evil. But in all cases, at a certain point in the crisis came an awareness of the whiteness of the surrounding world: "Why do people write in black on a white page, and not in white on a black page?" one of our Africans asked in astonishment, objectivizing, by his anguished query, his desire to be assimilated into white culture, to be white himself.

Since it is impossible to reproduce in this article the series of paintings done by this patient, which mark the successive phases of his illness up to the point where a cure was effected, we cannot analyse them in detail here, but at least we can give some general indications. To begin with we are in a nightmare world where all the colours turn against the patient, white denoting the hostility of the country which rejects and is hard to please, the colour of aggressive people, but black also possessing a sinister significance. The cure is effected when the patient realizes that colour has only a "phenomenological", and not an "ontological" value, not in itself constituting a reality, but belonging to the realm of appearances, since it is possible to paint the same individual in different colours. But this realization, which will enable the subject to discard his anxiety and adapt to the white world without rejecting himself as black, did not come suddenly but was acquired in stages. There were two main stages in the cure: at first, the patient's desire for whiteness was demonstrated by his rejection of his black face, which he painted in different colours; but during this first phase the dominant idea was not the possibility, demonstrated by paint, of separating the real person from the mere appearance of colour, but the rejection of a particular colour considered as a reality. The patient had to pass through a second phase, and destroy what amounted to the obsessive theme of the mirror. This he did by painting first the therapist—who was white but had shown interest in him, and demonstrated that whiteness is not necessarily hostility—then, by extension, other subjects, in "green" or "pink". It was only at this point, and because he was thinking more of other subjects than of himself, that he was able to realize that changing the colour does not destroy the likeness; thus he made the transition between colour as *trauma*, and colour as an aesthetic game. In our conclusion we shall return to the phenomenon of therapeutic transfer in cases where the doctor is of a different colour from his patient; for the moment, we have indicated the principal phases in the dispersal of a neurosis centring around colour.

The great majority of Africans who come to France grow progressively more accustomed to the white world, but it appears that there is very probably an initial shock, because in certain cases at least the juxtaposition of their blackness with the white body of a sexual partner upsets their precarious state of equilibrium. One of our subjects dreamed that he was sitting on his bed beside a young white girl who was completely naked, but they did not touch each other or even speak to one another; a white man appeared and made a sign, and the young girl got up to follow him; there ensued a quarrel between the two rivals which awoke the sleeper. Almost always, in the dreams we made a note of, the white woman was the subject of a fight, as if she were, on account of her colour, a forbidden creature, reserved for the Whites, belonging to a different world to which the Black had not, must not have access. It is interesting to note that these dreams of white girls do not appear to be accompanied by nocturnal emissions, while they often accompany dreams about black girls. Moreover, these dreams of struggles for the body which seemed to offer itself to the stronger rival were generally considered as "not ordinary dreams", because they were accompanied by violent palpitations and cephalic disturbances ("it seemed as if my brain was about to stop functioning"), and patients awoke feeling stiff; one of these Africans wrote: "return to reasonable sleep, then a normal dream".

Nevertheless, does not desire for the white girl constitute a betrayal of the black girl, who will also be forbidden in her turn? "Commotion about A.... But her parents, specially her mother, obstruct our plan. She tries her hardest to approach me. Each episode is accompanied by bathing in the *marigot* (branch of a stream) with friends, as in an enchanted land." The rest of the dream, although it no longer has a sexual character, expresses the same anxiety in a different register. It is a commemoration celebration in African surroundings, but Christians (symbolic Whites) are also participating, and the celebration ends in failure. We could give many other examples—like that of the subject who dreamed that he returned to his native village, but as he walked out of the plane and approached the huts, everybody ran away and disappeared, as if it were a white person arriving and not a son of the village.

Sexuality, therefore, only revives something deeper which is expressed through colour conflict. The dreams of which we are talking cannot be analysed out of the context of the patient's life history—it is this which gives significance to the nocturnal images. Desire for the white woman can operate at different levels, from normal desire to aggressiveness, but in most of the cases of neurosis which we were able to follow up, it symbolized the desire for whiteness, the desire for intimacy with, possession of and parti-cipation in the white world; and the rival was the man whose presence and look denounced the patient's blackness. It is precisely because this desire expresses the wish for whiteness, that it brings with it somatic disturbances and the feeling of racial culpability. Will the patient not be rejected upon his return, because he will be seen with a new colour, like a man who has become white? As if, by some magic effect of sexual relations, by coming into contact with and embracing the white girl's body, her whiteness rubbed off onto him.

Against our interpretations, one could of course object that the pheno-mena we have described merely demonstrate a well-known fact—namely, that the surrounding culture provides the pathological subject with means and forms of expression. In megalomania, the patient's choice of historical personages is related to his nationality: the French megalomaniac is more likely to become Charlemagne, Napoleon or the President of the Republic, than Cavour or Hitler. Up to the nineteenth century especially, the coen-aesthesic disturbances associated with chronic hallucinatory psychoses were interpreted as divine commandments, diabolical temptations or the effects of witchcraft; today, rays, waves and electricity are used as explanations—the patient is being electrocuted, brought under remote control, or bombarded with X-rays. Similarly, might not the motifs of blackness and whiteness which are provided by the two civilizations between which the African living in France is divided, be used merely through mental economy, as the most convenient and most readily available pseudological explanation for the pathological state? This is partially true, and we were careful to point out at the outset that the concept of colour was present in psychoses as a ration-alization. However, several additions to this statement are necessary: firstly, the sociologist who is interested in mental illness is able to achieve more than the psychiatrist; otherwise, it would not have been necessary to add to psychiatry the new branch of social psychiatry. The study of ideologies, mythologies and superstructures occupies a place of considerable importance in contemporary sociology, and no sociologist, even if he saw these only as "reflections", would be tempted to ignore them; the rationalizations of mental patients are their own ideologies, and as such present an analogous degree of interest. Moreover, societies provide the mentally sick, as well as the normal, with a set of collective representations, which are the same for both. But there are some representations which are above all images or signs, and are used essentially as means of communication, which makes them relatively neutral; there are others which are also values, and are strongly affectively charged; the values which they represent change according to the civilization, being sometimes positive, sometimes negative, and this quality in itself determines behaviour, various reactions and inhibitions. Blackness and whiteness fall in the second category of collective representations. In the first type of situation, as with electricity now and demonology formerly, or with the list of great men to be reincarnated, society provides the image, and the patient transforms it into a symbol. In the second type of situation, society provides an image which is already a symbol, with pathogenic content, which the neurotic weaves into the pattern of his conflict or distress. We believe that the examples we have given adequately demonstrate the difference between the two cases.

Colour therefore becomes the crystallizing element in the illness, the nucleus which has to be destroyed. Sometimes Africans think that they will be able to cure their friend by bringing him a white prostitute with whom he may free himself from his colour trauma. This generally produces a disastrous effect and increases the virulence of the crisis. What is needed is a psychotherapy of "disontogenization" or shattered identity: this is the first practical conclusion to emerge from our study. Naturally, we do not intend to imply that the problems of adaptation to a different way of life do not produce any other symbols—for instance, in the dreams and T.A.T.[1] responses of one of our subjects we found the theme of death, and more especially the "sense to be given to death". For him, death stood for the successive detachments from the traditional environment, and the detachments gave rise to an anxiety feeling as to how he could justify his life. If his detachment from African culture and his self-chosen goal of entering the white culture did not meet with success, he would find himself stripped of every possibility of positive integration and structuring; he would truly have died for nothing, and his death would not be the symbolic death of initiation

[1]*Editorial note.* Thematic Apperception Test.

into another world. Although the same affective content may find interpretation in various symbols, however it is still true to say that with Africans the most frequent and natural is the symbolic confrontation between the Black and the White, the rejection both of blackness and of the idea of growing white, or the symbolic recuperation of blackness as a response to the aggressiveness of whiteness. This means that the cure for the neurosis, however paradoxical this may seem, consists in the cure of its major symptom, so close in the connection between the expressed and the expressive.

Another conclusion which may be drawn, this time of theoretical interest, concerns the processes of transfer and counter-transfer in the therapeutic relationship. Devereux, in his attempt to elaborate a trans-cultural analysis, already observed that according to the prevalent family patterns the therapist might play the role of father or of mother's brother; but he paid no attention to the fact that the therapist belonged to a different race. In the case of the African and the white therapist, more clearly than with the Indians studied by Devereux, the colour difference demonstrates the importance of the element of ethnic participation. Within the patient–doctor relationship, the therapist will always enact the role of some family image with all its attendant ambiguity; Freud, who belonged to the same social and cultural environment as his patients, saw only the family image, and generally speaking his successors merely took up at this point where he left off. It seemed to us that in addition the counter-transfer made use of the collective images which one race has of another, and the doctor symbolized the world of the Whites, and that the ambiguity consisted also in the duality of the wicked White man and of the doctor who is tending the patient and trying to effect a cure; it seemed that psychotherapy was achieving a relativization of colour, which consequently lost its ontological character: the therapist could become the father, therefore—and this marked the beginning of the cure—the colour of the father was not of overriding importance. Thus the processes of transfer and counter-transfer are complicated in "trans-racial" therapy by the addition to the family images of sociological images symbolized by colour. It would be interesting to verify this conclusion by observing what happens when the therapist is black and the patient white. Only when we have accumulated a sufficient number of case analyses, and interchanged the colour of the participants, shall we be able to make a more effective assessment of the place of colour symbolism in transfer and counter-transfer, with all its social and cultural, as well as family, implications.

Lastly, it remains to examine the place of the Black and the White in projective tests. The Rorschach is obviously more significant here than the T.A.T., but a comparison of the two tests in this respect is of considerable interest. Before considering this subject, we should like to point out without drawing any conclusions, but merely as an additional relevant fact, that all our subjects up till now have dreamed in black and white only. But certain subjects give a meaning to these colours in their dreams: white is identified with the ward or hospital atmosphere and hence with illness; to leave behind this world of white overalls and white faces and return to the black, is proof of the cure. Are similarities encountered in the interpretation of the test images?

As regards content, the T.A.T. images evoke or impose the world of the Whites, while the Rorschach test leaves the imagination freer, and more readily allows the African personality to appear. This is very clearly seen when the two tests are compared for one subject. One of our patients related the T.A.T. pictures to memories of his school work: "This is a play similar to the tragedy of *Andromaque*"; "One is tempted to make a comparison with Lamartine when he had lost Elvire" (No. 7);[2] "That reminds me of Chateaubriand" (No. 9); "That rather reminds me of Pyrrhus when he said '*Vous me fuyez, Madame*' ('you seek to avoid me, Madam')". It is certain that these literary comparisons are, to some extent, defence mechanisms against an emotional content which is a strong anxiety source; the subject is avoiding involvement by projecting his personal experience into the dramatic roles. It is true, too, that these "dramatizations" may be thought to indicate hysterical tendencies, but one must not pursue this idea too far. The subject was still unaccustomed to our tests and examinations, and envisaged the T.A.T. as yet another end-of-term exam. He attempted to show the extent of his knowledge, he assumed the position of a pupil. On the contrary, when confronted with the Rorschach Test the same student talked about Africa: "That looks like an insect which is very common in Africa, it has two wings and antennae" (No. I);[3] "men draped in burnous, masked and wearing Phrygian bonnets" (No. II); "two women who are drawing water; the rest represents greenery; reminds me of pictures of my home" (No. III); "it seems to be a hyena (pink part); the image is reflected in the water" (No.

---

[2]*Editorial note.* These numbers refer to the cards of the Thematic Apperception Test issued by the National Foundation for Educational Research, Windsor. There are 20 in number.

[3]*Editorial note.* These roman numerals refer to the cards of the Rorschach Test published by Hans Huber, Publishers, Berne.

VIII). With other subjects the differentiation between the European and the African world is less manifest, but one receives the impression that the T.A.T. forces the subjects to represent their problems in the most general of human terms, with the least possible cultural and social bias, so that the particular problem of colour tends to be obscured—but only thinly, for there is one plate (No. 14) which can bring the whole question out into the open. A reticent subject who up till then had given no response, or a hesitant or incomplete response, began to speak at length when he came to this plate: ". . . very symbolic, we are in the black. We can see white through the window." The conversations incidental to the administering of the test often bring out what is hidden. One subject told the woman psychologist who was giving him the test that he was the illegitimate son of a Breton father; his mother had subsequently remarried with a Black man who was only his adoptive father. The well-known paranoiac saga of dual paternity is here transposed from the realm of social class (noble progenitor, plebeian adoptive father), in which form it has been the subject of study, to the domain of race and colour. The replies of this subject naturally revealed the adaptation difficulties of an individual who had broken with his environment to integrate into a new ethnic group symbolized by his white father, as well as remorse for having "killed" his black father ("his father has maybe committed suicide or else he has been killed, and his son beside him is thinking, perhaps he wants to find out who had murdered his father, so that he can avenge him").

The Rorschach test, however, has proved much more interesting to us in the perspective with which we are particularly concerned in this article. The suggestions arising from its application may be of theoretical interest when considering its wider application to the African world. As we know, red shock and colour shock are considered as symptoms of inadequate emotional adjustment. This appears to be as true of Black people as of Whites. Indeed, we obtained many explosive responses connected with the perception of red, and many alterations in the quality of responses to the colour plates. But in our Africans we also found black shock. Certain responses make this apparent: "very sad; reminds me of very black things in our country which we were very afraid of when we were young; especially the owl, which symbolises evil, and the unhappiness of its mournful cry; because of that massive image, black tinged with grey . . .". This shows that white and black are being regarded as colours, and not simply as contrasted forms; they awaken and precipitate the Black man's awareness of his confrontation with the Other, the White, and all the tensions this confrontation implies. The black–white contrast of the plates is used to express the conflicts and tensions resulting from adaptation, because the two worlds of Africa and Europe are the worlds of the Black and the White. Thus the feelings of pleasure, curiosity and hostility which the colour black arouses may be interpreted in a neurotic or even a psychotic sense.

Consequently the study of drawings, dreams or projective tests always brings us back to the same, or analogous, conclusions about the great importance of colour. Our research is not yet advanced or extensive enough for us to have been able to elaborate a theory of the relationship between sociological and pathological data within the framework of collaboration advocated by Mauss in relation to symbolism. But it seems to us that our research has already proved its usefulness by the suggestions it has furnished about treatment of mental illnesses in Africans (with colour used as a means to penetrate the patient's morbid world, and the cure resulting from the relativization of dualism), about the theory of transfer and counter-transfer in the therapeutic relationship, and the importance of black shock in the Rorschach test.

Color Gradation and Attitudes among Middle-income Negroes*

Howard E. Freeman, J. Michael Ross, David Armor and
Thomas F. Pettigrew

"If you're white, you're right; if you're brown, stick around; if you're black, step back!" So goes an often-repeated adage among color-sensitive Negroes in the United States. The apparent importance of skin color within the Negro-American community has long evoked research interest.

At the social-psychological level, a number of studies find that skin color is intertwined with identity and self-esteem among Negroes: young children often deny their color, prefer white dolls and white playmates, and reveal other symptoms of acute racial awareness and feelings of stigma because of dark skin.[1] Negro college students tend to judge attractiveness partly in terms of skin color, the most admired color being lighter than average but not at the extremely light end of the scale. These students also compromise between reality and wish-fulfillment and rate their own skin color in the

*The data presented here are from a study of middle-income Negroes and their housing by the Florence Heller Graduate School for Advanced Studies in Social Welfare of Brandeis University under contract with the Department of Commerce and Urban Development of the Commonwealth of Massachusetts and financed by the United States Housing and Home Finance Administration. See Lewis G. Watts, Howard E. Freeman et al., The Middle-income Negro Faces Urban Renewal, Waltham, Massachusetts: Brandeis University, 1964.

[1]K. B. Clark, Prejudice and Your Child, 2nd edition, Boston: Beacon Press, 1963; K. B. Clark and Mamie P. Clark, "Racial Identification and Preference in Negro Children", in T. M. Newcomb and E. L. Hartley (eds.), Readings in Social Psychology, 1st edition, New York: Holt, 1947, pp. 169–178; Mary E. Goodman, Race Awareness in Young Children, Cambridge, Massachusetts: Addison-Wesley, 1952; Catherine Landreth and Barbara C. Johnson, "Young Children's Responses to a Picture and Inset Test Designed to Reveal Reactions to Persons of Different Skin Color", Child Development, 24, (March 1953), pp. 63–80; J. K. Morland, "Racial Recognition by Nursery School Children in

direction of the preferred shade.[2] Negro adults also are attuned to skin color. For instance, dark Negroes tend to be more positive toward and informed about newly independent African nations than lighter skinned Negroes.[3] Some Negroes are so concerned with skin shade as to evoke the accusation from other Negroes of being "color struck".[4]

At the structural level, studies repeatedly have noted a link between skin color and social stratification within the Negro-American community. Prior to Emancipation, mulattoes had the highest value on the slave market, were most often the house servants and skilled artisans rather than field hands, and were disproportionately numerous among free Negroes.[5] After Emancipation, mulattoes enjoyed so great a head-start in education and property ownership that historically they have dominated the top social and occupational slots in the Negro community. Manifestations of this phenomenon have continued to be reported. Field studies in a variety of settings— Chicago,[6] Washington, D.C.,[7] and small towns in Mississippi[8]—consistently

---

Lynchburg, Virginia", *Social Forces*, **37** (December 1958), pp. 132–7; Judith D. R. Porter, "Racial Concept Formation in Preschool Age Children", Cornell University Unpublished Master's thesis, 1963; M. Seeman, "Skin Color Values in Three All-Negro School Classes", *American Sociological Review*, **11** (June 1946), pp. 315–21; H. W. Stevenson and E. C. Stewart, "A Developmental Study of Racial Awareness in Young Children", *Child Development*, **29** (September 1958), pp. 399–409; and Helen G. Trager and Marian R. Yarrow, *They Live What They Learn*, New York: Harpers, 1952.

[2]E. S. Marks, "Skin Color Judgments of Negro College Students", *Journal of Abnormal and Social Psychology*, **38** (July 1943), pp. 370–6. Similar findings had been reported earlier in field studies by E. F. Frazier, *Negro Youth at the Crossroads*, Washington, D.C.: American Council on Education, 1941; and C. S. Johnson, *Growing Up in the Black Belt*, Washington, D.C.: American Council on Education, 1941. See also M. Seeman, "Situational Approach to Intragroup Negro Attitudes", *Sociometry*, **9** (May–August 1946), pp. 199–206.

[3]T. F. Pettigrew, *A Profile of the Negro American*, Princeton, New Jersey: Van Nostrand, 1964, pp. 11–12.

[4]S. C. Drake and H. R. Cayton, *Black Metropolis*, Vol. II, Revised and Enlarged Edition, New York: Harper & Row, 1962 (originally published in 1945), pp. 496–500.

[5]G. F. Edwards, *The Negro Professional Class*, Glencoe, Illinois: Free Press, 1959, pp. 18, 104–8, 199; and G. Myrdal, *An American Dilemma*, New York: Harper, 1944, pp. 695–700.

[6]Drake and Cayton, *op. cit.*, pp. 495–506; and W. L. Warner, B. Junker, and W. Adams, *Color and Human Nature*, Washington, D.C.: American Youth Commission, 1940.

[7]Edwards, *op. cit.*; and Frazier, *op. cit.*, pp. 24–28.

[8]A. W. Davis, B. B. Gardner, and M. R. Gardner, *Deep South*, Chicago: University of Chicago Press, 1941, pp. 233–6, 244–8, 447–8; and J. Dollard, *Caste and Class in a Southern Town*, New Haven, Conn.: Yale University Press, 1937.

reveal that upper-status members of Negro communities tend to be lighter than lower-status members. Moreover, these studies uniformly note that skin color often plays a critical role in the selection of marriage partners, with light-skinned women preferred.

Obviously, skin color is only one attribute of social desirability among Negroes and, in comparison with more general status characteristics such as education and occupation, may be accorded exaggerated importance by students of ethnic groups. For example, skin color appears to rank well below occupation, education, income, and "respectability" as prestige factors.[9] Moreover, some studies indicate that skin color has become less critical in recent years. Edwards has shown that young Negro professionals in comparison with old ones are less likely to be extremely light or dark.[10] Finally, there is the suggestion of a centralizing tendency toward a medium brown shade because of the high rates of racially endogamous marriages.[11]

In this paper we report an analysis of the association between skin color and structural and sociopsychological measures among middle-income, residentially stable, urban Negro families. Although the characteristics of the study group limit the generality of the findings, at the same time the residential and economic homogeneity of the group provides an opportunity for a severe test of whether or not skin color continues to be an attribute that must be reckoned with in developing a sociological and social-psychological portrait of today's Negro American.[12] In terms of the empirical analysis, two questions are examined: Is skin color among middle-income Negroes associated with other attributes of social status? Is skin color

[9]N. D. Glenn, "Negro Prestige Criteria: A Case Study in the Bases of Prestige", *American Journal of Sociology*, **68** (March 1963), pp. 645–57. See also, S. Parker and R. Kleiner, "Status Position, Mobility, and Ethnic Identification of the Negro", *Journal of Social Issues*, **20** (April 1964), pp. 85–102.

[10]Edwards, *op. cit.*, pp. 108–13.

[11]Edwards, *op. cit.* In this connection, the Lees suggest a gradual darkening of the Negro-American group if miscegenation is in fact decreasing, and light, upper-status Negroes continue to have lower fertility rates than low-status Negroes. E. S. Lee and Anne S. Lee, "The Differential Fertility of the American Negro", *American Sociological Review*, **17** (August 1952), pp. 437–47.

[12]The severity of the test is a function of the restricted variance in status. The sample limitations, however, do raise problems: if dark Negroes are more often restricted from lucrative jobs, the study group may be somewhat biased against the inclusion of low-paid, but otherwise middle-class-oriented, dark Negroes. Such a problem is inevitable given any restriction on a sampling variable that is related to variables included in the analysis.

correlated with selected attitudinal responses of middle-income Negro women? At the inferential level, our first concern is whether skin color is a determinant of social class position when class is measured by the status characteristics that ordinarily operate in American society. In other words, does "light skin pay off?" Our second concern is with the question of whether skin color has an impact on attitudes of Negroes. Here our interest is not only whether skin color is a structural characteristic linked to individual characteristics among Negroes, but also whether it is characteristic of, superordinate to, or at least independent of, more general status characteristics in determining the personal world of the Negro American.

METHOD

As part of a broad study of middle-income Negroes, 250 wives were interviewed by Negro social workers using structured schedules. These 250 women represent the female heads of those Negro families in Boston's predominantly Negro Washington Park area in which the male head of the household is between 20 and 60 years of age and the family has an annual income of not less than $5200. (An additional 10 women were refusals or were otherwise unavailable for interviews.) The median interviewee is a 37-year-old northern-born homemaker who had completed high school and was living in a household with an annual income of $8500; her spouse had attended college for over a year, was 42 years old, and northern-born. In short, the sample is characteristic of today's intact middle-income family who lives in ghetto-like areas of large northern metropolitan areas—a rapidly expanding and especially crucial segment of the current urban population.

The key variable, skin color, is measured by a carefully lithographed chart of six shades, scored from one to six and representing white, yellow, light brown, dark brown, chocolate, and ebony black. Interviewers rated the skin color of each wife by judging the color of the dorsal surface of her hand. This part of the body was selected because it is exposed and generally free from cosmetics. The husband's skin color was similarly judged if he was present; otherwise it was necessary to make a rating from a photograph. The over-all study was a panel-type investigation with two interviews conducted some ten months apart. Approximately 90 per cent of the study group were re-interviewed and in the majority of the cases the interviews were conducted by different persons. Skin color was rated again in the

TABLE 1. DESCRIPTION OF ATTITUDE SCALES

Name of scale	Content	Number of items	Example of positive items	Example of negative items
Anti-White[1]	Resentment against Caucasians.	8	It is risky to trust a white person.	Most white people are not prejudiced and sincerely believe Negroes are equal.
Anti-Negro[2]	Resentment against the in-group.	4	White people should make more distinction between respectable Negroes who are like them and the poorly educated Negroes who live in a world all their own.	It makes me mad to see how little pride Negroes take in their own group.
Militancy	Attitude toward direct efforts to achieve racial change.	4	In seeking to end racial discrimination, Negro-Americans need to stop talking so much and start more economic boycotts and other direct actions.	A man gets ahead better by keeping out of trouble than by always demanding his rights.
Subjective-Victimization[3]	Perceived effects on self of racial restrictions.	4	I sometimes feel that prejudice in this country has hurt me personally.	Even if there were no racial prejudice and discrimination in America, I don't think my life would be any different.

| Authoritarian- ism[4] | The authoritarian personality syndrome. | 6 | People can be divided into two classes, the strong and the weak. | It may well be that children who talk back to their parents actually end up respecting them more. |
| Conformity[5] | Attitudes toward conforming behavior. | 6 | It is best not to express your views when in the company of friends who disagree. | Sometimes I rather enjoy going against the rules and doing things I'm not supposed to. |

[1]Some of the items for this scale are from R. Johnson, "Negro Reactions to Minority Group Status", in M. L. Barron (ed.), *American Minorities*, New York: Knopf, 1958, pp. 192–212; and G. A. Steckler, "Authoritarian Ideology in Negro College Students", *Journal of Abnormal and Social Psychology*, **54** (May 1957), pp. 396–9. See also E. S. Marks, "Standardization of a Race Attitude Test for Negro Youth", *Journal of Social Psychology*, **18** (November 1943), pp. 245–78.

[2]Some of the items for this scale are from R. Johnson, *op. cit.*, and Steckler, *op. cit.*

[3]The basic conceptualization and initial measurement for this variable appeared in G. W. Allport and B. M. Kramer, "Some Roots of Prejudice", *Journal of Psychology*, **22** (January 1946), pp. 9–39.

[4]All of the Authoritarianism scale items are from either T. W. Adorno, Else Frenkel-Brunswik, D. Levinson, and N. Sanford, *The Authoritarian Personality*, New York: Harper, 1950, or A. Couch and K. Keniston, "Yeasayers and Naysayers: Agreement Response Set as a Personality Variable", *Journal of Abnormal and Social Psychology*, **60** (March 1960), pp. 151–74.

[5]Items for the Conformity scale are from four sources: F. Barron, "Some Personality Correlates of Independence of Judgment", *Journal of Personality*, **21** (March 1953), pp. 287–97; R. S. Crutchfield, "Conformity and Character", *American Psychologist*, **10** (May 1955), pp. 191–8; M. L. Hoffman, "Some Psychodynamic Factors in Compulsive Conformity", *Journal of Abnormal and Social Psychology*, **48** (May 1953), pp. 383–93; and T. F. Pettigrew, "Personality and Sociocultural Factors in Intergroup Attitudes: A Cross-National Comparison", *Journal of Conflict Resolution*, **2** (March 1958), pp. 29–42.

second interview. The two independent ratings on skin color indicate that the measure is reliable; Robinson's coefficient of agreement is .86, and the intra-class correlation is .72.[13] We also examined the differences between the two ratings of skin color; the maximum possible difference is 5 if the two interviewers gave ratings of 1 and 6 for the same subject. The largest actual difference, however, was three, and this occurred in less than 1 per cent of the comparisons. A difference of two points occurred in 5 per cent of the ratings. Errors resulting from differences in ratings are further minimized in portions of the present analysis by trichotomizing skin color into light, medium, and dark. When this is done, the ratings are congruent for 94 per cent of the informants. Since the measure is reasonably reliable, we employed the ratings obtained in the first interview in order to utilize the full sample of 250.

The six attitude measures are brief scales composed of Likert-type statements drawn from the literature and answered by informants in terms of six response categories ranging from "agree strongly" to "disagree strongly". In each case, adequate internal reliabilities were obtained for gross research purposes, though not for individual diagnostic ones. Each scale is "balanced"; that is, they largely avoid the "response set" problem by containing both positive and negative items. The content of the six scales is described in Table 1.

SKIN COLOR AS A STRUCTURAL CHARACTERISTIC

It is apparent from the data presented in Table 2 that the skin color of both wife and husband are correlated with other characteristics of social status. Six separate associations are presented in this table; the skin color of the wife and of the husband is related to the wife's education, the husband's education, and the husband's occupation. In five of the six cases the associations are statistically significant. In the one case that is not significant, dark husbands are more likely to be in blue-collar than white-collar occupations. Certainly from the data presented here it is difficult to reach any other conclusion than that skin color is at least a concomitant, if not a determinant, of social status in terms of prestige attributes typically employed within the larger American society.

In addition to the three status variables reported in Table 2 (wife's edu-

[13]W. S. Robinson, "The Statistical Measurement of Agreement", *American Sociological Review*, **22** (February 1957), pp. 17–25.

cation, husband's education, and husband's occupation), income, class self-identification, and Warner's Index of Status Characteristics also were correlated with skin color. The Pearsonian coefficients between wife's skin color, measured on the six-point scale, and all six characteristics are significant at the .05 level or better. It is clear that, regardless of the mode of analysis, skin color is associated with the class-status of families. The weakest measure is income and in part this finding may be accounted for by the attenuation in income variance inherent in the selection of a medium-income study group.

TABLE 2. WIFE'S EDUCATION, HUSBAND'S EDUCATION, AND HUSBAND'S OCCUPATION, BY SKIN COLOR OF WIFE AND HUSBAND
(Per Cent)

	Skin color of wife			Skin color of husband		
Status measure	Light	Medium	Dark	Light	Medium	Dark
Wife's education						
High school or less	46.9	53.3	71.2	35.7	57.1	63.4
Some college	53.1	46.7	28.8	64.3	42.9	36.6
Number of cases	49	135	66	28	140	82
	$\chi^2 = 8.31$; $p < .05$			$\chi^2 = 6.52$; $p < .05$		
Husband's education						
High school or less	36.7	45.9	65.1	28.6	45.7	62.2
Some college	63.3	54.1	34.9	71.4	54.3	37.8
Number of cases	49	135	66	28	140	82
	$\chi^2 = 10.32$; $p < .01$			$\chi^2 = 11.00$; $p < .01$		
Husband's occupation[1]						
Blue-collar	33.3	47.0	75.8	46.4	47.8	61.0
White-collar	66.7	53.0	24.2	53.6	52.2	39.0
Number of cases	48	134	66	28	138	82
	$\chi^2 = 22.96$; $p < .01$			$\chi^2 = 3.96$; n.s.		

[1]Two wives did not clearly state husband's occupation.

The plausibility of the inference that skin color is indeed a determinant of social status, at least in the sense of being a selection factor, is supported by the data presented in Table 3. In this table we take three variables into account: the occupation of the husband, the occupation of the wife's father, and the disparity in skin color between the two spouses. The data provide evidence for the notion that skin color counts within the Negro world.

93

TABLE 3. FAMILY COLOR PATTERN BY HUSBAND'S OCCUPATION
AND OCCUPATION OF WIFE'S FATHER

Family color pattern	Blue-collar husband			White-collar husband		
	Wife's father blue-collar	Wife's father white-collar	Subtotal	Wife's father blue-collar	Wife's father white-collar	Subtotal
Wife lighter than husband	35	3	38	33	15	48
Wife and husband same skin color	42	4	46	23	11	34
Husband lighter than wife	22	11	33	14	6	20
Total	99	18	117	70	32	102

Note: For over-all table, $\chi^2 = 5.90$; n.s.

TABLE 4. FAMILY COLOR PATTERN BY WIFE'S AGE
(Per Cent)

Family color pattern	Wife's age		
	20–34	35–39	40–60
Wife lighter than husband	43.2	39.7	37.2
Wife and husband same skin color	35.8	35.3	39.5
Husband lighter than wife	21.1	25.0	23.3
Number of cases	95	68	86

Husbands in white-collar occupations are more likely to marry light-colored wives than husbands in blue-collar occupations; husbands in blue-collar occupations are more likely to obtain a wife lighter than they are if they marry a girl from a blue-collar family; the chances are higher for husbands in blue-collar occupations to marry a girl from a white-collar family if he is lighter than she is; and upwardly-mobile wives are more likely than downwardly-mobile wives to be lighter than husband. Although the over-all table is not statistically significant, each of the comparisons just described is significant ($p < .05$); the general pattern suggests a linkage between skin color and the class-mobility patterns among the families studied.

An interesting point is that the marriage patterns do not seem to have changed, at least during the lifetimes of the persons in the study group. In Table 4 we show the family color patterns by the wife's age; the selection patterns apparently have remained constant.

The relationship between class self-identification and skin color is also interesting (see Table 5).[14] When the husband's occupation is taken into account, it appears that skin color is more strongly associated with class

TABLE 5. CLASS IDENTIFICATION OF WIFE BY HUSBAND'S OCCUPATION AND WIFE'S SKIN COLOR

Class identification of wife[1]	Husband blue-collar		Husband white-collar	
	Wife's skin color		Wife's skin color	
	Light	Medium or Dark	Light	Medium or Dark
Working class	50.0	63.1	9.4	21.2
Middle class	50.0	36.9	90.6	78.8
Number of cases	16	111	32	85
	χ^2=n.s.		χ^2=4.8; $p < .05$	

[1]Six wives did not report class identification.

[14]The question used was adapted from R. Centers, *The Psychology of Social Classes*, Princeton, New Jersey: Princeton University Press, 1949: "Compared with Most People White and Negro—What Class Do You Consider Yourself In—Lower Class, Working Class, Middle Class, or Upper Class?" Two lower-class identifiers were combined with the working-class identifiers, and thirteen upper-class identifiers were combined with the middle-class identifiers.

TABLE 6. PRODUCT-MOMENT CORRELATIONS BETWEEN STATUS MEASURES AND ATTITUDE MEASURES

Status measure	Attitudes					
	Subjective-victimization	Authoritarianism	Conformity	Militancy	Anti-white	Anti-Negro
Occupation of husband	−.03	+.23**	+.28**	−.13	+.24**	−.14
Warner's I.S.C.	+.04	+.23**	+.18*	−.09	+.32**	−.17*
Class self-identification	+.03	−.09	−.13	+.12	−.10	+.19*
Education	+.10	−.20*	−.24**	+.09	−.28**	+.27**
Income	−.02	−.17*	−.19*	+.02	−.24**	+.17*

*p < .05.
**p < .01.

self-identification among white-collar families than amor
families, although the relationship is in the same direction amo
of families. In both groups, with occupation controlled, mid
identification is correlated with having light skin. Thus, the   ...uer
clearly indicate that skin color is a status variable, or at least a correlate of
more general status variables, among the study group.

SKIN COLOR AND ATTITUDE MEASURES

Given the substantial relationship between skin color and social status, the
issue of whether skin color operates as do other status variables—to structure
the individual's personal world—becomes pertinent. The first point that
needs to be established, of course, is that structural variables important within
the larger society are correlated with personal characteristics of the middle-
income Negroes studied. In Table 6, we show Pearsonian correlation coefficients between six attitude measures and five status variables: occupation,
Warner's I.S.C., class self-identification, education, and income. In this part
of the analysis, the personality measures are divided into ten categories but
the reader should be cautioned that the number of categories for the class
measures ranges from three in the case of self-identification to nine in the
case of Warner's I.S.C. Thus, the coefficients cannot be fully compared with
one another. Nevertheless, the conclusion is clear: with the exception of the
subjective-victimization and militancy scales, objective class characteristics
are associated with attitudes. An interesting point is that class self-identification is a weak predictor. But certainly in the case of the authoritarianism,
conformity, anti-white, and anti-Negro scales, objective status characteristics are associated with the attitudinal responses of the women.

What about skin color? Although the results are in a direction consistent
with the findings on the status measures, the differences in proportions are
not impressive (see Table 7). The question that remains is whether the
relation of the general class measures to wife's skin color is masking the
relationships. For this part of the analysis both a linear analysis of variance
and cross-tabular partial analyses were employed. In Table 7 we present the
proportion scoring above the median on each of five attitude measures by the
occupation of husband and the education of wife. This table indicates that
when objective status measures are taken into account, skin color does
operate differentially on those in high and low statuses, but the differences
are not marked and rarely approach statistical significance. This lack of

97

systematic differences would indicate that skin color mediates relationships between attitudes and objective status measures only to a very limited extent.

The findings on the sixth attitude measure, anti-white feelings, are presented in detail in Table 8. Here we show the proportion above the median on the anti-white attitude measure by five status variables; the conclusion is that skin color (of wife) as well as objective status is associated with anti-white feelings of middle-income Negroes. Although not all of the relationships in the sub-groups are statistically significant, it is apparent that within objective-status groups, dark-skinned Negroes are most likely to be anti-white. Certainly in terms of this measure, skin color appears to have an impact on the views of middle-income Negroes that is to some extent independent of objective class measures.

As a more formal means of analysis, F ratios were calculated using a linear model of analysis of variance. Under the conditions imposed by such an analysis, the findings confirm the interpretation offered for the previous two tables: namely, the wife's skin color has a significant independent effect only in the case of the anti-white scale, while the wife's education and her husband's occupation remain significantly correlated with the attitude measures in almost all cases (see Table 9). This does not deny, of course, that skin color has some impact on attitudes, but on balance it appears to be relatively small save for the anti-white scale.

An interesting point comes up when a similar analysis of variance is undertaken centered on the husband's skin color rather than wife's (see Table 10). Wife's education is still correlated independently with several of the measures, and husband's occupation is still an effective predictor of all but one of the six scales. However, husband's skin color is correlated with four of the attitude measures and *it is a stronger predictor of wife's attitudes than her own skin color.*

What does this last finding suggest? Here one must speculate on the dual role of skin color as a determinant of attitudes. On the one hand, skin color can be viewed as an ascribed status held from birth and related to the total life experience of the individual; on the other hand, it can operate within the Negro world as a contemporary status symbol, like occupation, for example, in shaping the individual's personal world. Given the middle-class character of the study group and the finding that the husband's skin color counts most in differentiating attitudes, the "contemporary-status explanation" of skin color appears to be the more reasonable.

TABLE 7. PROPORTION SCORING ABOVE MEDIAN ON ATTITUDE MEASURES,
BY WIFE'S SKIN COLOR, HUSBAND'S OCCUPATION, AND WIFE'S EDUCATION

Attitude measure and wife's skin color	Husband's occupation		Wife's education		Total study group
	Manual	Skilled or higher	High school or less	Some college	
Subjective-victimization					
Light	.38	.53	.39	.54	.47
Medium	.47	.63	.47	.65	.56
Dark	.48	.38	.49	.37	.46
Total	**.46**	**.57**	**.47**	**.57**	**.51**
Authoritarianism					
Light	.37	.41	.35	.46	.41
Medium	.64	.47	.68	.40	.55
Dark	.58	.44	.53	.60	.55
Total	**.59**	**.45**	**.58★**	**.45**	**.52**
Conformity					
Light	.38	.38	.35	.42	.39
Medium	.61	.27	.54	.30	.43
Dark	.64	.44	.66	.42	.59
Total	**.59**	**.32**	**.55★**	**.35**	**.46★**
Militancy					
Light	.63	.69	.61	.69	.65
Medium	.45	.54	.46	.54	.50
Dark	.42	.56	.43	.53	.46
Total	**.46**	**.58**	**.47**	**.57**	**.52**
Anti-Negro					
Light	.56	.53	.48	.62	.55
Medium	.42	.62	.46	.60	.53
Dark	.46	.38	.43	.47	.44
Total	**.45**	**.56**	**.45**	**.58**	**.51**
Number of cases	130	119	142	108	250

★$p < .05$, using χ^2 test.

These are middle-income families in which the male has a dominant place within the Negro community and structures his family's social relations in the larger community. This being the case, the husband's skin color, like his occupation, represents a status characteristic by which he and his family are judged. In the same sense in which skin color is a predictor of choice of a marital partner, it also serves as a screening variable with respect to current status position: just as with her husband's occupation, her husband's skin color makes a difference in her relations both within the Negro community

TABLE 8. PROPORTION SCORING ABOVE MEDIAN ON ANTI-WHITE ATTITUDE SCALE, FOR SELECTED STATUS MEASURES

Status Measure	Wife's skin color			
	Light	Medium	Dark	Total
Occupation of husband				
Manual	.38	.56	.66	.58 (130)
Skilled and higher	.22	.44	.38	.37 (119)
Warner's I.S.C.				
Lower	.57	.59	.74	.65 (110)
Middle	.17	.43	.33	.35*(140)
Class self-identification				
Working	.27	.56	.57	.53 (100)
Middle	.29	.45	.60	.44*(146)
Education				
High school or less	.35	.60	.68	.59*(142)
Some college	.23	.38	.37	.34 (108)
Income				
Less than $6500	.38	.57	.75	.59*(124)
$6500 and over	.22	.43	.40	.37 (115)
Total	.29 (49)	.50 (135)	.59**(66)	.48 (250)

*p < .05, using chi square test.
**p < .01, using chi square test.
Note: Numbers of cases shown in parentheses.

TABLE 9. F RATIOS FOR RELATIONSHIPS BETWEEN WIFE'S SKIN COLOR, STATUS MEASURES, AND ATTITUDE SCALES

Status measure and skin color	Degrees of freedom	Attitude scale					
		Subjective-victimization	Authoritarianism	Conformity	Militancy	Anti-white	Anti-Negro
Wife's skin color	2	0.7	0.5	1.2	0.5	4.1*	0.0
Wife's education	1	2.9	3.2	9.0**	0.2	11.6**	4.6*
Husband's occupation	1	0.0	13.9**	15.6**	4.3**	8.2**	7.5**
Skin color × education	2	0.6	3.5*	1.0	0.8	0.5	0.6
Skin color × occupation	2	1.4	0.8	0.3	0.7	0.2	1.5
Education × occupation	1	1.3	0.1	0.2	1.0	0.0	3.3
Skin color × education × occupation	2	0.5	0.3	1.1	0.0	0.1	0.0

*$p < .05$.
**$p < .01$.

TABLE 10. F RATIOS FOR RELATIONSHIPS BETWEEN HUSBAND'S SKIN COLOR, STATUS MEASURES, AND ATTITUDE SCALES

Status measure and skin color	Degrees of freedom	Attitude scale					
		Subjective-victimization	Authori-tarianism	Conformity	Militancy	Anti-white	Anti-Negro
Wife's skin color	2	0.7	3.0*	3.1*	1.5	7.6**	3.8*
Wife's education	1	1.9	1.5	4.0*	1.5	6.5*	0.1
Husband's occupation	1	0.0	14.0**	16.2**	4.6*	8.5**	7.6**
Skin color × education	2	1.5	1.5	2.0	2.8	1.7	2.0
Skin color × occupation	2	0.4	1.5	1.8	2.6	1.5	0.6
Education × occupation	1	2.2	0.0	3.8	2.3	0.1	0.3
Skin color × education × occupation	2	0.4	0.6	1.7	0.0	1.8	1.0

*$p < .05$.
**$p < .01$.

and in the larger social scene, and consequently, influences attitudes. Indeed, the contemporary influence of husbands' skin color upon wives' attitudes may interact with characteristics initially important in mate selection. Those most "color-struck" at the time of marriage still are probably the most sensitive to the prestige aspects of skin color.

CONCLUSION

We have presented here considerable data on the relationships of skin color to general structural characteristics and social-psychological variables. Skin color apparently clusters with the objective measures of social status that characterize the larger American society and seems to operate via marriage as a determinant of chances to achieve status. Its impact on attitudes is somewhat less sharply revealed by this investigation. In general, skin color does not appear to be as strongly correlated with the attitudes investigated as are objective class measures. Sub-group analyses that take into account both class measures and skin color simultaneously indicate, however, that in the case of anti-white feelings skin color does independently predict responses, with dark Negroes holding the least favorable attitudes towards whites. In the case of the other attitude measures, although there is a hint that color confuses, or perhaps mitigates, the basic relationships between objective class statuses and attitudes held by the wives, it is only to an appreciable degree.

When husband's skin color is taken into account, one finds that his color is more strongly correlated with the attitudes of the wife than her own color. One interpretation of this finding is that the skin color of the middle-income Negro represents an important objective status in a contextual sense; that is, it operates as do other family status indicators to limit and outline the course of their lives both within the Negro community and the larger American society. Just as the Negro professional holds attitudes different from those of the blue-collar worker by virtue of his place within the Negro community and the level of his interaction with the white community, so too, skin color may in part set the boundaries of the social worlds of these families.

Race, Religion
and Urbanization

Ethnic Differentiation: Ecological Aspects of a Multidimensional Concept

A. Gordon Darroch and Wilfred G. Marston

INTRODUCTION

Residential segregation is a key aspect of the social organization of the city. The spatial distance between social groups (such as ethnic groups or social classes) is not only a manifestation of urban social structure but, as a form of differentiation itself, directly affects the nature of social interaction and exchange. Many students of the city have contended that three constructs serve to describe the basic characteristics by which an urban area is differentiated. Although the constructs have been variously labelled, they can be referred to summarily as, (1) life style (or more specifically, type of family and household), (2) socioeconomic status and (3) ethnic status or ethnicity (Shevky and Bell, 1955; Greer, 1962; Schnore, 1967; Jones, 1968; Berry and Rees, 1969).

This classification scheme has been the subject of a continuing debate over both the adequacy of its theoretical derivation and the demonstration of its empirical validity (Hawley and Duncan, 1957; Jones, 1968). Nevertheless, a number of studies contend that at least for spatial differentiation the distinction is more than conceptually convenient. Evidence from several cultural contexts indicates that the broad classes of characteristics subsumed under each construct may be thought of as determining distinct patterns of residential clustering (Anderson and Egeland, 1961; Berry, 1965; Jones, 1967 and 1968; Berry and Rees, 1969). The most detailed theoretical and empirical works have focused particularly on the residential segregation of socioeconomic, immigrant, and racial groups (Duncan and Duncan, 1955a; Metha, 1968; Lieberson, 1963; Taeuber and Taeuber, 1965).

*We wish to acknowledge the assistance of G. Sabir Shakeel and Nilly Ackerman in various phases of the research.

The specific concern of this paper is *ethnic residential segregation*, the spatial referent of the ethnic construct. While the analysis is limited to examining patterns of segregation, the basic contention is that in this context ethnic status is properly conceived of as being multidimensional. Patterns of ethnic residential segregation have been defined in terms of a wide variety of characteristics, ranging from a single variable representing the racial composition of cities to multivariate indexes incorporating differentials in religion, nationality, language and the like. With the exception of studies of racial segregation, it has been commonly implied that a variety of these variables can be substituted for others and still delineate essentially similar patterns of ethnic segregation. This assumption raises a critical issue for a conception of the general process of social differentiation and, more specifically, for a theory of ethnic segregation. It is by no means established that any one or a unique combination of characteristics can sufficiently represent the complexity of ethnic and immigrant status as it is manifested in residential segregation and social differentiation. Since the often arbitrary selection of convenient indicators leaves unanswered questions regarding both the conceptual and empirical validation of a complex concept, it seems inadequate to rest the case on a demonstration of the tendency for some ethnic characteristics to be more or less related in their spatial distributions (Beshers, 1962, p. 91).

That ethnic status may be multidimensional is further suggested by the theoretical and empirical support for a multidimensional conception of socio-economic status (cf. Tilly, 1961). The latter has long been recognized as consisting of the more specific aspects of social rank defined at least in terms of occupational, educational and income criteria. As Duncan has emphasized, despite the utility of even well validated composite indexes, "it may well be that empirical studies should be so designed that 'socio-economic status' is handled in a multi-variate framework" (Duncan, 1961, p. 146).

It is argued here that perhaps such a diffuse status characteristic as ethnicity should similarly be specified in terms of component attributes. Some of these components may be clearly identified. They may also generate significantly different degrees and patterns of residential segregation. Milton Gordon has, in fact, recently attempted to define the basic elements of ethnicity in the North American context. In brief, he offers a model of ethnicity in which each dimension is defined as an aspect of self-identity. Beyond common citizenship, the core elements of ethnic affiliation proposed are race, religion and national origin (Gordon, 1964, pp. 26–27).

Since patterns of segregation for some religious groups, as for Negroes, have already been found not to exactly parallel those of nationality groups (Duncan, 1959), this initial distinction by Gordon is particularly useful. However, it does ignore several aggregate aspects of ethnic status known to manifest themselves in the structural plurality of urban populations and which may be considered as conceptually separate dimensions of ethnicity. For example, variations in degrees of assimilation[1] are in part a function of differences between the first and subsequent generations of immigrants, while variations in assimilation among the foreign-born themselves are apparently related to recency of arrival (Lieberson, 1963, ch. 3). In this sense, native birth and period of immigration together represent a continuum of differences in terms of familiarity with the dominant institutions and presumably in the opportunities for gaining full entrance into them.

Further specification calls for a less apparent, but nonetheless potentially important distinction. Where immigration continues to be significant for urban growth, place-of-birth itself must be considered a component of ethnicity separate from that of national origin. That is, dissimilarities in country of birth are not identical to differences in the ancestral heritage of an entire urban population. Moreover, national or ethnic origin, as Gordon implies, entails an awareness of a common culture which does not necessarily vary in accordance with birthplace even among immigrants (Montague, 1963).

Finally, an associated dimension is the more obvious one of language differences. It is probable that diversity in language is a crucial factor in the process of residential sorting and although many countries are essentially unilingual, the cultural pluralism of others, such as Belgium and Canada, sustains a plurality of mother tongues.

Tentatively, then, it is suggested that there are at least six analytically distinct but interrelated dimensions of ethnicity which enter into a consideration of residential segregation—national or ethnic origin, race, religion, immigrant status[2] (period of immigration), birthplace, and language.

---

[1]Hereafter, the term assimilation is used with its traditional connotations; that is, the process whereby, and/or the degree to which, minority groups become similar to the dominant group both culturally and socially. It should be recognized, however, that the validity of assimilation as a concept has been seriously questioned (Richmond, 1967).

[2]Herafter, immigrant status refers to a two-stage categorization of the population— first, a native vs. foreign-born distinction with foreign-born then tabulated by period of immigration.

A. G. Darroch and W. G. Marston

DATA AND MEASUREMENT

To the authors' knowledge, no attempt has been made to thoroughly examine the empirical implications of a multidimensional conception of ethnic segregation. Certainly a primary reason for this has been the difficulty in acquiring distributions of a population along several dimensions for any one urban area. For example, in the study of assimilation in American cities, census data permit dealing with ethnic segregation (as distinguished from race) only with reference to those who are either foreign-born themselves or who have at least one foreign-born parent (defined as foreign-stock). Clearly one unavoidable consequence of this unidimensional approach has been ignorance of the degree of ethnic differentiation within the numerically dominant "native-born of native parentage" population. In contrast, studies in Britain and Australia have been restricted to another dimension, with very different empirical implications. Collison in Oxford, England (1967), and Jones in Melbourne, Australia (1967), for example, employ birthplace data to delineate patterns of ethnic residential segregation for entire urban populations.

The situation for Canada is quite unusual, however, in that it is possible for one major metropolitan area to secure data representing all but one of the dimensions of ethnicity discussed above (the exception being race).[3] The Canadian decennial census provides tabulations for ethnic origin, religion, period of immigration, birthplace and mother tongue. Specifically, ethnic origin and religion are published by census tract for each Canadian metropolitan area (Census of Canada, 1961). For metropolitan Toronto it was also possible to secure unpublished period of immigration data[4] and by means of special census runs, birthplace and mother-tongue data by census tract.[5]

[3]No question is included on race in the Canadian census. Its exclusion for the urban area under study is not considered to be a serious omission, however, since the non-white population of Toronto in 1961, excluding Asiatics, was less than 1 per cent of the total.

[4]The published census tract data provides only a pre- and post-World War II breakdown of immigrants. It was possible, however, to secure from the Dominion Bureau of Statistics a finer breakdown of immigrants into six immigration periods.

[5]Birthplace and mother-tongue data were obtained from the Dominion Bureau of Statistics as a result of a special computer-run which was financed from a grant received from The Canada Council. Both sets of data are for the population 15 years of age and over, which raises some question as to comparability with the other three dimensions. It is contended, however, that this is not a serious discrepancy since the working-force population essentially determines the residential distribution of the under-15 population.

110

We do not contend that the classifications employed here are fully adequate in capturing the content of the conceptual dimensions or that the dimensions as specified are themselves fully refined or exhaustive. However, the tabulations are sufficiently unique and detailed to serve in an initial comparative analysis of the degree and pattern of residential segregation found along five distinct aspects of ethnic status in a single urban context (Toronto).

With a growth rate of over 50 per cent during the 1951–1961 decade, Toronto is one of the fastest growing metropolitan areas in North America. Of further significance is that, unlike American cities, immigration has been a major contributor to its recent population increase. In fact, of those immigrating to Canada between 1951 and 1961 and settling in urban areas, nearly 40 per cent resided in Toronto as of the latter year. Moreover, some conditions of size, growth, locale and ethnic representation suggest that Toronto is particularly suited for comparison with some cities of the United States during their period of greatest overseas immigration in the earlier part of this century. There are also, of course, good reasons for initially restricting direct inter-city and inter-nation comparisons, especially with regard to the presently unknown effects of housing shortage and immigration policy on segregation in Toronto.

It is argued, then, that a primary empirical step in the testing of a multi-dimensional conception of ethnicity should be the measurement of the actual extent and pattern of residential dissimilarity along as many potentially meaningful dimensions as possible. If ethnicity is correctly conceived as having multidimensional implications, we would expect to find a significant degree of residential segregation generated along each dimension. Although, in itself, such a finding would not suggest that each dimension is independent of the others it would make obvious their empirical content and, further, make explicit the task of validation faced in considering ethnicity a unidimensional status variable. With regard to the latter implication, given the restrictions of the data, only a limited analysis of the interrelationships between selected dimensions can be attempted here for illustrative purposes.

In order to examine the segregation generated by the several dimensions of ethnicity we employ a useful and now common measure of the spatial separation of any two populations, called the "index of dissimilarity". The index is defined as the sum of either the positive or negative differences between the respective percentage distributions of the two populations over the same areal subdivisions of a community. The subareas of Toronto used

111

here are its 301 tracts reported in 1961. The index ranges from 0, representing complete similarity in spatial distribution (no segregation) to 100, indicating complete dissimilarity or segregation between the two groups. A substantive interpretation of the values of the index is given in terms of the percentage of one population which would have to move to different sub-areas (tracts) in order to have the same per cent distribution over the spatial units as another population. The computation and meaning of the index have been extensively discussed elsewhere (Duncan and Duncan, 1955b; Taeuber and Taeuber, 1965, Appendix A).[6]

FINDINGS

Indexes of dissimilarity between pairs of groups for each of the five selected dimensions are presented in Tables 2 to 6. Except for period of immigration, the order in which the groups defined by the dimensions are arranged is determined by their increasing dissimilarity from a previously selected standard population. The selection of a standard is a more or less arbitrary one. For the purpose of this paper, in each case, it is both the numerically dominant category and the one likely to be representative of the most homogeneously integrated or assimilated population.

OVERVIEW OF FINDINGS

Cursory inspection of the tables suggests preliminary support for a multi-dimensional model of ethnicity. First, for all five dimensions, the indexes of dissimilarity reach substantively significant magnitudes. In fact, only the period of immigration dimension fails to reveal a pair of groups for which at least 60 per cent of one of them would have to alter their tract or residence in order to achieve complete similarity in residential distributions. Moreover, within each dimension there is considerable relative variation in the degree of residential dissimilarity found between different pairs of groups. Further inspection of the tables suggests that the ranking of the groups with respect to the standard populations yields overall patterns of residential segregation which are surprisingly consistent *within* each of the dimensions.

[6]The index of dissimilarity is recognized as measuring only one aspect of segregation, i.e. the unevenness of spatial distributions. Other aspects or dimensions of *segregation*, such as degree of concentration, location and the like, might well be examined for separate ethnic characteristics.

112

Just as noteworthy in the present context is the fact that there tend to be marked differences in the magnitudes of the indexes from one dimension to the next.[7] For the purposes of comparison the unweighted mean and range of the index values of each dimension are presented in Table 1. It will be noted that both the lowest mean and range of dissimilarity indexes are found for the period of immigration groups, whereas religious groups generate the highest range of scores and both mother-tongue and birthplace groups the highest mean (42).

TABLE 1. UNWEIGHTED MEAN AND RANGE OF INDEXES OF DISSIMILARITY, SELECTED ETHNIC DIMENSIONS, METROPOLITAN TORONTO, 1961

Dimensions	Unweighted mean	Range
Immigrant status	21	19
Religion	38	67
Origin	39	44
Mother tongue	42	38
Birthplace	42	59

SEGREGATION BY PERIOD OF IMMIGRATION

As suggested previously, the period of immigration dimension incorporates both a distinction between native-born and immigrants and distinctions in the time of arrival of immigrants. The Canadian-born category is employed primarily as a standard population with which the residential distributions of the immigrant groups may be compared and the combination of categories does serve to define differentials in a broadly interpreted "immigrant status" aspect of ethnicity for the entire urban population.

Table 2 reveals two patterns of interest. First, indexes of dissimilarity between each period of immigration group and the Canadian-born show a

[7]Since the dimensions consist of unequal numbers of categories some inconsistencies in the theoretically possible ranges of index values could result from extreme differences in the population sizes of the groups in comparison with the population of the spatial units. The conditions under which such attenuation occurs are not confronted for the dimensions and categories employed here (cf. Lieberson, 1963, pp. 36–37). The further possibility that a change in the number of categories would substantially affect the index values imposes a limitation on generalizing from a comparison of dimensions, but there is no systematic relationship between the number of categories used in this paper and general level of the segregation found along the dimensions.

113

very slight U-shaped pattern. Contrary to our expectations, those immigrating prior to 1921 and those arriving thirty or more years later have similar levels of segregation from the native-born. Since those immigrating in the earliest period were over 40 years of age in 1961, it should be noted that the pattern could result in part from the segregation of age groups. However, since the greatest dissimilarity is clearly found between the most recent immigrants and the Canadian-born, as might be predicted from a length of residence hypothesis, age differentials probably account for only a part of the variation in segregation.

Of more immediate interest is the fact that, excluding the Canadian-born category, the indexes consistently increase in magnitude as one reads upward and to the right of the main diagonal of the table. Although the increases are not large, the extent to which the pattern is orderly indicates that there is a close relationship between dissimilarity in time of arrival and the residential dissimilarity among immigrants, as has been found elsewhere (Lieberson, 1963, pp. 47–48).

TABLE 2. INDEXES OF DISSIMILARITY IN RESIDENTIAL DISTRIBUTION OF CANADIAN-BORN AND FOREIGN-BORN BY PERIOD OF IMMIGRATION, METROPOLITAN TORONTO, 1961

Period of immigration	Index of dissimilarity among Canadian-born and foreign-born					
	2	3	4	5	6	7
1. Canadian-born	23	19	17	22	24	31
2. Before 1921	—	12	21	25	28	30
3. 1921–30		—	14	17	23	26
4. 1931–45			—	16	23	27
5. 1946–50				—	15	21
6. 1951–55					—	13
7. 1956–61						—

SEGREGATION BY RELIGION

For this dimension the categories are arranged with respect to their increasing dissimilarity from the United Church group. Table 3 shows that in general the residential segregation between religious groups reaches very substantial levels and again is rather uniformly patterned given the initial ordering. The Protestant groups listed first display very little dissimilarity when the residential distributions of any two groups are compared, although the Lutherans are slightly more segregated from the others. The three Catholic or Orthodox groups are somewhat more segregated again but to a greater degree from the Protestants than among themselves. Finally, the Jewish religious group is equally and very highly segregated from both the Protestant and Catholic groups. This is to say that residential segregation by religious affiliation conforms basically to a Protestant, Catholic, Jewish continuum.[8]

TABLE 3. INDEXES OF DISSIMILARITY IN RESIDENTIAL DISTRIBUTION OF RELIGIOUS GROUPS, METROPOLITAN TORONTO, 1961

| Religious groups | Index of dissimilarity among religious groups | | | | | | | | |
	2	3	4	5	6	7	8	9	10
1. United Church of Canada	9	14	15	16	25	30	42	58	75
2. Anglican Church	—	13	12	15	23	29	42	58	75
3. Baptist		—	14	15	21	25	37	53	75
4. Presbyterian			—	15	21	25	38	54	75
5. Others[a]				—	19	24	36	53	72
6. Lutheran					—	25	32	47	70
7. Roman Catholic						—	25	36	70
8. Greek Orthodox							—	36	72
9. Ukrainian								—	76
10. Jewish									—

[a]Includes such religious groups as Adventists, Christian Reformed, Christian Science, Evangelical United Brethren, Jehovah's Witnesses, Mennonite, Pentecostal, and Salvation Army.

SEGREGATION BY ORIGIN, MOTHER TONGUE AND BIRTHPLACE

Indexes of dissimilarity for ethnic origin, mother-tongue and birthplace groups are presented in Tables 4, 5 and 6, respectively. A discussion of the three dimensions is facilitated by several points of comparability in their categories and in the levels and patterns of segregation they generate.

[8]Although the residential segregation between religious groups is lower in Toronto, a very similar pattern in the magnitude of dissimilarity indexes was found for Montreal using 1941 ward data (Duncan, 1959).

115

In the light of the doubt regarding the meaning of the ethnic origin classification, brief comment should be made concerning its use in representing national origin. As tabulated by the census the origin classification ostensibly captures the ethnic identifications of the population as traced through paternal ancestry. The notion of ethnic heritage as distinct from language and birthplace appears to be useful at a conceptual level. Empirically, however, there is still the severe criticism of the census tabulations arising from the demonstration of considerable variation in the responses of the same populations to the set of fixed categories over time (Ryder, 1955). Nevertheless, we have chosen to employ the dimension on the theoretical grounds proposed by Gordon that ethnic heritage is a central and separate element of ethnicity. The reader may decide whether or not for one point in time the classification at least serves to represent a sense of ethnic affiliation on the part of a population, in contrast to the admittedly more concrete characteristics of birthplace and mother tongue.[9]

For origin the British category clearly meets the criteria for selection as the standard population. Thus, with respect to increasing relative dissimilarity from the British, the northern and western European groups are listed first in Table 4, followed by the Asian and "Other" groups and finally by those with southern and eastern European origins. There is a rather low level of segregation between any two of the five groups from northern and western Europe, with the largest index being 28 per cent between the French and Netherlands categories. Groups from southern and eastern Europe are not only more highly segregated from each of the groups with north-western European origins than those five are among themselves, but they also tend to be quite highly segregated from each other. The highest index in the latter case is 59 per cent for Russian and Italian origin groups. In contrast the "Other", Asiatic and "other European" groups are in general less segregated from the northern and western European groups than from the southern and eastern ones.

The mother-tongue dimension presented in Table 5 is more restricted than origin in its representation of the full ethnic diversity of the city. It does, however, include each of the numerically most significant language groups.[10]

[9]In 1961 the census question regarding ethnic origin was "To what ethnic or cultural group did you or your ancestor (on the male side) belong on coming to this continent?"

[10]The apparently obvious exclusion of a French language category is less significant than it would seem at first glance. In an indirect manner this can be shown by the fact that in Toronto in 1961, the French *origin* group makes up just over 3 per cent of the metropolitan population and is over 60 per cent English speaking.

In addition, it should be noted that English is the mother tongue of a significant number of those in both non-British and foreign-born groups.

The groups are arranged with respect to increasing residential dissimilarity from the dominant population—those with English mother tongue. It can be seen that there is a similar tendency here for the two language groups representative of northern and western Europe to be less segregated from each other than from the mother-tongue groups of southern and eastern Europe. Furthermore, the indexes of residential dissimilarity between any two groups of German, Ukrainian, Polish or Italian mother tongue are similar in relative magnitude to those between the corresponding origin groups. Even the less obviously comparable English mother tongue and British origin categories exhibit similarity in the order of magnitude of their segregation from each of the other comparable groups of the respective dimensions. It is also true, however, that the level of residential segregation between pairs of mother-tongue groups is greater in each case than it is between corresponding pairs of origin groups. For example, although they represent the lowest index values of each table, the dissimilarity between

TABLE 4. INDEXES OF DISSIMILARITY IN RESIDENTIAL DISTRIBUTION OF ETHNIC ORIGIN GROUPS, METROPOLITAN TORONTO, 1961

Origin groups	Index of dissimilarity among ethnic groups										
	2	3	4	5	6	7	8	9	10	11	12
1. British	15	16	20	20	27	35	41	42	46	52	55
2. Scandinavian	—	17	23	19	28	37	39	43	45	50	56
3. German		—	18	23	30	32	33	33	36	47	51
4. French			—	28	29	30	38	37	42	50	53
5. Netherlands				—	29	43	46	46	49	54	58
6. Other					—	40	46	47	51	56	57
7. Asiatic						—	36	43	46	53	52
8. Other European[a]								—	38	30	35	48
9. Ukrainian									—	23	52	45
10. Polish										—	35	50
11. Russian											—	59
12. Italian												—

[a]Jewish origin group included in Other European Category.

117

British and German origin groups is 16 per cent, whereas, the dissimilarity between English and German mother-tongue groups is 26 per cent. A difference of similar magnitude is found for the indexes between those of Ukrainian and Italian origin (45 per cent) and those of Ukrainian and Italian mother tongue (54 per cent).

The standard birthplace population is, of course, the Canadian-born (Table 6). Indexes among birthplace groups are quite similar in magnitude to those for the origin and mother tongue dimensions. For example, the index value between the Canadian and Italian-born is only one percent point higher than the value between the English and Italian mother tongue groups. The similarity between Canadian-born and English tongue also holds when comparing corresponding German and Polish groups (although in both cases the birthplace indexes are higher). Moreover, indexes of dissimilarity *among* any of the German, Russian, Polish or Italian birthplace groups are, on the whole, similar in degree to those indexes for corresponding origin and mother tongue groups.

TABLE 5. INDEXES OF DISSIMILARITY IN RESIDENTIAL DISTRIBUTION OF MOTHER-TONGUE GROUPS,* METROPOLITAN TORONTO, 1961

Mother-tongue groups	Index of dissimilarity among mother-tongue groups				
	2	3	4	5	6
1. English	26	33	49	50	62
2. German	—	26	38	37	56
3. Other		—	39	36	52
4. Ukrainian			—	24	54
5. Polish				—	55
6. Italian					—

*Population 15 years old and over.

Two exceptions to this similarity in magnitude among the three dimensions are the relatively large index values between United States and (1) Italian-born (72) and (2) Polish-born (59). In fact for each of all the other groups, the degree of residential dissimilarity from the United States group is higher than it is from either the United Kingdom or Canadian-born group. For that matter, the first generation immigrants from both the

118

United States and the United Kingdom are segregated more from other immigrant groups than are native-born Canadians. That the Continental European groups are not more highly segregated from the native-born is probably due to the fact that a substantial proportion of the native-born group is of European parentage.

TABLE 6. INDEXES OF DISSIMILARITY IN RESIDENTIAL DISTRIBUTION OF BIRTHPLACE GROUPS, METROPOLITAN TORONTO, 1961*

Birthplace groups	Index of dissimilarity among birthplace groups							
	2	3	4	5	6	7	8	9
1. Canada	13	22	26	28	28	45	54	63
2. United Kingdom	—	29	28	29	29	46	56	62
3. United States		—	37	42	41	51	59	72
4. Other			—	29	25	38	48	60
5. German				—	26	32	42	57
6. Other European					—	31	37	51
7. Russian						—	29	55
8. Polish							—	55
9. Italian								—

*Population 15 years old and over.

SUMMARY AND IMPLICATIONS

The data presented permit two summary observations. *First*, the magnitude and pattern of segregation found along each dimension suggests that each is worthy of consideration in its own right and further that a comparison of their empirical implications, as separate aspects of ethnic status, may be quite instructive with respect to a full analysis of ethnic residential segregation. *Second*, the fact that there is substantial variation between the dimensions in the general level of segregation observed implies that it makes a considerable difference which dimension serves as an analysis of ethnic differentiation.

With respect to the first observation, the analysis suggested that each dimension exhibited a rather consistent pattern of internal variation in the degree of residential dissimilarity among the various urban subpopulations. That is, the initial ranking of the groups tended to result in orderly patterns

119

of increasing segregation in a fashion conforming to the well-known proposition that a positive relationship holds between social and spatial distances. In the case of the period of immigration classification, which displays the lowest levels of residential dissimilarity overall, the pattern of indexes strongly supports a contention that the more dissimilar two groups of immigrants are in their length of residence, the greater their residential dissimilarity. More or less similar patterns of variation are also observed for each of the other four dimensions. In these cases the initial ranking is made in terms of increasing residential dissimilarity from a standard population selected essentially on the basis of numerical dominance and thus is not equivalent to employing some external status criterion. Nevertheless, neither the choice of the standard population nor the initial ranking itself is sufficient to produce the observed uniformity of the patterns of segregation.[11]

The similarity of the patterns of segregation indexes over several dimensions of ethnicity appears to have broader implications. As suggested above, the variation in residential dissimilarity among religious groups is clearly patterned as if there were a consistent ranking in ethnic status among the Protestant, Catholic, and Jewish groups, and in that order. Furthermore, the variation in the dissimilarity of residential distributions along the origin, mother-tongue and birthplace dimensions reflects not only this religious differentiation but also suggests a more embracing form of status differentiation in terms of the geographic origins of the groups. That is, as has elsewhere been suggested, those groups which have native-Canadian or northern and western European backgrounds exhibit the lowest degrees of segregation from each other, while those with southern and eastern European backgrounds are more segregated from each other and from the former groups (Duncan and Lieberson, 1959).

With respect to the second observation, the analysis suggests that a representation of the degree of residential integration and assimilation among ethnic groups may depend to a large extent on the particular dimension to which reference is made. For example, one could argue on the basis of the relatively low (although patterned) degree of segregation along the immigrant status (length of residence) dimension, that Toronto's population is relatively integrated. On the other hand, one could argue, on the basis of

[11]There is some restriction of the theoretically possible range of values of the dissimilarity index between two groups once the dissimilarity of both from a third (in this case the standard) is known. For all dimensions, however, the possible variation in the pattern of indexes remains much greater than that observed.

the relatively high degree of segregation according to birthplace differences (e.g. United States vs. Italian-born) that Toronto's population is highly pluralistic. Moreover, a somewhat different picture, as to the pattern of residential integration and assimilation, may be inferred from either the religion, origin or mother-tongue dimensions.

The fact that it does matter which dimension one uses does not necessarily suggest that one is more representative of ethnic status than the others, but rather that each dimension reflects at least in part, a particular aspect of ethnicity to which the other dimensions are not analytically sensitive. To the extent that this is the case in a given urban area it argues strongly for a multi-dimensional conception of ethnicity.

There is the further obvious consideration, that despite distinct differences, the dimensions are empirically interrelated. The issue here is not that an assumption of close functional interrelationships between the dimensions is false, but rather that the extent of the interrelationships is an empirical question, subject to demonstration. That is, to what degree can the pattern and magnitude of segregation found along any dimension be directly attributed to the effects of another? It is beyond the scope and capacity of the present analysis to systematically approach all aspects of this question. It is possible, however, to present some preliminary assessment of the inter-relationships between three of the dimensions—period of immigration, origin and religion.[12]

One initial question to be raised in such an analysis concerns the temporal order in which variables are related. For example, the process of residential integration for immigrant groups (as one aspect of their social integration) has been considered to be partially a function of their length of residence in urban areas. Presumably, then, period of immigration could be considered a dimension of ethnicity partly determining the degree of segregation of origin groups.

The question of temporal order is not so clear, however, with regard to the relationship between religion and origin. Considering the apparent similarity between these two dimensions in their patterns of residential segregation, the more appropriate question to be raised here is whether or not they are measuring the same variation in residential distribution. That is, many observers have contended that religious differences, especially between Protestants, Catholics and Jews, have tended to predominate in effecting the

[12]The availability of appropriate data for the following computations has determined this selection.

121

social structure of a community; differences in origins, on the other hand, have become residual in their effects (Kennedy, 1952; Herberg, 1955; Laumann, 1969). Perhaps the pattern of religious segregation essentially accounts for the pattern of origin segregation and therefore these two are not, in fact, empirically separate ethnic dimensions.[13]

The technique employed in examining these relationships has been thoroughly discussed in earlier studies (Duncan, 1959; Lieberson, 1963, ch. 3; Taeuber and Taeuber, 1965, ch. 4). The application of the procedure may be shown with reference to the effect that differences in the periods of immigration of the origin groups have on their residential patterns. As a variant of the method of indirect standardization the procedure yields the residential distributions of origin groups which would be "expected" solely as a result of residential distributions of period of immigration groups.[14] For the expected distributions of the origin groups, indexes of dissimilarity may also be computed and the ratio between the expected and actual indexes for each pair of origin groups indicates the degree to which segregation by period of immigration accounts for their residential segregation. For this analysis Table 7 presents the expected indexes of dissimilarity above the diagonal and the ratio of expected to actual in percentage terms below the diagonal. (The expected indexes, of course, may be directly compared to the actual of Table 4.)

Given that the period of immigration dimension itself generates a lesser degree of segregation than any of the others considered, it could not be expected to come close to fully accounting for the observed segregation of origin groups (see Tables 1 and 3). However, Table 7 reveals that there is even less overall relationship between the two dimensions than a conventional conception of the processes of residential integration and assimilation would lead us to believe. To exemplify the point, if together foreign birth and

[13]It could be argued that religious affiliation is largely a product of one's heritage and, therefore, the segregation of religious groups would be based on the segregation of origin groups (Duncan, 1959). We chose to examine the former interpretation, because it allows a comparison of the relative significance of religion and period of immigration as factors accounting for origin segregation.

[14]Period of immigration again includes the non-immigrant category. In metropolitan Toronto as a whole the period of immigration-specific proportional distributions of each ethnic origin group are given. These proportions are applied to the known distribution of period of immigration groups among the tracts of the city, generating the number of each origin group *expected* to reside in each tract on the basis of their period of immigration composition alone.

length of residence in Canada were the only operative segregating characteristics of the metropolitan population, then a maximum of 17 per cent of one of any pair of origin groups would have to relocate in order to achieve full residential integration (i.e. the case of the French and Italian origin groups). In fact, the mean index of dissimilarity expected on the basis of differences in period of immigration alone is only 6.4 (S.D. $= 3.6$) and, in the average, the expected indexes account for only 18 per cent of the actual ($\bar{X} = 18.2$, S.D. $= 12.8$).

In Canadian cities at least, the notion that time and familiarity with the dominant institutions are the main conditions of acculturation and ultimately of residential dispersion and integration is insufficient to account for the extent of the observed residential segregation of origin groups. There is also a very wide variation in the degree to which the period of immigration dimension accounts for the residential dissimilarity of origin groups, ranging from over 69 per cent of the segregation of the French and German groups to less than 5 per cent of that, say, of the British and Russian. The variation suggests that the interrelationship of the two variables is complex enough that a more adequate conceptualization of the process of ethnic differentiation will be gained by further specification of the effects of separate components of ethnic status and of their relationships, rather than through summary indexes.

Table 8 presents the expected indexes of dissimilarity between origin groups based on their religious composition. The results are in striking contrast to those of the former table. In general the expected indexes are very high, and in two cases predict a greater degree of segregation between origin groups than is actually observed. Religion, thus, may be considered to be at the opposite extreme from period of immigration in terms of the similarity to the origin dimension in the implications for ethnic segregation. Whatever the predominant direction of the effects between origin and religion they are, at least in general, highly interrelated. It can be seen from the ratio of expected to actual indexes that differences in religious affiliations best approximate the magnitude of the segregation of southern and eastern European origin groups. In the case of the Russians, for example, a knowledge of their religious composition and of the residential distributions of the religious groups serves to account for a very high percent of their segregation from others. In the case of those of Italian origin, however, the religious dimension is relatively ineffective in describing the segregation of the origin group.

123

TABLE 7. EXPECTED INDEXES OF DISSIMILARITY FOR ORIGIN GROUPS BASED ON INDIRECT STANDARDIZATION FOR PERIOD OF IMMIGRATION; PER CENT EXPECTED INDEX IS OF ACTUAL INDEX, TORONTO, 1961

Ethnic origin groups	1	2	3	4	5	6	7	8	9	10	11	12
1. British Isles	—	6	10	4	7	3	5	9	4	6	3	14
2. Scandinavian	39.2	—	5	9	2	8	2	4	3	2	4	8
3. German	62.7	26.5	—	13	3	12	6	3	7	6	9	4
4. French	17.0	37.9	69.4	—	10	1	8	12	8	9	6	17
5. Netherlands	36.4	11.8	13.6	33.9	—	9	4	12	5	4	6	7
6. Other	9.8	27.5	39.7	3.2	29.9	—	7	12	6	8	5	16
7. Asiatic	13.0	4.5	19.1	26.5	8.7	17.5	—	5	3	2	3	10
8. Other European	23.0	9.7	7.5	33.1	7.5	24.9	14.1	—	6	4	8	5
9. Ukrainian	9.1	7.6	21.9	18.4	9.9	12.9	6.4	16.3	—	2	2	11
10. Polish	13.2	5.1	15.4	22.1	7.3	16.5	5.0	13.2	10.3	—	4	9
11. Russian	4.9	8.9	19.0	11.9	11.6	9.3	5.6	21.9	4.4	11.8	—	13
12. Italian	25.3	14.6	7.6	31.5	12.0	27.2	18.5	10.6	24.3	18.0	21.3	—

Note: Expected indexes above diagonal; ratio E/A below diagonal.
Per cent expected of actual computed on basis of indexes taken to two decimal places.

TABLE 8. EXPECTED INDEXES OF DISSIMILARITY FOR ORIGIN GROUPS BASED ON INDIRECT STANDARDIZATION FOR RELIGION; PER CENT EXPECTED INDEX IS OF ACTUAL INDEX, TORONTO, 1961

Ethnic origin groups	1	2	3	4	5	6	7	8	9	10	11	12
1. British Isles	—	7	11	15	5	2	7	32	30	30	48	23
2. Scandinavian	50.7	—	6	14	6	7	12	29	27	28	47	21
3. German	68.5	32.1	—	10	7	10	16	25	23	24	44	16
4. French	75.7	61.9	53.6	—	11	14	21	23	19	20	44	8
5. Netherlands	26.5	32.6	30.6	39.5	—	4	11	28	26	26	46	19
6. Other	6.2	24.0	33.0	49.1	13.1	—	8	30	29	29	47	22
7. Asiatic	18.9	31.9	50.6	70.7	25.7	20.0	—	37	35	35	51	28
8. Other European	77.5	73.0	74.9	61.6	47.4	65.5	102.5	—	26	6	21	23
9. Ukrainian	70.7	62.2	67.5	51.9	56.4	61.0	81.2	67.8	—	25	45	17
10. Polish	65.5	61.9	64.7	47.0	53.6	56.7	75.7	19.7	105.9	—	25	19
11. Russian	91.9	93.6	94.1	86.9	85.9	84.3	97.1	60.9	87.6	69.9	—	43
12. Italian	41.5	37.2	31.6	14.5	32.1	37.6	54.1	34.2	37.6	38.1	73.5	—

Note: Expected indexes above diagonal; ratio E/A below diagonal.
Per cent expected of actual computed on basis of indexes taken to two decimal places.

Although on the average the expected indexes of dissimilarity amount to 55 per cent of the actual ($\overline{X} = 55.7$, S.D. $= 23.8$) there is again a relatively wide variation in the degree of interrelationships between the religion and origin dimensions.[15] Thus, despite the magnitude of the effects of one on the other, the origin dimension cannot in this sense be interchanged with that of religious differentiation if a full analysis of the role of ethnicity in residential segregation is intended.

CONCLUSIONS

Our purpose has been to present a theoretical rationale and some preliminary empirical support for a multidimensional conception of ethnic status. Due to a lack of appropriate data and perhaps, also, to the ideological assumption of the inevitability of ethnic assimilation, the variety of characteristics contributing to ethnic status has not been adequately investigated. Availability of data for Toronto provides the opportunity to partially correct this inadequacy. It was possible to determine the degree of residential segregation for each of five social characteristics assumed to represent separate dimensions of ethnic status. The analysis revealed that each characteristic generates both a significant degree and a socially meaningful pattern of residential segregation. Furthermore, evidence was presented regarding the interrelationships of selected ethnic variables which initially supports the validity of conceiving ethnic status along more than one dimension.

That a more rigorous test of the multidimensional conception is needed is obvious. One such test is currently in progress by the present authors employing cross-classified census tract data for birthplace by mother tongue. This will allow a more direct test of the extent to which one dimension accounts for another.

A continuing emphasis in urban ecology concerns the validity of, and the extent of empirical support for, social area analysis. Specifically, attention is focused on the degree to which the three basic dimensions (constructs) of social area analysis—life style, socio-economic status and ethnic status— capture the basic patterns of urban social differentiation in societies of differing scale. Recent studies suggest that in certain urban areas perhaps two

[15]The zero order correlation of the expected and actual indexes is .658, thus the variation between expected indexes statistically accounts for a relatively small proportion of the total variation between the actual indexes of segregation, i.e. the square of .658 is .43. For expected indexes based on period of immigration, the correlation with the actual is .170, and the proportion accounted for is virtually insignificant (.03).

or possibly only one dimension is needed (Abu-Lughod, 1969). Considerable attention has been given, for example, to the extent to which socio-economic status differences account for ethnic segregation. There is no question that further clarification of this relationship is needed. But even when ethnic segregation is to a large extent a function of socio-economic differences, it is not an argument for minimizing the differences within the ethnic construct. Rather, it is our contention that further specification of each construct is needed. We do not yet know, for example, either the manner in which all the various dimensions of ethnicity are interrelated, or perhaps more strategically, how they relate to the separate dimensions of socio-economic status. To claim sufficiency for only three (or even fewer) dimensions is to close prematurely the theoretical arguments concerning the dynamics of differentiation and integration in the urban community.

REFERENCES

ABU-LUGHOD, JANET L. (1969) "Testing the theory of social area analysis: the ecology of Cairo, Egypt." *American Sociological Review* **34** (April), 198–212.

ANDERSON, THEODORE and EGELAND, JANICE (1961) "Spatial aspects of social area analysis." *American Sociological Review* **26** (June), 392–398.

BERRY, BRIAN J. L. (1965) "Internal structure of the city" in EVERETT and LEACH (eds.), *Urban Problems and Prospect.* Dobbs Ferry: Oceana Publications Inc.

BERRY, BRIAN J. L. and REES, PHILIP H. (1969) "The factorial ecology of Calcutta." *American Journal of Sociology* **74** (March), 445–491.

BESHERS, JAMES (1962) *Urban Social Structure.* New York: The Free Press.

CENSUS OF CANADA (1961) *Population and Housing Characteristics by Census Tracts.* Ottawa: Dominion Bureau of Statistics.

COLLISON, PETER (1967) "Immigrants and residence." *Sociology* **1** (September), 277–292.

DUNCAN, OTIS D. (1959) "Residential segregation and social differentiation." *International Population Conference, Vienna.* (International Union for the Scientific Study of Population), pp. 571–577.

DUNCAN, OTIS, D. (1961) "A socio-economic index for all occupations" in Albert J. Reiss, Jr., *Occupations and Social Status.* New York: The Free Press of Glencoe.

DUNCAN, OTIS D. and DUNCAN, BEVERLY (1955a) "Residential distribution and occupational stratification." *American Journal of Sociology* **60** (March), 493–503.

DUNCAN, OTIS D. and DUNCAN, BEVERLY (1955b) "A methodological analysis of segregation indexes." *American Sociological Review* **20** (April), 210–217.

GORDON, MILTON (1964) *Assimilation in American Life.* New York: Oxford University Press.

GREER, SCOTT (1962) *The Emerging City: Myth and Reality.* New York: The Free Press of Glencoe.

127

HAWLEY, AMOS and DUNCAN, OTIS DUDLEY (1957) "Social area analysis: a critical appraisal." *Land Economics* **33** (November), 337–345.

HERBERG, WILL (1955) *Protestant—Catholic—Jew*. New York: Doubleday and Co.

JONES, F. LANCASTER (1967) "Ethnic concentration and assimilation: an Australian case study." *Social Forces* **45** (March), 412–423.

JONES, F. LANCASTER (1968) "Social area analysis: some theoretical and methodological comments illustrated with Australian data." *The British Journal of Sociology* **19** (December), 424–444.

KENNEDY, RUBY JO REEVES (1952) "Single or triple melting pot? Intermarriage trends in New Haven, 1870–1940." *American Journal of Sociology* **49** (April), 331–339.

LAUMANN, EDWARD O. (1969) "The social structure of religious and ethnoreligious groups in a metropolitan community." *American Sociological Review* **34** (April), 182–197.

LIEBERSON, STANLEY (1963) *Ethnic Patterns in American Cities*. Glencoe: The Free Press.

METHA, SURINDER K. (1968) "Patterns of residence in Poona (India) by income, education and occupation (1937–1965)." *American Journal of Sociology* **73** (January), 496–508.

MONTAGUE, JOEL B., JR. (1963) *Class and Nationality: English and American Studies*. New Haven: College and University Press.

RICHMOND, ANTHONY H. (1967) *Post-War Immigrants in Canada*. Toronto: University of Toronto Press.

RYDER, NORMAN (1955) "The interpretation of origin statistics." *Canadian Journal of Economics and Political Science* **21**, 466–479.

SCHNORE, LEO F. (1967) "Community" in NEIL J. SMELSER (ed.), *Sociology: An Introduction*. New York: John Wiley & Sons, Inc.

SHEVKY, ESHREF and BELL, WENDELL (1955) *Social Area Analysis: Theory Illustrative Application and Computational Procedures*. Stanford University Series in Sociology No. 1, Stanford: Stanford University Press.

TAEUBER, KARL E. and TAEUBER, ALMA F. (1965) *Negroes in Cities*. Chicago: Aldine Publishing Co.

TILLY, CHARLES (1961) "Occupational rank and grade of residence in a metropolis." *American Journal of Sociology* **67** (November), 323–330.

Religion and Urbanization in Africa*

Leo Kuper

I HAVE chosen as a basis for the discussion in this paper two sociological theories relevant to the relations between religion and urbanization. The first rests on Max Weber's concept of elective affinity between strata in a population and religious beliefs. I think the concept of elective affinity is broad enough to encompass Marxist theories of the ideological and utopian functions of religious beliefs. The second theory rests on Durkheim's analysis of the social consequences of the division of labour, and similar formulations of this central theme in sociological thought.

I

Weber's thesis that strata or classes in a population have certain affinities for different forms of religious expression by no means implies an economic determinism. Certainly Weber acknowledges the importance of such material factors as occupation and possessions, and freely relates material conditions to religious perspectives. Thus he writes that non-privileged classes are disposed to accept a rational world view incorporating an ethic of compensation, replacing what they cannot be by that which they will one day become, and that their sense of honour rests on a concealed promise for the future which implies the assignment of some function, mission or vocation to them. By contrast the privileged classes require from religion the psychological reassurance of the legitimacy of their good fortune; for

*Revision of a paper given to the Third Conference of Scholars, Frank L. Weil Institute, on The Effects of Urbanization on Religion, October 1963. I am indebted to Professor Monica Wilson, University of Capetown, for her comments on an earlier version of the paper, and to the Weil Institute for Studies in Religion and the Humanities for permission to publish this paper.

129

L. Kuper

such sated strata as warriors, bureaucrats and plutocrats the need for salvation is remote and alien.[1]

This is the familiar concept of belief as ideology for the upper classes and as utopia for the lower, and clearly in the tradition of Marxist analysis. There is no antithesis between Marx and Weber, nor does Weber substitute a determinism by ideas for an economic determinism. But while Weber emphasizes the significance of material factors, he is quite flexible in his interpretation of their influence on ideas, and equally concerned with the reciprocal influence of ideas on material factors. In the first place, following Weber, the material factors apparently act with different force on the religious attitudes of different strata, or at any rate, there is an increase in the diversity of religious attitudes among classes of lower social and economic privilege, indicating that there cannot be a uniform economic determination of religion. In the second place, the influence of the material factors is interpreted within a broader context which includes concepts of honour and style of life. All these elements, for example, seemingly influence Weber's interpretation of the distinctive attitude of bureaucracies as involving the rejection of orgiastic forms of religious expression. In the third place, Weber gives purely religious interests an independent role in the genesis of religious beliefs, and much of his research has been directed to show how these interests and beliefs motivate men to act in the economic and other spheres. The role of ideas, as expressed in the following passage, is quite central. "Not ideas, but material and ideal interests, directly govern men's conduct. Yet very frequently the 'world images' that have been created by 'ideas' have, like switchmen, determined the tracks along which action has been pushed by the dynamic of interest. 'From what' and 'for what' one wished to be redeemed and, let us not forget, 'could be' redeemed, depended upon one's image of the world."[2]

Relating the concept of elective affinity to the subject of this paper, the problem becomes that of deriving, on a purely theoretical basis, a series of propositions as to the expected religious behaviour of typical strata in the population of African cities, which can then be tested against the actual observed behaviour. Quite apart from the intellectual challenge of the task, an immediate difficulty in this approach is that available fragments of knowledge of the actual religious behaviour immediately suggest appropriate

[1]Max Weber, The Sociology of Religion (The Religion of Non-Privileged Classes), Boston: Beacon-Press, 1963.
[2]H. Gerth and C. Wright Mills, From Max Weber (Oxford University Press, 1958). p. 280.

130

theoretical formulations. For example, the utopian functions of religious beliefs in the independent African religious movements, or the ideological functions of religious beliefs among the ruling strata, are sufficiently clear in many cases to confirm in advance the significant influence of class interests, though not of course to define the weight of these interests relative to other interests. An alternate approach is to analyse the observed regularities in urban religious behaviour in Africa, and thereafter to reflect on the implications of these regularities for theories as to the forms of religious expression characteristic of typical strata.

The phrase "typical strata in the population of African cities" is deceptively simple for a continent of such diversity that valid generalizations about African societies are likely to be valid generalizations about human societies. There are the sharp contrasts between the Islamic North and the Christian South, quite apart from the variety of indigenous religions in Sub-Saharan Africa. There are the contrasts between types of city, such as the old cities of Northern Africa, or the traditional cities among the Yoruba, or the new and rapidly expanding industrial cities established during the colonial era. And then there are the contrasts in the milieus of urban growth, involving a range of traditional societies from centralized states to the seemingly amorphous clusters of kinship units, and a range of countries from an overwhelming predominance of subsistence agriculture with a scattering of urban nuclei to countries with a high degree of industrialization and urbanization relative to African standards.

Given this immense variety, I have selected a specific situation close to my own experience of African life, that of the white settler South, and I use this as the main core of the analysis, with only limited comparisons to other areas. I concentrate on the urban African population, but in the broader context of the plural structure of the society, since African urban religions must be seen in part as a form of race relations. And I make certain assumptions about the social situation and the characteristics of African traditional religions in the plural societies of the South.

The social situation in the South, as I define it for the purposes of this paper, involves domination by white settlers and a high rate of urban and industrial growth in cities established by whites and based on African labour, initially migrant but increasingly settled. In this process of migration and urbanization, Africans are detached from the "natural" territorially based and homogeneous tribal communities, and obliged to establish new patterns of social relationship in a new society. These are circumstances which might be

131

expected to influence religious affiliation, the "gathered community" of the church fulfilling some of the functions of the kinship unit and of the "natural" community. The detachment from the tribal matrix should, however, be seen in perspective. In the early stages of urbanization, migrants from the same area may form intimate groups within the city and maintain continuous relations with the tribal home, to which they return for rest periods and for ceremonial occasions; and in the later stages of urbanization, the city becomes the "natural" community for new generations of urban-born citizens.

The tribal composition of the urban African population, whether drawn from many tribes or mainly from a single tribe in the vicinity of the city, may have some relevance for religious participation. Perhaps diversity may encourage new forms of association transcending the tribal bonds, while homogeneity encourages the persistence of tribal sentiments. I have assumed that even in the case where the city draws its African residents mainly from a single tribe, the cultural differences between the tribal and urban milieus far exceed those which the individual must bridge in situations of rural–urban migration arising from changes internal to the society rather than changes imposed by foreign conquest. Extreme subordination of the conquered, and barriers raised against social mobility, impede cultural adaptation. The inordinate privileges of ruling strata in key positions and preferred occupations confront the debased status of African masses labouring in unskilled employment. Thus racial and class differences converge with cultural differences to promote extreme social cleavage. Acquisition of the culture and learning of the white man gains Africans neither exemption from civil disability nor social acceptance; and a growing African urban middle class now stands poised for the forceful assumption of power.

The traditional forms of the tribal religions may also be expected to influence religious affiliations in the city. Edwin Smith discerns three phases or categories of African religious beliefs, namely theism, spiritism, and dynamism.[3] I will assume that Africans in the South traditionally believed in a High God, but vaguely define, remote from everyday life and not expressed in a cult, nor indeed in any form of regular observance or ritual. And I will assume that this concept of a High God was too tenuous to draw together in a universal religion, men of different tribes and races, such as would be found in an African city; or alternatively that the African concept of a High God was overwhelmed by the spiritual power of Christianity, with its concept of a universal God, in much the same way (and perhaps in

[3] Edwin Smith, *African Ideas of God* (London: Edinburgh House Press, 1950).

part by reason of the fact) that African traditional societies were overwhelmed by the military and political power of the bearers of Christianity.

As for spiritism, I will assume that this consists mainly in beliefs and rites connected with the ancestors, that the ancestral cult is practised within the family under the guidance of a senior member and does not call for highly specialized training nor for priestly ministrations nor indeed for spiritual virtuosity. It consists of routine observances associated with the ancestral homestead and the ancestral graves in the rural areas of tribal jurisdiction. Hence there are no traditional priests to carry religious organization into the cities or to found new urban religions, though the wide dispersal of religious leadership among family elders may favour the spread of small intimate sect-like religious groups in the cities. The social arrangements in the southern cities are likely to be antipathetic to the ancestral cult. The ancestral lines are submerged by the sheer density of urban African life, they are lost in its mobility and insecurity, and buried in its impersonal and relatively anonymous mass cemeteries. And conversely the ancestral cult is antipathetic to the tribal and racial diversity of the urban populace, since the main basis of association is the exclusive principle of family membership. Nevertheless, the ancestral cult may persist in a modified form in the uncongenial environment of southern cities, and it may find a more congenial and enduring basis in the urban family compounds of other areas.

Dynamism in Edwin Smith's usage refers to the belief in an impersonal pervasive power and the practices associated with this belief. The power which resides in persons and things may be directed for the benefit of an individual or destructively against him. I will assume the presence of dynamism in the religious thought of Africans as well as some belief in spirits other than the ancestral, such as nature spirits and strange supernatural beings. I will assume the practice of magic and witchcraft derived from dynamism and spiritism, and the presence of specialists, who heal through divination or destroy by sorcery. To the extent that magic and witchcraft are a response to insecurity, the city may foster a desperate reliance on these supports as it throws together unrelated families and tribal foreigners and subjects them to the tensions of a raw industrial urban life.

These then are my assumptions as to the traditional beliefs and social situation of African urban strata in the plural societies of the South. I enquire, in terms of Weber's concept of elective affinity, whether such urban African strata can be expected to display, or do in fact display, forms of religious

133

expression which may be attributed to the conditions of their social existence. I also refer briefly to the social conditions of existence in the cities and ask in effect whether there are religious beliefs and rituals and organization characteristic of urban life. There are thus the two complementary aspects, of the religious affinity of strata, and the religious affinity of cities.

II

The second theory, of a progressive differentiation in structures and functions with an increase in the division of labour, is related by Durkheim to the contrast between mechanical and organic solidarity. In societies characterized by mechanical solidarity, there is little specialization of labour or differentiation of structures. In consequence, social relationships tend to be diffuse, encompassing many activities, rights and obligations. The family is the main unit of organization, and fulfils wide economic, political, educational and religious functions. Social solidarity rests on sympathy between similar units engaged in similar activities, or alternatively on a common and consistent web of understandings. By reason in part of the extensive nature of these common understandings, sacred values tend to permeate social life.

By contrast, as a result of specialization in tasks and differentiation in structure, social relationships in the complex society with organic solidarity tend to be more specific and based on contract. Many of the functions of the family in simple societies are now carried by separate economic, political, educational and religious social structures. Diversity encourages individualization, since it offers opportunity for varied participation. Solidarity rests on the interdependence of persons, and of the special-interest and other groups to which they belong. The area of common understanding contracts. Society becomes more secular as beliefs and rites are segregated in separate institutions and structures. The boundaries of the religious and the "natural" community diverge, and religious bodies take on some of the qualities of voluntary organizations. Perhaps universal criteria of religious membership tend to replace the particular bonds of common ancestry, corresponding to the ascendancy of contractual relationships over blood ties.

This is all very schematic and misleading if applied uncritically as descriptive of the contrast between rural and urban communities in homogenous western societies. It is also misleading if taken as descriptive of the contrast between tribal society and the old traditional cities of Africa. Le

Tourneau's study of the North African city of Fez[4] shows the persistence of sacred values and intimate groupings in association with a massive organization of handicraft industry. The prototype for the complex society was certainly derived by Durkheim from western industrial cities, and some of the ascribed qualities are no doubt characteristic of western culture and industry rather than of complex society as such. But it is precisely for this reason that these ideal types are appropriate to the present discussion of the new cities of southern Africa, established by white men on a western industrial model and in a milieu of rural tribal societies. And I use them in a general way to indicate some of the contrasts between the tribal and urban milieus. I also enquire whether the forms of African urban religion are to be conceived as part of a process of progressive differentiation from the simple sacred tribal society to the complex secular urban society.

III

In applying these theories an immediate difficulty arises from the plural character of the southern states and their origin in conquest. Both Weber and Durkheim deal mainly with change internal to the society. Weber emphasizes the role of the charismatic leader, the prophet, as the agent of change, and analyses the genesis and adoption of religious ideas, and the interaction between the bearers of the religious ideas and the ideas themselves. Durkheim finds the source of change in an increase in social density, from which flows the stimulus to the division of labour and increasing complexity. But neither is specifically concerned with directed or imposed social change, which is a crucial element in the interpretation of contemporary African religions.

Thus the elective affinities of whites may be as decisive an influence on African religious expression as the elective affinities of Africans themselves. I am thinking for example, that the missionary call to bear Christian witness in Africa must be interpreted in part as an expression of the religious needs and aspirations of congregations in Europe and the United States of America, and in part as influenced by the relations between the metropolitan power and the African area of missionary enterprise. The missionary himself brings attitudes and conceptions shaped in non-African cultures which may have a direct relevance for the relations between religion and urbanization in Africa. A reluctance to establish mission stations in the urban industrial areas—as,

[4]Roger Le Tourneau, *Fez in the Age of the Marinides* (University of Oklahoma Press, 1961).

for example, reported by Taylor with reference to the Northern Rhodesian Copperbelt[5]—may well be rooted in an image of the city as ungodly, based on experience in European cities or a traditional depreciation of city life. And these conceptions then influence the direction of missionary effort. It is easy to understand the desire of a missionary to establish his station in a rural area on specially reserved mission lands, where he can hope to build Christian communities, and not merely to gain individual converts in tension with what he feels to be the inhospitable and threatening environment of the city. But this means that the basic distribution of rural and urban religions among Africans may be greatly affected by these predispositions among missionaries.

Where white settlers establish themselves, and the church ministers both to new African converts and to whites whose ancestors were born into the Christian religion, then many further influences act upon African Christians. Again the focus cannot be simply the elective affinities of Africans. The evangelical effort is affected by the structure of the wider society and the privileged position of whites in that society. Thus I think it is correct to say that the Dutch Reformed Church in South Africa was more inclined to carry the gospel to Africans in the northern territories of Nyasaland and Northern Rhodesia than to the African peasants and workers in South Africa. Without in any way impugning the integrity and dedication of the missionaries themselves, the effect of the former case would be to extend Afrikaner influence, in the latter case to undermine it. But if there is this selective factor, then a comparison of the appeal of Calvinism to, say, Nyasas and Zulus must take account of the material and ideal interests of Afrikaners.

The interests of white settlers may profoundly affect the organization and ritual of the church, and perhaps even the dogma. Or if the integrity of the dogma is maintained, there may nevertheless be a selective emphasis in greater harmony with the material interests of the settlers, or different emphases in white and non-white congregations appropriate to their respective stations in life. The multi-racial church adjusts to the wider society. There may be dogmatic tension between the religious beliefs and the political ideologies of the ruling strata, but a practical adjustment, as has been the case with the English-speaking churches in South Africa. Though they reject *apartheid*, most of them carry over to the Christian community the segregation and discrimination of the secular society. Or there may be both practical and dogmatic adjustment as in the case of the Afrikaans-speaking churches.

[5] John Taylor, *Christians of the Copperbelt* (London: SCM Press, 1961).

Tension with the world is not eliminated but it is much reduced in the political sphere by harmonizing religious belief with traditional racial attitudes and contemporary political ideology. Syncretism between traditional beliefs and Christianity is not the prerogative of converts; it is also to be observed among the bearers of Christianity. And in fact missionaries brought to Africans a Christianity much confounded with western society and culture.

Hence there is an interplay between the elective affinities of Africans and whites, and Africans react to a situation which includes the religious and secular expression of white interests. Perhaps I might suggest, though this oversimplifies the facts, that the African separatist (Ethiopian) church movement is in part a response to white domination in the mission churches, and that the African syncretist (Zionist) church movement is in part a response to secular domination.

My argument is that both Weber's approach and the theory of increasing differentiation must be related to the specific situation of a plural society. Under the conditions of a plural society, the process of differentiation assumes special forms, since there is a confrontation between the highly differentiated society of the dominant group and the relatively undifferentiated tribal society. The conversion to Christianity may involve not only a new faith, but also the renunciation of the ties of blood and locality and the acceptance of a whole complex of culture items—western education, employment in a bureaucracy as a teacher, or clerk, or interpreter, and change to monogamous marriage and a more nuclear type of family structure. An African may move almost directly from his own society into a complex western type of society, a process which creates sharp divisions within African society. Social change within the indigenous society is greatly affected by the cultural mobility open to its members and by the imposition of change. It is therefore necessary to separate, if at all possible, some of the consequences of pluralism from those of urbanization, or alternatively to interpret African urban religion in the context of pluralism.

IV

In the plural context of Southern African society, African urban religion may be viewed in part as a mode of relationship between the racial groups. There may be total acceptance of Christianity, or at the other extreme, total rejection (which may or may not involve the adherence to traditional religious beliefs) or complex combinations of both acceptance and rejection.

Probably neither acceptance nor rejection is found in purity: there is always some effect of culture contact.

The response to Christianity as a form of race relations with the conqueror or the alien may be illustrated by the varied reactions of the Xhosa people, crystallized in the distinction between *abantu ababomvu* (that is "Red people" smeared with ochre) and the *abantu basesikolweni* (or "School people"). The "School people" as Philip Mayer describes them[6] are products of the mission and the school, committed to Christianity, literacy and other western ways as ideals, whereas the "Red people" are conservatives who stand by the indigenous way of life, including the pagan Xhosa religion and, as commitment to a moral principle, resist the "new" ways. The "School" Xhosa may have four or five generations of "School" ancestors behind them, whose social horizons also included the town and its opportunities for employment. The "Red" Xhosa are those who have been looking askance at white people and their ways in every successive generation since the time of George IV. These differences reflect in part the conflicting reactions to conquest. The "Red" pattern, in a sense, is the domesticated equivalent of the wars waged by the Xhosa in the eighteenth and nineteenth centuries against white domination: the "School" pattern, in a sense, is or was the cultural equivalent of the submission to domination and the identification with the conqueror. The contrast is most graphically expressed in the different interpretations of the Xhosa term for the converts to Christianity, the *amagqoboka* or "people having a hole". "Red" Xhosa explain this in a derogatory sense, the converts being the quislings who originally "opened a hole" in the Xhosa nation and let in the white-skinned enemy, while Christians prefer to say that the "hole" is where the heart has been pierced by the word of Christ.[7]

The division between the "Red" and the "School" Xhosa is rooted in the countryside and carried over into the town, where it represents varied propensities for religious and other forms of expression. While the "School" Xhosa are relatively open to urban influences, by reason of their training in school and church and their acceptance of western culture, the "Red" migrant may "incapsulate" himself in traditional and country-oriented associations and practices. His identity, his goals and his ideals are defined with reference to the ancestral home and the ancestral spirits which seek to draw him back to the countryside, opposing the evil designs of the witches for his urbanization. Certainly these different propensities constitute elective

[6]Philip Mayer, *Townsmen or Tribesmen* (Oxford University Press, 1961).

[7]Mayer, *op. cit.*, p. 30.

affinities in terms of which the different religious behaviour of the "Red" and the "School" in town may be interpreted. But the affinities are themsleves, at any rate in part, reactions toward or against whites, and the urban milieus in which they operate are shaped and dominated by whites. Hence allowance must be made for the plural structure of the society in any discussions of the relations between religion and urbanization, and this is the point I want to establish.

So too, there is certainly a process of religious differentiation. I assume that this differentiation is to be measured by a continuity in the forms of a phenomenon. If, for example, the differentiating factor is the conversion to Christianity from a religion of ancestral beliefs and rites, then a whole range of variations and combinations between Christianity and the ancestral cult would be represented, and indeed Mayer reports this for the Xhosa. There are pagans, pagan Christians, Christian pagans, and Christians, "Red" people who dabble in Christianity, and Christians committed to the ancestor cult. But there is also the discontinuity between the persistent rejection over the generations of Christianity and associated items of western culture in favour of tribal institutions, and the positive affirmation of western institutions as synonymous with civilization, separating "Red" and "School" almost as two nations, and representing opposed reactions to conquest.

The rejection of Christianity may be quite detached from any commitment to the traditional way of life, and the acceptance may be selective or compounded with rejection, and influenced as much by race relations as theological concerns. The Ethiopian Church is in part a phenomenon of race relations, combining adherence to the dogma and rituals of the mother church with the repudiation of white control of the church. Since there is an affinity between Ethiopian Church movements and movements of national independence, and since African movements of national independence have drawn inspiration from the cities, Ethiopianism may similarly derive an urban impetus. The influence of race relations is more pervasive in the Zionist Churches, expressed in the role of prophets, in church organization and in dogma.[8] One of the consequences of pluralism, and of contact between

---

[8] I have relied very largely on the analysis of the Ethiopian and Zionist Churches by Bengt G. M. Sundkler (*Bantu Prophets in South Africa*, Oxford University Press, 1961). B. A. Pauw (in his study of *Religion in a Tswana Chiefdom*, Oxford University Press, 1960, pp. 142–5) did not find as much concern with the inter-racial situation in the churches he studied in Taung. In many respects, his results are different from those of Sundkler, who was concerned largely with the independent Zulu churches.

a highly differentiated conquering group, offering Christianity and other elements of its culture, and a relatively undifferentiated and subordinated African society, with quite diverse culture and obliged to adjust to the demands of the conqueror, is that it is the subordinates who function as phophets. In general, the white man is the priest, transmitting the knowledge he has acquired in the seminary, while the charisma of religious invention is reserved for Africans. And particularly in South Africa, there has been an efflorescence of African prophetic movements.

In the organization of the Zionist Churches, Africans may achieve, as prophets or as bishops, an honoured status denied them in the plural society. The immense proliferation of over 2000 independent African sects in South Africa answers in some measure the need for recognition among non-privileged groups. Racial prerogatives in the persons of the Biblical prophets, or in the exalted positions of the church hierarchy, are circumvented by the creation of new churches, both Zionist and Ethiopian, in which the highest aspirations may be fulfilled. At the annual general conference of the Federation of Bantu Churches in May 1960, attended by about 280 delegates (160 men and 120 women) and representing some 200 sects, there were, according to a tally made on my behalf, among the men 51 bishops (26 of them on the committee), 39 prophets, 58 ministers, the rest being laymen, and among the women 10 bishops and 9 pastors. Sundkler comments on the paradox that the Zionists and sections of the Ethiopians somehow stem from American Protestant Churches, professing a sturdy individualism and democratic ideals.

> But let these democratic groups operate in a Bantu context in Natal and Zululand, and the result is paradoxical. Throw out the bishops in the name of democracy, and next day your cook or garage attendant will turn up as an Archbishop in mitre and vestments. Wrench the gilded crozier or pastoral staff out of the hand of your bishop, and next day you will find every member of the Zionist congregation with a staff and cross—not of gold this time, but of the wood of a special tree, the thorny sondeza.[9]

The doctrinal reaction in the Zionist Churches to white dominance is shown by Sundkler in dogmas establishing an independent sacred genealogy for the Bantu Churches, mystical and Biblical credentials not derived from the whites, and in the role of the Bantu prophet, the Bantu Messiah who stands at the Gate. Millenarian prophecies reflect the utopian functions of

[9] *The Concept of Christianity in the African Independent Churches*, Institute for Social Research, University of Natal, 1958.

140

religious beliefs in the context of pluralism, and the influence of race relations on revelation. The social situation is such as to inspire a spiritual trans- migration into the Biblical world of the Old Testament and a quest for the New Jerusalem and release from bondage. Sundkler links "the dramatic, hectic formation of Separatist Churches with an apocalyptic programme" to the quest for living space in South Africa, a quest which persists under descriminatory laws reserving most of the land to whites. And since Africans can only establish themselves with some semblance of security on land in the rural areas, it is natural that Rome or the New Jerusalem should be, for the most part, in the countryside rather than in the towns. Ethiopianism would seem to be more urban, Zionism more rural or peri-urban or migrant. It is, however, difficult to test this. The category of Native Separatist Churches in the published census statistics for South Africa includes both Ethiopian and Zionist sects. (According to the 1951 census, there were 524,485 African members of the "Native Separatist Churches" in the urban areas and 1,069,454 in the rural areas. These figures correspond to 22.5% of urban Africans and 17.1% of rural Africans respectively.) Sundkler writes that even though the city congregations are small as a rule, and the overwhelming numbers of church members live in the rural areas, many Ethiopian and Zionist bishops and metropolitans have chosen the Golden City (Johannes- burg) as their see for reasons of prestige. For both, the City is the breeding ground, the Reserve the hatching ground, but he suggests that for the Zionists, in contrast to the Ethiopians, "the Reserve is the Canaan with Bethesdas and Jordans, the pools and the rivers where the sick are healed, and Hills of Zion, the holy hilltops where prayers and sacrifices are presented to Jehovah".[10] The great prophets reside in the country.

Separatism and messianic type movements are not exclusively phenomena of pluralism, but they express social cleavages and hence are quite character- istic of plural societies. The genesis in particular of messianic prophecies and nativistic religions throughout the world under conditions of domination which the subject peoples perceive as oppressive, has been widely docu- mented. The studies in Africa describe local variants of human condition, arising out of suffering and despair, and expressed in a dramatic and exotic form, which has attracted the sympathetic interest of scholars. There can be little doubt of an affinity between pluralism and religious protest and separatism, and the very strength of this affinity obscures other relationships. Thus the problem raised by Andersson of the relations between messianic

[10]Sundkler, *Bantu Prophets . . ., op cit.*, pp. 85–93.

L. Kuper

mythologies and the Protestant religion becomes somewhat intractable.[11] He refers to the arguments that the Catholic Church creates a climate unfavourable to messianic movements, since the individual is subjected to the church by the doctrine that the salvation of the individual takes place through the institution, whereas the personal struggle for salvation demanded in Protestantism often leads to failure and resentment. But he questions the thesis that the adoption of the messianic mythology is characteristic of Protestants, and not of Catholics, and the confirmation offered by Bastide that in Africa the messianic movement "est toujours sorti . . . des milieux prealablement evangelises par les missionnaires protestants, et non par les missionnaires catholiques". The difficulty in advancing the argument further is that of separating the specifically religious promise of salvation from the social relationships of the religious organization and the environing society, so that what appears to be a characteristic reaction of Protestant converts may in fact be a reaction to the associated forms of race relations and colonial domination.

The analysis of the devout acceptance of Christianity as transmitted is so complicated by pluralism that there can be no simple translation into religious affinity of the statistical distribution of Africans in different denominations. Nor can one argue from the known forms of religious observance in a denomination to the emotional mood and appeal of the services, since segregation may permit the containment within one denomination of the perfunctory monotones of genteel devotion, and the loud acclaim and joyous discovery of the Lord. The zeal of converts may not be impervious to the pattern of race relations either within the church community or outside in the wider society. Within the church, converts may be as responsive to opportunities for leadership and for security in a religious fraternity as they are to the specifically religious content of the doctrine and the manner in which it guides the quest for salvation. The different modes of organizing authority, episcopal, methodist, presbyterian or congregational, acquire an added significance because of their relation to the forms of authority in the wider white-dominated society. And the theological significance of the church may be profoundly affected by the stand it takes on the secular politics of race, or by a contagion of disillusionment where the white man is perceived as the exemplar of Christianity.

[11]Efraim Andersson, *Messianic Popular Movements in the Lower Congo*, Studia Ethnographica Upsaliensia, 1958.

142

V

When separate societies of different structure and culture are drawn together in a single society, as in the colonial situation, new social structures and social standards emerge to regulate the new relationships. From this point of view, religious conversion serves the important function of relating strangers to each other by membership in the same church, participation in the same rituals, and adherence to the same moral principles, enjoining the peaceful adjustment of interests and the muting of egoism. Many Africans, in some disillusionment with the practice of Christianity, tend to emphasize the domesticating functions of conversion, and to underestimate the role of disinterested good faith and the importance of the more basic function of providing a framework for co-operative relationships. No doubt, conversion at times, perhaps quite generally, served to nurture among Africans attitudes of subordination, and among whites the self-righteous assurance of the right to dominate as agents of civilization. Common beliefs legitimated the good fortune of the white colonizers in this world, directing them to its enhancement, and guided Africans away from concern for wealth, land and property in this world toward the idyllic compensations of the next. Possibly the concept of a transcendental omnipotent God is specially congruent with the colonial situation. But whatever the ideological functions of conversion to Christianity, it is a basis for relating urban dwellers of different race and tribe.

For Africans, conversion has the further aspect of a process of acculturation. Christianity is not received in isolation from other elements of western culture. At the very least it is associated with some measure of western education. Andersson comments that in the Belgian Congo, children and their parents usually regarded the school and the new religion as inseparable phenomena, and this is true for southern Africa. Conversion is an initiation into western culture and signifies a readiness to enter western society. Since the cities of southern Africa were built on the initiative of white men and after the model of western industrial cities, it seems self-evident that urbanization will be selective, sifting Christians from pagans, and settling Christians in greater proportions in the cities. This proposition can be roughly tested by a comparison of the distribution of the religious affiliations of Africans in urban and rural areas. Allowance should, however, be made for the type of urban industrial development (which is likely to be an important variable, because the extractive industries, such as gold mining, seem to rely more

143

largely on pagan labour), and for rates of pay in different cities (since Christians seem more likely to move to areas of higher wages).[12]

The affinity between Christianity and urbanism—if such is indeed the case under the conditions stated—may be strengthened by intertribal diversity in the towns. The ancestor cult on the other hand is likely to be undermined by this diversity. It is, of course, remarkably persistent, surviving, as a domestic institution, radical change in political structure and transplantation to the town. But it is exclusive, and it does not offer a basis for relating members of different tribal and ethnic groups. If conditions in the towns promote a social effervescence among townsmen of varied ethnic origin, and a consequent exploration of forms of association in which the new relationships may be expressed, then the exclusiveness of the ancestor cult may be in some tension with the growing inclusiveness of social relationships. Or to phrase the matter differently, the universal ethic of Christianity will be more congruent with the developing patterns of social relationship.

This is not to deny that the response to urban change may involve selective emphases in different situations.[13] Intertribal relations may be expressed in the context of work through trade unions, while purely tribal norms prevail in the domestic situation. Nor do I imply that there cannot be adjustment between a universal religious ethic, and exclusive systems of social relationships. Christianity has accommodated racialism. It has fused with tribal exclusiveness, as for example in the independent "Tembu Church" founded by Nehemiah Tile in 1884. Even within the intertribal mission churches in the cities, there may be an indulgence of exclusive tribal sentiment through the use of tribal languages to impart the gospel, and hence a tribal constitution of congregations. Michael Banton reports a similar situation in the context of Islam, tribal groups establishing their tribal mosques and schools.[14] But presumably these practices are in conflict with the ethic of universal brother-

---

[12]Some crude confirmation of a selective religious factor in African urbanization may be derived, for South Africa, from the census for 1951, which showed the percentage of rural Africans returned as heathen to be over twice as high as that of urban Africans. In East London, the second generation of town-born Xhosa were mostly children of "School" Xhosa (B. A. Pauw, *The Second Generation*, Oxford University Press, 1963). Monica Wilson thought that the opportunity for higher wages was a factor in the different pattern of migration to Cape Town as compared with East London, largely "School" in the former, "Red" in the latter.

[13]Cf. Arnold L. Epstein, *Politics in an African Urban Community* (Manchester University Press, 1958).

[14]Michael Banton, *West African City* (Oxford University Press, 1960).

hood, and there must be some basis for association in a common religion, though under certain conditions denominationalism can be as divisive as tribalism. In any event, the towns are likely to be areas of greater intertribal and perhaps interracial worship, and the broader social base of religious membership may be expected to inhibit the intrusion of specifically tribal elements of belief and ritual.

This statement must, however, be qualified by reference to class differences in religious affiliation. There is some evidence that African professionals belong to the main denominations established among whites, that is to day, Methodist, Anglican, Catholic, Congregationalist, Lutheran, Presbyterian. They may be members of such well-known African independent churches as the African Methodist Episcopal Church or the African Congregational Church of the Presbyterian Church of Africa, but they are not likely to worship in churches of the minor Christian sects, whether interracial, Ethiopian or Zionist. For professionals there is almost an element of impropriety in membership of a Zionist sect, save perhaps in quest of healing. The religions of social protest, Utopian compensation, millenarian vindication are not for the African middle classes, though they are non-privileged classes and labour under grave discrimination. Their identification is seemingly with whites, their affiliation is to the churches within which they or their parents were educated, and they have taken over, not single items of culture, but a whole way of life, highly differentiated, with a clear distinction between religious and political functions. This distinction is, of course, more apparent than real, and more proclaimed than practiced. Indeed a source of disillusionment or of apostasy among Africans has been the discovery of the interpenetration of religion and politics, and the realization that the seemingly differentiated structures and functions are integrated by common racial interests.

The minor Christian sects, above all the Zionists, express the aspirations of lowly strata disrupted from their accustomed way of life. In the theodicies of the Zionist sects, working-class men and women, Africans in the interstices of the new society, or transient between the old and new, may find an immediate significance and an ultimate compensation. Dogma and ritual effect a syncretism between traditional African beliefs and Christianity. Under the inspiration of an apocalyptic Church in the United States, the Christian Catholic Apostolic Church in Zion, which taught "divine healing", "triune immersion", and that the second coming of the Lord was near at hand, and under the later inspiration of Pentecostal or Apostolic Faith

145

missionaries, also from the United States, Zionists have interwoven with Christianity traditional purification rites, elements of the ancestor cult, spirit possession, divination and healing. Zionism is a bridge over which men may move from tribal society toward western urban society. It is also a bridge by which they may return. Accommodation tends to replace the earlier rejection of western education and medicine, so that Zionism begins to mediate between the societies in these fields as in religion.[15]

The great profusion of urban African voluntary associations is usually interpreted as, in part, a response to the change from the relatively undifferentiated traditional societies in which most needs are satisfied within the kin group. The abundance of purposive associations between strangers somehow functions for the ties of blood. The gathered community replaces the natural community. This quality is perhaps most marked in the religious fraternities of the Zionists as they relate to each other in small groups, bounded by distinctive insignia and ascetic and other practices, and drawn together by the shared experience of deeply emotional forms of religious worship. But it is also to be found within the mission churches in the *manyanos*, sect-like associations of African women, who attain in Christianity some release from their traditionally subordinate status. The religious base of social security may ease the transition to urban society; or it may insulate, though perhaps temporarily, against urban involvement where the religious bond diffuses over a wide range of social relationships.

VI

To conclude, African religious behaviour must be interpreted in the context of the plural structure of the societies in which they live. Their religious affiliations are partly motivated by the relations between the races. In the early periods of domination, Africans related themselves to the white conquerors by the very act of conversion to Christianity. And though with the growth of independent African churches, this is no longer clearly the case, nevertheless the independent churches, Ethiopian and Zionist, and the mission churches, all express different forms of race relations with the white man. They involve different types of reaction to the racial structure of the society outside the church and to the racial structure of authority within it. In their religious affiliations, Africans may be motivated as much by worldly

[15]See Sundkler, *Bantu Prophets . . ., op. cit.*, pp. 307–10.

146

reactions to race and politics as by the religious appeal of a specific promise of salvation. And the range of religious affiliation, from the positive affirmation of traditional religion and the rejection of Christianity (as among the"Red" Xhosa) to membership of interracial churches, has its counterpart in the range of political choice from exclusive nationalism to multi-racialism.

The influence of the specifically religious elements of dogma and ritual, and of the worldly factors of society, race and politics, are likely to vary with different strata of the African population. Weber, in his analysis of affinities, relates the social situation of various strata to such qualities of dogma as appeal to the intellect, spiritual promise, implicit concept of honour, and so on. I have no doubt that these are relevant for the interpretation of the membership of middle-class Africans in Methodist, Anglican, Catholic, Con-gregationalist, Lutheran and Presbyterian Churches. But I would suppose that the class status of these churches in white society is also relevant and that to some extent the affiliation is with middle-class white society. That is to say, the affinity may be as much for the spiritually irrelevant class symbolism of membership in the church as for sobriety of worship or the elimination of magic or the promise of salvation or the active asceticism or other elements of belief and ritual and ethic.

My argument assumes that middle-class Africans chose the churches of their affiliation, whereas to an appreciable extent they were chosen. It was the churches which made the election. Since the major English-speaking churches pioneered African education and since education was the avenue of social mobility for Africans, there was inevitably an historical association between these churches and the African middle class. And presumably the churches fostered among their members a feeling for a certain mood of worship and devotion.

I am suggesting then, that it is difficult to apply to the African middle class the concept of an elective affinity for a religious ethic or style. The member-ship of African workers and peasants in the same churches as the African middle class adds to the difficulty. By contrast, in the free synthesis of Christian and traditional dogma and ritual, and in the re-creation of the Holy Land, in messianic prophecy, and in the role of black prophet and priest, the Zionist churches clearly reflect the social situation of marginal strata seeking security and dignity under white domination in a changing world.

The progressive differentiation of structures and functions, consequent upon the increasing division of labour, is affected by social differentiation among Africans and by the racial structure of the wider society. Seen as a

147

whole, African social structure has become more highly differentiated under the domination of white industrial society. But different strata in the African population have played very different roles in this process. Partly for the reason that Christianity was introduced by whites as a separate institution in a highly differentiated society. Africans were able to move more directly from relatively simple traditional societies into modern complex societies. For many middle-class Africans, the process was one of abrupt change and discontinuity rather than a process of gradual and progressive change. Conversely, the very sharpness of the contrast between the traditional and industrial societies has the opposite consequence for many Zionists in the cities. Having accepted the separate religious institution of the church, they integrate the most varied aspects of life round this nucleus, so that the church begins to approximate the undifferentiated "natural" community. But presumably this is only a transitional phase in a process of differentiation: Zionists work in urban industries and businesses, and as Sundkler reports, they increasingly use the schools and hospitals. The racial divisions naturally impede the progressive differentiation of structures and functions even within each racial group. This partly explains the overlapping of functions in African voluntary associations, so that a sports association or a church may have a significant political role. So too, the Dutch Reformed Churches in South Africa, in their totalitarian form (not unlike Zionist Churches) and in the extent to which they are integrated with political, educational, economic and other social structures and functions, show the restraint on progressive differentiation imposed by racial divisions.

The specific relations between religion and urbanization are not easily abstracted from the broader context of race and culture contact. The interest of the early missionaries in rural mission stations has resulted in a more equal distribution of African Christians in town and country: but in general, there is a tendency for the industrial cities in the South to be selective of Christians. The environment of the cities is by no means hospitable to the traditional observance of ancestral rites, nor do the ancestral cults offer a basis of religious association between people of different tribe and race. In this respect, too, urbanization may encourage worship in Christian churches. On the other hand, if a more secular view of life is one of the consequences of urbanism and differentiation, then it may also be encouraged by a cynical appraisal of the political role of Christianity in the plural societies of southern Africa.

Contrasts in the Community Organization of Chinese and Japanese in North America*

Stanford M. Lyman

Race relations theory and policy in North America have for the most part been built upon examination of the experiences and difficulties of European immigrants and Negroes. As a result contrasting ideas and programmes, emphazing integration for the latter and cultural pluralism for the former, have been generated primarily in consideration of each group's most manifest problems.[1] However, relatively little work has been done to ascertain the conditions under which an ethnic group is likely to follow an integration-oriented or a pluralist-oriented path.[2] Two racial groups found in North America—the Chinese and the Japanese—are likely candidates for the focus of such research, since they have superficially similar outward appearances, a long history as victims of oppression, discrimination, and prejudice, but quite different developments in community organization and cohesion.[3] In this paper an attempt is made to ascertain the distinctive feature of the culture and social organization of the two immigrant groups that played significant roles in directing the mode of community organization in North America.

*Revised version of a paper presented at the University of California under the sponsorship of the Committee for Arts and Lectures, August 23, 1966. I am indebted to Herbert Blumer, Jean Burnet and Marvin Scott for criticisms of earlier versions of this paper.

[1] Cf. Horace M. Kallen, *Culture and Democracy in the United States* (New York, 1924) with Gunnar Myrdal, *An American Dilemma* (New York, 1944).

[2] See Clyde V. Kiser, "Cultural Pluralism", *The Annals of the American Academy of Political and Social Science,* **262** (March 1949), 118–129. An approach to such a theory is found in William Petersen, *Population* (New York, 1961), pp. 114–49.

[3] For an extended analysis see Standford M. Lyman, "The Structure of Chinese Society in Nineteenth-Century America" (unpublished Ph.D. dissertation, University of California, Berkeley, 1961).

S. M. Lyman

There is sound theoretical ground for reconsidering the role of Old World culture and social organization on immigrant communities in North America. Even in what might seem the paradigm case of cultural destruction in the New World—that of the Negro—there is evidence to suggest at least vestiges of cultural survival.[4] In those ethnic communities unmarred by so culturally demoralizing a condition as slavery, there survives what Nathan Glazer calls elements of a "ghost nation", so that despite its fires social life goes on at least in part "beyond the melting pot".[5] American ideology has stressed assimilation, but its society is marked by European, Asian, and some African survivals; Canadian ideology has stressed the "mosaic" of cultures, but at least some of its peoples show definite signs of being Canadianized. The immigrants' cultural baggage needs sociological inspection to ascertain its effects on community organization and acculturation. Fortunately, the Chinese and Japanese communities provide opportunities for this research because of new knowledge about the Old Asian World[6] and extensive material on their lives in North America.

THE CHINESE

In contrast to the Japanese and several European groups, the Chinese in Canada and the United States present an instance of unusually persistent social isolation and preservation of Old World values and institutions.[7] To the present day a great many Chinese work, play, eat, and sleep in the

[4]Melville Herskovitz, *The Myth of the Negro Past* (Boston, 1958). See also Charles Keil, *Urban Blues* (Chicago, 1966), 1–69.

[5]Nathan Glazer, "Ethnic Groups in America: From National Culture to Ideology", in Morroe Berger, Theodore Abel, and Charles H. Page, Editors, *Freedom and Control in Modern Society* (New York, 1954), pp. 158–76, Nathan Glazer and Daniel Patrick Moynihan, *Beyond the Melting Pot: The Negroes, Puerto Ricans, Jews, Italians and Irish of New York City* (Cambridge, 1963).

[6]The "knowledge explosion" on China has been prodigious since 1949 despite the difficulties in obtaining first-hand field materials. Much research was inspired by interest in the Chinese in Southeast Asia. See Maurice Freedman, "A Chinese Phase in Social Anthropology", *British Journal of Sociology*, **16**, 1 (March 1963), 1–18.

[7]Sources for the material reported are Lyman, "The Structure of Chinese Society in Nineteenth-Century America", *passim;* Leong Gor Yun, *Chinatown Inside Out* (New York, 1936), 26–106, 182–235; Calvin Lee, *Chinatown, U.S.A.: A History and Guide* (Garden City, 1955); Stuart H. Cattell, *Health, Welfare and Social Organization in China-town, New York City* (New York, August 1962), pp. 1–4, 20–68, 81–185. For the origins of organized labour's hostility to the Chinese see Herbert Hill, "The Racial Practices of

150

Chinese ghettos known throughout North America as "Chinatowns". The business ethics of Chinatown's restaurants and bazaars are institutionalized in guild and trade associations more reflective of nineteenth-century Cathay than twentieth-century North America. Newly arrived Chinese lads work a twelve to sixteen-hour day as waiters and busboys totally unprotected by labor unions. Immigrant Chinese mothers sit in rows in tiny "sweatshops" sewing dresses for downtown shops while infants crawl at their feet. In basements below the street level or in rooms high above the colorfully-lit avenue, old men gather round small tables to gamble at *f'an t'an, p'ai kop piu*, or other games of chance. Above the hubbub of activity in the basements, streets, stores, and sweatshops are the offices of clan associations, speech and territorial clubs, and secret societies. And behind the invisible wall that separates Chinatown from the metropolis the élites of these organizations conduct an unofficial government, legislating, executing, and adjudicating matters for their constituents.

Not every Chinese in Canada or the United States today recognizes the sovereignty of Chinatown's power élite or receives its benefits and protections.[8] At one time San Francisco's "Chinese Six Companies" and Vancouver's Chinese Benevolent Association could quite properly claim to speak for all the Chinese in the two countries. But that time is now past. Students from Hong Kong and Taiwan and Chinese intellectuals, separated in social origins, status, and aspirations from other Chinese, have cut themselves off from their Chinatown compatriots. Another segment of the Chinese population, the Canadian-born and American-born, who have

---

Organized Labor—The Age of Gompers and After", in Arthur Ross and Herbert Hill, Editors, *Employment, Race, and Poverty: A Critical Study of the Disadvantaged Status of Negro Workers from 1865 to 1965* (New York, 1967), pp. 365–402. For a detailed description of Chinese games of chance see the several articles by Stewart Culin, "Chinese Games with Dice" (Philadelphia, 1889), pp. 5–21; "The Gambling Games of the Chinese in America", *Publications of the University of Pennsylvania, Series in Philology, Literature, and Archaeology*, I, 4, 1891; "Chinese Games with Dice and Dominoes", *Report of the United States National Museum, Smithsonian Institution*, 1893, pp. 489–537. The sweatshops of San Francisco's Chinatown are described in James Benet, *A Guide to San Francisco and the Bay Region* (New York, 1963), pp. 73–74.

[8] See Rose Hum Lee, *The Chinese in the United States of America* (Hong Kong, 1960), pp. 86–131, 231–51, 373–404. See also *Chinese Students in the United States, 1948–1955: A Study in Government Policy* (New York, March 1956). For a Canadian–Chinese view of his own generation's adjustment to Chinese and Canadian ways of life see William Wong, "The Younger Generation", *Chinatown News*, **11,** 13 (March 18, 1964), 6–7.

acquired citizenship in the country of their birth, not only exhibits outward signs of acculturation in dress, language, and behaviour, but also grants little if any obeisance to Chinatown's élites. Some of this generation now find it possible to penetrate the racial barrier, and pass into the workaday world of the outer society with impunity. Others still work or reside in Chinatown but are too acculturated to be subject to its private law. Still a few others are active in the traditional associations seeking power and status within the framework of the old order.

That North America's Chinatowns are not merely creatures of the American environment is indicated by the relatively similar institutionalization of Chinese communities in other parts of the world.[9] The diaspora of Chinese in the last two centuries has populated Southeast Asia, the Americas, Europe, and Africa with Oriental colonies. Should the tourists who today pass along Grant Avenue in San Franscico, Pender Street in Vancouver, and Pell and Mott Streets in New York City, peering at exotic food and art, and experiencing the sights, sounds, and smells of these cities' Chinatowns, be whisked away to Manila, Bangkok, Singapore, or Semarang, or suddenly find themselves in Calcutta, Liverpool or the capital of the Malagasy Republic, they would discover, amidst the unfamiliarity of the several national cultures, still other "Chinatowns" not unlike their North American counterparts. Recognition of the recalcitrance of overseas Chinese to their surroundings takes different forms in different places. In the United States sociologists marvel at their resistance to the fires of the melting pot; in Indonesia the government questions the loyalty of this alien people; in Malaysia native farmers and laborers resent the vivid contrast between their

[9] Material for the following is drawn from Maurice Freedman and William Willmott, "Southeast Asia, with Special Reference to the Chinese", *International Social Science Journal*, **13**, 2 (1961), 245–70; Victor Purcell, *The Chinese in Southeast Asia* (London, 1965), Second edition; Jacques Amyot, S. J., *The Chinese Community of Manila: A Study of Adaptation of Chinese Familism to the Philippine Environment* (Chicago, 1960); Richard J. Coughlin, "The Chinese in Bangkok: A Commercial-Oriented Minority", *American Sociological Review*, **20** (June 1955), 311–16; Maurice Freedman, *Chinese Family and Marriage in Singapore* (London, 1957); Donald Willmott, *The Chinese of Semarang: A Changing Minority Community in Indonesia* (Ithaca, 1960); Shelland Bradley, "Calcutta's Chinatown", *Cornhill Magazine*, **57** (September 1924), 277–85; Christopher Driver, "The Tiger Balm Community", *The Guardian* (January 2, 1962); Tsien Tche-Hao, "La vie sociale des Chinois à Madagascar", *Comparative Studies in Society and History*, **3**, 2 (January 1961), 170–81; Justus M. van der Kroef, "Chinease Assimilation in Indonesia", *Social Research*, **20** (January 1954), 445–72; Leonard Broom, "The Social Differentiation of Jamaica", *American Sociological Review*, **19** (April 1954), 115–24.

own poverty and Chinese commercial affluence; in Jamaica Chinese are urged to quit their exclusiveness and become part of the larger community. But everywhere the issue is acculturation. Despite more than a century of migration, the Chinese have not fully adopted the culture, language, behaviour—the ways of life—of the countries in which they have settled. Their cultural exclusiveness—especially as it finds its expression in geographically compact and socially distant communities within the host societies' cities—is a world-historical event deserving far more discussion and research than it has yet been given.

THE JAPANESE

The rapid acculturation of the Japanese in North America has been a source of frequent discussion. The fact that "Japan-town" is not as familiar a term to North Americans as "Chinatown" is an unobtrusive measure of this difference between the two peoples. Such local names as "Li'l Tokyo" or "Li'l Yokohama" have been short-lived references for Japanese communities isolated through discrimination, but these have rarely been characterized by such peculiar institutions and private government as are found in the Chinese quarter. Japanese-owned businesses are not organized on the basis of guilds or *zaibatsu*; prefectural associations exist primarily for nostalgic and ceremonial purposes, playing no effective part in political organization in the community; and secret societies like those so prominent among the Chinese are not found in North American Japanese communities. Neither sweatshops nor gambling houses are established institutions of Japanese-American or Japanese-Canadian communities. Indeed, in the geographic sense, the North American Japanese communities show increasing signs of disintegration.

Although overseas Chinese communities exhibit the characteristics of colonization with a superordinate organization to represent them to the larger society, the Japanese are organized on patterns closer to that of a reluctant minority group.[10] The earliest associations among immigrant Japanese emphasized defense against prejudice and support for the larger

[10]Material for the following is based on Michinari Fujita, "Japanese Associations in America", *Sociology and Social Research* (January–February 1929), pp. 211–28; T. Obana, "The American-born Japanese," *Sociology and Social Research* (November–December 1934), pp. 161–5; Joseph Roucek, "Japanese Americans", *in* Francis J. Brown and Joseph S. Roucek, Editors, *One America: The History, Contributions, and Present Problems of Our Racial and National Minorities* (New York, 1952), pp. 319–84; Forrest E. la Violette, "Canada and Its Japanese", in Edgar T. Thompson and Everett C. Hughes,

society's laws and customs, and these organizations have been supplanted by even more acculturation-oriented organizations in the second generation. Japanese are the only ethnic group to emphasize geo-generational distinctions by a separate nomenclature and a belief in the unique character structure of each generational group. Today the third and fourth generations in North America (*Sansei* and *Yonsei*, respectively) exhibit definite signs of a "Hansen effect"—that is, interest in recovering Old World culture—and also show concern over the appropriate allocation of their energies and activities to things American or Canadian and things Japanese. Ties to a Japanese community are tenuous and find their realization primarily in courtship and marriage and in recreational pursuits.

Although the situation is by no means so clear, overseas Japanese communities outside North America exhibit some patterns similar to and some quite different from those of the continental United States and Canada. In the most extensive study of acculturation among Japanese in pre-war Kona, Hawaii, the community appeared organized less along Japanese than Hawaiian–American lines. Other studies of Japanese in Hawaii have emphasized the innovative food habits, decline of the patriarch, and changing moral bases of family life. On the other hand, Japanese in Peru, where Japan's official policy of emigration played a significant role in establishing the colony and supervising its affairs, had maintained a generally separate though financially successful and occupationally diversified community until 1942; postwar developments indicate that the Peruvian-born Japanese will seek and obtain increasing entrance into Peruvian society and further estrangement from all-Japanese associations. In Brazil, a situation similar to that of Peru developed: sponsored migration reached great heights during the period of Japan's imperialist development, and, although Brazil welcomed Japanese until 1934, a policy of coerced assimilation motivated by suspicion of Japanese intent led to a closing of many all-Japanese institutions before the outbreak of World War II. In the postwar period, Brazilian-born Japanese indicated a greater interest than their parents had in integration into Brazilian society. In Paraguay, where the first Japanese colony began in La Colmena as

Editors, *Race: Individual and Collective Behavior* (Glencoe, 1958), pp. 149–55; Charles Young, Helen R. Y. Reid and W. A. Carrothers, *The Japanese Canadians* (Toronto, 1938), edited by H. A. Innis; Ken Adachi, *A History of the Japanese Canadians in British Columbia* (Vancouver (?) 1958); T. Scott Miyakawa, "The Los Angeles Sansei", *Kashu Mainichi* (December 20, 1962), Part 2, 1; Harry Kitano, "Is There Sansei Delinquency?", *Kashu Mainichi* (December 20, 1962), Part 2, 1.

recently as 1936, signs of acculturation and community break-down have been reported by cultural geographers surveying the area.[11] Generally, this cursory survey of overseas Japanese communities suggests that when such communities are not governed by agencies of the homeland and where, as the researches of Caudill and de Vos indicate,[12] Japanese values find opportunity for interpenetration and complementarity with those of the host society (as in the United States and Canada), the speed with which community isolation declines is accelerated.

Contrasts between the Chinese and Japanese have been noticed frequently but rarely researched.[13] As early as 1909 Chester Rowell, a Fresno, California journalist, pointed to the Japanese refusal to be losers in unprofitable

[11]For the Japanese in Hawaii, see John Embree, "New and Local Kin Groups Among the Japanese Farmers of Kona, Hawaii", *American Anthropologist*, 41 (July 1939), 400–7; John Embree "Acculturation Among the Japanese of Kona, Hawaii", *Memoirs of the American Anthropological Association*, No. 59; Supplement to *American Anthropologist*, 43, 4:2 (1941); Jitsuichi Masuoka, "The Life Cycle of an Immigrant Institution in Hawaii: The Family", *Social Forces*, 23 (October 1944), 60–64; Masuoka, "The Japanese Patriarch in Hawaii", *Social Forces*, 17 (December 1938), 240–8; Masuoka, "Changing Food Habits of the Japanese in Hawaii", *American Sociological Review*, 10 (December 1945), 759–65; Masuoka, "Changing Moral Bases of the Japanese Family in Hawaii", *Sociology and Social Research*, 21 (November 1936), 158–69; Andrew M. Lind, *Hawaii's Japanese, An Experiment in Democracy* (Princeton, 1946). For the Japanese in Peru see Toraji Irie: "History of Japanese Migration to Peru", *Hispanic–American Historical Review*, 32 (August–October, 1951) 437–52, 648–64; (February 1952), 73–82; Mischa Titiev, "The Japanese Colony in Peru", *Far Eastern Quarterly*, 10 (May 1951), 227–47. For Japanese in Brazil see J. F. Normano "Japanese Emigration to Brazil", *Pacific Affairs*, 7 (March 1934), 42–61; Emilio Willems and Herbert Baldus, "Cultural Change Among Japanese Immigrants in Brazil in the Ribeira Valley of Sao Paulo", *Sociology and Social Research*, 26 (July 1943), 525–37; Emilio Willems, "The Japanese in Brazil", *Far Eastern Quarterly*, 18 (January 12, 1949), 6–8; John P. Augelli, "Cultural and Economic Changes of Bastos, a Japanese Colony on Brazil's Paulista Frontier", *Annals of the Association of American Geographers*, 48, 1 (March 1958), 3–19. For Paraguay see Norman R. Stewart, *Japanese Colonization in Eastern Paraguay* (Washington, D.C., 1967).

[12]William Caudill, "Japanese American Personality and Acculturation", *Genetic Psychology Monographs*, 45 (1952), 3–102; George de Vos, "A Comparison of the Personality Differences in Two Generations of Japanese Americans by Means of the Rorschach Test", *Nagoya Journal of Medicine*, 17, 3 (August 1954), 153–265; William Caudill and George de Vos, "Achievement, Culture and Personality: The Case of the Japanese Americans", *American Anthropologist*, 58 (December 1956), 110–226.

[13]Materials in this section are based on Chester Rowell, "Chinese and Japanese Immigrants—a Comparison", *Annals of the American Academy of Political and Social Science*, 24, 2 (September 1909), 223–30; Winifred Raushenbush, "Their Place in the Sun", and "The Great Wall of Chinatown", *The Survey Graphic*, 56, 3 (May 1, 1926), 141–5,

contracts, to their unwillingness to be tied to a "Jap-town", and to their geniality and politeness; in contrast he praised the Chinese subordination to contracts and headmen, their accommodation to a ghetto existence, and their cold but efficient and loyal service as domestics. Similar observations were made by Winifred Raushenbush, Robert Park's assistant in his famous race relations survey of the Pacific coast. More recently the late Rose Hum Lee has vividly remarked upon the contrast between the two Oriental groups. Professor Lee asserts that the *Nisei* "exhibit within sixty years, greater degrees of integration into American society, than has been the case with the Chinese, whose settlement is twice as long". Other sociologists have frequently commented on the speed with which Japanese adopted at least the outward signs of Occidental culture and attained success in North America. Broom and Kitsuse summed up the impressive record of the Japanese by declaring it "an achievement perhaps rarely equalled in the history of human migration". More recently, Petersen has pointed to the same record of achievement and challenged sociologists to develop a theory which could adequately explain it as well as the less spectacular records of other ethnic groups.

Although the differences between the Chinese and Japanese in North America have excited more comparative comment than concrete investigation, an early statement by Walter G. Beach deserves more attention than it has received. In a much neglected article[14] Beach observed the contrast between the speed of acculturation of Chinese and Japanese and attributed it to those conditions within and extrinsic to the ethnic groups which fostered either segregation and retention of old world culture traits or rapid breakdown of the ethnic community. Noting that ethnic cultures were an important aspect of the kind of community an immigrant group would form he pointed out that the Chinese came to America "before Chinese culture had been greatly influenced by Westerd Civilization". More specifically, he suggested that "they came from an old, conservative and stationary social organization and system of custom-control of life; and that the great

---

154–8; Rose Hum Lee, *The Chinese in the United States of America*, p. 425; Leonard Broom and John I. Kitsuse, "The Validation of Acculturation: A Condition of Ethnic Assimilation", *American Anthropologist*, **57** (1955), 44–8; William Petersen, "Family Structure and Social Mobility Among Japanese Americans". Paper presented at the annual meetings of the American Sociological Association, San Francisco, August, 1967.

[14]Walter G. Beach, "Some Considerations in Regard to Race Segregation in California", *Sociology and Social Research*, **18** (March 1934), 340–50.

majority came from the lower and least independent social stratum of that life". By contrast, he observed that the Japanese "came at a time when their national political system had felt the influence of Western thought and ambitions". He went on to say: "Japan was recognized among the world's powers, and its people were self-conscious in respect to this fact; their pride was not in a past culture, unintelligible to Americans (as the Chinese), but in a growing position of recognition and authority among the world's powers". It was because of these differences in culture and outlook, Beach argued, that Japanese tended to resist discrimination more vigorously and to adopt Occidental ways more readily, while Chinese produced a "Chop-suey culture" in segregated communities. Stripped of its ethnocentrism, Beach's analysis suggests that acculturation is affected not only by the action of the larger society upon immigrants, but also, and more fundamentally, by the nature and quality of the immigrant culture and institutions.

The present study specifies and clarifies the features of Japanese and Chinese culture which Beach only hinted at, and details the interplay between Old-World cultures and North American society. Certain key conditions of life in China and Japan at the times of emigration produced two quite different kinds of immigrant social organization. The responses of the American economy and society to Chinese and Japanese certainly had their effects. But these alone did not shape Chinese and Japanese life. Rather they acted as "accelerators" to the direction of and catalysts or inhibitors of the development of the immigrants' own culture and institutions.[1ᴇ] Prejudice and discrimination added considerable hardship to the necessarily onerous lives of the immigrating Orientals, but did not wrench away their culture, nor deprive them completely of those familial, political, and social institutions which they had transported across the Pacific.[16] The Chinese and Japanese were never reduced to the wretchedness of the first Africans in America, who experienced a forcible stripping away of their original

[15]See the discussion in Lyman, "The Structure of Chinese Society in Nineteenth-century America", pp. 370–77.

[16]One difference with respect to hostility toward the Chinese and Japanese had to do with whether either was perceived as an "enemy" people. Although the Chinese were occasionally accused of harboring subversive intentions toward America—(see, e.g. P. W. Dooner, *Last Days of the Republic* (San Francisco, 1880))—it was the Japanese who suffered a half-century of such suspicions. See Jacabus tenBroek, Edward N. Barnhart, and Floyd Matson, *Prejudice, War and the Constitution* (Berkeley, 1954), pp. 11–99; Forrest E. La Violette, *The Canadian Japanese and World War II* (Toronto, 1948). Undoubtedly these deep-seated suspicions led Japanese to try very hard to prove their

culture, and then a coercive assimilation into selected and subordinated elements of white America. Thus, although both Chinese and Japanese share a nearly identical distinction from the dominant American racial stock, and although both have been oppressed by prejudice, discrimination, segregation and exclusion, a fundamental source of their markedly different rates of acculturation is to be found in the particular developmental patterns taken by their respective cultures[17] in America.

EMIGRATION

The conditions of emigration for Chinese and Japanese reflected respectively their different cultures. The Chinese migrated from a state that was not a nation, and they conceived of themselves primarily as members of

loyalty and assimilability. In this respect see Mike Masaoka, "The Japanese American Creed", *Common Ground*, **2**, 3 (1942), 11; and "A Tribute to Japanese American Military Service in World War II", Speech of Hon. Hiram Fong in the Senate of the United States, *Congressional Record*, 88th Congress, First Session, May 21, 1963, pp. 1–13; "Tributes to Japanese American Military Service in World War II", Speeches of Twenty-four Congressmen, *Congressional Record*, 88th Congress, First Session, June 11, 1963, pp. 1–16; Senator Daniel Ken Inouye (with Lawrence Elliott), *Journey to Washington* (Englewood Cliffs, 1967), pp. 87–200.

[17] In the tradition of Max Weber, religion might properly be supposed to have played a significant role in the orientations of overseas Chinese and Japanese. However, certain problems make any adoption of the Weberian thesis difficult. First, although Confucianism was the state religion of China, local villages practiced syncretic forms combining ancestor worship, Buddhism, Christianity, and homage to local deities. Maurice Freedman, *Lineage Organization in Southeastern China* (London, 1958), p. 116. Abroad Chinese temples were definitely syncretic and functioned to support a non-rationalist idea of luck and the maintenance of merchant power. See A. J. A. Elliott, *Chinese Spirit Medium Cults in Singapore* (London, 1955), pp. 24–45; Stewart Culin, *The Religious Ceremonies of the Chinese in the Eastern Cities of the United States* (Philadelphia, 1887); Wolfram Eberhard, "Economic Activities of a Chinese Temple in California", *Journal of the American Oriental Society*, **82**, 3 (July–September 1962), pp. 362–71. In the case of Japanese, the Tokugawa religion certainly facilitated a limited achievement orientation. Robert Bellah, *Tokugawa Religion: The Values of Pre-industrial Japan* (Glencoe, 1957), pp. 107–132. But both in Japan and the United States, Japanese exhibit a remarkable indifference to religious affiliation, even countenacing denominational and church differences within the same nuclear family and relatively little anxiety about religious intermarriage. See Kiyomi Morioka, "Christianity in the Japanese Rural Community: Acceptance and Rejection", *Japanese Sociological Studies. The Sociological Review*, Monograph X (Sept. 1966), 183–98; Leonard D. Cain, Jr., "Japanese-American Protestants: Acculturation and Assimilation," *Review of Religious Research* **3**, 3 (Winter 1962), 113–21; Cain, "The Integration Dilemma of Japanese-American Protestants", Paper presented at the annual meetings of the Pacific Sociological Association, April 5, 1962.

local extended kin units, bound together by ties of blood and language and only secondarily, if at all, as "citizens" of the Chinese empire.[18] Chinese emigration was an organized affair in which kinsmen or fellow villagers who had achieved some wealth or status acted as agents and sponsors for their compatriots. Benevolently despotic, this emigration acted to transfer the loyalties and institutions of the village to the overseas community. In the village, composed for the most part of his kinsmen, the individual looked to elders as leaders; in emigrating the individual reposed his loyalty and submitted his fate to the overseas representative of his clan or village. Loans, protection, and jobs were provided within a framework of kin and language solidarity that stretched from the village in Kwangtung to the clan building in "Chinatown". Emigrants regarded their journey as temporary and their return as certain. Abroad the Chinese, as homeless men, never fully accepted any permanence to their sojourn. They identified themselves with their Old-World clan, village, dialect grouping, or secret society whose overseas leaders were recognized as legitimate substitutes for homeland groups. These institutional leaders further insinuated themselves into the overseas immigrant's life by acting as his representative to white society, by pioneering new settlements, and by providing badly-needed goods and services, protection against depredations, and punishment for wrong-doing.

The Japanese emigrant departed from an entirely different kind of society.[19]

[18]For information on nineteenth-century Chinese social organization in the provinces from which North America's immigrants came, see Maurice Freedman, *Chinese Lineage and Society: Fukien and Kwangtung* (New York, 1966); Kung-Chuan Hsiao, *Rural China: Imperial Control in the Nineteenth Century* (Seattle, 1960). On the Chinese as sojourners see Paul C. P. Siu, "The Sojourner", *American Journal of Sociology*, 8 (July 1952), 32–44 and Siu, "The Isolation of the Chinese Laundryman", in Ernest W. Burgess and Donald Bogue, Editors, *Contributions to Urban Sociology* (Chicago, 1964), pp. 429–42. On the role of immigrant associations, see William Hoy, *The Chinese Six Companies* (San Francisco, 1942); Tin-Yuke Char, "Immigrant Chinese Societies in Hawaii", *Sixty-First Annual Report of the Hawaiian Historical Society* (1953), pp. 29–32; William Willmott, "Chinese Clan Associations in Vancouver", *Man*, **64,** 49 (March–April, 1964), 33–7.

[19]Material for the following is based on George B. Sansom, *Japan: A Short Cultural History* (New York, 1943); Takashi Koyama, "The Significance of Relatives at the Turning Point of the Family System in Japan", *Japanese Sociological Studies. Sociological Review*, 10 (September 1966), 95–114; Lafcadio Hearn, *Japan: An Interpretation* (Tokyo, 1955), pp. 81–106; Ronald P. Dore, *City Life in Japan: A Study of a Tokyo Ward* (Berkeley, 1958), pp. 91–190; Irene Taeuber, "Family, Migration, and Industrialization in Japan", *American Sociological Review* (April, 1951), pp. 149–57; Ezra F. Vogel, "Kinship Structure, Migration to the City, and Modernization", in R. P. Dore, *Aspects of Social Change in Modern Japan* (Princeton, 1967), pp. 91–112.

Japan was a nation as well as a state, and its villages reflected this fact. Village life had long ceased to be circumscribed by kinship, and the individual family rather than the extended kinship group was the locus of loyalty and solidarity. When children departed their homes they left unencumbered by a network of obligations. Unless he had been born first or last, a Japanese son was not obligated as was a Chinese to remain in the home of his parents. After 1868 emigration was sometimes sponsored by the government and certainly encouraged. When Japanese departed the homeland they, like the Chinese, expected only to sojourn, but they were not called back to the home village by the knowledge that a long-patient wife awaited them or that kinsmen fully depended on their return. Moreover, the men who inspired Japanese emigration were not pioneer leaders but exemplary individuals whose singular fame and fortune seemed to promise everyone great opportunity abroad. They did not serve as overseas community leaders or even very often as agents of migration, but only as shining examples of how others might succeed.

MARITAL STATUS

The respective marital situation of these two Asian peoples reflected fundamental differences in Chinese and Japanese kinship and profoundly influenced community life overseas. Custom required that a Chinese man sojourn abroad without his wife. A man's return to hearth and village was thus secured, and he laboured overseas in order that he might some day again enjoy the warmth of domesticity and the blessings of children. Abroad he lived a lonely life of labour, dependent on kinsmen and compatriots for fellowship and on prostitutes and vice for outlet and recreation. When in 1882 restrictive American legislation unwittingly converted Chinese custom into legal prohibition by prohibiting the coming of wives of Chinese labourers it exaggerated and lengthened the separation of husbands from wives and, more significantly, delayed for nearly two generations the birth in America of a substantial "second generation" among the immigrant Chinese. Canadian immigration restrictions had a similar consequence.[20] Barred from intermarriage by custom and law and unable to bring wives to Canada

[20]For discussions of United States restrictive legislation see Mary Coolidge, *Chinese Immigration* (New York, 1909), pp. 145–336; S. W. Kung, *Chinese in American Life: Some Aspects of Their History, Status, Problems and Contributions* (Seattle, 1962), pp. 64–165. A discussion of both American and Canadian restrictive legislation will be found in Huang Tsen-ming, *The Legal Status of the Chinese Abroad* (Taipei, 1954). See also Tin-Yuke Char, "Legal Restrictions on Chinese in English Speaking Countries, I",

or the United States, Chinese men sired children on their infrequent return visits to China, and these China-born sons later partially replenished the Chinese population in North America as they joined their fathers in the overseas venture. Like their fathers the sons also depended on Chinatown institutions. Their lack of independence from the same community controls which had earlier circumscribed the lives of their fathers stood in sharp contrast to the manner of life of the Canadian and American born.

Neither custom nor law barred the Japanese from bringing wives to Canada or America.[21] Within two decades of their arrival the Japanese had

---

Chinese Social and Political Science Review (January 4, 1933,) pp. 479–94. Careful analyses of Canadian legislation are found in Duncan McArthur, "What is the Immigration Problem?", *Queen's Quarterly* (Autumn 1928), pp. 603–14; three articles by H. F. Angus, "Canadian Immigration: The Law and its Administration", *American Journal of International Law*, **18,** 1 (January 1934), 74–89; "The Future of Immigration into Canada", *Canadian Journal of Economics and Political Science*, **12** (August 1946), 379–86; Jean Mercier, "Immigration and Provincial Rights", *Canadian Bar Review*, **22** (1944), 856–69; Hugh L. Keenleyside, "Canadian Immigration Policy and Its Administration", *External Affairs* (May 1949), pp. 3–11; Bora Laskin, "Naturalization and Aliens: Immigration, Exclusion, and Deportation", *Canadian Constitutional Law* (Toronto, 1960), pp. 958–77. In general see David C. Corbett, *Canada's Immigration Policy: A Critique* (Toronto, 1957).

[21]For Japanese immigration see Yamato Ichihashi, *Japanese in the United States* (Stanford, 1932), pp. 401–9; Dorothy Swaine Thomas, Charles Kikuchi, and J. Sakoda, *The Salvage* (Berkeley, 1952), pp. 3–18, 571–626; H. A. Millis, *The Japanese Problem in the United States* (New York, 1915); K. K. Kawakami, *The Real Japanese Question* (New York, 1921); T. Iyenaga and Kenosuke Sato, *Japan and the California Problem* (New York, 1921); Iichiro Tokutomi, *Japanese–American Relations* (New York, 1922), pp. 65–88 (translated by Sukeshige Yanagiwara); R. D. McKenzie, *Oriental Exclusion* (Chicago, 1928). For Japanese immigration to Canada see Young, Reid, and Carrothers, *The Japanese Canadians;* A. R. M. Lower, *Canada and the Far East—1940* (New York, 1941), pp. 61–89; H. F. Angus, *Canada and the Far East, 1940-1953* (Toronto, 1953), pp. 99–100. For a statement by a pessimistic *Nisei* see Kazuo Kawai, "Three Roads, and None Easy", *Survey Graphic*, **56,** 3 (May 1, 1926), 1964–6. For further discussions see Tsutoma Obana, "Problems of the American-born Japanese", *Sociology and Social Research*, **19** (November 1934), 161–5; Emory S. Bogardus, "Current Problems of Japanese Americans", *Sociology and Social Research*, **25** (July 1941), 562–71; For the development of new associations among *Nisei* see Adachi, *A History of the Japanese in British Columbia, 1877–1958*, pp. 11–14; *Better Americans in a Greater America*, booklet published by the Japanese American Citizens' League, undated (1967), 24 pp. For an ecological analysis of the distribution and diffusion of achievement orientations among Japanese in America see Paul T. Tagagi, "The Japanese Family in the United States: A Hypothesis on the Social Mobility of The Nisei", revision of an earlier paper presented at the annual meeting of the Kroeber Anthropological Society, Berkeley, California (April 30, 1966).

brought over enough women to guarantee that, although husbands might be quite a bit older than their wives, a domestic life would be established in America. Japanese thus had little need for the brothels and gambling halls which characterized Chinese communities in the late nineteenth century and which, not incidentally, provided a continuous source of wealth and power to those who owned or controlled them. Japanese quickly produced a second generation in both Canada and the United States, and by 1930 this *Nisei* generation began to claim a place for itself in North America and in Japanese–American and Japanese–Canadian life. The independence and acculturation of the *Nisei* was indicated in their social and political style of life. They did not accept the organizations of their parents' community and established *ad hoc* associations dedicated to civil rights and penetration beyond Canada's and America's racial barrier. Some Japanese immigrants educated one of their children in Japan. These few Japan-educated offspring (*Kibei*) did not enjoy the same status in North America as *Nisei*, and in their marginality and problems of adjustment they resembled the China-born offspring of Chinese immigrants. Educated in Canadian or American schools and possessed of Canadian or American culture and values, the *Nisei* found that prejudice and discrimination acted as the most significant obstacle to their success.

OCCUPATIONS AND LOCATIONS

Jobs and settlement patterns tended to reinforce and accelerate the different development patterns of Chinese and Japanese communities in America.[22] Except for a small but powerful merchant élite the Chinese began and remained as wage labourers. First employed in the arduous and menial tasks of mining and railroad-building, the Chinese later gravitated into unskilled, clerical and service work inside the Chinese community. Such work necessitated living in cities or returning to cities when unemployment drove the contract labourers to seek new jobs. The city always meant the Chinese quarter, a ghetto set aside for Chinese in which their special needs could be met and by which the white population could segregate itself from them. Inside the ghetto Old-World societies ministered to their members' wants,

[22]For information on occupations and settlement patterns see Lyman, "The Structure of Chinese Society in Nineteenth-century America", pp. 111–27; Milton L. Barnett, "Kinship as a Factor Affecting Cantonese Economic Adaptation in the United States", *Human Organization*, **19** (Spring, 1960), 40–6; Ping Chiu, *Chinese Labor in California: An Economic Study* (Madison, 1963).

exploited their needs, and represented their interests. When primary industry could no longer use Chinese and white hostility drove them out of the labour market and into Chinatown, the power of these associations and their merchant leaders was reconfirmed and enhanced. The single most important feature of the occupations of Chinese immigrants was their tendency to keep the Chinese in a state of dependency on bosses, contractors, merchants— ultimately on the merchant élite of Chinatown.

The Japanese, after a brief stint as labourers in several primary industries then on the wane in western America, pioneered the cultivation of truck crops.[23] Small-scale agriculturalists, separated from one another as well as from the urban anti-Orientalism of the labor unions, Japanese farmers did not retain the kind of ethnic solidarity characteristic of the urban Chinese. Whatever traditional élites had existed among the early Japanese immigrants fell from power or were supplanted. In their place *ad hoc* associations arose to meet particular needs. When Japanese did become labourers and city dwellers they too became segregated in "li'l Tokyos" presided over by Old-World associations for a time. But the early concentration in agriculture and the later demands of the *Nisei* tended to weaken the power even of the city-bred immigrant associations.

COMMUNITY POWER AND CONFLICT

Finally, the different bases for solidarity in the two Oriental communities tended to confirm their respective modes of social organization. The Japanese community has remained isolated primarily because of discriminatory barriers to integration and secondarily because of the sense of congregation among fellow Japanese. The isolated Chinese community is, to be sure, a product of white aversion and is also characterized by congregative sentiments, but, much more than that of the Japanese, it rests on communal

[23]For the Japanese as agriculturalists see Masakazu Iwata, "The Japanese Immigrants in California Agriculture", *Agricultural History*, **36** (January 1962),25–37; Thomas *et al.*, *The Salvage*, pp. 23–5; Adon Poli, *Japanese Farm Holdings on the Pacific Coast* (Berkeley, 1944). For farming and fishing communities in Canada see Tadashi Fukutake, *Man and Society in Japan* (Tokyo, 1962), pp. 146–79. For the rise and decline of urban ghettos among Japanese in the United States see Shotaro Frank Miyamoto, *Social Solidarity Among the Japanese in Seattle*, University of Washington Publications in the Social Sciences XI, 4 (December 1939), 57–129; Toshio Mori, "Li'l' Yokohama" *Common Ground*, **1**, 2 (1941), 54–6; Larry Tajiri, "Farewell to Little Tokyo", *Common Ground*, **4**, 2 (1942) 90–5; Robert W. O'Brien, "Selective Dispersion as a Factor in the Solution of the Nisei Problem", *Social Forces*, **23** (Dec. 1944), 140–7.

foundations. Political life in Chinatown has rarely been tranquil.[24] The traditional clans and *Landsmannschaften* controlled immigration, settled disputes, levied taxes and fines, regulated commerce, and meted out punishments. Opposition to their rule took the form it had taken in China. Secret societies, chapters of or modeled after the well-known Triad Society, took over the functions of law, protection, and revenge for their members. In addition the secret societies owned or controlled the gambling houses and brothels which emerged to satisfy the recreational and sex needs of homeless Chinese men and displayed occasional interest in the restive politics of China. Struggles for power, blood feuds, and "wars" of vengeance were not infrequent in the early days of Chinatown. These conflicts entrenched the loyalties of men to their respective associations. More important with respect to non-acculturation, these intramural fights isolated the Chinese from the uncomprehending larger society and bound them together in antagonistic cooperation. Since the turn of the century, the grounds of such battles have shifted on to a commercial and political plane, but violence is not unknown. Chinatown's organizational solidarity and its intra-community conflicts have thus acted as agents of non-acculturation.

POSITION AND PROSPECTS OF THE ORIENTAL IN NORTH AMERICA

The conditions for the political and economic integration of the Chinese appear to be at hand now.[25] This is largely because the forces which spawned

[24]On power and conflict in Chinatown see Lyman, "The Structure of Chinese Society in Nineteenth Century America", pp. 272–369. For secret societies see Stanford M. Lyman, "Chinese Secret Societies in the Occident: Notes and Suggestions for Research in the Sociology of Secrecy", *Canadian Review of Sociology and Anthropology*, **1**, 2 (1964), 79–102; Stanford M. Lyman, W. E. Willmott, Berching Ho, "Rules of a Chinese Secret Society in British Columbia", *Bulletin of The School of Oriental and African Studies*, **27**, 3 (1964), 530–9. See also D. Y. Yuan, "Voluntary Segregation: A Study of New Chinatown", *Phylon Quarterly* (Fall 1963), pp. 255–65.

[25]For an extended discussion of the progress in eliminating discrimination in Canada and the United States see Stanford M. Lyman, *The Oriental in North America* (Vancouver, 1962), Lecture No. 11: "Position and Prospects of the Oriental since World War II". On immigration matters to 1962 see S. W. Kung, "Chinese Immigration into North America", *Queen's Quarterly*, **68**, 4 (Winter 1962), 610–20. Information about Chinese in Canada and the United States is regularly reported in the *Chinatown News*, a Vancouver, B.C. publication and in *East–West*, a San Francisco Journal. For problems of recent Chinese immigrants see *San Francisco Chronicle* (March 18, 1968) 2; for those of American born, *ibid.* (March 19, 1968), 42.

and maintained Chinatown are now weakened. The near balancing of the sex ratio has made possible the birth and maturation in America of second and third generation Chinese. Their presence, in greater and greater numbers, poses a serious threat to old-world power élites. The breakdown of discriminatory barriers to occupations and residency brought about by a new assertion of civil rights heralds an end to Chinatown economic and domestic monopoly. The relative openness of Canadian and American society to American-born and Canadian-born Chinese reduces their dependency on traditional goods and services and their recruitment into communal associations. Concomitantly, the *casus belli* of the earlier era disappears and conflict's group-binding and isolating effect loses force. What remains of Chinatown eventually is its new immigrants, its culturally acceptable economic base—restaurants and shops—and its congregative value for ethnic Chinese. Recent events in San Francisco suggest that the young and newly-arrived immigrants from Hong Kong and Taiwan and the American-born Chinese school drop-outs are estranged from both the Chinatown élites and white America. Many of their activities resemble those of protesting and militant Negro groups.

The Japanese are entering a new phase of relations with the larger society in North America. There is a significant amount of anxiety in Japanese circles about the decline of Japanese values and the appearance of the more undesirable features of Canadian and American life—primarily juvenile delinquency but also a certain lack of old-world propriety which had survived through the *Nisei* generation—among the *Sansei* and *Yonsei*.[26] Moreover, like those Negroes who share E. Franklin Frazier's disillusion with the rise of a black bourgeoisie, some Japanese–Americans are questioning the social and personal price paid for entrance into American society. Scholars such as Daisuke Kitagawa have wondered just how *Nisei* and *Sansei* might preserve elements of Japanese culture in America. At the same time one European Japanophile has bitterly assailed the Americanization of the *Nisei*.[27] Nothing similar to a black power movement has developed among the Japanese, and, indeed, such a movement is extremely unlikely

---

[26]On April 15, 1965, in response to a rash of teenage burglaries among Japanese in Sacramento, parents and other interested adults met and discussed how the community might act to prevent delinquency.

[27]Daisuke Kitagawa, "Assimilation of Pluralism?" in Arnold M. Rose and Caroline B. Rose, *Minority Problems* (New York, 1965), pp. 285–7. Fosco Maraini has written "The *ni-sei* has generally been taught to despise his Asian roots; on the other hand, all he

given Japanese–American and Canadian material success and the decrease in social distance between Japanese and white Americans. At most there is a quiet concern. But even such mild phenomena are deserving of sociological attention.

THEORETICAL CONSIDERATIONS

This survey of Oriental community organization suggests the need to take seriously Robert Park's reconsideration of his own race relations cycle. Park at first had supposed that assimilation was a natural and inevitable outcome of race contact marked off by stages of competition, conflict, and accommodation before there occurred the eventual absorption of one people by another.[28] In addition to its faults as a natural history, a criticism so often discussed by other sociologists,[29] Park's original statement of the cycle took no account of what, in a related context, Wagley and Harris refer to as the "adaptive capacity" of the immigrant group.[30] However, Park himself reconsidered the cycle and in 1937 wrote that it might terminate in one of three outcomes: a caste system as was the case in India; complete assimilation, as he imagined had occurred in China; or a permanent institutionalization of minority status within a larger society, as was the case of Jews in Europe. Park concluded that race relations occur as phases of a cycle "which, once initiated, inevitably continues until it terminates in some predestined racial configuration, and one consistent with the established social order of which it is a part".[31] Park's later emphasis on alternative outcomes and his consideration of the peculiar social context in which any ethnic groups' history occurs implicitly recall attention to the interplay between native and host society cultures. As Herskovitz's researches on West African and American

has taken from the west is a two-dimensional duralumin Christianity, ultra-modernism, the cultivation of jazz as a sacred rite, a California veneer." *Meeting with Japan*, New York, 1960 (translated by Eric Mosbacher), p. 169.

[28]Robert E. Park, "Our Racial Frontier on the Pacific", *Survey Graphic*, **56**, 3 (May 1, 1926), 196.

[29]Seymour Martin Lipset, "Changing Social Status and Prejudice: The Race Theories of a Pioneering American Sociologist", *Commentary*, **9** (May 1950), 475–9; Amitai Etzioni, "The Ghetto—A Re-evaluation", *Social Forces*, **37** (March 1959), 255–62.

[30]Charles Wagley and Marvin Harris, *Minorities in the New World* (New York, 1958).

[31]Robert E. Park, "The Race Relations Cycle in Hawaii", *Race and Culture* (Glencoe, 1950), pp. 194–5. For an extended discussion of the race cycle see Stanford M. Lyman, "The Race Relations Cycle of Robert E. Park", *Pacific Sociological Review* **11**, 1 (Spring 1968), 16–22.

Negro cultures indicate, the immigrant group, even if oppressed *in transitu*, does not arrive with a cultural *tabula rasa* waiting to be filled in by the host culture. Rather it possesses a culture and social organization which in contact with and in the several contexts of the host culture will be supplanted, inhibited, subordinated, modified or enhanced. Kinship, occupations, patterns of settlement and community organization are each factors in such developments. Assimilation, or for that matter pluralism, is not simply an inevitable state of human affairs, as those who cling to "natural history" models assert, but rather is an existential possibility. Social factors contribute to the state of being of a people and to changes in that state. The Chinese and Japanese communities in America illustrate two modes of development and suggest the need to refine even further our knowledge of the factors which affect whatever mode of development an immigrant group chooses.

Racial Integration
in a Transition Community[1]

HARVEY MOLOTCH

ALTHOUGH the in-migration of blacks into previously white areas generally leads to eventual all-black occupancy, thus continuing the pattern of residential racial segregation in U.S. cities (cf. Taeuber and Taeuber, 1965), it is possible that at least during the transition period, geographical propinquity may lead to some degree of racial integration. Three possible forms of integration may conceivably realize themselves during the transition process: (1) *demographic* integration, whereby a given setting contains both blacks and whites in some specified proportions; (2) *Biracial interaction*, whereby non-antagonistic social interaction is occurring between blacks and whites to some specifiable extent; (3) *Transracial solidarity*, defined as conditions in which whites and blacks interact freely and without constraint, and in a manner such that race ceases to function as an important source of social cleavage or as a criteria for friendship and primary group selection. This report describes the extent, form, and most common contexts of these various sorts of integration in one changing area on the South Side of Chicago—the community of South Shore. Utilizing the data gathered, an attempt will be made to explicate the more general processes at work which, in the context of black–white propinquity, inhibit or promote the cross-racial sharing of social life. (In another publication, the author has described the speed and ecological patterns of South Shore's transition; cf. Molotch, 1969.)

[1]The author wishes to thank Tamotsu Shibutani and J. Michael Ross for helpful comments on an earlier draft of this manuscript and John Dyckman for his assistance in carrying out observations. Financial support was provided by a grant from the Bowman C. Lingle Foundation to the Center for Urban Studies, University of Chicago, and by a Faculty Research Fellowship, University of California, Santa Barbara.

GENERAL STRATEGY

There have been many descriptions of communities striving for integration, yet seldom do data on the subject of actual interracial contact go beyond the anecdotal level. Many community studies (cf. Johnson, 1965 Biddle and Biddle, 1965) cheerfully recount instances when whites and blacks serve on the same committee or come together in a constructive joint enterprise. Precise information is lacking which would indicate the frequency of such contacts, the contexts in which they most often appear, or the dynamics of their development. The absence of such information inhibits the development of a sound theory of cross-racial interaction and, at a more practical level, precludes rigorous comparative analysis or evaluation of various forms of intervention which have integration as their goal.

An attempt is thus made in the present study to depict objectively the extent and forms of integration in South Shore. Basic to the more mechanical means utilized to carry out this task was a two-year (July 1965–July 1967) participant observation study in the community—particularly of the area's major community organization and its subsidiary committees and groups (cf. Molotch, 1967, 1968, 1969). Data of a more precise sort were gathered by taking simple head counts of the racial composition of various local settings—including schools, churches, recreation facilities, retail shops and voluntary organizations. In some instances, reports of organizational officers were utilized; in others, organizational group-photographs appearing in the local community newspaper or on bulletin boards were inspected. In most instances, however, actual visits were made to the setting and the numbers of whites and blacks present were recorded. The racial mix of such settings is taken as an important clue to the possible existence of other forms of integration as well.

THE STUDY AREA

"South Shore" commonly denotes not only a specific aerial unit of the city of Chicago, but also a certain "community". That is, the phrase brings to the mind of Chicagoans, and specially those living in the South Side, an image of certain geographical boundaries, certain landscapes and landmarks and a certain life style. Both residents and non-residents utilize the concept "South Shore" as a means of identifying those living within its boundaries. The imagery has traditionally been one of middle-class living, lakeside recreation and well-kept lawns, homes and buildings. South Shore has long

169

been administratively utilized by local politicians, religious denominations, public and private civic agencies and businesses in distributing services and in naming stores and branch offices. Persons indigenous to the area have used the term "South Shore" to name their own shops and organizations and to adopt as constituencies for such institutions those persons living within its boundaries.

That South Shore is an entity which continues to have an existence in the minds of local residents was documented by a series of informal interviews carried out by the writer on the major business arteries of the area (cf. Molotch, 1966, 1968, Chap. 2). Passersby were stopped and asked such questions as: "What area is this?" "What part of town is this?" The answer would almost always be South Shore, although additional probing would often reveal additional place names corresponding to the smaller-scale elementary school districts which serve the region. Community boundaries were established by utilizing the answers to such questions as "How far does South Shore go?" or "Where does this area end?" Under varying conditions of context and an individual's purposes in reporting such information, the relevant unit of "community" might be smaller than South Shore (e.g. an elementary school district) or considerably larger (e.g. the South Side, or Chicago). For present purposes it is asserted that South Shore is one important source of community identification utilized by both local and non-local residents and that, in this sense, it is a meaningful unit of analysis. Further, the common recognition of the area and wide-spread tendency to self-identify oneself as a resident of "South Shore" is indicative of a common stake in the area, and thus a basis for the commonalty of interests and the "we feeling" which McKenzie (1923:344) held to be the defining attribute of community.

Approximately 80% of South Shore's 70,000 residents have come to live in basically sound apartment structures—generally of the walk-up variety, mostly constructed in the early 1930's.[2] In terms of the characteristics of its population, housing and geographic location, it is generally prototypical of racially changing communities in the United States (cf. Taeuber and Taeuber, 1965; Fishbein, 1962). Its residents were, at least when racial change began in 1960, Protestant, Catholic and Jew in approximately equal proportions.[3] By the time the data for this study was gathered, South Shore's population was

[2]Data are based on 1960 census reports as contained in Kitagawa and Taeuber (1963). (South Shore is taken to constitute census tracts 635 through 644 and the northerly portion [above 83rd Street] of tracts 662 through 665.)

[3]Impressionistic estimates based on reports of local clergymen.

approximately one-third black, with blacks preponderant in the North-western portion of the area (contiguous to the previously existing ghetto), whites predominant in the southeastern region (adjoining the Chicago lake shore) and mixed occupancy in more central areas.

A strong community organization, the South Shore Commission was formed in anticipation of racial change and eventually came to subscribe explicitly to the goal of "stable racial integration" for the area. By the close of the study period, the Commission was widely cited for its success—success at organizational growth (a $90,000 annual budget and a paid staff of six), and success in the near-achievement of "stable racial integration" in the area. The city government, school authorities, and private welfare groups were all enthusiastic Commission supporters; both local and national media touted it for its "grass roots success" at "preserving" racial integration in the community.[4]

ORDERED SEGMENTATION IN SOUTH SHORE

It needs to be noted that the inhibitions to integration in an area such as South Shore can not be properly understood by reliance upon such concepts as "prejudiced attitudes", "bigotry", or white "status anxiety", as these terms are ordinarily employed to "explain" interracial avoidance behavior. It is reasonable to anticipate that what Suttles (1968) refers to as "ordered segmentation" is natural to any community; thus, the fact that South Shore blacks differed from South Shore whites in terms of religion (few black Catholics, no Jews), ethnicity, economic status (blacks lower),[5] stage of life cycle (blacks younger with more children), and length of residency in the area would all act to deter many sorts of biracial contact. That is, racial distinctions coincided with other commonly utilized bases for social differentiation.

Urban settings have as their critical social characteristic the fact that intimate relationships between all parties are precluded by the sheer vastness

[4]See, for example, "Self-Help Pays Off in South Chicago", *Christian Science Monitor* (Boston), July 21, 1967; "The South Shore Plan", *Chicago Sun Times*, April 14, 1967.

[5]Changes in South Shore's welfare case loads, crime rates, etc., provide some evidence documenting this point (see Molotch, 1968). Although differences in net income between black and white family units is generally small (or nonexistent) in changing areas, the fact that black households are more likely to have multiple breadwinners and that black males are more likely to hold blue-collar jobs, are differences indicative of real status differences. (See Taeuber and Taeuber, 1965, Chaps. 7, 8.)

171

of the numbers involved (cf. Wirth, 1938). Selection is thus necessary. In South Shore, as everywhere else in American society, people are "up tight" in the presence of persons who are unknown, unproven, and thus, to them, undependable. The genuine psychic (and occasionally, physical) risks, which accompany encounters with strangers, lead local residents to develop certain techniques for "gaining associates, avoiding enemies and establishing each other's intentions" (Suttles, 1968:234). These techniques evolve in the search for cues which bespeak similarity, or existence of some other form of personal tie (e.g. mutual friendship, blood relationship) which would imply dependability and trustworthiness. Where such cues are not forthcoming, mutual avoidance behavior (or outright hostility) results.

In the case at hand not only authentic social and demographic differences exist between the black and white populations, taken as a whole, but there are also differences of a more subtle sort in virtually all black–white confrontations. A few examples may be cited. Whites and blacks in South Shore *sound* different; among whites, speach varies with length of residence in Chicago, family status background, and ethnicity. Blacks have an analogous internal pattern of speech differentiation—in addition to a common touch of Southern Negro dialect, not quite absent even among the most "middle-class" of Chicago-born blacks. Young blacks *walk* differently from young whites; many of the boys, especially, utilize a swagger which sets them apart from their white school mates (cf. Suttles, 1968; Finestone, 1957). Without carrying out a complete inventory of black and white habits and folkways, we know these differences exist, and that, whether they speak of them or not, both blacks and whites in South Shore were sensitive to them.

PUBLIC PLACES AND PRIVATE BEHAVIOR

All of these distinctions, some obvious and some subtle, are more or less problematic for the persons involved, depending upon the public place in which whites and blacks happen to come together. "Public" places are defined, for the present discussion, as settings in which no *explicit* criteria exist for the exclusion of any person or group. Yet public places vary in the degree to which they tend to actually exclude certain types of persons or social groups. Given the inhibitions to random intimacy which exist in urban settings, public places can be viewed as exclusive in the degree to which they serve as arenas for the kinds of informal, intimate, and uninhibited sorts of behaviors ordinarily associated with informal peer group activity. In contrast, public places are inclusive in so far as they act as settings in which formalized roles are routinely attended to carefully by participants —places in which participants expect that they, as well as others, will guardedly attend to the performance of prescribed activity and behavior. Thus, public places may be differentiated according to the degree to which they serve as arenas for public as opposed to more "private" behavior.

RETAIL STORES

An example of a relatively *public* place for *public* behavior is the local retail store. Such settings in South Shore are rather formal in that patrons arrive to purchase merchandise and then exit. Although various forms of informal activity occur, including chats between owners and customers, the usual undirected patter and diffuse banter evident in lower-class business settings (cf. Suttles, 1968) tend to be absent.

Yet despite the relatively formal nature of shopping in South Shore (relative both to shopping in other kinds of areas and to other South Shore public settings), it is indeed a social activity as well as a utilitarian one. Shopping is the social activity which most frequently takes adult residents out of their homes and into the community. An examination of racial compositions of shopping settings may, in addition to providing benchmark data on the status of "demographic" integration in this important social setting, also indicate something of the extent to which a significant "opportunity context" exists for the promotion of other kinds of integration.

South Shore has two major internal shopping strips (71st and 79th Streets) both of which run east–west traversing black, mixed, and white residential areas. These streets are depicted in Fig. 1 along with a portrayal of the approximate racial composition of the surrounding neighborhoods. Each of the shopping strips was visited during business hours of shopping days, and racial headcounts were made for all street-level retail establishments (including restaurants and taverns) on both streets.[6]

Racial retail shopping patterns were found to generally coincide with racial residential patterns. That is, individual stores and business blocks surrounded by predominantly black residents were patronized almost exclusively by

[6]For some types of establishments, such as beauty shops, there was no way to make a complete count unobtrusively; in such instances, only those patrons visible through plate glass windows were counted. Employees, detectable by uniforms, positions behind counters, or general demeanor, were excluded from the counts.

H. Molotch

TABLE 1. RACIAL COMPOSITION OF SOUTH SHORE SHOPPING AREAS[a]

Street and hundred block[b]	Number of black patrons in shops	Number of white patrons in shops	Total both races	Percent of all patrons white
71st Street				
1600, 1700	35	6	41	15
1800, 1900	67	36	103	35
2000, 2100	74	142	216	66
2200, 2300	19	148	167	89
79th Street				
1600, 1700	49	3	52	6
1800, 1900	33	40	73	55
2000, 2100	2	29	31	94
2200, 2300	5	36	41	88
2400, 2500	0	41	41	100
2600, 2700	8	211	219	96
2800, 2900	5	92	97	95
3000 . . .	1	93	94	99

[a]Based on a single visit, daytime weekday count, April 1967.
[b]Each row represents two sides of two shopping blocks.

blacks; those in white areas by whites, those in mixed areas by members of both races. Table 1 presents the results of headcounts taken of shopping blocks; Table 2 presents results of the same operation in terms of composition of individual stores.

If a setting is arbitrarily considered to be demographically integrated if at least 10% of its population consists of members of each race, then it can be said that the 71st Street area is integrated for its entire length and that 70% of its shops are integrated. However, 79th Street is generally segregated in its entire length with only 22% of its shops integrated. The congruence of this pattern with the nature of the surrounding residential areas would indicate that the factor of distance outweighs other possible considerations (e.g. the desire for psychically "safe" shopping territory) in determining shopping patterns.

Certain interesting exceptions to this pattern are provided by those establishments which by their nature or traditional neighborhood usage render

174

personal services and/or which serve as settings for informal, more intimate interaction. All barber and beauty shops, regardless of location, were segregated. Establishments catering to recreational and social needs were often segregated; three of seven restaurants on otherwise integrated 71st Street were

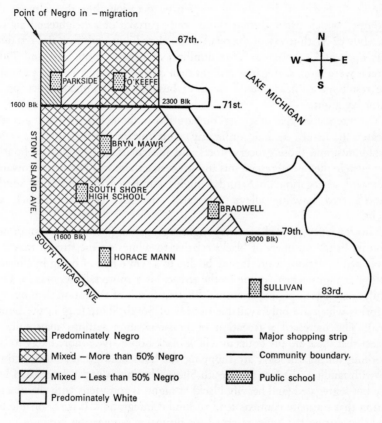

Fig. 1.

serving only whites, whereas all six supermarkets on the same street were integrated. Perhaps consistent not only with its attraction for customers of a particular ethnicity, but also with its function as a social setting, the kosher butcher shop was the only food store which was not serving a biracial clientele.

175

H. Molotch

SATURDAY NIGHT RACIAL PATTERNS

This tendency toward greater segregation of social and recreational settings is confirmed by analogous data collected on a Saturday night during the same time period. Not only is it the case that Americans typically reserve Saturday night as a social, festive occasion, but that almost all activities which occur during those hours partake of a heightened air of sociability.[7] With many of the retail stores closed, but with bars and restaurants open and catering to large numbers of persons, both 71st and 79th Streets were more segregated at night than during the day.[8] Table 3 presents the results of a "head-count" made of business establishments open on a Saturday night.

The integrated types of settings on Saturday night included motion picture theaters (a leisure setting, ordinarily with minimal interaction), several restaurants, and those grocery stores and supermarkets keeping late hours. Yet even in the case of restaurants and groceries, there was a tendency toward increased segregation on Saturday night, compared to weekdays. South Shore's two bowling alleys, integrated by day, become all-black at night.

This tendency toward Saturday night segregation (including a significant increase in the numbers of blacks relative to whites on the streets) may be explained in various ways. It may be due to a white fear of being in a black setting at night when "crime in the streets" is a more salient concern. Or, whites may be simply experiencing different forms of recreation than blacks —forms which are only available outside of South Shore (e.g. in the Loop area). The increased segregation of non-recreation settings may simply reflect that these are the hours in which black housewives, more likely to be working during the day, are shopping for household goods. Such factors notwithstanding, the fact that South Shore's business district, integrated by day but segregated (and heavily black) at night, is consistent with the observation that intimate contexts tend to inhibit integration. It is reasonable to find that during the hours reserved for intimacy, segregation increases.

[7]It is for this reason that for persons excluded from social activity on Saturday night, these hours are, as the lyrics of the popular song imply, "the loneliest night of the week".

[8]For example, the 71st Street daytime count included only one segregated bar whereas the night count included six segregated bars. Given the fact that many retail shops are closed at night, the prevalence of open bars has the consequence of dramatically increasing the *proportion* of establishments which are segregated as well as the absolute number of segregated establishments.

176

TABLE 2. RACIAL COMPOSITION OF INDIVIDUAL STORES ON TWO SHOPPING STRIPS, DAYTIME SOUTH SHORE[a]

Shopping street	Number of "white" stores[b]	Number of persons in "white" stores	Number of "black" stores[b]	Number of persons in "black" stores	Number of integrated stores[b]	Number of persons in integrated stores	Percent of all stores integrated	Percent of all persons integrated
71st Street	4	85	2	16	14	235	70	70
79th Street	12	212	2	21	4	67	22	22

[a]Consideration was given only to shops serving 8 or more persons.
[b]Stores classified as "White" or "Black" were those in which at least 90% of persons on the premises were of the same race. "Integrated" stores were those in which fewer than 90% of persons on the premises were of the same race.

177

Special scrutiny of one sort of segregated leisure setting, the neighborhood tavern, can provide some insight into explaining the metamorphosis of places from white to black status. There was almost total racial segregation in taverns with, in certain places, *alternating* black and white establishments along a given block.[9] Tavern owners can themselves influence racial patterns by, in the words of one bartender-owner, "give them (blacks) the big hello". But the several tavern owners who were interviewed felt that although the owner can influence the racial process, he cannot determine it. A bar "just becomes colored" as blacks patronize it with increasing frequency. For white tavern patrons, it is simply a matter of "the colored took the place over" or "the colored forced everybody out". Such were the phrases used to explain again and again "what happened" to a particular establishment which was once frequented by whites but eventually became a black setting.

To make sense of this "explanation" of tavern change, it must be noted that of all public settings in South Shore, probably none was more private than the neighborhood tavern. That is, although the tavern is officially open to the public, it is in fact (at least in South Shore) an intimate setting frequented by a small and stable group of "regulars" who use the establishment as the very focal point of their social lives.[10] For the few middle-class taverns in South Shore (which also were segregated) this characterization is likely less accurate than for working-class establishments. But even here, the tavern is a place where people "let their hair down", where back-stage and on-stage behavioral routines (cf. Goffman, 1959) tend to merge and thus where increased social vulnerability makes for anxiety in the presence of persons who fail to emit satisfactory signals of trustworthiness and forgiving acceptance of what may be transgressions of various normative codes. Thus blacks, who share mannerisms, clothing tastes, musical preferences and other tavern-specific behavior habits at variance with white cultural counterparts, are "outsiders" in the white environment. Their very presence can thus serve to inhibit the very kind of interactions for which the tavern is sought

[9]Except for one bar which was observed as having one black patron and nine white patrons, all 21 South Shore taverns were completely segregated on Saturday night.

[10]Gans (1962) has confirmed that this pattern is also the case for Italian-American working-class males.

out by neighborhood whites; they can thus "take over" an establishment by simply being in it.[11]

OUTDOOR RECREATION

Parks are a day-time setting in which informal social activity is routine.[12] A headcount was made at South Shore's largest park ("Rainbow Beach"), which provides facilities (e.g. tennis, beach bathing, formal gardens, field houses) available nowhere else in South Shore. On a sunny Sunday in May 1967, only two of the several thousand persons at the park were black, and these were small children in the company of white adults. It should be noted that Rainbow Beach Park in 1962 was the scene of a nonviolent civil rights "wade-in", protesting the racial segregation of some of the city's beaches (including Rainbow). Ironically, this much publicized event and the accompanying acrominious remarks by whites, may have served to dramatize Rainbow Beach's *de facto* status as a white public place, thus deterring blacks from risking the cost of a subsequent spontaneous visit. That Rainbow Beach was also a place where individuals routinely appear in abbreviated costume (bathing suits, tennis clothes, etc.), and thus routinely expose body areas ordinarily considered private, would act to increase anxieties stemming from interpersonal vulnerability.

Yet the special circumstances of Rainbow Beach were actually not significant since almost all of South Shore's parks were racially segregated—including those completely internal to the community and without any known history of "incidents". Seven smaller parks and playlots were inspected on the same warm Sunday; almost all were catering exclusively to small children with a few parents supervising. The only park catering to adult "passive recreation" (located on South Shore Drive at 68th Street) was occupied by 13 white adults and three white children, all of whom sat on benches, and one black child who sat with his dog on the grass at an opposite end of the small greensward.

South Shore's six remaining parks were all scenes of active recreation. In

[11]The same phenomenon can be observed in the case of houseguests' "taking over" a home by simply being in it for a period longer than that desired by the hosts. Guests, who often cannot "understand" if confronted with such an accusation, can avoid the problem by either "becoming just like a member of the family" (i.e. host accepts guest as an intimate) or by devising schemes whereby extensive absences from the scene can be gracefully arranged.

[12]The situation is not strictly comparable to taverns, however, in that the relative expansiveness of space may permit a greater degree of insularity to an intimate gathering.

179

Table 3. Racial Composition of South Shore Shopping Areas, Saturday Night[a]

Shopping street	Number of "white" stores[b]	Number of persons in "white" stores	Number of "black" stores[b]	Number of persons in "black" stores	Number of integrated stores[b]	Number of persons in integrated stores	Percent of all stores integrated	Percent of all persons integrated
71st Street	4	120	10	300	10	141	42	34
79th Street	14	359	7	272	2	19	9	3

[a]Consideration was given only to establishments observed to be serving 8 or more persons.
[b]Stores classified as "White" or "Black" were those in which at least 90% of persons on the premises were of the same race. "Integrated" stores were those in which fewer than 90% of persons on the premises were of the same race.

those parks located in segregated areas (either all black or all white), participation was limited to persons of the same race as the surrounding area. Thus at a soccer field at Phillips and 82nd, all game participants and spectators (approximately 200) were white; only black children were present at two playlots (one at Parkside School, 69th at East End, and one at O'Keeffe School, 69th at Merrill) located in predominately (although not exclusively) black areas.

One park located in a racially mixed residential area (69th at Oglesby) served only black children. The playlot at Bryn Mawr School (74th at Chappel), also located in a biracial residential area, was being utilized by approximately 50 black children and 40 white children. One ball game was in progress; all players were white. Of the various playgroups, only one— a dyad—was racially mixed, although the two playlots were serving equal numbers of white and black children.

Rosenblum Park, at 76th Street and Bennett, stands contiguous to both black and white residential areas. Seven ball games were in simultaneous progress at the time observations were made, all consisting of adolescent boys. Four games were all-black; two were all-white; one was racially mixed. The two tot lots in the park are situated in diagonally opposite corners of the recreation area, with clear visibility from one to the other. The tot lot in the Northwest corner was being utilized by approximately 35 black children, one white child, and seven supervising black adult women. The tot lot in the Southwest corner of the park showed an opposite racial pattern; it was being utilized by 20 white children, one black child and four white supervisors. It is noteworthy that two such playlots in the same part situated at a distance of no more than 200 feet from one another should be almost completely racially segregated.

The lack of evidence of demographic integration leads to the suspicion that South Shore residents, when taking outdoor recreation as well as public indoor recreation, do not lead integrated social lives. Members of different races do not accompany one another to parks and do not mingle once they arrive in parks. For children, some limited cross-racial contact seems to occur; for adults, there seems to be none whatsoever.

SCHOOLS

Schools in a community are a crucial determinant of the social lives of children; they provide settings for intimate interaction and their attendance

boundaries tend to circumscribe a child's opportunities for friendship formation (Roper, 1934). For some parents, schools are also a social setting (e.g.
PTA, volunteer work), but because of parents' more numerous alternative
sources of social interaction, and because of the relatively small proportion
of their time spent in school contexts, the school is of much less social
significance.

TABLE 4. RACIAL COMPOSITION OF SOUTH SHORE PUBLIC SCHOOLS,
1963, 1964, 1965, 1966

School	Proportion of student body black			
	1963	1964	1965	1966
Parkside	90.3	96.6	97.8	99.1
O'Keeffe	39.8	67.3	85.4	93.9
Bryn Mawr	16.3	37.2	55.2	66.1
Mann	7.0	26.6	43.0	55.1
Bradwell	0.1	0.2	0.7	3.7
Sullivan	0.0	0.0	0.0	2.3
South Shore High[a]	1.5	7.0	24.8	41.8

Sources: 1963 data: *Chicago Sun-Times*, October 24, 1963; 1964, 1965 data: *Southeast
Economist* (Chicago), October 17, 1965; 1966 data: *Southeast Economist* (Chicago),
October 23, 1966.

[a]High school boundary zone was modified between 1964 and 1965 with the inclusion
of Parkside and O'Keeffe and the exclusion of a larger all-black elementary school as
"feeder" schools in the fall, 1965. The net effect of this change on the high school's
racial composition was negligible.

The racial composition of South Shore's public schools for 1963 through
1966 is presented in Table 4. As is common in transition areas in which
attendance is based on the "neighborhood" principle, schools closest to the
original point of Negro in-migration (the area's northwest corner) are most
heavily black, with an increasing number of schools becoming predominately
black over time. In 1966, two of the community's six elementary schools
were demographically integrated (again, using the 10% convention). The
South Shore High School and one of the three Catholic schools were also
demographically integrated.[13]

[13]Unfortunately, no intensive observations were made of student life within schools.

PTA meetings held in 1966 at the three integrated public schools (Mann, Bryn Mawr, and the high school) were attended by members of both races —as were PTA meetings at the predominately black O'Keeffe school which drew an approximately equal number of whites and blacks to its meetings, although its student body was 74% black. In general, whites participated most in South Shore's school affairs, including in its biracial schools. In all schools in which any appreciable number of white children were enrolled, whites dominated the adult organizations. Thus all newly elected officers of the high school PTA were white despite the fact that over 42% of the school's student body were black at the time of the 1967 PTA Spring elections. In other biracial schools, as in almost all of South Shore's biracial settings, blacks were always under-represented in top leadership positions.

RELIGIOUS INSTITUTIONS

South Shore's religious organizations provide settings which are a mix of formality and informality. During worship services individuals find themselves in a situation whereby virtually every move of every participant, including gestures and signs of effect, is determined either by explicit ritual, tradition or local habit. In other types of church activity, such as funerals, weddings, bowling games, club meetings, etc., social interaction is more spontaneous, intense, and intimate.

It is thus not surprising to find that whatever integration existed in church organizations, existed primarily in terms of worship activity and not in terms of church para-religious social life. Four of South Shore's 16 Protestant churches hold integrated (again, by the 10% criterion) church services; one had an integrated *membership* list. Table 5 presents a detailed summary of the racial composition of South Shore's churches and church-related schools.[14]

Church life, outside of worship services, was virtually completedly segregated and completely white. Two church membership screening committees had a black member (to help find the "good element", according to the white chairman); several churches had black Sunday school teachers and one

[14]Interviews with local clergy were carried out during the Summer of 1965 and Spring of 1966. The author personally interviewed 12 clergymen; additional interview material was provided by E. Maynard Moore III, who based part of his interview schedule upon that of the author's, thus generating a total of 23 comparable cases. Respondents interviewed by both investigators generally gave identical responses to the two researchers. (Cf. Moore, 1966.)

church had two black women helping to establish a youth program. Of these "active" blacks (as was true of most black church members in South Shore), all were women.

In part, the near-total absence of blacks from church social life was a result of deliberate white exclusion. In one case, revealed with dismay by the pastor of the church involved (and subsequently confirmed by an interview with the "victim"), a black woman, upon invitation of the pastor's wife, joined a church bowling team which previously had only white members. The other bowlers' resultant demand that the woman be excluded was resisted by the clergyman. In consequence, the bowling team severed formal ties with the church. Rather than force such issues, thereby risking damage to church programs, most South Shore clergymen seemed to handle the inevitable role strain by insisting upon "welcoming" blacks to church services (thus fulfilling official denominational dictates as well as their own stated positions of "conscience") while permitting social activities to continue in a segregated fashion. This "compromise" can be said to have "worked", given the formality and constrained behavior characteristic of the church service, in contrast to the very different nature of other church-related activity.

Another important variation in church racial patterns, one strikingly revealed in Table 5, was the difference in the degree to which black children, compared to black adults, were being served by South Shore churches. Eight church Sunday schools were at least 10% black; in one case a church with only 10% black membership had a Sunday school which was 98% black. Fully 48% of Protestant Sunday school attenders were black; 11% of those enrolled in Catholic day schools were black.

This contrast between adult and child integration in church settings is again suggestive of the significance of interpersonal vulnerability as a determinant of racial patterns. Parents (of both races) were willing to place their children in racially mixed settings because such settings provided no psychic difficulties for *them* (the parents). Children, perhaps having different criteria for mutual identification and for establishing boundaries of community (e.g. sex, age, territory, athletic standing), were possibly less likely to find such settings painful, although the segregation patterns at play, as well as evidence presented by Suttles (1968, Chapters 9, 10), would suggest otherwise. In any event, children are not as free as their parents to pick and choose their social settings, regardless of the inconvenience or personal discomfort they might experience.

An Exception: The Baptist Church. A fundamentalist Baptist church, located in a predominately Negro area, stood apart from all other religious institutions in South Shore in that equal numbers of whites and blacks attended services; it was, in other respects as well, the most completely integrated of all South Shore religious institutions.[15] It was also distinct in that worship services were a more basic part of the life of the church than in other denominations. Worship was a time of spontaneity and much animated social interaction. Church members were working class and lower-middle class; it was the poorest church in South Shore—poor in terms of the income of it worshippers, and almost the poorest in terms of annual church budget. Among South Shore clergy, its minister had the least familiarity with the "liberal" conventional wisdom concerning the role of the urban ministry, the "crisis in the city", etc.—utterances which permeated interview responses from most other area clergy. This fundamentalist minister was the only South Shore clergyman to ever indicate a past history of "prejudice" toward blacks.

That such conditions gave rise to the only case of trans-racial solidarity in a church context is perhaps surprising; for this reason the Baptist church and several other such "deviant" cases will be discussed at length in a later discussion. For the present, however, it should be noted that the conditions of spontaneity and intimacy characteristic of fundamentalist religion could lead *only* to one of two states: either complete racial exclusion *or* complete racial integration with concomitant total acceptance. If blacks were to be present at all, their presence would have to be unreservedly accepted; otherwise, the resultant inhibitions would have destroyed the nature of the religious experience and thus the very reason for the coming together.

VOLUNTARY ASSOCIATIONS

Many national charity and service organizations (e.g. Lions, American Legion, Veterans of Foreign Wars, B'nai B'rith) had chapters serving the South Shore area and all were exclusively white.[16] Of over 50 organizational

[15]The divergence in this church between the number of Negro *attenders* and number of black *members* (as indicated by data in Table 5) was due to the fact that a "personal revelation" was a requisite for formal membership; many blacks were thus in the situation of having formal induction pending such a revelation.

[16]The author has been advised that a tutoring center at the South Shore YMCA was being operated during the study period on a racially integrated basis. Pressures of time did not permit a first-hand investigation of this program.

TABLE 5. RACIAL COMPOSITION OF SOUTH SHORE'S CHRISTIAN CHURCHES AND CHURCH-RELATED SCHOOLS

Denomination of church	Number of church members (parishioners)	Number of blacks in membership	Percent of membership black	Number Sunday attenders	Number black Sunday attenders	Percent Sunday attenders black	Number enrolled in Sunday school	Number of blacks in Sunday school	Percent of Sunday school black
Protestant:									
Community	1,775	14	0.8%	625	27	4.3%	350	160	45.0%
Episcopal	450	30	6.6%	250	25	10.0%	87	20	23.0%
Lutheran	305	25	8.0%	113	10	8.8%	45	25	55.0%
Methodist	650	25	3.8%	200	30	15.0%	390	250	64.0%
Methodist	210	21	10.0%	90	9	10.0%	159	157	99.0%
Christian Science	250	1	0.4%	250	7	2.8%	160	12	7.5%
Bible Church	75	5	6.6%	65	35	53.0%	150	100	66.0%
Sub-Totals	3,715	121	3.3%	1,593	143	8.9%	1,360	724	53.0%
Nine Other Prot. Churches	2,285	0	—	994	0	—	140	0	—
Prot. Totals	6,000	121	2.0%	2,587	143	5.5%	1,500	724	48.0%
Catholic:[a]									
1) Catholic	1,200[b]	70[b]	5.0%	4,000	100	2.5%	485	110	23.0%
2) Catholic	1,900[b]	1[b]	0.5%	3,000	0	—	200	10	5.0%
3) Catholic	2,700[b]	325[b]	12.0%	9,000	477	53.0%	732	40	5.5%
Catholic Totals	5,800[b]	396[b]	6.8%	16,000	577	3.6%	1,417	160	11.0%

[a]Catholic school data refer to day school enrolments, not Sunday school. Except for Church No. 3, attendance data based on actual headcounts on a Sunday, Spring, 1966.

[b]Refers to number of families, rather than individuals.

Other sources: Reports of clergymen to the writer and to E. Maynard Moore, III (cf. Moore, 1966).

group photographs published in the *Southeast Economist*[17] (the community newspaper serving the area), none which involved South Shore residents included blacks. The South Shore Country Club, the boards and officer corps of two local hospitals and of the Chamber of Commerce were also without black participants.

That charity and service groups, organizations which are generally based in friendship cliques, were not integrated is not surprising. That the governing bodies of major local institutions were also exclusively white can be taken to simply reflect a combination of similar social patterning of organizational participation linked with the positions of the two races in the American stratification system.

THE SOUTH SHORE COMMISSION

The most prominent exception to the general pattern of black exclusion (or omission) from the ranks of important community groups was the South Shore Commission which, at least after 1964, was biracial in its leadership as well as in membership. Although blacks remained greatly underrepresented in Commission leadership positions during the study period, several on the Board of Directors and one of six officers were black. Many of the Commission's sub-groups were also biracial, including several committees and various block club organizations. But it is quite safe to say that since only a small proportion of South Shore's residents involved themselves in any block club or other Commission activity,[18] its effectiveness in creating biracial contacts was probably limited to a small leadership group in the community.

From its very inception, the Commission was not an informal social organization; as an association of Protestants, Catholics and Jews, it had from the beginning brought together persons who were less than at complete ease in each other's presence. It continued to function primarily as an instrumental organization, and not as a setting for intimate socializing as blacks were brought into membership. Thus, the Commission provided a series of

[17] *The Southeast Economist* serves South Shore as well as a much larger region of the South Side as a "community newspaper". An organization was considered to be located in South Shore if at least half of all addresses of those photographed were within the study area.

[18] The Commission's "grass roots" were actually rather shallow. It is likely that there were no more than 12 block clubs operating during the study period, although statements printed about South Shore in national and local media implied there were many more. (Cf. Molotch, 1968:71.)

public meetings, outings, and fund-raising entertainments wherein public behavior was the accepted norm.

In the context of Commission activity, as in the case of other biracial voluntary organizations in South Shore, cross-racial interaction was more formal and guarded than were interactions (also quite formal) between members of the same race. Because of the uniqueness of biracial interaction in American society, blacks and whites were in the difficult situation of having to create *de novo* a formal mode for social interaction, given the obvious and subtle differences between blacks and whites and the lack of mutual knowledge of what the other party might consider "appropriate" talking behavior. Thus there was a need to avoid the unknown transgressions which might occur if spontaneous behavior were to run its course. This was accomplished by both blacks and whites by resort to a zealous interpersonal courtesy (to ward off any conceivable slight or "misunderstanding"), unrelenting pleasantness, and a well-understood, tacit, mutual agreement to limit the subject of all conversation to small talk. Behavior was carefully guarded; words and expressions were selected with extraordinary care.

For blacks, this heightened self-consciousness generally resulted in deferential postures toward their white colleagues, and an ongoing monitoring of behaviour to avoid any possible controversy which might set them in opposition to policies favored by any significant number of whites. Several substantive examples may be cited. The Commission was known by black members to be cooperating through its tenant referral service with landlords who refused to rent housing to non-whites. The actions entailed in such cooperation were probably illegal under the Chicago Fair Housing Ordinance and were a source of distress to black Commission members. Yet they preferred, in the words of one, not to "make a fuss" against a policy which they indicated (to the writer) they found obnoxious. Similarly, black Commission members assented to quota systems for maintaining whites in buildings and blocks which otherwise would have become predominately black. Again, there was public acquiescence in spite of privately held feelings that such policies were improper and also in violation of the Housing Ordinance.

That this effect of biracial interaction was most pronounced in the case of blacks, and not whites, is perhaps explicable in terms of another important feature of biracial interaction in South Shore: blacks and whites seldom come together as equals. This fact thus adds an additional dimension to the vulnerability of the "alien" persons who were not only in a numerical minority but, because of such status differences, were especially vulnerable to

188

the sanctions of those who possessed so disproportionate an amount of wealth, power and expertise.

These status differences were pervasive. In general, blacks moving into South Shore were of lower socioeconomic status than the whites they replaced.[19] The same status differentiation was reflected within organizational contexts such as the Commission. Thus, white males of the Commissions' governing board were almost all proprietors, lawyers, physicians, and stockbrokers, and black members were salesmen, school teachers, and low-level supervisors.

Furthermore, unlike white leaders, blacks did not find their way to the Board because of their state of personal wealth, power, or expertise, but instead because of their race and an acceptance of Commission goals. The Commision originally "took in" blacks in order to be more "representative" and to avoid being labeled "racist" or "bigoted", and blacks were thus largely interchangeable with any number of other blacks, with the consequence that their status vis-à-vis their white "colleagues" could only suffer. Several black members were viewed approvingly by whites as "real work horses" who make a "fine contribution", but none had the contacts with the political, religious, and business leaders of Chicago which were seen to be the really important determinants of South Shore's future. A good "work horse" may be hard to find, but a member of the Chicago School Board or the editor of a Chicago daily newspaper is impossible to replace. Such differences in the degree to which people are important to an organization's goals do not bode well for parity in interpersonal relationships.

The case of biracial interaction in the Commission would seen to provide an explanation for the findings generated by tests of the "contact hypothesis". A large body of literature suggests that more "favourable" white attitudes toward blacks results from biracial interaction in which whites and blacks share the same status, are in mutually dependent roles, and where contact is "intimate" rather than superficial.[20] These are precisely the conditions in

[19]See note 5.

[20]Various studies have yielded somewhat conflicting evidence on the validity of the "contact hypothesis". Three classic studies which indicate a positive relationship between "improvement" in white attitudes toward blacks with increasing contact are Deutsch and Collins (1951); Starr *et al.* (1949); and Merton *et al.* (1949). Three reports providing evidence for the opposite conclusion are Allport and Kramer (1946); Kramer (1950); and Winder (1952). A synthesis of these mixed findings, one which is consistent with the criteria for effective positive attitude change as specified in the above text, appears in Wilner *et al.* (1955).

which social vulnerability to alien and unknown individuals is minimized for members of both races. Where such conditions are not present, the contact hypothesis suggests that biracial interaction is expected to yield either no effects or an increased amount of "negative" white evaluation of blacks.

Indeed, these latter results were the consequences in such groups as the Commission. For whites, participation with blacks led to the observation that they (blacks) "aren't real leaders", or, in the words of one of the area's most liberal clergymen, they aren't "take charge people". The middle-class analogue of the "lazy colored boy" remained the dominant white stereotype. For blacks, interaction in such settings would seem to debilitate energies as whites come to be seen as the real makers of decisions and holders of power (cf. Piven and Cloward, 1967). The really crucial organizational skills which blacks observed were those involving the utilization of contacts (e.g. friends in high places) and resources (e.g. personal fortunes) which they neither possessed nor stood a very good chance of ever possessing.

"MARGINAL GROUPS": INSTANCES OF
TRANSRACIAL SOLIDARITY

In addition to the case of the Baptist church, of which mention has been previously made, there were three other contexts in South Shore which seemed to have provided settings in which transracial solidarity could be said to have been extant. These were "marginal" organizations—marginal in that meetings were held only on an irregular basis and in that they were organizations founded on premises of dissent and protest which limited their appeal to only a small number of participants. One such group was a local branch of Veterans for Peace in Vietnam, an organization with leftist political orientations (including several persons of militant Marxist ideology) which held occasional meetings above a South Shore store during the study period. Another group was the O'Keeffe Area Council—technically a part of the South Shore Commission but with an active leadership which, because of its rather "pro-Negro", anti-"establishment" orientation, was often independent of the Commission in spirit and in action.

Finally, there was the South Shore Organization for Human Rights, a group active in fostering open occupancy and other civil rights goals in South Shore and metropolitan Chicago. This group was indigenous to South Shore, having been stimulated by a young clergyman during his rather brief association with a South Shore Protestant church. Like Veterans for Peace and the O'Keeffe Area Council, its active membership consisted of only a handful of persons, but, unlike the other groups, it carried out independent programs such as "testing" the racial practices of local real estate firms, as well as the racial policies of a tenant referral service managed by the South Shore Commission.

These three organizations differed from other South Shore institutions not only in terms of their militancy and marginality, but also in terms of the "tone" of biracial interactions shared by members. In all of these contexts, as in the case of the Baptist Church, interaction across racial lines seemed to come easily; interaction was unstilted, informal and direct. Except possibly for the Veterans for Peace, these were all informal social organizations, with blacks and whites living out shared social as well as shared institutional lives. Race ceased to operate as a source of cleavage or determinant of institutional roles.

In other respects, these groups were quite diverse. The Baptist Church was largely working-class with many recent migrants from the South and Appalachia. The O'Keeffe Council consisted of young well-educated professionals; to a lesser extent, the same was true of the Organization for Human Rights. Veterans for Peace was an extremely diverse group of blue-collar workers, small businessmen, and a few professionals. Congregators of the Bible Church were apolitical, religious fundamentalists; members of the other groups were identified with secular, left-leaning ideologies.[21]

Yet there were certain important similarities. Within each of these groups, race and status differences were not correlated; businessmen or professionals within each were as likely to be black as white.[22] In addition, these groups

[21]These findings are consistent with other studies which have uncovered the extremely diverse conditions under which racial integration occurs and the seeming irrelevance of "prejudice" or racial "attitude" in determining when and where integration exists. Grier and Grier (1960) found integrated housing developments to be heterogeneous in terms of the income, education, ethnicity, stage of life cycle, and geographical origin of residents. Supporting findings are also reported in Rapkin and Grigsby (1960) and Mayer (1960).

[22]Membership status of the Baptist church was relatively homogenous. Veterans for Peace was led by a well-to-do black funeral director and several of his black business colleagues, whereas whites included in their ranks (along with a few professionals) a TV repairman and a sign painter. The O'Keeffe Council included in its top leadership cadre a black businessman and a black lawyer along with a white businessman and a white engineer. The Organization for Human Rights was dominated by a white clergyman and a group of black and white women who were either white-collar workers or had lower middle-class husbands.

191

were alike in that members were in an alien environment. The church was surrounded by more stolid, richer congregations; Veterans for Peace, the Organization for Human Rights, and the O'Keeffe Council existed in the shadow of the powerful South Shore Commission and other "moderate" or conservative institutions which supported Chicago's and the nation's ongoing political arrangements. The various deviant traits of these groups' members thus created a situation in which organizational alternatives within the South Shore area were lacking. The result may have been an organizational commitment of sufficient strength to overcome any inhibitions which racial differences might have created. Finally, members of these groups were similar in that most were either new to the South Shore area, or, because of their youth, new to South Shore organizational life. A lack of previous ties to existing structures may thus similarly facilitate commitments to organizations which, in that they are biracial, operate with new kinds of *modus vivendi*.

SUMMARY

Although South Shore's total racial composition provided initial evidence of some forms of racial integration in the area, social life is essentially segregated. The nature of the contexts in which varying forms of integration are found suggests that fear of exposure and mutual suspiciousness between members of the two races inhibit biracial sharing of public places which serve as loci of private behavior. Thus some degree of demographic integration and a slight amount of biracial interaction can occur in public places in which public behavior traditionally ensues. That is, extensive integration (primarily by demographic indices) occurs in places such as retail shops, church chapels and formal organizations oriented toward the accomplishment of instrumental goals. In such settings, social interaction across racial lines is not reflective of transracial solidarity. Nor can the results of such interaction be assumed to promote eventual solidarity, given the problematic power disparities which are general concomitants of such black–white interaction. Presumably because of the greater psychic and practical dilemmas it would create, integration of any sort is absent from informal settings such as church socials, service clubs, taverns, Saturday night bowling and parks.

Women, because they are more local in their activity and interests, are more likely than men to find themselves in biracial circumstances. Protestants are more likely than are Catholics or Jews, and children—perhaps because they are less free to vary their milieu according to preference—to have the most experience of biracial contact.

Although there are some communalities in the problems which both blacks and whites face under conditions of biracial propinquity and contact, the consequences on the two groups are not identical. In South Shore, as in the rest of the society, the integration "experiment" opens with the most important and useful institutions, organizations and settings as white, and the "challengers" or "invaders" as black. *The circumstances are thus not parallel.* The widely shared community conceptions so generated of "intruders" versus "preservers", applied to blacks and whites respectively, provide still another distinction consistent with the status and power disparities widely observed to exist between blacks and whites. Not only is the development of transracial solidarity made more difficult as a result, but, in addition, the psychic difficulties which blacks must face when entering the alien white context are further intensified.[23] That is, biracial interaction challenges members of both races to overcome certain fears of the dissimilar, the unproven, and the threatening. But for blacks, there is the added problem of knowing that in presenting oneself in a biracial setting, one is challenging and "pushing" to gain something otherwise unavailable. The modal black response would seem to be either a show of hostility (as in some manifestations of the current phase of the civil rights movement) or, as was common in South Shore, a show of deference and total capitulation to white preferences.

Integration of a thoroughgoing type, what has been termed "transracial solidarity", occurred in South Shore in only a few settings. These were instances in which there were cross-racial communalities of a shared and deviant ideology (mutual recognition of which provided bases for the development of needed social alternatives); an equality in occupational status and organizational usefulness (thus providing cross-racial parity in interpersonal vulnerability); and, among both blacks and whites, a lack of previously constituted local organizational ties (thus precluding habit and/or social pressures from inhibiting affiliation with groups which have integration as one of their innovative features).

All settings observed in South Shore (an attempt was made to be exhaustive) which shared these characteristics were found to approximate the

[23]Levy (1968) provides a description of an instance (whites in the southern civil rights movement) in which the tables are turned, that is, where biracial interaction occurs in a black-dominated context (with analogous intensification of difficulties for *whites*).

circumstance of transracial solidarity; no other instances of this form of integration were found. If other possible contingencies to racial integration are to be uncovered, or if those observed in South Shore are to be confirmed as determinant (either singly, or in some "value-added" combination), additional case studies and eventual comparative analysis will be necessary. But for the present, it is well to note that the conditions cited as concomitants of transracial solidarity in South Shore are precisely those which are likely to provide the overarching cues of similarity, reliability, and trust which would seem requisite for the building and maintenance of racially integrated associations, institutions, and community.

REFERENCES

ALLPORT, GORDON and KRAMER, BERNARD (1946) "Some roots of prejudice." *Journal of Psychology* **21** (Fall), 9–39.

BIDDLE, WILLIAM and BIDDLE, LOUREIDE (1965) *The Community Development Process: The Rediscovery of Local Initiative.* New York: Holt, Rinehart and Winston.

DEUTSCH, MORTON and COLLINS, MARY (1951) *Interracial Housing. A Psychological Evaluation of a Social Experiment.* Minneapolis: University of Minnesota Press.

FINESTONE, HAROLD (1957) "Cats, kicks and color." *Social Problems* **5** (July), 3–13.

FISHBEIN, ANNETTE (1962) The Expansion of Negro Residential Areas in Chicago. Unpublished Master's dissertation, Department of Sociology, University of Chicago.

GANS, HERBERT (1962) *The Urban Villagers.* New York: The Free Press.

GOFFMAN, ERVING (1959) *The Presentation of Self in Everyday Life.* New York: Doubleday.

GRIER, GEORGE and GRIER, EUNICE (1960) *Privately Developed Interracial Housing: An Analysis of Experience.* Berkeley: University of California Press.

JOHNSON, PHILIP A. (1965) *Call Me Neighbor, Call Me Friend.* New York: Doubleday.

KITAGAWA, EVELYN and TAEUBER, KARL (eds.) (1963) *Local Community Fact Book: Chicago Metropolitan Area, 1960.* Chicago: Chicago Community Inventory, University of Chicago.

KRAMER, BERNARD M. (1950) Residential Contact as a Determinant of Attitudes Toward Negroes. Unpublished Ph.D. dissertation, Department of Social Relations, Harvard University.

LEVY, CHARLES J. (1968) *Voluntary Servitude: Whites in the Negro Movement.* New York: Appleton-Century-Crofts.

McKENZIE, RODERICK O. (1923) *The Neighborhood: A Study of Local Life in the City of Columbus, Ohio.* Chicago: University of Chicago Press.

MAYER, ALBERT J. (1960) "Russel Woods: Change without conflict: A case study of neighborhood racial transition in Detroit." In NATHAN GLAZER and DAVIS McENTIRE (eds.), *Studies in Housing and Minority Groups.* Berkeley: University of California Press.

MERTON, ROBERT et al. (1949) "Social facts and social fictions: The dynamics of race relations in Milltown". New York: Columbia University Bureau of Applied Social Research.

MOLOTCH, HARVEY (1966) "Urban community boundaries: A case study". Working Paper No. 60, Center for Social Organization Studies, University of Chicago, multilith.

MOLOTCH, HARVEY (1967) "Toward a more human human ecology: An urban research strategy" *Land Economics* **43**:3 (August), 336–41.

MOLOTCH, HARVEY (1968) Community Action to Control Racial Change. Unpublished Ph.D. dissertation, Department of Sociology, University of Chicago.

MOLOTCH, HARVEY (1969) "Racial change in a stable community." *American Journal of Sociology* **75** (forthcoming).

MOORE, E. MAYNARD, III. (1966) The Church and Racial Change in South Shore. Unpublished paper. The Divinity School, University of Chicago.

PIVEN, FRANCIS FOX and CLOWARD, RICHARD (1967) "The case against racial integration." *Social Work* **12** (January), 12–21.

RAPKIN, CHESTER and GRIGSBY, WILLIAM (1960) *The Demand for Housing in Racially Mixed Areas*. Berkeley: University of California Press.

ROPER, MARIAN (1934) The City and the Primary Group. Unpublished Ph.D. dissertation, Department of Sociology, University of Chicago.

STAR, SHIRLEY, WILLIAMS, ROBIN M. JR. and STOUFFER, SAMUEL A. (1949) "Negro Soldiers" in Samuel Stouffer et al., *The American Soldier: Adjustment During Army Life*, Vol. I. Princeton: Princeton University Press.

SUTTLES, GERALD (1968) *The Social Order of the Slum*. Chicago: University of Chicago Press.

TAEUBER, KARL and TAEUBER, ALMA (1965) *Negroes in Cities*. Chicago: Aldine.

WILNER, DANIEL, WALKLEY, ROSABELLE and COOK, STUART (1955) *Human Relations in Interracial Housing: A Study of the Contact Hypothesis*. Minneapolis: University of Minnesota Press.

WINDER, ALVIN (1952) White Attitudes Towards Negro–White Interaction in an Area of Changing Racial Composition. Unpublished Ph.D. dissertation, Committee on Human Development, University of Chicago.

WIRTH, LOUIS (1938) "Urbanism as a way of life." *American Journal of Sociology* **44** (July).

Race and Ethnic Stratification

Stratification and Ethnic Groups

STANLEY LIEBERSON

DOES an ethnic stratification system differ significantly from those based on economic, age, or sex characteristics? Or is ethnic stratification but another form of general stratification? This paper compares ethnic hierarchies with other types of stratification in terms of two issues: first, the distinctive qualities of ethnic stratification; second, the ways in which ethnic stratification influences economic stratification in the same society. The term "ethnic" is used here in its broadest context, including groups that are differentiated on either cultural or physical criteria. This includes groups that are commonly called races, as well as populations that are distinguished on the basis of language, religion, foreign origin, history, or other cultural characteristics.

Most stratification theories are concerned primarily with economic dimensions such as the unequal distribution of rewards and privileges to labor and capital or to occupational groups. Indeed there are some who would hold that ethnic groups are not even a possible basis of stratification. But if, following Sorokin (1959, p. 11), stratification is defined as the differentiation of a population into a hierarchy of layers, and if this means an unequal distribution of rights and privileges, power and influence, then it is clear that ethnic differentiation may be the basis of a stratification system. To be sure, ethnic groups may differ in their aggregate positions on these dimensions without there necessarily being a system of ethnic stratification in the society. This would occur if the ethnic differences were *solely* a function of their positions on other characteristics such as education or occupation that were, in turn, not influenced by ethnic membership. However, it is clear that most often ethnic groups differ in their occupational opportunities as well as their positions of power and influence, rewards and privileges, at least in part because of their ethnic group membership *per se*. In such instances, the society can be viewed as stratified along ethnic lines as well as other dimensions. In other words, stratification exists *between* ethnic groups that goes beyond the stratification that occurs *within* each ethnic group.

Determination of an ethnic ranking system raises some serious methodological difficulties and the evidence on the United States is not altogether clear (see Jackson and Curtis, 1968, pp. 125–6). It is difficult to decide whether ethnic groups should be classified in terms of prestige or political-economic position, or some other attribute. The dimensions used here are two-fold; discrimination against a group in terms of economic opportunity and/or political power. This means that a society with two or more ethnic groups will be viewed as stratified along these lines if the ethnic groups have differential access to either economic position or political power in a way that cannot be explained through the operation of other forms of stratification in the society.

MAINTENANCE OF THE NATION

The most fundamental difference between ethnic and other forms of stratification lies in the fact that the former is nearly always the basis for the internal disintegration of the existing boundaries of a nation-state. On both theoretical and empirical grounds, only ethnic groups are likely to generate a movement towards creating a separate nation-state. Ethnic groups are the only strata that have the inherent potential to carve their own autonomous and permanent society from the existing nation without, in effect, re-creating its earlier form of stratification all over again. Political separatism offers a solution to disadvantaged groups in an ethnic stratification system that is not possible for groups disadvantaged on the basis of age, sex, or economic stratification.

In the case of sex stratification, it is clear that a crucial dependence exists between the sexes such that neither has the potential for maintaining a society without the other. Although there are striking analogies between the position of women and ethnic groups in societies generally (Hacker, 1951) and between Negroes and women in the United States (Myrdal, 1944, pp. 1073–8; Hodge and Hodge, 1965), they clearly differ with respect to the potential for maintaining separate nation-states. As a consequence, efforts to reduce or eliminate stratification along sex lines must occur within the context of the existing nation.

With respect to stratification based on age, no single age segment could maintain itself indefinitely in a society. If the age strata forming a new society was in the child-bearing ages, then new age groups would be produced. If past the child-bearing ages, then it would not even be possible to produce a new generation. Under any circumstances, it is clear that separation would not eliminate age stratification since the new society, if it were to be viable, would soon re-create the age differences.

Likewise, it is not normally possible for an economic class to split off to form its own society since almost certainly this would re-create a set of economic classes. Except for the simplest systems, an economic group is normally not self-sufficient. Hence, it would be necessary for the abandoned functions to be re-created if a given class were to form its own nation-state. Unless a classless society were to be formed, a separatist movement among a subordinate economic class would be self-defeating.

By contrast, an ethnic group possesses this potential for creating an autonomous nation-state that would eliminate its subordination in an ethnic hierarchy. An ethnic group has all of the existing age and sex divisions. If subordinate in the existing economic system, then there are always members willing to assume the new opportunities for power and wealth that an autonomous state would offer. This theoretical potential for fission that marks ethnic strata also corresponds to the empirical reality. Generally, separatist movements or movements towards political decentralization are in fact based on ethnic group movements. In the former Belgian Congo, where Katanga province attempted to secede, there were distinctive ethnic factors as well as the influence of the outside mining interests. The creation of Biafra is a product of an ethnic group, the Ibos. The separatist threat in Canada is clearly an ethnic group movement. Likewise the political decentralization of India is deeply bound to linguistic issues that tear apart that nation. Ethnic forces were also the basis for the new nations that sprang into being after the First World War in Europe. To be sure, the ethnic divisions may mask or greatly overlap with socio-economic divisions, but still the separation issue is normally cloaked in an ethnic form. Likewise, most regional forms of separation are usually based on ethnic differences between the groups residing in the various parts of the larger, established political union.[1]

In political terms, all nations are unions that incorporate heterogeneous populations with inherently conflicting goals and ambitions. In some nations these cleavages are based on forms of stratification that do not normally undermine the political boundaries of the nation. Although the means for seeking a resolution to these conflicting interests may vary from competition for power between political parties (or the wings of a one-party state) to

[1]Civil wars, such as the one in the United States, are notable exceptions to the role of conflicting ethnic groups in separatism.

201

demonstrations and revolution, the existing nation-state is generally maintained. Political parties differ in their responsiveness to the conflicting demands within the nation, but they are geared to the continuity of the political union itself. Even the revolution in Russia had very little effect on the continuation of the Czarist position in Asia (Wheeler, 1960).

Although the probability of a separatist movement and its chances for success varies enormously between nations with ethnic stratification, the underlying potential for such movements exists in virtually all nations with diverse ethnic groups. Accordingly, the existing political union cannot be assumed to hold the inevitable and unvarying consent of those governed by it. The issue here, unlike economic stratification, is not replacement of one party by another or even a revolutionary change in the political system, but whether the ethnic segments will consent to participation within the confines of the existing nation-state. Nationalism is essentially an ethnic movement in which the distinctive characteristics of a "people" are emphasized and praised, and where the true and full expression of their unique qualities requires that a separate nation exist. To be sure, there may be economic interests compatible with such a movement, and international politics may play its role, but the key to nation-making are ethnic groups. Ethnic groups can and do exist side-by-side in pluralistic nations, but nevertheless only such groups hold the potential for the creation of new, and separate, nations.

The position of each ethnic group is often an important source of conflict within the existing nation. One need only consider such nations as Belgium, the United States, Ceylon, and Malaysia to recognize that societies at all levels of development can be deeply torn by issues revolving about the positions of the various ethnic groups. To be sure these conflicts are often linked to economic stratification. Nevertheless, it is clear that a government's ethnic policy is often potentially a very sensitive issue for the stability of the nation. Language conflict, for example, can occur in such domains as: the official recognition of the language in the legislature, courts, and government documents; availability of government-supported education in each group's own mother tongue; government actions with respect to the discrimination against the speakers of a given language; maintenance of the language through mass media such as publications, radio and television; special budgetary privileges, and the like (see United Nations, 1950).

In short, the position of each ethnic group within the existing nation-state is often a major source of discontent which may, in turn, generate a movement towards political disassociation. In so far as the national government

202

fails to meet the demands of its dominant ethnic group, a change in government provides a suitable mechanism for introducing reforms within the context of the present political union. For ethnic groups that are unable to achieve their goals through the existing nation-state, however, there is the possibility that they will seek to undo the political union which thwarts these goals. Barring the use of extremely repressive measures, no political party of coalition in power can afford to completely ignore a minority segment even if this segment is not the source of voting support.

IMPACT ON OTHER STRATIFICATION SYSTEMS

Obviously, the existence of an ethnic group hierarchy does not prevent a society from stratifying along other axes as well. Thus ethnic stratification is relevant to other forms of stratification even in nations where separatism is not a threat. There are a number of ways in which the presence of an ethnic stratification system modifies other forms of stratification and, in turn, is influenced by them. I shall describe several of these modifications, paying particular attention to the influence of ethnic stratification on economic stratification. This analysis is restricted to societies whose ethnic and economic strata are not mutually exclusive, but overlap to some degree. In the United States, for example, not all of the lower income positions are occupied by members of a single subordinate ethnic group, even if there is an obvious differential economic distribution between ethnic groups.

Class solidarity

There is reason to suspect that the presence of an ethnic stratification system will affect the development of class solidarity. It is clear that the existence of economic stratification does not automatically generate class unity with respect to either political or union activities. One may hypothesize that the presence of ethnic stratification that cross-cuts economic groups will tend to reduce the cohesiveness of the classes. If, for example, some members of the working class belong to one ethnic stratum and others belong to a lower ethnic stratum, then the unity within the economic class will be less developed than might otherwise occur in a nation with ethnic homogeneity.

The conflict between Negroes and whites in the United States, for example, undoubtedly undermines political unity between members of the groups who share common economic interests. This is particularly noteworthy in the South, where the conflict along ethnic lines definitely weakens

203

both the union movement as well as a unified political approach. It is easy to understand how such divisions along ethnic lines might undermine or reduce economic classes. For the working-class member of a subordinate ethnic group, there are two channels of social action that may be beneficial. Movements to raise the rewards available to either his economic or his ethnic group will offer rewards. Likewise, for working-class members of the dominant ethnic group, any movement towards raising his economic group's position or reducing the position of subordinate ethnic groups offers rewards. By comparison, a homogeneous working-class population does not face these conflicting and alternative paths for gains within the stratification system.

If one goes to a very simple extreme, it can be argued that the lowest economic stratum within the dominant ethnic group has a vested interest in ethnic stratification since it permits members of this group to look down on another segment of the population. But this perspective allows certain symbolic prestige advantages to override any economic advantages that the lower economic segment of the dominant group might gain through political or working alliances with other ethnic groups in the same economic position. Undoubtedly, symbolic advantages are of significance, but can be readily overdone. It would be of considerable value to work out models of the economic gains that might accrue to the economically subordinate sector of the dominant ethnic group in various settings. If these theoretical advantages are compared with the actual degree of cross-ethnic economic unity, it should be possible to determine the actual significance of such symbolic features for economic class behavior. Blalock (1967, pp. 84–92) has offered a useful beginning to such an approach by adopting the coalition theories of Gamson and Caplow to the union situation in the United States.

The hypothesis is that class polarization tends to be reduced when such an alignment would conflict with ethnic statification. In view of the rather wide variety of ethnic stratification systems existing in nations of roughly comparable economic and industrial development, it would be possible to test this proposition through a comparative study.

Mobility

There is an inherent linkage between economic mobility and the structural methods for maintaining ethnic stratification. In a society where there is no inter-generational mobility within each ethnic stratum, including the dominant one, then a caste-like situation exists in which discrimination is not necessary for the maintenance of ethnic stratification. The initial gaps between ethnic groups will remain unaltered over time and between generations without the need for discrimination against ethnic groups. If, however, the advantages enjoyed by one ethnic group over another are to be maintained in a system where inter-generational occupational mobility exists, then discrimination is necessary (see Lieberson and Fuguitt, 1967).

The importance of discrimination for maintaining ethnic stratification will vary with the magnitude of the inter-generational mobility patterns. If there is no relationship between father's occupation and those of their sons, to take the extreme case, then discrimination would be the only means whereby ethnic stratification in the occupational world could be maintained. If, however, the magnitude of inter-generational mobility is slight, then discrimination would be less necessary. Approaching mobility in terms of Markov chains, in the absence of discrimination the number of generations necessary to eliminate occupational differences between ethnic groups is a function of the rates of mobility. The level of difference at any given point in time would reflect the initial dissimilarity between the group in their occupational composition (Lieberson and Fuguitt, 1967, pp. 199–200).

In effect, then, there is a relationship between the nature of the economic mobility system within the dominant ethnic group and the kinds of institutional activities necessary to keep some other ethnic stratum subordinate. If the actual rates of inter-generational mobility are high within the dominant ethnic group, then the maintenance of ethnic stratification will require severe forms of discrimination and repression in order to keep the subordinate ethnic groups from moving out of their subordinate economic positions. If, on the other hand, occupational mobility is less easily obtained, then such forms of discrimination are less necessary for maintaining ethnic stratification.

Creation of economic classes

New economic classes within a given ethnic population are sometimes created by the subordination of another ethnic group. The expansion of Europeans into the remainder of the world often meant the introduction of new economic enterprises that, in turn, created a new economic stratum of considerable wealth within the white group. The plantation economy, mining, and industries developed by Europeans overseas were often deeply dependent on large new labor forces that were supplied by other ethnic groups. Large-scale pineapple and sugar plantations in Hawaii, for example, required laborers from new ethnic groups (Lind, 1955, pp. 65–7). Africans and Asian Indians were used extensively in many parts of Africa as whites developed new industrial activities. The role of Indians in Natal provides a good illustration. They were first brought to South Africa to meet the new industrial needs created by whites. In no way were they encouraged to remain permanently, but only to meet these needs (Kuper, Watts, and Davies, 1958). Accordingly, the subordination of this ethnic group formed the basis of the creation of a wealthy economic class within the white population.

There are other instances where a new economic class within the dominant ethnic group is predicated on the availability of a cheap and subordinate labor force. The use of Negro slaves in the New World was undoubtedly crucial to the development of the cotton economy. Slave and quasi-slave systems of forced labor usually mean the subordination of one ethnic group by another. Hence, these systems are often an extreme illustration of the means by which an economic class within the dominant ethnic group creates and maintains its wealth through ethnic subordination. Since often not all members of the dominant ethnic group are able to use slaves to their advantage, it is noteworthy that the subordination of one ethnic group by another does not eliminate classes within the dominant ethnic group.

But even if the historical origins of a wealthy class are due to the initial ethnic stratification system, it does not necessarily follow that this wealthy class later remains the main source of ethnic stratification. A hierarchy may continue long after the initial causes have disappeared. Initially, an ethnic group may be used by a wealthy class exclusively and thus form no competition for other members of the dominant ethnic group. But the nature of the situation can change radically. In the United States, due to technological and economic changes, the need for Negroes in the cotton fields declined, but their threat to other economic segments of the dominant white group increased.

In short, the historical origins of an ethnic stratification system are sometimes linked with basic characteristics of an economic system. But, on the other hand, these earlier needs may later dissolve and may no longer be the basic impetus for maintaining the ethnic hierarchy after it is established in a society.

Proliferation of statuses

Hughes (1962, pp. 162–75) has described the wide array of status contradictions and dilemmas that may be formed when the various stratification systems are combined. The occupational role of a female Negro physician, for example, obviously clashes with her other role expectations. If we consider a society in which there are various combinations of age, sex, economic, and ethnic stratification, it becomes clear that the relative importance of each stratification system may vary considerably. This proliferation of status combinations can provide a powerful empirical clue to the nature of the stratification system since it is possible to attribute causal weights for each of these stratification factors as determinants of, say, income. Moreover, it is not unlikely that "interaction" effects will exist such that the importance of each status system will change in different combinations. Siegel (1965) and Blau and Duncan (1967, pp. 211–12) report such an interaction, for example, between education and income for Negroes. Compared with whites, the more educated Negroes suffer a greater income disadvantage than do those with lower levels of education.

The presence of ethnic stratification also means that many of the conflicts involving economic, age, and sex strata are more complex. This, of course, is not a unique quality of ethnic stratification since the same can be said for each of the other stratification systems. However, in comparing homogeneous with heterogeneous ethnic societies, issues are compounded in the latter. Suppose, for example, there are three major economic classes and three major age strata, then the homogeneous society will have eighteen age-economic-sex specific combinations. The addition of two major ethnic strata means a doubling to thirty-six combinations. If there were three major ethnic strata, then there would be fifty-four combinations and so forth.

One significant question revolves about the development of unity within an ethnic group that is potentially also divided by economic and other forms of stratification. There are some basically conflicting interests if a subordinate ethnic group contains members of more than one economic strata. The more prosperous members of the ethnic group face special issues that deal with the conversion of their income into the rewards normally enjoyed by equivalent class members within the dominant ethnic group. Such problems arise as housing, education, prestige, political power, recreation, and the like. For those members of the same ethnic group who also occupy poorly paying positions, employment and occupation may become the dominant issue. The conditions under which the different class segments of an ethnic group will unite on the ethnic stratification issue, as opposed to pursuing their somewhat independent class interests, requires further empirical study. This is a particularly crucial problem since it may atomize the potential power of

207

the subordinate ethnic group. Such contradictions may also be confusing for the political leaders of the dominant ethnic groups.

The conditions under which class or ethnic stratification will become most salient for the dominant ethnic group also require further investigation. In the case of the South, for example, civil rights may override other issues and hence mould both the parties and the electorate accordingly. Other issues that are class-specific may become subordinated and neglected because of the confounding of ethnic stratification. In the case of public housing, welfare, and other forms of aid for the lower income segments in the United States, undoubtedly the issues are far more complex because of the ramifications any decision holds for ethnic stratification independently of the class interests.

A CONCLUDING NOTE

There are two main points to this essay. First, ethnic relations is a distinctive form of stratification since only these strata hold the potential for forming their own separate nation-state. As a consequence, there are certain unique theoretical issues in the study of such groups that cannot be resolved through an application of other stratification theories. The conditions under which subordinate ethnic groups will accept or not accept the existing political entity is one that requires further elaboration. But it is also necessary to consider the ways in which the potential threat of separatism may modify and affect the existing nation-state in terms of its existing economic stratification and its power structure.

The second point revolves about the relations between ethnic stratification and other hierarchical systems in the society such as those based on age, sex, and wealth. Even when separatism is not a particularly salient issue, the presence of stratified ethnic groups will tend to alter and affect some of the remaining stratification systems. In this regard, for example, it is likely that economic class alliances will be weaker than in comparable countries that are homogeneous in their ethnic composition. Likewise, the presence of an ethnic stratification system is often a basic prerequisite to the creation of certain economic strata among the dominant ethnic group.

REFERENCES

BLALOCK, HUBERT M., JR. (1967) *Toward a Theory of Minority-group Relations.* New York: John Wiley & Sons, Inc.

BLAU, PETER M. and DUNCAN, OTIS DUDLEY (1967) *The American Occupational Structure.* New York: John Wiley & Sons, Inc.

HACKER, HELEN MAYER (1951) "Women as a minority group." *Social Forces* 30 (October), 60–69.

HODGE, ROBERT W. and HODGE, PATRICIA (1965) "Occupational assimilation as a competitive process." *The American Journal of Sociology* 71 (November), 249–64.

HUGHES, EVERETT CHERRINGTON and HUGHES, HELEN MACGILL (1952) *Where Peoples Meet.* Glencoe, Illinois: The Free Press.

JACKSON, ELTON F. and CURTIS, RICHARD F. (1968) "Conceptualization and measurement in the study of social stratification", pp. 112–49 in HUBERT M. BLALOCK, Jr. and ANN B. BLALOCK (eds.), *Methodology in Social Research.* New York: McGraw-Hill Book Co.

KUPER, LEO, WATTS, HILSTON and DAVIES, RONALD (1958) *Durban: a Study in Racial Ecology.* London: Jonathan Cape.

LIEBERSON, STANLEY and FUGUITT, GLEN V. (1967) "Negro–white occupational differences in the absence of discrimination." *The American Journal of Sociology* 73 (September), 188–200.

LIND, ANDREW W. (1955) "Occupation and race on certain frontiers", pp. 49–70 in ANDREW W. LIND (ed.), *Race Relations in World Perspective.* Honolulu, Hawaii: University of Hawaii Press.

MYRDAL, GUNNAR (1944) *An American Dilemma.* New York: Harper & Brothers, Publishers.

SIEGEL, PAUL M. (1965) "On the cost of being a negro." *Sociological Inquiry* 35 (Winter), 41–57.

SOROKIN, PITIRIM A. (1959) *Social and Cultural Mobility.* Glencoe, Illinois: The Free Press.

UNITED NATIONS—COMMISSION ON HUMAN RIGHTS (1950) *Definition and Classification of Minorities.* Lake Success, New York: United Nations Publications.

WHEELER, GEOFFREY (1960) *Racial Problems in Soviet Muslim Asia.* London: Oxford University Press.

Distance Mechanisms of Stratification[*]

Pierre L. van den Berghe

Many observers and students of race relations have pointed to an apparent paradox in the practice of segregation in the Southern United States and elsewhere. Although the majority of Southern whites believe in school segregation between Negro and white pupils, they have no objection to entrusting their children to colored servants.[1] At the height of Jim Crowism in the South, Negro nurses in charge of white children were admitted without question to "white" railway carriages, public parks, and the like.[2] Although many white Southerners would not think of inviting a Negro university professor to dinner in their home, they do not object to having their food cooked and served by a colored servant. To cite a more macabre illustration from another culture, Indian medical students in South Africa are not allowed to watch a postmortem examination performed on a white corpse, but that very corpse is sewed up after the autopsy by a black hospital attendant.[3]

Incongruous though such attitudes and practices may seem, the paradox is only apparent. As observed by several social scientists, the key to the problem is *social status*.[4] As long as the social status of the "races" is unequal, segre-

[*]We are indebted to Professors Talcott Parsons and Gordon W. Allport for stimulating advice and criticism, but the responsibility for the views contained in this paper is entirely our own.

[1]Cf. Charles S. Johnson, *Patterns of Negro Segregation* (New York: Harper & Brothers, 1943), p. 118.

[2]Cf. Robert E. Park, *Race and Culture* (Glencoe: The Free Press, 1950), p. 241.

[3]Cf. G. H. Calpin, *Indians in South Africa* (Pietermaritzburg: Shuter & Shester, 1949), p. 105.

[4]Cf. Park, *op. cit.*, pp. 181–2, 232–3; Gunnar Myrdal, *An American Dilemma* (New York: Harper & Brothers, 1944), p. 582; G. W. Allport, *The Nature of Prejudice* (Cambridge: Addison-Wesley Publishing Company, 1954), pp. 234, 276, 319–23; J. Greenblum and L. I. Pearlin, "Vertical Mobility and Prejudice", in R. Bendix and S. Lipset, *Class, Status and Power* (Glencoe: The Free Press, 1953), pp. 480–500.

gation need not be enforced. In the field of "social therapy", the importance of the status variable in changing prevailing stereotypes and attitudes has been demonstrated by many empirical studies.[5] Contact *per se* does not reduce prejudice, but equal status contact does, barring conditions of competition whether real or perceived. In this paper we shall attempt to draw more general theoretical conclusions from these observations and findings.

The central concept to be used here is that of *distance* as a mechanism of stratification. Some form of distance is presumably a functional prerequisite in any social situation involving authority, hierarchy, or stratification. For analytical purposes, forms of distance can be classified as *spatial* (of which segregation is a notable instance) and *social* (e.g. etiquette and sumptuary regulations). No formal definitions of the two terms are required, as the meaning of the first term is self-evident, and the second term already has a long history in social science.[6]

Presumably, a combination of both forms of distance will be present in any hierarchical or authoritative situation, though in various combinations. Distance is a major mechanism of social control for the maintenance of authority and hierarchy. If everything else remains constant, close physical or social contact can be achieved only at a "cost" in authority and hierarchization.

In order to illustrate the generality of the above propositions, three examples will be given before drawing the implications of the concept of distance for the field of race and ethnic relations.

In the relations between the sexes in Western culture, "gallantry" is a form of social distance. It has been repeatedly observed that, at least in Western societies, the lower the status of women is in relation to that of men, the more punctilious the rules of gallantry are. In Italy, Spain, Portugal, and Latin America, where the status of women is the lowest of all Western countries, both gallantry and spatial distance (chaperonage, etc.) are the

[5]Cf. M. Deutsch and M. B. Collins, *Interracial Housing* (Minneapolis: University of Minnesota Press, 1951); Allport, *op. cit.*, pp. 261–81; D. M. Wilner, R. P. Walkley, and S. W. Cook, "Residential Proximity and Intergroup Relations in Public Housing Projects", *Journal of Social Issues*, **8**, 45–69; F. T. Smith, "An Experiment in Modifying Attitudes Toward the Negro", *Teachers College Contributions to Education*, No. 887, 1943; M. Jahoda and P. S. West, "Race Relations in Public Housing", *Journal of Social Issues* **7**, 132–9.
[6]Cf. Park, *op. cit.*, p. 183; E. S. Bogardus, *Sociology* (New York: The Macmillan Company, 1954), p. 536.

211

most developed. The reverse is true of the Anglo-Saxon and Scandinavian countries. Other European nations occupy an intermediate position; modern France, for example, still practices much gallantry (though hand-kissing is rapidly disappearing), but relatively little segregation of the sexes. The hope of some American women to revive gallantry while preserving a measure of status equality with men seems to be a forlorn Utopia. Similarly, as the status gap between the sexes decreases, differences in dress become less (sumptuary regulations are also a form of social distance). In the Islamic countries, the relatively low status of women is accompanied by a great amount of segregation.

The problem of authority of adults over children in the family, whether nuclear or extended, offers another illustration of the principle of distance. In order to maintain such authority, a combination of spatial and social distance is at work. Though spatial distance is minimal, some form of "segregation" in sleeping or eating arrangements is generally present. But social distance is of paramount importance here. Homans and Schneider have indicated that the child must show respect and restraint toward the adult who has authority over him—his father in patrilineal societies, his mother's brother in the matrilineal case.[7]

The military is another illustration of the institutionalization of distance. Since the military hierarchy is very rigid, a high degree of both spatial and social distance separates commissioned officers from the lower ranks. In the case of a peace-time army, spatial distance between officers and men is very great indeed. Living quarters, dining halls, recreation facilities, and the like are segregated. Whatever physical contact officers and men have is ritualized under a rigid etiquette known in the U.S. Armed Forces as "military courtesy". This etiquette, which most enlisted men (excepting a few old "accommodated" N.C.O.'s) find irksome and superfluous, is probably a "safety margin" intended for war-time conditions, when spatial distance breaks down to a large extent. Besides close physical contact under battle conditions, one of the two main kinds of *social* distance to which the Army resorts, namely, uniform differences (i.e. a form of sumptuary regulation), is

---

[7]Cf. G. C. Homans and D. M. Schneider, *Marriage, Authority and Final Causes*, p. 58. Interestingly enough, the authority relationship seems to preclude a close affective relationship to the same person. This finding is further corroborated by Bales' polarity between the "idea-man" and the "best-liked" man in his small group studies. Cf. T. Parsons, R. F. Bales, and E. A. Shils, *Working Papers in the Theory of Action* (Glencoe: The Free Press, 1953), p. 147.

also reduced in combat. Battle uniforms are nearly identical for all ranks in modern armies. Hence, etiquette remains as the principal mainstay of authority under the conditions which constitute the very *raison d'être* of military organizations. It is, therefore, little wonder that "military courtesy" should be cultivated in peace time to a degree which appears excessive to most people concerned.

In the above illustration, we have indicated that spatial and social forms of distance can be not only complementary, but also alternative to each other. As a further indication of this, it may be pointed out that the Navy, in which spatial distance aboard ships in peace time is by necessity lesser than in peace-time Army units on land, has an even more rigid etiquette than the Army. Furthermore, sumptuary regulations (another device of social distance) are much more pronounced in the Navy than in the Army. Whereas Army uniforms have become "democratized", the difference between the uniform of a sailor and that of a Navy officer is still very great. Given a like requirement for authority as between Navy and Army, it may be said that the Navy "compensates" for its lesser degree of spatial distance with a greater degree of social distance.

We can now turn to some implications of the above considerations for the field of race relations. In a previous paper we have suggested a typology of racial prejudice.[8] We distinguish two ideal-types which we call *paternalistic* and *competitive*. The paternalistic type is characterized among other traits by the existence of a rigid and elaborate etiquette of race relations, and the relative absence of segregation. In the competitive type, the reverse relationship between spatial and social distance prevails: the etiquette is ill-defined and not complex, whereas segregation is pronounced.

In the paternalistic situation, where the type-role between members of different racial castes is the master–servant relationship, close physical and emotional ties between the castes prevail.[9] Doyle and Park were among the first social scientists to recognize the crucial importance of etiquette in such an "accommodative" sort of race relations. Park defines etiquette as a social ritual which maintains social distance. Etiquette, concludes Doyle, makes a measure of cooperation possible by preserving rank and order of precedence

---

[8]Cf. Pierre L. van den Berghe, "The Dynamics of Racial Prejudice: An Ideal-type Dichotomy", *Social Forces*, **37**, 128–41.

[9]One of the important corollaries of these close ties is the prevalence of miscegenation under a system of institutionalized concubinage. Cf. Pierre L. van den Berghe, *ibid.*, p. 139.

between the groups in presence. Myrdal speaks of etiquette as one of the primary mechanisms of social control that permits intimacy of contact coupled with status inequality.[10]

When because of a complex of factors such as social and geographical mobility brought about by industrialization and urbanization, the paternalistic type of race relations breaks down, etiquette ceases to be an effective mechanism to preserve distance between the racial castes in presence. One of the requirements for an effective functioning of etiquette is that the roles be *unambiguous*; this condition ceases to prevail when the traditional master–servant ties are disrupted. As the situation evolves toward what we have called the competitive type of race relations, segregation is introduced as an alternative means of maintenance of the caste hierarchy.

In the context of race relations, segregation and etiquette emerge, then, as two primary mechanisms of spatial and social distance, respectively. Both are aimed at preserving a caste hierarchy of socially defined "races".[11] In so far as etiquette and segregation in this case are both based on the ascriptive criterion of "race", they involve a "cost" in efficiency, at least in the sense of *Zwecksrationalität*. There is, however, an important respect in which etiquette and segregation are functionally different from each other. Etiquette involves a great measure of *functional differentiation* in the sense that members of the various castes perform tasks which are largely *complementary*. Segregation, on the contrary, involves a large degree of *segmentation without differentiation* in so far as tasks, facilities, and functions are *duplicatory* rather than complementary. If the "separate but equal" doctrine is applied, the "cost" of segregation is maximized. This fact is one of the reasons why the "separate but equal" precept has remained a Utopia, even when interpreted in purely physical terms, quite apart from subjective, psychological considerations.

If these considerations are correct, we can see that segregation involves an even greater "cost" in the efficiency of the social system than etiquette. Indeed, etiquette in a relatively stable, preindustrial, paternalistic type of society can perform a definitely adjustive function. To the extent that roles are ritualized and unambiguous, and that everyone "knows his place", race

[10]Cf. Doyle, *op. cit.*, p. 171; Myrdal, *op. cit.*, p. 612; Park, *op. cit.*, p. 183.

[11]In the use of the term "caste", we follow the Warner–Dollard–Myrdal–Davis, and Gardner definition. Cf. John Dollard, *Caste and Class in a Southern Town* (New Haven: Yale University Press, 1937), pp. 62–97; Myrdal, *op. cit.*, pp. 674–5; W. L. Warner, "American Caste and Class", *American Journal of Sociology*, **42**: 234. We dissent from Cox' usage of the term. Cf. Cox, *Caste, Class and Race* (New York: Doubleday and Company, 1948), pp. 3–5, 427–8, 489–98, 539.

relations will be relatively stable and peaceful.[12] On the other hand, segregation in an industrial competitive society is inherently dysfunctional for the social system as a whole. The extent of "functionality" as between the two types of prejudice is one of the major differences between the paternalistic and the competitive types.[13]

We can now turn to two brief illustrations of etiquette and segregation as alternative mechanisms of color-caste hierachization. It is a well-known fact that segregation in the Southern United States increased markedly after the Civil War. In the ante-bellum paternalistic South, the type-role between whites and Negroes was the master–slave relationship.[14] This is, of course, not to say that *all* Negroes were slaves and *all* whites, or even a majority of whites, were slaveholders. But most Negro–white contacts up to Emancipation were of the master–slave variety. There was some spatial segregation between whites and Negroes, particularly for field slaves. But house servants lived in very close spatial contact with their masters, as chambermaids, concubines, "mammies", body servants, etc. They often lived in the "big house" of the plantation as members of the patriarchal household; they worshipped in the same churches as their masters; white and Negro children played together.[15] It is far from our intention to romanticize the past and evoke images of happy singing slaves. But the fact remains that masters and slaves lived in comparatively close spatial symbiosis, and that most whites did not look with horror on physical contact with Negroes. Miscegenation was widely tolerated and frequent, though, of course, intermarriage was unknown.[16] Nevertheless, there existed a rigid caste line, which, in the relative absence of segregation, was maintained by a complex etiquette. The Negro had to "know his place", exhibit the proper marks of subservience, use the appropriate titles in addressing whites. Ideally, he internalized his lower caste status, and accepted his master's estimate of his own worth.[17]

---

[12]This is *not* to say that "efficiency" in the sense of economic rationality will be maximized.

[13]Cf. Pierre, L. van den Berghe, *op. cit.*, p. 141.

[14]Cf. Myrdal, *op. cit.*, p. 592–3.

[15]Cf. C. Vann Woodward, *The Strange Career of Jim Crow* (New York: Oxford University Press, 1955), pp. 24–5; Charles Wagley and Marvin Harris, *Minorities in the New World* (New York: Columbia University Press, 1958), pp. 89, 122.

[16]Cf. Mydral, *op. cit.*, pp. 124–6; L. Wirth and H. Goldhamer, "The Hybrid and the Problem of Miscegenation", in Otto Klineberg, editor, *Characteristics of the American Negro* (New York: Harper & Brothers, 1944), p. 267.

[17]Cf. Myrdal, p. 701; Wagley and Harris, *op. cit.*, p. 122.

Of course, much of that etiquette has survived Emancipation in the South, particularly in the rural regions of the Black Belt. The Civil War, however, disrupted very abruptly the old master–slave relationship, with the result that the South moved from paternalistic to a competitive type of race relations. With the subsequent migration of Negroes to cities, and the rise of industrialization in the South, the old etiquette, which was based on stable, highly particularistic and personalized ties, became rapidly incompatible with the changing situation. The increased mobility of Negroes, both spatially and socially, made the crystallization of a new etiquette difficult.[18] Whatever was left of the old etiquette was only a vanishing survival of another era. If the color-caste order was to be maintained, new mechanisms had to be devised.

One of these new mechanisms was the lynching of Negroes, which increased very rapidly at the end of the Civil War. Another mechanism was segregation. In his history of segregation, C. Vann Woodward rightly points out that the main wave of Jim Crowism did not set in until some twenty years after the end of the Reconstruction era. But some important aspects of segregation were introduced during the Reconstruction period, notably segregation in churches and in schools.[19]

The lull in the implementation of segregation between the end of the Reconstruction period and the wave of Jim Crowism of the 1890's is to be accounted for, in large part, by the fact that the "Redeemer" politicians were mostly members of the old slave-owning aristocracy, with a strong tradition of paternalism. With the downfall of this upper-class white rule, segregation and political disenfranchisement followed. Extralegal segregation anticipated even the most drastic Jim Crow laws.[20] A whole set of rationalizations was developed to justify segregation. Negroes were considered unclean, smelly, lascivious, and hence, the thought of close physical contact became abhorrent to most whites. Miscegenation was seriously condemned and probably much less common.[21]

A dramatic illustration of etiquette and segregation as alternative mechanisms of caste hierarchy is provided by the housing situation in American cities. In the older cities of the South, such as Charleston, South Carolina, which had a sizeable Negro population before the Civil War, there is relatively little racial segregation in housing. Many Negroes live in back alleys

[18]Cf. Johnson, *op. cit.*, pp. 119, 139; Myrdal, *op. cit.*, pp. 611, 614.
[19]Cf. Woodward, *op. cit.*, pp. 14–15; Doyle, *op. cit.*, pp. 122–3.
[20]Cf. Woodward, *op. cit.*, pp. 29–30, 38–9, 51–2, 66–9, 81–4.
[21]Cf. Wirth and Goldhamer, *op. cit.*, pp. 273–4.

near "white" houses, in what were formerly servants' quarters. In these cities, which are little industrialized, the traditional etiquette of race relations is still operative. This situation contrasts markedly with the high degree of residential segregation in the newer industrial cities of the South and in the Negro ghettos of the Northern cities. In these cities, conditions of rapid migration and industrialization prevent the establishment of a rigid racial etiquette.[22]

From this very cursory examination of the racial situation in the Southern United States, we would suggest that etiquette and segregation are two main mechanisms of caste hierarchization in a multiracial society.[23] Segregation, the more "costly" of the two major mechanisms, was introduced as an attempt to salvage the color-caste system, which was undermined by the decay of the old etiquette. If these conclusions are correct, then it would be safe to predict that the present attack on segregation in the United States must lead to a decline in the importance of color as a criterion of hierarchization.[24]

Another illustration of the shift from etiquette to segregation is the case of South Africa. The Cape Colony in the seventeenth and eighteenth centuries had a paternalistic slave-owning type of society similar in many ways to that of the Southern United States, though on a much smaller scale. Masters and slaves lived in close, intimate physical contact. Miscegenation was common, and interracial concubinage was institutionalized. Masters and slaves worshipped together. Household servants often lived in the same house as their masters; female slaves did sewing and embroidery work together with their mistresses in the family parlor.[25]

Yet, there was a rigid color-caste system, which was maintained by an

---

[22]Cf. Wagley and Harris, *op. cit.*, pp. 143–6.

[23]Other mechanisms, such as sumptuary regulations, lynchings, and pogroms, may also be present, but are of secondary importance. Lynching in the American South, for example, seems to have been resorted to mostly when and where other mechanisms had been unsuccessful in preserving the traditional caste hierarchy, and when the breakdown of that hierarchy was perceived as a threat by the dominant caste. In that sense, lynching was a "last resort" mechanism.

[24]This is, of course, not to say that *racial prejudice* will disappear, but rather that a rigid system of color-caste will be seriously undermined, as, indeed, it already is.

[25]Cf. C. G. Botha, *Social Life in the Cape Colony in the 18th Century* (Cape Town: Juta & Co., 1926), pp. 45, 97; I. D. MacCrone, *Race Attitudes in South Africa* (London: Oxford University Press, 1937), p. 69; J. S. Marias, *The Cape Coloured People*, 1652–1937 (New York: Longmans, Green and Co., 1939), pp. 162–7, 169.

elaborate etiquette of race relations with a wealth of terms of address.[26] With the abolition of slavery in 1834, the discovery of the diamond and gold mines later in the nineteenth century, and the large-scale industrialization and urbanization since the Anglo–Boer War of 1899–1902, South Africa has moved steadily toward a competitive type of prejudice. Although, as in the Southern United States, relics of the old system of race relations can still be found, etiquette as a mechanism of caste hierarchy has been seriously undermined, and racial segregation has been substituted for it.

Since 1948, the *apartheid* policies of the Nationalist Government have received much publicity. Because of space limitations, it is impossible to review all the segregation legislation passed by the South African Parliament. *Apartheid*, to be sure, represents a post-World War II intensification of the segregation doctrines, but it is merely a new label for a long-standing practice in South Africa. The *apartheid* program is the culmination of a trend that started with the establishment of Native Reserves under a British administration in the middle of the nineteenth century. By now, the wave of color-bar legislation and extralegal segregation has covered most aspects of life.[27]

Contrary to the recent trend in the United States, South Africa has been moving toward increasing segregation in the last decade. But powerful economic and ideological forces militate against the long-range success of *apartheid*. In both countries, the built-in dysfunctional nature of racial segregation in an industrial society is well illustrated. Though segregation was introduced in both cases, at least in part, in response to changing conditions of industrialization and urbanization, segregation conflicts with certain functional prerequisites of any industrial society. Among these necessary conditions are mobility of the labor force, "rational" criteria of recruitment based on achievement and universalism, and functional differentiation, all of which are impeded by racial segregation.

Besides economic forces, segregation also undergoes a powerful ideological onslaught in the United States. South Africa, in spite of her relative cultural isolation, cannot escape a similar onslaught on *apartheid*. It seems,

[26]Cf. Botha, *op. cit.*, p. 50; Sheila Patterson, *Colour and Culture in South Africa* (London: Routledge and Kegan Paul, 1953), pp. 139–40.

[27]Cf. G. H. Calpin, *op. cit.*, pp. 23, 33, 91, 169–71; G. M. Carter, *The Politics of Inequality, South Africa Since 1948* (New York: Frederick A. Praeger, 1958); E. P. Dvorin, *Racial Separation in South Africa* (Chicago: University of Chicago Press, 1952); Leo Kuper, "The Control of Social Change, A South African Experiment", *Social Forces*, October 1954.

thus, that racial segregation, at least in a Western industrial society, truly contains the "seeds of its own destruction".

In summary, we have suggested that: (1) some form of distance, whether spatial or social, is basic to any situation involving authority, hierarchy, or stratification; (2) etiquette, i.e. social distance, and segregation, i.e. spatial distance, are basic mechanisms of hierarchization in a racial caste situation; (3) these two mechanisms have tended to vary in inverse relation to each other during the transition of multiracial societies from a paternalistic to a competitive type of race relations; (4) whereas etiquette in a preindustrial, paternalistic society can be an adjustive mechanism, segregation in a competitive industrial society is inherently dysfunctional; (5) given the failure of both etiquette and segregation as mechanisms of color-caste hierarchization, physical appearance or "race" must decrease in importance as a criterion of status, at least in Western industrial societies. This does not mean, however, that racial prejudice will disappear in any forseeable future.

Patterns of Occupational Mobility among Negro Men

OTIS DUDLEY DUNCAN*

THE first reasonably adequate data on occupational mobility of American men became available only in 1964.[1] The initial tabulations did not include a breakdown by race, but this information is now at hand. Previous reports on patterns of mobility in the total male population[2] may be supplemented by a comparison of the patterns observed among Negro and non-Negro men.

The reader should note the departure from the conventional pattern of presentation by color—white and "nonwhite". In the population under study, estimated at 39,969,000 men aged 25 to 64 years in March, 1962 (all civilians in this age group plus some 718,000 members of the armed forces who were living off post or with their families on post), there were 3,514,000 Negroes, 459,000 other nonwhites, and 35,996,000 whites. Classifying the "other nonwhites" with the whites hardly disturbs the latter category, but removes a serious contamination of the "nonwhite" group when that group is to be studied primarily for the information it conveys about Negroes (as is usually the case).

*University of Michigan. This report was supported by contract No. OE-5-85-072 with the United States Office of Education, for a project, "Socio-economic Background and Occupational Achievement". The data were collected by the United States Bureau of the Census under a grant from the National Science Foundation.

[1]U.S. Bureau of the Census, "Lifetime Occupational Mobility of Adult Males: March 1962", *Current Population Reports*, Series P-23, No. 11, May 12, 1964.

[2]Peter M. Blau, "The Flow of Occupational Supply and Recruitment", *American Sociological Review*, 30 (August 1965), 475–90; Otis Dudley Duncan, "Occupation Trends and Patterns of Net Mobility in the United States", *Demography*, 3, 1 (1966), 1–18.

NET SHIFTS

Respondents to the questionnaire on "Occupational Changes in a Generation", administered as a supplement to the March, 1962 Current Population Survey, were classified by occupation at three stages in the life cycle: the occupation of the father (or other family head) as of the respondent's sixteenth year; the respondent's first full-time civilian job; and the respondent's current occupation in March 1962. (This pertained to the job held during the survey week for the employed, and to the last job held for the experienced unemployed.) The occupation classification is the conventional census major occupation grouping, extended by sub-classifications according to industry or class of worker, or condensed by combining major groups into broader categories. There are three mobility tables, representing the transition from father's occupation to first job, from first job to 1962 occupation, and from father's occupation to 1962 occupation. Marginal distributions of these tables, using the extended classification, are shown for Negro and non-Negro men in Table 1.

A significant shift is observed, between the distributions at the first and second stages of the life cycle and again between the second and third. When classified by father's occupation, Negro men are "over-represented" at the level of service occupations and all lower categories and "underrepresented" among all higher categories.[3] When the classification is by first job, the same pattern prevails, except that there is overrepresentation in one additional category—nonmanufacturing operatives. In terms of 1962 occupations, there are two further variations: underrepresentation among farmers and overrepresentation among both categories of operatives.

There is considerable resemblance between the patterns of net shifts between career stages for Negroes and non-Negroes, but some major dissimilarities warrant notice. From father's occupation to first job, there is a net shift into service jobs and sales work (other than retail) for Negroes, but not for non-Negroes. Non-Negroes experienced net shifts into salaried professional employment, while the Negroes did not. From first job to 1962, net shifts occurred for Negroes, but not for non-Negroes, into nonmanufac-

---

[3]To avoid misunderstanding, it should be stated that the terms "over-" and "underrepresentation" refer merely to the relative size of the percentages of Negro and non-Negro men in a category, without regard to whether that situation is desirable or not. Reference to "higher" and "lower" categories, moreover, is simply a convenience in discussing the occupation groups as arranged in Table 1, where the ordering corresponds only very roughly to a socioeconomic ranking of occupations.

221

TABLE 1. PERCENTAGE DISTRIBUTION BY OCCUPATIONAL ORIGINS AND
DESTINATIONS (EXTENDED CLASSIFICATION), BY RACE, FOR CIVILIAN MEN
AGED 25–64 YEARS, FOR THE UNITED STATES, MARCH 1962

Occupation	Father's occupation		First job		1962 occupation	
	Negro	Non-Negro	Negro	Non-Negro	Negro	Non-Negro
Professional, technical and kindred workers						
1. Self-employed	0.4	1.3	0.3	0.7	0.2	1.6
2. Salaried	2.2	3.1	1.5	7.8	2.5	10.9
Managers, officials, and proprietors, except farm						
3. Salaried	0.4	3.8	0.2	1.3	1.1	8.6
4. Self-employed	0.9	7.7	0.1	0.6	1.4	7.5
Sales						
5. Other	0.1	2.1	0.2	1.5	0.1	3.4
6. Retail	0.5	1.8	1.2	5.1	0.5	1.6
7. Clerical	1.0	3.3	3.6	11.3	4.8	6.3
Craftsmen, foremen, and kindred workers						
8. Manufacturing	1.6	6.1	1.1	3.4	3.1	7.6
9. Construction	3.2	5.0	1.1	2.3	2.9	5.1
10. Other	2.3	6.8	1.7	4.0	3.5	7.5
Operatives and kindred workers						
11. Manufacturing	4.7	7.9	12.0	15.2	11.6	9.8
12. Other	4.3	6.8	11.2	11.0	11.4	7.2
13. Service	5.5	4.2	10.4	3.2	15.2	4.5
Laborers						
14. Manufacturing	4.0	1.5	7.8	4.8	6.4	1.7
15. Others	9.2	3.7	14.4	7.4	17.6	3.0
16. Farmers	34.5	25.0	3.2	3.1	3.1	5.4
17. Farm laborers	5.0	2.4	21.2	13.6	4.6	1.4
18. Not reported[a]	20.3	7.3	8.9	3.7	10.0	6.9
Total	100.0	100.0	100.0	100.0	100.0	100.0
Number (000)	3,514	36,455	3,514	36,455	3,514	36,455

turing laborer and operative pursuits and into clerical occupations. Non-Negroes, unlike Negroes, underwent net shifts into farming (owners and tenants), non-retail sales jobs, and professional self-employment. Among the seventeen occupations, there were six for which the composite pattern of net shifts, father's to first occupation and first to 1962 occupation, showed disparity by race. Negroes failed to match the non-Negro pattern of net shifts into self-employed professional jobs in 1962, into salaried professional first jobs, and into farming in 1962, and failed to match the net shifts out of clerical first jobs, out of first jobs as manufacturing operatives, and away from father's occupation in nonmanufacturing operative pursuits. Although only net shifts have been discussed thus far, it is clear that the occupational history of Negroes differs in many particulars from that of whites.

The Negro sample is too small to permit analysis of gross mobility in the 18×18 mobility tables. Nevertheless, some striking results at this level of occupational detail can be obtained by an indirect method. For the total male sample, it is possible to compute the transition matrix from each of the mobility tables, showing the probability that a man originating in occupation group i finds his destination in occupation group j, for each of the 324 (i,j) pairs. The "expected" destination distribution for either Negroes or non-Negroes is obtained by multiplying the origin distribution of that racial category by the transition matrix for all men. The assumption, in other words, is that the pattern of gross mobility is the same for Negroes and non-Negroes. The "expected" distributions so derived appear in Table 2. Differences between the "expected" destination distributions of Negroes and non-Negroes are solely a function of the differences in origin distributions. These differences may be taken to measure the impact of differentials in origin status, apart from differentials in subsequent mobility experience.

It is apparent from the strong patterning of the differences in Table 2 that the differences in origins are consequential. Even with the same probabilities of mobility, but given the difference in father's occupation, Negro first jobs manifest overrepresentation among service workers and all lower categories and underrepresentation in all higher categories. Similarly, when

---

[a]Father's occupation or first job was not reported, or the respondent was not experienced in the civilian labor force (1962).

Source: March 1962 Current Population Survey and supplementary questionnaire, "Occupational Changes in a Generation" (unpublished tables). See "Lifetime Occupational Mobility of Adult Males: March 1962", *Current Population Reports*, p. 23, No. 11, May 12, 1964, for definitions and explanations.

TABLE 2. PERCENTAGE DISTRIBUTION BY "EXPECTED" OCCUPATIONAL
DESTINATIONS (EXTENDED CLASSIFICATION), BY RACE, FOR CIVILIAN MEN AGED
25–64 YEARS, FOR THE UNITED STATES, MARCH 1962

Occupation	First job, from father's occupation		1962 occupation, from first job		1962 occupation, from father's occupation	
	Negro	Non-Negro	Negro	Non-Negro	Negro	Non-Negro
Professional, technical and kindred workers						
1. Self-employed	0.4	0.7	0.7	1.5	0.9	1.5
2. Salaried	4.8	7.5	6.1	10.6	7.1	10.5
Managers, officials, and proprietors, except farm						
3. Salaried	0.7	1.3	5.5	8.2	5.7	8.2
4. Self-employed	0.3	0.6	6.1	7.1	6.0	7.1
Sales						
5. Other	0.7	1.4	2.1	3.2	2.0	3.2
6. Retail	3.7	4.8	1.4	1.6	1.4	1.6
7. Clerical	8.4	10.8	4.8	6.3	5.9	6.2
Craftsmen, foremen, and kindred workers						
8. Manufacturing	2.6	3.3	6.9	7.2	7.0	7.2
9. Construction	2.0	2.2	5.4	4.8	5.2	4.9
10. Other	3.3	3.9	7.5	7.1	7.3	7.1
Operatives and kindred workers						
11. Manufacturing	14.2	15.0	11.3	9.8	11.3	9.8
12. Other	10.8	11.0	8.9	7.4	8.6	7.5
13. Service	4.1	3.8	7.4	5.3	6.7	5.3
Laborers						
14. Manufacturing	5.7	5.0	2.7	2.1	2.7	2.1
15. Other	9.3	7.9	5.7	4.1	5.8	4.1
16. Farmers	4.2	3.0	6.5	5.0	6.8	5.0
17. Farm laborers	19.8	13.7	2.3	1.6	2.4	1.6
18. Not reported[a]	5.1	4.1	8.7	7.0	7.4	7.2
Total	100.0	100.0	100.0	100.0	100.0	100.0

[a]Father's occupation or first job was not reported or the respondent was not experienced in the civilian labor force 1962.

224

mobility from first job to 1962 occupation is (hypothetically) the same for Negroes and non-Negroes, the former are overrepresented in the last nine categories and underrepresented in the first nine. Using the same kind of hypothesis for mobility over the total span from father's occupation to 1962, we find Negro overrepresentation in all farm and manual occupations, except manufacturing craftsmen (where there is near parity), and under-representation at all white-collar levels.

Despite the evident importance of origins in producing occupational differentials at the time of working-force entry or as of 1962, the same analysis shows that this source of disparity is much less important than are differentials in mobility patterns. This conclusion is reached by summarizing the differences between Negroes and non-Negroes in both actual and "expected" destination distributions, as well as in origin distributions, by means of the index of dissimilarity (the sum of the positive percentage-point differences between corresponding entries in the respective Negro and non-Negro distributions). Index values are shown in Table 3.

Consider the transition from father's occupation to first job. In terms of

TABLE 3. INDEXES OF DISSIMILARITY AND NET MOBILITY, SUMMARIZING COMPARISONS OF OCCUPATIONAL MOBILITY (EXTENDED CLASSIFICATION) OF NEGRO AND NON-NEGRO MEN AGED 25–64 YEARS, FOR THE UNITED STATES, MARCH 1962

Comparison	Father's occupation to first job	First job to 1962 occupation	Father's occupation to 1962 occupation
Dissimilarity between Negro and Non-Negro, with respect to:			
Origins	34.4	30.4	34.4
Destinations	30.4	42.3	42.3
"Expected" destinations	10.7	12.1	9.5
Net Mobility, Origin to Destination			
Negro	47.6	19.3	42.6
Non-Negro	45. 6	37.3	22.1

Source: Tables 1 and 2.

225

origins (in this case, father's occupation) the dissimilarity between Negroes and non-Negroes amounts to 34.4 percent. Given this disparity, but assuming that Negroes and non-Negroes have the same probabilities of moving from a given origin to each destination, a dissimilarity of only 10.7 percent would be observed in terms of first jobs. This "expected" dissimilarity is only one-third as large as the actual dissimilarity of first jobs—30.4 percent.

Similarly, given a common matrix of transition probabilities to describe the movement from first jobs to 1962 occupations, the dissimilarity of 30.4 percent observed at the origin stage would shrink to 12.1 percent at the destination. The actual result, however, is a dissimilarity of 42.3 percent at the destination, or about three and one-half times the "expected" dissimilarity.

Looking finally at the whole period, father's occupation to 1962 occupation, we see that the initial dissimilarity of 34.4 percent is transformed into a dissimilarity of 42.3 percent at the destination, although the latter would have been only two-ninths as great (9.5 percent) had Negroes and non-Negroes been subject to the same probabilities of occupational mobility.

If the data had been available for a sufficiently large sample, the foregoing mental experiment could have been designed in a different way. Assume Negroes and non-Negroes have the same origin distributions (say, that of all men), but their actual transition matrices. The resulting differences in destination distributions, as compared with the actual differences, would then measure the relative importance of the mobility patterns as against the differentials at origin. A comparison of the two types of experiment (which correspond, respectively, to the demographer's conventional indirect and direct standardization) in another case[4] suggests that the conclusion would be much the same: most of the difference in destinations is produced by differences in mobility patterns, and only the lesser part is due to the difference in origins.

For those concerned with rectification of racial inequalities in occupational status, the conclusion may seem either encouraging or discouraging. On the one hand, if barriers to Negro mobility (call them "discrimination" if you like) could be removed, there would ensue a rapid convergence of Negro and non-Negro occupation distributions. On the other hand, raising the level of the Negro "input" to the mobility process, but leaving that process

[4]Otis Dudley Duncan, "Methodological Issues in the Analysis of Social Mobility", *Social Structure and Mobility in Economic Development*, ed. N. J. Smelser and S. M. Lipset Chicago: Aldine Pub. Co., 1966), pp. 70–72.

itself intact, results in only a modest gain for Negroes. This has been the disquieting conclusion of analyses of the role of education in Negro occupational advancement.[5]

It may be noted in passing that "removing the barriers to Negro mobility" does not merely mean engendering a large amount of mobility. In *net* terms, the mobility of Negroes from father's to 1962 occupation was 42.6 percent and that of whites was 22.1 per cent (Table 3). In large part, however, this striking net change in the Negro distributions between the two stages of the life cycle merely represents a diminution of the heavy concentration in farming and its replacement by concentrations at the lower manual levels. How this comes about will become clearer momentarily.

There is an important qualification on the entire analysis to this point, insofar as it involves father's occupation as the origin. Respondents were instructed to state the occupation of the father in the event that he was the head of the respondent's family when the respondent was about 16 years old. If this condition did not obtain, the occupation was to be given for such other person, male or female, as was the family head. About two-thirds of the Negro respondents reported that they grew up in an intact family (both father and mother present), as compared with five-sixths of the non-Negroes. For both Negroes and non-Negroes, non-response on the "father's occupation" question was higher for those who did not grow up in intact families than for those who had modal family experience. Nonresponse for Negroes was higher than for non-Negroes irrespective of family history. Altogether, some three-fourths of the nonresponse on father's occupation among Negroes, compared to three-fifths among non-Negroes, was contributed by respondents who did not grow up in an intact family. A considerable part of category 18 in the Negro origin distribution, therefore, consists of men who lacked a father on whom to report. Since category 18 has been treated statistically as though it were merely another occupation group, to some extent the influence of occupational origins is confounded with that of family background. (Conclusions as to the locus of under- and overrepresentation, however, would not be altered by recomputing percentages on a basis excluding nonrespondents.)

[5]Nathan Hare, "Recent Trends in the Occupational Mobility of Negroes, 1930–1960; An Intracohort Analysis", *Social Forces*, **44** (December 1965), 166–73; Paul M. Siegel "On the Cost of Being a Negro", *Sociological Inquiry*, **35** (Winter, 1965), 41–57.

PATTERNS OF MOVEMENT

To study gross changes in occupational status between stages of the life cycle, it is necessary to collapse the occupational categories rather drastically. In the Occupational Change in a Generation sample, each respondent represents, on the average, about 2170 members of the population, although the effective sampling ratio varies over strata. Hence the number of Negroes under study is of the order of 1500. The five-fold occupational classification used in subsequent tables provides about the maximum amount of detail that can be presented even with an appreciable liberalization of the Census Bureau's criterion for minimum base populations. Unfortunately, the degree of aggregation thus imposed is such as to impair comparability between Negroes and non-Negroes, since their distributions by specific occupations within broad categories may be quite different. Conclusions must be appropriately qualified.

Table 4 shows the percentages of men with specified father's occupation who found first jobs at each of the five levels of the condensed occupational classification. At every level of origin, Negroes enjoyed less access to the higher levels of working force entry than did non-Negroes. Indeed, the modal experience of Negroes in all four categories of nonfarm origin was to find lower manual first jobs. If the figures can be trusted, it is especially noteworthy that higher white-collar origins were of little value to Negroes for setting the stage for entry into white-collar work. The greatest similarity between Negro and non-Negro entry patterns occurred for men with farm origins. Approximately one-half of both groups found their first regular employment on the farm (predominantly as farm laborers, as one can infer from Table 1). Yet among those who moved from the farm, Negroes were rather more likely than non-Negroes to go into lower manual jobs, while an appreciable fraction of non-Negroes found work at the higher manual or white-collar levels.

Not only was the lower manual job the typical level of working-force entry for Negroes, the bulk of the Negro men starting there remained there while the majority of non-Negro men were able to rise to a higher level in their subsequent careers, as Table 5 shows. No less than 70 percent of Negroes who entered this type of employment were still at this level in 1962, as compared with a proportion only one-half as large for non-Negroes. Broadly speaking, therefore, the first job represents only a temporary lowering of occupational status for many non-Negroes, but a permanent lowering

228

TABLE 4. TRANSITION PERCENTAGES, FATHER'S OCCUPATION TO FIRST JOB (CONDENSED CLASSIFICATION), BY RACE, FOR CIVILIAN MEN AGED 25–64 YEARS, FOR THE UNITED STATES, MARCH 1962

Race and father's occupation[a]	First job[a]						Total	
	Higher white collar (1-4)	Lower white collar (5-7)	Higher manual (8-10)	Lower manual (11-15)	Farm (16-17)	Not reported (18)	Percent	Number (000)
NEGRO								
Higher white collar (1-4)	2.9	5.9	14.7	71.3	0.0	5.1	100.0	136
Lower white collar (5-7)	13.0	29.6	0.0	53.7	3.7	0.0	100.0	54
Higher manual (8-10)	4.1	12.3	7.0	62.6	1.2	12.8	100.0	243
Lower manual (11-15)	3.1	4.6	3.8	74.7	6.7	7.2	100.0	976
Farm (16-17)	0.5	2.3	1.9	39.7	49.6	6.0	100.0	1,389
Not reported (18)[b]	1.7	6.2	4.8	56.3	13.9	17.2	100.0	714
Total percent	2.0	5.0	3.8	55.8	24.4	8.9	100.0	—
Number (000)	70	175	134	1,961	858	314	—	3,512
NON-NEGRO								
Higher white collar (1-4)	28.2	27.6	9.3	29.0	2.3	3.5	100.0	5,834
Lower white collar (5-7)	20.4	32.0	7.8	32.9	2.8	4.1	100.0	2,653
Higher manual (8-10)	7.3	20.2	17.2	48.0	4.6	2.8	100.0	6,520
Lower manual (11-15)	6.1	17.0	9.1	59.6	4.6	3.5	100.0	8,795
Farm (16-17)	4.5	7.1	6.2	30.9	48.7	2.7	100.0	9,991
Not reported (18)[b]	6.8	18.8	9.0	42.6	12.0	10.7	100.0	2,664
Total percent	10.5	17.8	9.7	41.6	16.7	3.7	100.0	—
Number (000)	3,831	6,484	3,532	15,156	6,094	1,360	—	36,457

[a]See Table 1 for code identifications of occupation groups combined.

[b]See Table 1, n. (a).

Source: see Table 1.

TABLE 5. TRANSITION PERCENTAGES, FIRST JOB TO 1962 OCCUPATION (CONDENSED CLASSIFICATION), BY RACE, FOR CIVILIAN MEN AGED 25–64 YEARS, FOR THE UNITED STATES, MARCH 1962

Race and first job[a]	1962 occupation[a]						Total	
	Higher white collar (1–4)	Lower white collar (5–7)	Higher manual (8–10)	Lower manual (11–15)	Farm (16–17)	Not reported (18)	Percent	Number (000)
NEGRO								
Higher white collar (1–4)	53.5	2.8	7.0	25.4	2.8	8.5	100.0	71
Lower white collar (5–7)	12.0	33.1	3.4	44.6	1.7	5.1	100.0	175
Higher manual (8–10)	4.4	11.8	36.8	31.6	1.5	14.0	100.0	136
Lower manual (11–15)	4.2	5.0	9.6	70.3	2.6	8.3	100.0	1,960
Farm (16–17)	1.4	1.3	6.5	56.2	23.3	11.2	100.0	857
Not reported (18)[b]	7.0	1.6	8.3	59.9	4.5	18.8	100.0	314
Total percent	5.2	5.4	9.4	62.3	7.7	10.0	100.0	—
Number (000)	181	191	331	2,188	271	351	—	3,513
NON-NEGRO								
Higher white collar (1–4)	77.1	8.9	4.5	4.3	1.2	4.0	100.0	3,830
Lower white collar (5–7)	39.4	26.1	11.4	16.6	1.2	5.4	100.0	6,484
Higher manual (8–10)	26.9	7.5	38.7	18.6	2.3	6.1	100.0	3,530
Lower manual (11–15)	20.1	9.3	24.8	36.5	2.7	6.6	100.0	15,157
Farm (16–17)	10.1	5.3	18.3	29.5	29.7	7.1	100.0	6,095
Not reported (18)[b]	22.1	7.1	15.9	23.8	3.6	27.5	100.0	1,360
Total percent	28.6	11.3	20.2	26.2	6.8	6.9	100.0	—
Number (000)	10,415	4,129	7,362	9,556	2,476	2,518	—	36,456

[a]See Table 1 for code identifications of occupation groups combined. [b]See Table 1, n. (a). Source: see Table 1.

TABLE 6. TRANSITION PERCENTAGES, FATHER'S OCCUPATION TO 1962 OCCUPATION (CONDENSED CLASSIFICATION), BY RACE, FOR CIVILIAN MEN AGED 25–64 YEARS, FOR THE UNITED STATES, MARCH 1962

Race and father's occupation(a)	1962 occupation(a)						Total	
	Higher white collar (1–4)	Lower white collar (5–7)	Higher manual (8–10)	Lower manual (11–15)	Farm (16–17)	Not reported (18)	Percent	Number (000)
NEGRO								
Higher white collar (1–4)	10.4	9.7	19.4	53.0	0.0	7.5	100.0	134
Lower white collar (5–7)	14.5	9.1	0.0	69.1	0.0	7.3	100.0	55
Higher manual (8–10)	8.8	6.8	11.2	64.1	2.8	6.4	100.0	251
Lower manual (11–15)	8.0	7.0	11.5	63.2	1.8	8.4	100.0	973
Farm (16–17)	3.1	3.0	6.4	59.8	16.2	11.6	100.0	1,389
Not reported (18)(b)	2.4	6.5	11.1	65.9	3.1	11.1	100.0	712
Total percent	5.2	5.4	9.5	62.2	7.7	10.0	100.0	—
Number (000)	182	190	334	2,184	272	352	—	3,514
NON-NEGRO								
Higher white collar (1–4)	54.3	15.3	11.5	11.9	1.3	5.6	100.0	5,836
Lower white collar (5–7)	45.1	18.3	13.5	14.6	1.5	7.1	100.0	2,652
Higher manual (8–10)	28.1	11.8	27.9	24.0	1.0	7.3	100.0	6,512
Lower manual (11–15)	21.3	11.5	22.5	36.0	1.7	6.9	100.0	8,798
Farm (16–17)	16.5	7.0	19.8	28.8	20.4	7.5	100.0	9,991
Not reported (18)(b)	26.0	10.3	21.0	32.5	3.9	6.4	100.0	2,666
Total percent	28.6	11.3	20.2	26.2	6.8	6.9	100.0	—
Number (000)	10,414	4,130	7,359	9,560	2,475	2,517	—	36,455

(a)See Table 1 for code identifications of occupation groups combined. (b)See Table 1, n. (a). Source: see Table 1.

of status for many Negroes. Even among the Negroes who managed to enter the work force at a higher level, moreover, the first job did not provide as auspicious a career beginning as for whites. Downward mobility from first job to 1962 among men who began at the white-collar or higher manual levels was much more frequent for Negroes than for non-Negroes.

Presenting mobility over the whole life cycle to the date of the survey, Table 6 demonstrates that the "holding power" of higher levels of origin is considerably less for Negroes than for non-Negroes, while the holding power of lower manual origins is much greater. Negroes left the farm in greater proportions than did whites, but the bulk of them were in lower manual pursuits in 1962, whereas about three in seven non-Negro men who originated on farms had achieved a white-collar or higher manual status.

To reduce the comparison between Negroes and non-Negroes in Table 6 to a pair of summary measures, we may compute Pearson's coefficient of mean square contingency between father's occupation and 1962 occupation: for Negroes it is 0.30; for non-Negroes, 0.42. It makes more difference what your father did if you were not a Negro than if you were. From one point of view, the occupational mobility data suggest that the Negro family has a lesser impact on its son's occupational chances than does the non-Negro family. Or, to put it another way, the intergenerational transmission of a strictly occupational advantage or handicap is greater for non-Negroes than for Negroes. In this respect, the Negro occupational mobility pattern is a more "open" or "equalitarian" one, but it is an equality that consists in the sharing by all members of the race in a lack of access to skilled or prestigious occupations.

Some of the details of the processes that produce this contrast are coming to light in analyses whose conclusions may be summarily stated here. Family background of Negroes—in the sense of the level of socioeconomic status, stability, and structural integrity of the family—is less favorable than that of non-Negroes. This initial handicap is translated into a lower level of educational attainment on the part of Negro youth. Yet, the disparity in educational attainment is too great to be attributed solely to measureable background handicaps. There is a residual difference that appears as a coefficient for "race" in a statistical model and that may be tentatively interpreted as an estimate of "racial discrimination" in educational opportunity.[6]

[6]Beverly Duncan, *Family Factors and School Dropout: 1920–1960* (Ann Arbor: The University of Michigan, 1965); Otis Dudley Duncan, "Discrimination against Negroes", *Annals of the American Academy of Political and Social Science*, **371** (May 1967), 86–103.

TABLE 7. INFLOW PERCENTAGES, 1962 OCCUPATION BY FATHER'S OCCUPATION (CONDENSED CLASSIFICATION), BY RACE, FOR CIVILIAN MEN AGED 25–64 YEARS, FOR THE UNITED STATES, MARCH 1962

Race and father's occupation[a]	1962 occupation[a]						
	Higher white collar (1–4)	Lower white collar (5–7)	Higher manual (8–10)	Lower manual (11–15)	Farm (16–17)	Not reported (18)	Total
NEGRO							
Higher white collar (1–4)	7.7	6.8	7.8	3.2	0.0	2.9	3.8
Lower white collar (5–7)	4.4	2.6	0.0	1.7	0.0	1.1	1.6
Higher manual (8–10)	12.1	8.9	8.4	7.4	2.6	4.5	7.1
Lower manual (11–15)	42.9	35.8	33.5	28.2	6.6	23.3	27.7
Farm (16–17)	23.6	21.6	26.6	38.0	82.7	45.7	39.5
Not reported (18)[b]	9.3	24.2	23.7	21.5	8.1	22.5	20.3
Total	100.0	100.0	100.0	100.0	100.0	100.0	100.0
NON-NEGRO							
Higher white collar (1–4)	30.4	21.6	9.1	7.3	3.1	12.9	16.0
Lower white collar (5–7)	11.5	11.7	4.8	4.0	1.6	7.4	7.3
Higher manual (8–10)	17.6	18.6	24.7	16.3	2.7	18.8	17.9
Lower manual (11–15)	18.0	24.6	26.9	33.1	6.2	24.3	24.1
Farm (16–17)	15.9	16.9	26.9	30.1	82.2	29.8	27.4
Not reported (18)[b]	6.6	6.6	7.6	9.1	4.2	6.8	7.3
Total	100.0	100.0	100.0	100.0	100.0	100.0	100.0

[a]See Table 1 for code identifications of occupation groups combined; see Table 6 for marginal totals.
[b]See Table 1, n. (a).
Source: see Table 1.

TABLE 8. PERCENTAGE NEGRO FOR EACH COMBINATION OF FATHER'S OCCUPATION AND 1962 OCCUPATION, FOR CIVILIAN MEN AGED 25–64 YEARS, FOR THE UNITED STATES, MARCH 1962

Father's occupation[a]	1962 occupation[a]						Total
	Higher white collar (1–4)	Lower white collar (5–7)	Higher manual (8–10)	Lower manual (11–15)	Farm (16–17)	Not reported (18)	
Higher white collar (1–4)	0.4	1.4	3.7	9.2	0.0	3.0	2.2
Lower white collar (5–7)	0.7	1.0	0.0	8.9	0.0	2.1	2.0
Higher manual (8–10)	1.2	2.2	1.5	9.3	9.6	3.3	3.7
Lower manual (11–15)	4.0	6.3	5.4	16.3	10.5	11.8	10.0
Farm (16–17)	2.5	5.6	4.3	22.4	10.0	17.7	12.2
Not reported (18)[b]	2.4	14.4	12.4	35.1	17.6	31.6	21.1
Total	1.7	4.4	4.3	18.6	9.9	12.3	8.8

[a] See Table 1 for code identifications of occupation groups combined; see Table 6 for marginal totals.
[b] See Table 1, n. (a).
Source: see Table 1.

The handicap of educational disadvantage is naturally translated into inferior occupational achievement on the part of Negroes. But again, the occupational differential cannot be fully accounted for by educational disadvantage, nor even by the combination of educational disadvantage and handicaps of family background. A specifically racial differential remains.[7] Finally, although it is not yet possible to assemble all the components into a single quantitative representation of the stratification process, it is virtually certain that the entire configuration of family background factors, educational levels, and occupational achievement is insufficient to account for differences between Negroes and non-Negroes in earnings and family income.[8] There is a residual effect for "race", whether it can legitimately be taken to be a measure of "discrimination" in some strict sense of the term or not.

OUTCOMES OF MOBILITY

Returning to the materials at hand, which concern occupational mobility *per se* abstracted from the complex of socioeconomic factors involved in the process of mobility, we may indicate two other ways to summarize the data in order to bring out some consequences of racial differences in mobility patterns.

First, the array of inflow percentages (Table 7), although derived from data already reviewed, puts a somewhat different perspective on the relative prevalence of upward and downward mobility among Negro and non-Negro men. Whereas we have seen that the probability of movement into the higher white-collar level is small for Negroes, irrespective of origin, Table 7 shows that of the men who do achieve this level, a much higher proportion of Negroes than of non-Negroes have moved up from humble origins. Over two-fifths of the Negroes, but less than one-fifth of non-Negroes, who were in higher white-collar occupations in 1962 had fathers who occupations were classified as lower manual. A similar though smaller differential is noted for inflow into lower white-collar occupations. In sociological jargon, then, an overwhelming preponderance of the small Negro "middle class" is composed of men new to that status, while a very substantial minority of the non-Negro "middle class" consists of men who originated there.

[7]Peter M. Blau and Otis Dudley Duncan, *The American Occupational Structure* (New York: John Wiley and Sons, 1967).

[8]Siegel, *op. cit.*

235

Second, Table 8 makes explicit the racial composition of the several sets of men defined by contrasting mobility experience. Since Negroes are under-represented at the upper occupational levels, both in terms of origins and in terms of destinations, it is not surprising that they are extremely under-represented among men who originated at a high level and who remained there. Less than one-half of one percent of men who "inherited" higher white-collar status are Negroes. Correlatively, there is marked overrepresentation of Negroes among men who "inherited" lower manual status or who achieved this status via mobility from a farm origin. Indeed, disregarding the "not reported" row and column, there is only one cell in which the percentage of Negroes is greater than both the corresponding row and column percentages; namely, the cell referring to movement from farm origins to lower manual occupations in 1962. When we speak of people "inheriting poverty"—as distinguished from those who find themselves in poverty despite a more favourable start in life—we are referring to a group that is quite disproportionately made up of Negroes. At least, that is the inference if we assume that patterns of mobility among income groups are somewhat like those among occupations.

COMMENT

There is little basis except conjecture for an estimate of how different the current pattern of racial differentials in occupational mobility may be from those prevailing in the past. It is virtually certain, however, that this pattern cannot prevail indefinitely in the future. For both Negro and non-Negro men aged 25–64 years in 1962, but especially for the former, the experience recorded in the intergenerational table is, in large measure, the story of a massive movement out of the farm sector. Such a movement cannot recur for future cohorts for the simple reason that much smaller proportions will have farm origins. It may prove to be true that the historical movement of Negroes from the farm into lower manual occupations is a prelude to their achieving a more nearly representative distribution in the entire occupation structure in the future. But, for this to happen, Negroes must have much greater access to higher occupational positions than in the past.

Race and Class in Latin America

OCTAVIO IANNI

CURRENT racial problems in Latin-American countries can be better under-stood if viewed in the light of the structural requirements of a society whose classes are in the process of formation. National variations are due to ethnic, racial or cultural traditions and heritage, to the rate of expansion, the persistence of regimes based on slavery and the type of economy involved. Despite these variations it cannot be denied that the significance of racial tensions which have arisen in these countries is determined by a developing capitalist system. Manifestations of prejudice, such as racial barriers, stereotypes or racial ideologies, are phenomena which reflect realistic situations, involving contact between different groups. These can only be understood when the analysis is taken beyond the surface manifestations and reaches down to the roots of the problem, which is neither ethnic nor racial nor cultural, although it may be expressed in these areas. The dilemmas generated by the co-existence of these groups within nations cannot be resolved on the level of their purely cultural, social, political or demographic manifestations. They can only be understood when they are analysed in the context of the socio-economic structure, bearing in mind their dominant social characteristic, which is the formation of classes within society. In other words, the racial problem can be explained if it is studied in terms of the structure which is dominant at the time; that is, in the light of the conditions of, and opportunities (whether real or imaginary) for mobility, including the processes, channels and obstacles concerned.

In the social sciences it is postulated that, in class-societies, relationships between men are governed by two fundamental and complementary principles: (a) the control by private ownership of the means of production, or to put it another way, the method of appropriation of the products of the society's labour, (b) the relationships of domination–subordination brought about by the conditions, manifestations and tendencies of the division of

237

labour, that is ultimately based on the types of appropriation of the products of collective effort. It is on the basis of these two principles that relationships between individuals, groups and social classes are organized and undergo changes, although these relationships generally appear on the face of it to vary significantly from each other. Consequently, in superficial observation the relations between given human groups look "social" or "cultural", as if these aspects of social reality possessed an autonomy and a deterministic significance, rather than being derivative. Thus, the problems are posed in terms of prejudice, barriers, or racial ideologies, as if in these limited spheres it were possible to discover significant correlations which would throw light on the nature of tensions or restrictive social relationships between relatively homogeneous racial or ethno-cultural groups. In other words, as the true nature of the relationships between those groups is neither racial nor cultural, a scientific explanation of them cannot be confined to that sphere. Although an analysis cannot exclude cultural, racial or ethnic characteristics, or indeed demographic, social and psychological factors, it is of fundamental importance that the explanation should not confine itself to these spheres. On the contrary, it should take the complete social system as its basis. Only when the phenomenon, in all its particular forms, is seen as part of a global system, does the analysis achieve its ultimate explanatory synthesis, comprehending its many and sometimes conflicting meanings.

Note that no attempt is being made to abandon altogether current interpretations, which focus on the "racial situation" or "race relations", as if these had only a descriptive value. This is not how we see the question under consideration. What we do aim to do is reformulate the question on a different basis, going beyond the limits which have been imposed on it in the past. But this does not mean abandoning the work that has been done in the field of description and explanation of racial problems. On the contrary, the approach adopted here will give added value to earlier contributions, implicitly incorporating their positive achievements.

The present study will deal with the problem from the standpoint of an historico-cultural understanding, remembering that, basically, it reflects a particular aspect of the power structure emerging in Latin-American countries. Industrial capitalism is being established in societies developing from a system in which slavery determined production and the organization of social relationships. Thus, we shall pay attention to an area of the democratization process which has not been explored. The negative, or discriminatory effects of relationships between racially distinctive groups, are fundamental elements for the clarification of some structural limitations on the expansion of democracy. For example, the possibility of, and restrictions upon, the formation of a democratic personality is an inevitable by-product of the ideas developed here.

Rather than an ethnic, racial, demographic or cultural phenomenon, the "race question" is a reflection of the tendency of the labour market to absorb, readjust and expand, whether on a regional or a national level. This is its fundamental nature, which gives meaning to its social, cultural, demographic and political manifestations. The latter does little to throw light on the problem if they are taken in isolation. In countries of emigration, just as in countries where immigrants or their descendants are being absorbed, the same determining structural feature (namely the labour force) is basic to the problem.

The socio-economic and political importance of the labour force clarifies and explains cultural, racial and other manifestations which have been obscured or rendered abstract by the analyses of some sociologists and anthropologists. In other words, certain transformations, taking place in the primary, secondary and tertiary sectors of the economy of countries in the process of industrialization, are found at the root of the "race problem". To the extent that the breakup of the slave regime freed productive forces capable of initiating the industrial expansion and reintegrating and differentiating the overall structure these transformations occur. As the conditions of production change and become more varied, due to the weakening of the slave structure and the redirecting of the colonial-style economy in favour of national production, the structure and the significance of the labour market alter and labour demands are accentuated. As a result, changes in the demographic structure take place, including population movements from one nation to another, especially from Europe to America. Thus, on the Spanish–African–Indian and Portuguese–African–Indian admixtures are superimposed new groups of Germans, Italians, Poles, Sirio-Lebanese, Russians and others, including the Japanese.

With the diminishing potential for expansion of a socio-economic system based on slave labour, changes of varying degree and importance became evident. These were destined to reformulate the economy and the social structure on a new basis. Hence the establishment of free labour which met new needs and created other demands. While, at the time when European capitalism was in the making, slavery in the Americas had shown itself to be the most productive way of organizing the labour force, when that same

239

system entered its period of maturity, slavery proved incapable of meeting the new production needs for "tropical goods" and the commercial distribution of merchandise produced in the first instance primarily in England and France and later in Germany and the U.S.A. Hence the abolitionist revolution, which took place in varying degrees in Latin-American countries, the regression of monetary economies to subsistence economies, the preservation of pre-existing economic orders, the modification of subsistence systems and trading systems or the expansion of monetary ones. Whatever the circumstance, slave labour as the fundamental institution was destroyed, although some of its elements continued in disguise in many regions. Free labour gained ground little by little, in line with the strength of the productive forces set free by abolition, or created subsequently. Yet, whenever there was expansion, whenever the socio-economic structure showed signs of development or diversification, the governments or private concerns encouraged immigration of workers, with the aim of promoting colonization programmes for uninhabited areas, or increasing the availability of labour in the most vigorous centres of the economy. As a consequence, immigrants and their descendants formed groups with distinctive ethnic, racial or cultural features. In this way we can locate hidden dimensions of the problem. As national societies are formed in Latin-America, so their ethnic, racial and cultural structure becomes diversified. At every important stage in the formation of nations, the new human contacts render even more complex the culture, demography and society. With the beginning of European colonization, after the discovery of the New World, slave labour was established, using the natives, the Africans or their *mestizos*.[1] It was a consequence of the process of primitive accumulation of capital, which accompanied the birth of European industrial capitalism. Afterwards, when the first signs of crisis in the slave structure were apparent, due to internal and

[1] For a study of the structural conditions of emergence and development of social identification between castes and races in the slave period in Latin America, see, for example: Sergio Bagu, *Economía de la Sociedad Colonial*, Ensayo de Historia Comparada de América Latina, Librería "El Ateneo" Editorial, Buenos Aires, 1949; Demetrio Ramos Perez, *Historia de la Colonización Española en América*, Pegaso, Madrid, 1947; Manuel Eduardo Hubner, *México en Marcha*, Zig-zag, Santiago de Chile, 1936; Caio Prado Junior, *Formação do Brasil Contemporâneo, Colonia*, 4th ed., Editora Brasiliense, São Paulo, 1953; Florestan Fernandes, "Côr e Estrutura Social em Mudança", in *Brancos e Negros em São Paulo* by R. Bastide and F. Fernandes, 2nd ed., Companhia Editora Nacional, São Paulo, 1959, pp. 77–161.

external conditions which we need not examine here,[2] there began a new period of socio-economic development and there was an increasing need, as a result, for a free working force. To these countries flowed immigrants who had been made redundant by socio-economic changes in England, Germany, Italy, France, Poland, Russia, etc. In short, the migratory process was directly linked to structural changes in the country of emigration just as in the country of immigration. We shall leave those aside, however.

Here it is proposed to examine the explanatory potential of clearly visible relationships between certain stages in the structural transformation and certain manifestations of "race relations". Thereby, an attempt will be made to understand the probable future development of the phenomenon. As the problem is to clarify the scientific significance of racial prejudice[3] in its various forms, the conditions which must have formed the background to the migratory movement in the countries of origin are of no explanatory value. Generally, the domination–subordination relationships which govern interaction between racial groups in Latin-American countries are independent of the study of economic, social, political, religious, demographic or psychological conditions which formed the basis of emigration.[4] This does not mean, however, that the theoretical importance of these conditions in

[2]The subject was dealt with in detail by Eric Williams, *Capitalism and Slavery*, University of North Carolina Press, Chapel Hill, 1944; and Celso Furtado, *Formação Econômica do Brasil*, Editora Fundo de Cultura S.A., Rio de Janeiro, 1959.

[3]In sociological terms race is a social category constituted by the integration of a number of socially derived evaluations according to which the persons or groups, due to the real or imaginary position which they occupy in the social system, are considered to belong to different genetic stocks. In this sense the category is defined beginning with certain conditions of social existence of the groups in interaction, and of their products, passing through a careful consideration of the auto-evaluation of one group by another, and taking into account the closeness or remoteness of their relationships. This category, as can be seen, involves racial prejudice in that the auto-evaluations which differentiate between distinct racial groups operate in an atmosphere of actual or prospective behaviour among those people or groups. It is by means of racial prejudice that the social significance of race is apparent, being oriented in such a way as to facilitate or guarantee the domination–subordination relationship represented in the racial ideologies. In other words, prejudice operates as a social technique for the ordering and reorienting of actions and relationships between persons and groups, obscuring the real basis of the types of domination which are current in society as a whole.

[4]On this subject see Julius Isaac, *Economics of Migration*, Kegan Paul, London, 1947; Alfred Sauvy, *Théorie Générale de la Population*, 2 vols., Presses Universitaires de France, Paris, 1952; Pierre Fromont, *Démographie Economique*, Payot, Paris, 1947.

determining social behaviour among the immigrants is underestimated.[5] Nor does it indicate the slightest contempt for the political and cultural activities of governments or national bodies concerned with immigration, which is also of interest in understanding the process of absorption of immigrants or their descendants.[6] As these events are not constant, they do not affect the underlying conditions although they may affect the outcome. The structural analysis of the relationships between ethnic groups or racial minorities and society as a whole omits those events which do not affect the essence of the relationships and those which obscure or render more complex certain cultural or political manifestations of structural connections.

STRUCTURES AND RACE RELATIONS

The theoretical concepts outlined above have the advantage of explaining both minor and major manifestations of racial tensions. They throw light on the significance of social barriers between Negroes, Mulattoes and Whites; between natives and their descendants with other groups; between Poles, Japanese, Sirio-Lebanese, Germans and Italians amongst themselves, and between their descendants and the charter group. The interpretation is sufficiently general to explain significant characteristics and tendencies in the relationship between the most distinct racial and cultural groups as they appear in Latin America, particularly Brazil. But it does not appear to be rigorous enough also to clarify the particular phenomena which arise with the operation of the social systems. However, that the analysis is basically correct can be seen clearly in the specific instances discussed below. As scientific studies of race situations in other Latin–American countries are not available, the present considerations are based on Brazilian society, which has been studied by sociologists and anthropologists.

[5]Cf. S. N. Eisenstadt, *The Absorption of Immigrants*, Routledge & Kegan Paul, London, 1954.

[6]With reference to the relationships between governments or emigration organizations, with the groups or their descendants, in the country of immigration, see Aurelio da Silva Py, *A Coluna no Brasil*, Edição da Livraria do Globo, Porto Alegre, 1942; Mario Martins, *Hitler Guerreia o Brasil há Dez Anos*, Empresa Editora "O Dia". S.A., Curitiba; José Arthur Rios, *Aspectos Políticos da Assimilação do Italiano no Brasil*, edition by Revista de Sociologia, São Paulo, 1959; Constantino Ianni, *Inchiesta Sull' Emigrazione*, MS, 1960, in press; Lindolfo Collor, *Sinais dos Tempos*, Editora Pan Americana, Rio de Janeiro, 1942, especially pp. 190–220.

(a) *The Negro and the Mulatto*

The present state of relations between Whites, Negroes and Mulattoes only becomes clear when we study the structural conditions in which the slaves became free. Understanding manifestations of race prejudice which permeate their relationships today[7] depends on a study of socio-economic crisis which led to the abolition of slavery and the origins of the class society. Where a society based on caste ceases to be viable as a consequence of internal dynamics and international socio-economic conditions, the prerequisites of a new system begin to be established. Due fundamentally to the limitations shown by the slave labour force in the face of new demands for expansion and diversification of the economy, the free worker begins to establish himself, at a rate commensurate with the strength of the productive forces which are operative or which are being established. During this time the abolitionist movement acquires a special drive and takes on a revolutionary character, producing changes in doctrines and traditional ideas which the "closed society" condoned.[8] Abolition has the notable effect, among others, of producing a redefinition of labour, raising it to a dignified activity, which is a requirement of growing industrial capitalism. The liberty allegedly given to the slaves was the freedom to work, the freedom of a labour force with no restrictions over the means of production, since the slave himself was the means of production. Thus the Negro and the Mulatto were "declared free", workers at liberty to offer themselves on the labour market, in accordance with the need for unified production open to technical innovations and rationalization.[9]

The former slave was not redefined as a citizen in the full sense of the word. Even today he is more of an ex-slave, whether Negro or Mulatto. When the general emancipation of slaves came about, a transformation of

[7]On present-day relationships between whites and blacks in Brazil, see Roger Bastide and Florestan Fernandes, *op. cit.*, Octavio Ianni and Fernando Henrique Cardoso, *Côr e Mobilidade Social em Florianópolis*, Companhia Editora Nacional, São Paulo, 1960; L. A. da Costa Pinto, *O Negro no Rio de Janeiro*, Companhia Editora Nacional, São Paulo, 1953; Donald Pierson, *Brancos e Pretos na Bahia*, Companhia Editora Nacional, São Paulo, 1945; Thales de Azevedo, *As Elites de Côr*, Companhia Editora Nacional, São Paulo, 1955; René Riberio, *Religião e Relações Raciais*, edition by Serviço de Documentação do Ministerio da Educação e Cultura, Rio de Janeiro, 1956; Charles Wagley *et al.*, *Races et Classes dans le Brésil Rural*, Unesco, 1951.

[8]Cf. Octavio Ianni, *As Metamorfoses do Escravo*, Difusao Europeia do Livro, São Paulo, 1962, pp. 232–5.

[9]*Ibid.*, pp. 207–32.

the caste into a mass of available workers resulted and these were gradually incorporated into the production process as a free labour force.

> As the Negro and the Mulatto are once more embraced by a socio-economic system which also divides its people hierarchically and since, along with them, there will be white workers of various origins who provide competition, colour becomes a significant factor and the group or the individual is defined as Negro or Mulatto. For those who resist the domination of society, it will prove easier to distribute men according to their colour, according to their religion or by their national origin or some other such attribute, rather than dividing them according to their position in the social structure. Thus there will be Negroes, Mulattoes, Italians, Poles, Jews, Germans, identified socially as distinct one from another, even when they live together in the same social group and work in conditions which are the same.[10]

This is what lies beneath the racial ideology of the dominant white group in whose mind colour is a reified abstraction which defines the totality of the person to whom it is attributed. As the social concept of Negro and Mulatto is attributed to the ranks of employees, Negroes, Mulattoes and Whites are correspondingly redefined.[11] As a consequence this creates the ideological conditions necessary for social behaviour in a specifically class society.

> As colour is selected as a social determinant and attribute, everyone comes to have at his disposal yet another element which is socially defined and which is bound to guide reciprocal expectations of behaviour. Following on the ideas of Wirth, the ideology of a social group is not merely the formulation of aims but an instrument for the realisation of those aims, that is, a weapon destined to establish and preserve connections. Paradoxically, in the case of the white man's racial ideology, even the Negro and the Mulatto themselves, given the historico-social conditions in which they are raised, also come to be adherents, even though passively. As a result of the way in which they were socially integrated they come to conform to the situation and values which the whites develop, and also have to attune their behaviour to their expectations.[12]

Thus the ideology of the Negro and the Mulatto will be a social expression of the other ideology, in the terms in which the domination–subordination relationship is posed and delimited by the white man's racial ideology.

> In the end, it facilitates the adjustment of the Negroes and Mulattoes to the emerging social situations where they come face to face with whites, be it in the

---

[10] *Ibid.*, p. 268.

[11] Cf. Louis Wirth, *Community Life and Social Policy*, University of Chicago Press, Chicago, 1956, p. 202.

[12] Cf. Octavio Ianni, *op. cit.*, p. 260.

context of social interaction, or when we consider other levels of social structure. Primarily, it works to diminish the subjective and negative effects of the standards of interracial behaviour which have been inherited from the past and which operate nowadays. Consequently it can be defined as *a compromise ideology*. . . . Its effect is to guide the behaviour of the "coloured person" in the matter of his social integration and betterment. Therefore it takes into account a variety of concessions which are offered in exchange for the social successes which mean the possibility of breaking into or surpassing groups dominated by whites. This ideology comprises elements which are geared specifically to allow concessions while taking in the adjustment to contact situations in which the white dominates. In this sense the ideal of becoming more white is one of the best examples we have for understanding this facet of the Negro and Mulatto ideology.[13]

On the other hand, the white man's racial ideology "has the effect of promoting or facilitating the adjustment and predomination of white men in social situations where Negroes and Mulattoes also play a part, whether we are considering face to face contact or whether we are concerned with levels of social structure".[14]

Further analysis confirms that the racial ideologies concerning Negro, Mulatto and White signify the creation of social consciences which are incapable of understanding the real significance of situations. They do not go beyond the superficial aspects of relationships between persons and groups, never relating them to the class structure. On the level of these ideologies, individuals and groups are not perceived as being in a particular situation because of the conditions of production or the domination–subordination imposed upon them through their relation to the labour force. They express abstractions concerning human relationships never synthesized in the totality of an historico-structural view. For this reason, these ideologies have another significance until now unsuspected. As now understood the ideology of the white man is only comprehensible as a component of the dominant social conscience in which the white man himself is represented as superior to others, having the right to control them. Stereotyped evaluations concerning the Negro and the Mulatto, based upon alleged moral and intellectual inferiority to the white man, reflect aspects of a dominant conscience which perceives relationships between people in an abstract and absurd way.

The racial ideology of the black man, on the other hand, which is based on

---

[13]Cf. Octavio Ianni, "A Ideologia Racial do Negro e do Mulato", in O. Ianni and Fernando Henrique Cardoso, *op. cit.*, pp. 225–6.
[14]Cf. Octavio Ianni, "A Ideologia Racial do Branco", *ibid.*, p. 210.

a status inferior to that of the white man, who presumably retains the power, expresses a submissive conscience. Accordingly the Negro imagines himself altogether in the terms in which he is viewed by the white man. Hence the alienation of the Negro is more acute since his self-image is a reflection of the false abstractions engendered in the mind of the white man. Therefore, attempts at self-definition on the part of the Negro are often unsuccessful and utopian. As he begins from an erroneous starting point, from the premises provided by the dominant consciousness of the white man, the Negro can never identify himself correctly. Unless he abandons his basic premises—trying to become more like the white man or to achieve the "superior" attributes claimed by the white man—his struggle will always be a succession of frustrations. For him to surpass the narrow barriers which surround him in a process of false consciousness, he must first re-establish the basis of the problem and begin from the real foundations which gave rise to his consciousness. In this way, the Negro must see himself above all starting from the social position which he occupies in the social system, and the way in which his "blackness" was generated by the class system which gave rise to his consciousness.

Following this line of thought, the peculiar ideology of the Mulatto has an explanatory value as it throws light on the domination–subordination which permeates the ideologies of Black and White. The bipolarization of the consciousness of the Mulatto, with respect to the Negro and the white man, is typical of the person who sees himself as mobile. Beginning with the abstractions of other people's ideologies, he sees himself in an obscure way, marginally, and turned in upon himself, in search of an impossible security so long as he is seen as the descendant of the Negro, of the ex-slave. Therefore his consciousness is ambiguous. But precisely for this reason it emphasizes even more the falsification of consciousness (of domination and of submission), since it reflects the vacillation between the social situation of privileged groups, ideologically identified with the white man, and the social situation of the underdogs, ideologically identified with the Negro. Seeing himself in this equivocal fashion, as a person who has a right to social ascent in spite of belonging to the lower stratum (to the class of people who sell their labour) the Mulatto shows up the black–white relationship as a false relationship, in which the black and the white, like the Mulatto himself, are abstractions.

To locate certain social relations in terms of "Negroes", "Mulattoes" and "Whites" is to set them on the wrong foundation, for it means trying to take as real something which is no more than an abstraction. When racial problems are viewed within the realm of interracial relations, even if defined socially as such, one is considering the question with the confused and confusing restrictions which are placed on it by the ideology of the people concerned. To treat the matter simply on that level and to try to explain it is to see it in terms of some of its abstract manifestations as if that were the whole picture. That is why a number of sociological, anthropological and psychological analyses have a strictly documentary value, without satisfactorily elucidating any aspect of the subject. These studies deal with the question within the limits imposed by the participants themselves, never going further than the empirical bases in which human relationships are revealed. Therefore, the examination of relationships between social groups assigned, explicitly or implicitly, in an asymmetrical fashion within the social structure, is reduced to a description of attitudes, opinions, stereotypes or ideologies, without taking into account historico-structural situations and configurations or questions of consciousness.

(b) *Polish immigrants*

Understanding of the structure of the problems posed by race relations, along the lines laid down in the present essay, is further corroborated if we consider these relations in other historico-structural contexts. This is the case with European groups in some areas of Brazil. In particular, the phenomenon was apparent in the situation of the Poles in the region of Curitiba.[15]

Leaving aside the fact that numbers of Poles who emigrated to the Paraná region dispersed and were absorbed with varying results, special attention is drawn to the creation, in the receiving society, of a social category with a negative connotation. At present, the Pole and many of his descendants have still not been accepted as Brazilian by social consensus. Characteristics or attributes, viewed as racial by other groups which make up the society, still associate him with a supposed "world of the Pole" in which the latter is allegedly given to alcoholism, excessively religious, always fair-haired, inclined to take to crude manual tasks and therefore intellectually inferior,

---

[15]On the situation of other immigrant groups in Brazil, see Emilio Willelms, *A aculturação dos Alemães no Brasil*, Companhia Editora Nacional, São Paulo, 1946; by the same author, *Aspectos da Aculturação dos Japoneses no Estado de São Paulo*, Faculdade de Filosofia, USP, São Paulo, 1948; Hiroshi Saito, *O Japonês no Brasil*, Editora Sociologia e Politica, São Paulo, 1961; Clark S. Knowlton, *Sirios e Libaneses*, Anhembi, São Paulo, undated.

247

and inclined to pair up with Negroes. In the context of the predominant racial ideology, as soon as the immigrant—whether first generation or later —is socially recognized as such, he is neither Polish (*polonês*) nor Brazilian but *polaco*, which is a separate and inferior category comparable to the Negro.

Nevertheless, when we examine what underlies this concept, we discover in the end that it arose in a typical historico-structural context in the past. To put it briefly, on arriving in Brazil in the third quarter of the nineteenth century, the Poles did not find a socio-economic system which could absorb them productively. Although the economy of the Curitiba region was expanding and diversifying, the rate of change was relatively slow and it was faced with the increasing availability of labour brought about by the arrival of immigrants. This was precisely the time the Poles arrived; they came to the area of Curitiba when economic activity could not develop any faster, especially following the arrival of the Germans. In structural terms the availability of labour had exceeded the opportunities provided by the economic system which had been created. Although they had arrived at a time when the receiving community needed workers in order to expand certain sectors of production, it appears that the Poles tried to enter industries which were not essential to the economy and also those which were already well developed by other groups. In particular, the situation resulting from the latter case created conditions which encouraged resistance in the most varied social forms. These restrictions, which to an extent still operate, have the effect of limiting the possibilities of social mobility among the Poles, or of hindering their resocialization. This means that integration of the immigrants in given sectors or institutions of his society of adoption depends on a functional dynamic balance among those very sectors and institutions, and the consequence is absorption or rejection, depending on their state and their tendencies. In a nutshell, "the Pole would be rejected in certain economic organizations because the labour market or the sector of production would be saturated, that is, because those economic organizations only take in labour or investments which result from internal expansion. By contrast, he would be accepted, as in the case of domestic servants, at one time, if conditions of the market were favourable."[16]

As a consequence, a swing of public opinion against the new arrivals became apparent, and there was a crystallization of criticisms concerning incidental attributes, presupposed on ideological grounds, equivocal ab-

[16]Cf. Octavio Ianni, "Do Polonês ao Polaco", *Revista do Museu Paulista*, Nova Serie, Vol. XII, São Paulo, 1960; pp. 315–38; quotation from p. 336.

stractions which came to be accepted as representative of the Pole in general, to the point of defining him completely. Hence the stereotypes and the systematic identification of the *polaco* with that which is inferior in moral, racial and intellectual terms. A complete doctrine of the moral and intellectual inferiority of the Poles was erected just as had taken place, in the time of slavery, with the doctrine of innate inferiority of the African or his descendants. As in the relationships between blacks and whites, where the bases of the relationships were obscured, from the relationships between Poles and other groups there arose ideological representations which confused the real situation. For the people discriminated against, just as for those who developed the stereotypes, the concrete basis of the situation was hidden. The relationships came to be formulated on the basis of those abstract representations as if they were real. Therefore, what was worker, immigrant, a competitor on the labour market or a tradesman, became, quite simply, *polaco*, just as the former slave became "Negro" and "Mulatto", instead of taking on the role of a free worker without means of production.

(c) *The Indian*

The history of the Americas is full of events which involve the Indians in all sorts of ways. In some nations, this history is confused with the epic of detribalization. Even nowadays, the Indian is still the object of "colonialist" politics which, despite having taken on several forms, still represents a movement destined to swallow up lands, workers and consumers. The most recent manifestations of contact between Indian groups, or their rustic members, and "Whites" or "Christians" reveal a particular way of organizing social relationships which rely principally on the exploitation of Indian land and labour. For this reason the interaction of one with another assumes, or tends to acquire, the nature of a domination–subordination relationship, and this is made legitimate by the "rights" which the leaders of the commercial system claim for themselves. Following on the general lines of the theory of race relations, outlined here, the coexistence of Indians and whites allows us to clarify better the interpretation developed so far. Now, as in the past, the outcome of social commitments between these contingents is made explicit when the analysis goes beyond the narrow limits in which these results are obtained and explores the level of the structural significance into which they fit.

In those studies where social scientists take their investigation beyond the cultural sphere of the groups in contact, there is a tendency to reveal at least

249

one part of the real basis of these links. When we examine not only the results of the socio-cultural coexistence of ethnically different groups, but also investigate their conditions and tendencies, we build up a picture of the true nature of contact between Indians and "nationals", which is much more complex and realistic. In these cases, the economic or political basis of expansion of the dynamic nuclei of the national economy become evident and they clarify the importance of social and cultural changes in the ecological and demographic processes. And so in some Brazilian regions, according to Roberto Cardoso de Oliveira, "the extractive economy, livestock and agriculture, which shaped the peasant both socially and economically, also drew in the native population". Most of the time, however, what dominates is "the pre-capitalist exploitation of work, which wage-earning did not even touch—credit vouchers, barter and forced labour".[17]

In fact, the national society assumes different forms when faced with the Indian and the peasant members of this group. In every aspect, however, intermittent or continuous relationships characterized the "nationals" as those who exploit the land and the work of both. When the vanguard of "Brazilian civilization" comes across Indians, they always organize themselves around economic activities which are absolutely characteristic. For example, according to Darcy Ribeiro, "when the nuclei of extractive economy are faced with an Indian group their tendency is to displace it violently from its lands and, if possible, to try to get them into their service, enticing the men into building up new reserves of forest products and into jobs such as oarsmen, porters, etc.; and the women they take as their mistresses or employ to produce foodstuffs". As the pastoral economy spreads, "reactions to the Indian are guided above all by the need to rid their land of its human inhabitants in order to give it over to the cattle, and to stop the Indian, who now has nothing to hunt, from attacking their flocks instead". Finally, the vanguard of agricultural expansion "sees in the Indian nothing more than an obstacle to its expansion and embarks on struggles to move them from the fern boxes which they occupy in order to confiscate them and thus increase their arable land."[18] Even so, once the

[17]Cf. Roberto Cardoso de Oliveira, "O Problema Indígena Brasileiro e o Serviço de Proteção aos índios", *Revista Brasiliense*, No. 9, São Paulo, 1957, pp. 72–87; quoted from p. 85.

[18]Cf. Darcy Ribeiro, "Culturas e Línguas Indígenas do Brasil", *Educação e Ciências Socials*, Ano II, Vol. 2, No. 6, Rio de Janeiro, 1957, pp. 5–102; quotations from pp. 23–4.

initial conflict is past, the groups in contact become used to each other and there tends to be co-operation based on the utilization of the Indian labour force in the most varied activities which are the basis of economic life in those regions. At the same time racial prejudice comes about, as a necessary outcome of the domination–subordination relationship. The expressions *bugre*, *selvagem*, *ignorante*, *bruto* express the lower limit of the human scale, while the term *cristão* (Christian) encompasses all the ideal attributes which are personified by the *Brazilians* who control the means of production and the instruments of power.[19] In this context, the Indian Protection Service acts as an organization which perpetuates conditions favourable to the reproduction of the life of the employer, while taking refuge in humanitarian doctrines. In the activities of this organization there are often concrete, more long-term aims which the very agents of economic expansion, because of their immediate concerns, are not in a position to understand.

At the root of manifestations of racial prejudice, then, there is more than simply ethnocentricity or contact between different cultural systems. Without doubt these spheres of reality are important to the analysis but they do not explain the whole significance of the phenomenon. Only when we set these manifestations against the background of the socio-economic structure in which they occur do we reach a full understanding of their basic meaning. It follows that racial ideology, social and cultural changes, certain crises of personality, or other phenomena, appear as expressions of a particular kind of social organization, affecting the lives of people who are allocated to different points in the system. In this situation, particular products of social relationships between different racial or cultural groups are, clearly, dynamic components of the domination–subordination relationship which are formed on the basis of certain kinds of appropriation of the products of the society's labour.

RACE AND DEMOCRACY

Thus new variables become relevant to the analysis of the power structure which operates in countries which are populated by different racial and

[19]Concerning evidence of race prejudice developed by the "colonizers" in their relationships with the Indians and their descendants, see R. Cardoso de Oliveira, *op. cit.*, especially pp. 85–7; Darcy Ribeiro, "Atividades Científicas da Secção de Estudos do Serviço de Proteção aos Indios", *Sociologia*, **13,** No. 4, São Paulo, 1951, pp. 363–85; especially p. 372.

cultural groups. We have not the slightest intention of defending the idea that there will be purely ethno-cultural or racial obstacles to the democratization of social systems and personalities. Following on the thoughts developed in the preceding paragraphs, we wish simply to emphasize that the heterogeneity (which, furthermore, is not just confined to few nations) creates conditions which prevent or hinder the expansion of democracy. As evidence of discrimination generally plays a part in techniques used to preserve interests and privileges, for purposes of interpretation we can consider it as an element which impedes or hinders the establishment or expansion of democratic relations, by obstructing the circulation of men according to their competence or qualifications. Therefore, *the myth of racial democracy* is an ideological expression in a society which does not and cannot allow democracy to make advances. The myth reverses the real conditions of existence and the standards of organization of relationships between men. While it denies racial inequality, implicitly it reaffirms it by recognizing that the Negro can become White and that the Pole can become Brazilian, that the savage can become "Christian". However, this metamorphosis, conceived in ideological terms, scarcely exists on the level of individuals, while collectively it will continue to exist in *negros, mulattos, polacos, bugres, brasileiros, cristãos.*

Prejudice, then, blocks the diffusion of democratic norms. As we see a crystallization of the products of asymmetrical social relationships, involving employers and employees, prejudice turns into a powerful obstacle to the advancement of the ways of democracy, both in the case of institutions and social classes and in the case of personalities. In these two spheres, evidence of discrimination, expressed in stereotypes, attitudes, opinions, doctrines, norms and standards of behaviour, restrict the possibilities of spreading the benefits of democracy, insofar as democracy imposes ever-increasing demands on schools, professions, intellectual activities and persons in authority. Together with the establishment of systems of occupational stratification, there is a crystallization of evaluations concerning social status and personality types. Men are classified, not according to their relative position *vis-à-vis* the social situation in which they find themselves, but by means of isolated attributes which may or may not be structurally connected with the situation. This encourages the emergence of racial ideologies which consider men on an abstract level ignoring their real involvement with the overall socio-economic structure. It explains how the categories *negro, mulatto, polaco, bugre* and others take shape, solidify and persist, as if there were no general concrete determinants defining men on the basis of the historical conditions which produced them.

Consequently, the myth of racial democracy arises as a particular expression of the much greater myth of the "open" society, in which men—whether rich or poor, of whatever race, sex, or religion—are defined ideologically as equal. With the formation of a class society, following on a crisis in the precapitalist socio-economic system in privileged areas, there was a reconstruction of the auto-representation of the new social order. In those, society as a whole is represented as appears to the ruling class, since this is a condition for the preservation of the power structure, which is inherent in a capitalist-style organization of relationships between men. Nevertheless, these representations are permeated by the social products of real relationships in which mankind has come to be subdivided according to race, sex, religion, national origin, so that the hierarchical relations in certain spheres or in the realm of society as a whole become even more complex. Therefore the components of racial ideologies run through and break up both collective and individual habits, dividing men and making them strangers to each other.

> By discriminating on racial grounds the members of social groups, whether organized hierarchically or not, are not aware of the true bases of the tensions they face. These tensions are made objective in colour or other ideologically constituted attributes and do not touch the social conscience of the members of the society as members of classes. Prejudice penetrates the ranks of those who are discriminated against, dividing them by the shades of their skin, as if phenotypical marks were the basis of social distinction.[20]

Democratization inevitably comes up against some of the obstacles which are inherent in the kind of social organization which is brought about by a capitalist system of production. Therefore, together with the natural impediments, which are brought about by the very structure of classes, must be added several consequences of social relationships that are generated in an atmosphere of racial and cultural interaction, when the population is distributed, as a result, in "minorities" of Negroes, Mulattoes, Whites, foreigners, natives and nationals. Consequently, the situation of groups and social classes faced with the power structure becomes more complex, whether we have in view the workings of democracy, whether we are considering man's freedom of access to the benefits of the regime, or whether we are interested in the political movement of social classes and their members.

[20]Cf. Octavio Ianni, *As Metamorfoses do Escravo*, p. 282.

CONCLUSIONS

Racial prejudice is a social process derived from particular ideological components of social relationships between groups who come to be defined as belonging to different races. It is a way of governing the coexistence of people and groups who, from an ideological point of view, are considered different. But this is no more than an empirical expression of the phenomenon and follows from rather distant observation. If we look at it more closely, however, this formulation is seen to be based on other elements and we are thus able to broaden our understanding of it.

On the one hand, racial prejudice is engendered by, and manifests itself in, situations where people or groups come face to face in competition for social privileges (especially in questions of status in economic or political institutions), although it may express itself in abstractions linked with "race" or "culture". Depending on the state of structural configurations, which have the effect of reinforcing or weakening competition between people and groups, signs of prejudice tend to become apparent in varying degrees of intensity. Due to degrees of integration, differentiation and change in structure, and following on the kind of rivalry for privileges or status in economic, social and political matters, racial groups accentuate or modify their reciprocal discrimination. At a time of economic crisis, for example, when the availability of labour increases or the demand drops sharply, workers tend to develop, accentuate, or reorient their reciprocal auto-representations; they subdivide themselves, discriminate against each other and reintegrate themselves in professional, "racial", sexual, religious groups, etc., as if these attributes were at the root of the crisis itself. As individual or group conscience is a product of, and is modified by, concrete situations, the crisis of the recurrent configurations of such situations, generates uneven, false and reified representations of reality. This stresses, then, particular contingent manifestations of their consciousness, such as prejudice, which divides classes internally while contradicting their structural position or their destiny. Besides this, in view of the fact that the means of domination can only work with the actual social elements of the system, it incorporates the components of racial ideologies and simplifies actions designed to preserve the balance of power. Clearly there are other elements and conditions of class consciousness which are involved in this class process. For example, together with the revitalization of ideological manifestations, which conspire to separate the members of a given class, some basic, decisive and more general conditions also play a part, conditions which make possible, or tend to facilitate, the formation of a radical class consciousness. The negative relationship which is brought about between "races", or other abstract categories, is only a partial expression of the deeper relationship which becomes explicit in the realm of class tensions. For, at the critical juncture, there is a tendency for the underlying internal factors of the whole historical structure to become apparent.

In "normal" situations, however, when there is some balance between the supply and demand of labour, the workers are led to abandon or to attribute less importance to reciprocal auto-representations and the evidence of discrimination is obliterated or reduced. In any case, racial ideologies, just like certain other ideological representations, must be viewed as components of a social consciousness. Although these ideologies may possess a certain degree of internal consistency and autonomy, and they are consequently diffused and adopted among various groups and social classes, they cannot be explained in isolation as if they themselves contained all their significance.

On the other hand, since it is a phenomenon which is apparent above all on an ideological level, the dynamics of race prejudice are relatively autonomous, as if prejudice arose solely in the realm of symbols, which run through race relations, independently of the nature of the socio-economic structure. Meanwhile, as this is a process derived from the context of certain kinds of social relations, whose secondary significance is constantly changing, it can become set or modified in the form of stereotypes, attitudes, opinions, moral attributes and so forth—that is, in an ideology which subsists outside the fundamental socio-economic conditions which gave rise to it. The fact that it is preserved, although it can be invigorated or weakened, becomes comprehensible when we set it against the background of class structure, which holds the key to its essential importance. In other words, prejudice is kept alive (whether or not modified, in accordance with the state of society) because of the preservation of the basic structure from which it was derived. In the vast process of mystification of the true bases of human relations, racial ideologies play the role of social techniques for governing the behaviour of individuals or groups, by dividing them or throwing them together, in the same way as, for example, religious or political ideologies; and often these are bound up with racial ideologies.

To sum up, we may say that the discrimination, barriers and stereotypes which go with racial ideologies, operate as recurrent and active features in a

255

social system which, in accordance with the power structure of the day, "must" be preserved. Distinctions and divisions, among groups which are defined as different on racial grounds, are manifestations which will express, in a confused way, the domination–subordination relationship which stemmed originally from appropriating the products of the society's labour —and, for that matter, the products of the men themselves, as commercial agents. Crystallization on the level of social relations has the effect of legitimizing particular hierarchical distributions of human beings.

Race, Politics and Conflict

The Precipitants and Underlying Conditions of Race Riots*

Stanley Lieberson and Arnold R. Silverman

The immediate precipitants and underlying conditions of race riots in the U.S. during the past half century are the subject of this paper. Using both "hard" and "soft" data, employing journalistic accounts as well as census data, we consider in a somewhat more systematic fashion the influence of diverse factors suggested as causes of riots in sociological case studies and texts on collective behavior.[1] Riots, as distinguished from lynchings and other forms of collective violence, involve an assault on persons and property simply because they are part of a given subgroup of the community. In contrast, lynchings and other types of violence are directed toward a particular individual as a collective response to some specific act. In practice,

*The comments of Alma and Karl Taeuber, and David Heise are gratefully acknowledged.

[1]Herbert Blumer, "Collective Behavior", in Alfred McClung Lee (ed.), *New Outline of the Principles of Sociology*, New York: Barnes and Noble, 1951, pp. 165–222; Chicago Commission on Race Relations, *The Negro in Chicago*, Chicago: University of Chicago Press, 1922, pp. 1–78; Allen D. Grimshaw, "Three Major Cases of Colour Violence in the United States", *Race*, 5 (1963), pp. 76–86, and "Factors Contributing to Colour Violence in the United States and Britain", *ibid.* 3 (May 1962), pp. 3–19; Allen D. Grimshaw, "Urban Racial Violence in the United States: Changing Ecological Considerations", *American Journal of Sociology*, 66 (1960), pp. 109–19; Kurt Lang and Gladys Engel Lang, *Collective Dynamics*, New York: Thomas Y. Crowell, 1961; Alfred McClung Lee and Norman Daymond Humphrey, *Race Riot*, New York: Dryden Press, 1943; Elliott M. Rudwick, *Race Riot at East St. Louis, July 2, 1917*, Carbondale: Southern Illinois University Press, 1964; Neil J. Smelser, *Theory of Collective Behavior*, New York: Free Press of Glencoe, 1963; Ralph H. Turner and Lewis M. Killian, *Collective Behavior*, Englewood Cliffs, N.J.: Prentice-Hall, 1957; Ralph H. Turner and Samuel J. Surace, "Zoot-Suiters and Mexicans: Symbols in Crowd Behavior", *American Journal of Sociology*, 62 (1956), pp. 14–20.

this distinction is sometimes difficult to apply, particularly in deciding when a localized racial incident has become a riot.[2] We have excluded some of the housing "riots" from our analysis because they were directed specifically at Negroes attempting to move into an area rather than at Negroes *per se* or some other more generalized target.

Using the *New York Times Index* for the period between 1913 and 1963 we found 72 different events that might be properly classified as Negro–white race riots. Descriptions of riots in various editions of the *Negro Year-book* supplemented some of the *Times* reports and also provided reports of four additional riots. In several instances, magazines and local newspapers were used for further information. Finally, we employed the sociological descriptions available for some race riots. Reliance on journalistic accounts for our basic sample of riots means the study is vulnerable to any selectivity in the riots actually reported in the newspaper. Our analysis of the immediate precipitants of race riots is similarly limited by the brevity of some of the descriptive accounts as well as by possible distortions in reporting.[3] For the underlying community conditions of riots, we relied largely on census data.

IMMEDIATE PRECIPITANT

As one might expect, race riots are usually sparked by a provocation involving members of the two races. At most only four of the 76 riots occurred without a precipitating event, and even in these few cases, the apparent lack of precipitant may be due to the scantiness of the accounts rather than the absence of an immediate cause. In riots, life and property are treated with an indifference and recklessness contrary to basic values in western society (except in wartime), and it is therefore important to ask what kind of events precipitate such an acute breakdown of social control, and whether these precipitants are uncommon occurrences of an exceptionally provocative nature.

Although lynchings are not riots, data gathered on the immediate causes

[2]Lynchings, for example, are sometimes followed by riots. No doubt we would have included some of these events and excluded others had more detail been available.

[3]See, for example, Raoul Naroll, *Data Quality Control—A New Research Technique*, New York: Free Press of Glencoe, 1962.

of the 3700 lynchings in the U.S. between 1889 and 1930 are illuminating. Of the known accusations, more than a third (37.7 per cent) were murder; in nearly a quarter (23.4 per cent) the accusation was rape or attempted rape; assault was the charge in 5.8 per cent and theft in 7.1 per cent.[4] Compared with the frequency of these felonies in the South, murder and rape—violations of strong social taboos—are greatly over-represented as precipitants of lynchings.

In the same fashion, we suggest, the immediate precipitants of race riots almost always involve some confrontation between the groups in which members of one race are deeply "wronged" in fact or in rumor by members of the other. Precipitants tend to be transgressions of strongly held mores by a representative of the other group. The difficulty is to obtain an independent judgment of the severity of offenses that precipitate riots.

For two rather frequent types of precipitants, we can offer some independent evidence of their intensity. First, riots are often precipitated in the U.S. by crimes—particularly alleged crimes against persons rather than property alone, or the public order. Murder, rape, assault, manslaughter, and theft by means of violence or intimidation arouse the greatest concern and receive the most publicity in the mass media.[5] In 1950, the median sentence received by men found guilty of offenses against persons was 9.9 years, whereas it was 3.9 years for those charged with other felonies.[6] Even excluding murder, sentences for other felonies against persons were more than twice as long as those for offenses solely against property or the public order. Since punishment reflects the public's values with respect to the intrinsic "evil" of various acts, it is in this sense an independent measure of the severity of acts that precipitate race riots.

Another class of events that apparently violate strongly held norms involve Negroes crossing the various segregation barriers erected against them. Particularly frequent as precipitants in recent years, these acts are "bad" only because Negro–white interaction occurs in a form gener-

[4]Arthur F. Raper, *The Tragedy of Lynching*, Chapel Hill: University of North Carolina Press, 1933, p. 36.

[5]Marshall B. Clinard, *Sociology of Deviant Behavior*, New York: Holt, Rinehart and Winston, 1957, p. 196. We include robbery as a crime against persons throughout this analysis.

[6]Based on data reported in Federal Bureau of Prisons, *National Prisoner Statistics: Prisoners in State and Federal Institutions, 1950*, Leavenworth, Kansas: U.S. Penitentiary, 1954, Tables 37 and 38. Determinate and maximum indeterminate sentences are combined.

ally prohibited, e.g. when Negroes use the same swimming pool as whites.[7]

We have classified the 72 riots for which data are available in terms of the nature of the immediate precipitant of the violence. (See Table 1.) The reader

TABLE 1. IMMEDIATE PRECIPITANTS OF RACE RIOTS, 1913–1963

Rape, murder, attack, or hold-up of white women by Negro men	10
Killings, arrest, interference, assault, or search of Negro men by white policemen	15
Other inter-racial murder or shooting	11
Inter-racial fight, no mention of lethal weapons	16
Civil liberties, public facilities, segregation, political events, and housing	14
Negro strikebreakers, upgrading, or other job-based conflicts	5
Burning of an American flag by Negroes	1
No information available	4
Total number	76

should recognize that it is not always clear which event triggered a riot, especially when a chain of inter-related events occurs. Not only is it difficult to specify where the riot begins and the precipitant ends, but often there are several precipitants. In these cases we have determined whether at least some of the events involve offenses against relatively sacred values.

A sizeable majority of the precipitants do involve an actual or rumored violation of one group by a member of the other. The ten cases in which white women were attacked by Negro men are highly inflammatory; apparently these involve violations of an extremely strong taboo. Highly charged acts to begin with, the murder, rape, or assault of women is even more serious an offense when offender and victim are of different races. Negroes were almost half of all persons executed for murder by civil

[7]Myrdal hypothesizes a rank order of discrimination in which whites object most strongly to close personal contact with Negroes. See Gunnar Myrdal, *An American Dilemma*, New York: Harper, 1944, pp. 60–61. Although a follow-up study suggested some modifications of this thesis, the areas of highest white resistance to Negroes remained unaltered. See Lewis M. Killian and Charles M. Grigg, "Rank Orders of Discrimination of Negroes and Whites in a Southern City", *Social Forces*, **39** (1961), p. 238.

authorities in the United States between 1930 and 1952 and nearly 90 per cent of those executed for rape.[8] In their analysis of the 1943 Los Angeles zoot-suiter riot, Turner and Surace describe sexual assault as the dominant trigger:

> The most prominent charge from each side was that the other had molested its girls. It was reported that sailors became enraged by the rumor that zoot-suiters were guilty of "assaults on female relatives of servicemen". Similarly, the claim against sailors was that they persisted in molesting and insulting Mexican girls. While many other charges were reported in the newspapers, including unsubstantiated suggestions of sabotage of the war effort, the sex charges dominated the precipitating context.[9]

The second type of precipitant, offenses committed by white law-enforcement officials against Negroes, involves white transgression of norms no less sacred than those involved in the rape of white women by Negro men. The Harlem riot during World War II started when a Negro woman was arrested by a white policeman for disorderly conduct. A Negro soldier, on leave, tried to stop him and the ensuing fight ended with both men in the hospital, the policeman with a battered head and the soldier with a pistol wound in the shoulder. Of greatest interest here is the account of the incident that spread through the Negro community: a Negro soldier was said to have been shot in the back and killed by a white policeman in the presence of the Negro's mother.[10]

The Harlem riot of July 1964 was precipitated by a demonstration protesting the slaying of a 15-year-old Negro boy by a white policeman, an act viewed as a wanton exercise of police brutality. The Bedford-Stuyvesant, Rochester, Jersey City, and Philadelphia riots of 1964—also outside the period covered in our study—were also precipitated by arrests or the presence of police.[11]

Both the fatal shooting of the boy and the rumored treacherous shooting of a soldier during wartime, in front of his mother, are highly inflammatory acts because they arouse some of the strongest sentiments the population holds, and they are especially inflammatory because they were committed by members of one race against another. In addition, offenses committed by

[8]Federal Bureau of Prisons, *op. cit.*, pp. 30–1.
[9]Turner and Surace, *op. cit.*, pp. 16–17.
[10]*Time*, August 9, 1943, p. 19; *New Republic*, August 16, 1943, pp. 220–2.
[11]"Background of Northern Negro Riots", *New York Times*, September 27, 1964, p. 81.

white law-enforcement officials, highly inflammatory in themselves, are aggravated when they involve actual or alleged wrong-doing on the part of officials expected to uphold and administer the law in an impartial manner. A number of recent race riots over civil-rights issues have been precipitated by police behavior, particularly in breaking up demonstrations.[12] We shall have more to say about the role of the police in our discussion of the underlying conditions of race riots.

The next category of precipitants, "Other inter-racial murder or shooting", calls for little additional comment. The shooting of white policemen by Negro men (three cases), although intrinsically not as inflammatory as inter-racial offenses against women and children, nevertheless involves murder or attempted murder of a representative of the government. The rumored beating to death of a Negro boy in a New York department store after he was seized for shoplifting, and the rumors of brutal assaults on women and children that circulated among both races during the Detroit race riot of World War II, are clearly in accord with our thesis that the precipitants tend to be violations of important mores. In two cases rumors of impending violence precipitated actual riots. In one instance there was a rumor of a forthcoming riot and in the other, anticipation of a lynching. In both instances, the rumors involved inter-racial violation of rights widely accepted as fundamental. Finally, two of the other four inter-racial murders or shootings were accompanied by Negro offenses against white women: as we noted earlier, more than one element may be involved in the precipitation of a race riot. In one of these incidents, a white man was murdered by three Negroes and a rumor arose that he had been trying to protect a white woman from these men.[13] In the other, a Negro had made derogatory statements about a white woman over whom a Negro had been lynched some weeks before.[14]

Most of the 16 race riots precipitated by inter-racial fights without the use of lethal weapons do not appear to involve offenses of the most intense nature. One difficulty here is that the accounts of these riots are so scanty that we do not know whether rumors existed, over what issue the fights started, or other features that may have made the incident especially in-

[12]This is particularly evident in the South.

[13]*New York Times*, September 21, 1920, p. 1; *Chicago Daily Tribune*, September 2, 1920, pp. 1–2.

[14]Monroe N. Work (ed.), *Negro Year Book, 1921–1922*, Tuskegee Institute, Ala. Negro Year Book Publishing Co., p. 75.

flammatory, e.g. a young adult attacking an elderly person or a cripple. A fairly common element in riots with this type of precipitant is a chain of events in which members of each racial group come to the assistance of others already engaged in the fight. This tends to excite the onlookers who arrive after the initial provocation, particularly if members of one race appear to be receiving the worse part of the battle.

"Civil liberties, public facilities, segregation, political events, and housing" is a residual category involving diverse precipitants. Some of the precipitants fit the thesis that sacred values were violated. For example, a riot in upstate New York in the mid-thirties was precipitated by whites attempting to break up a meeting called to rally support for a Negro accused of attacking a white girl.[15] From the white point of view this involves the not uncommon theme of sexual molesting; from the other side, it is a white attempt to prevent Negroes' efforts to insure fair treatment for a Negro accused of a provocative act. A riot in Athens, Ala. in 1946 involved whites protesting police favoritism after a brawl for which two whites had been arrested and a Negro escaped.[16] But for the most part, it is difficult to establish conclusively the extent to which the precipitants in this category were offenses against inter-racial mores. In some cases we are tempted to say that they were—the two just mentioned, or the Negro boy attempting to dance with a white girl at a city-sponsored dance—but in others, we are less certain about the nature of the acts.

Of the five job-based riots, three involved the allegation that Negroes were or had been strike breakers, one was over the up-grading of jobs held by Negroes, and one was simply in an industrial setting. Taking a conservative stance, we would not be inclined to label these as violations of sacred norms.

Burning an American flag is a different type of offense, for it violates neither the person nor any segregation taboo, but it is clearly an offense against one of the nation's most sacred symbols. We shall say more about this type of precipitant, which is unusual for riots in the U.S., when we discuss racial and ethnic riots elsewhere in the world.

In brief, at least a sizeable proportion of the immediate precipitants of race riots appear to involve inter-racial violations of intense societal norms.

[15]*New York Times*, August 28, 1934, p. 3.
[16]Charles R. Lawrence, Jr., "Race Riots in the United States 1942–1946" in Jessie Parkhurst Guzman (ed.), *Negro Year Book, 1941–46*, Tuskegee Institute, Ala.: Department of Records and Research, 1947, pp. 253–4.

S. Lieberson and A. R. Silverman

Noteworthy are the large number of events in which bodily injury is the precipitant as well as the smaller number of cases precipitated by violations of inter-racial segregation taboos.

UNDERLYING CONDITIONS

Applying Durkheim's typology, we observe that many of the immediate precipitants were acts that call for repressive sanctions, that is, they "consisted essentially in an act contrary to strong and defined states of the common conscience".[17] Repressive sanctions are normally administered under penal law by courts in the U.S. For example, murder, rape, and other acts of physical violence are strongly disapproved and severely punished in our society. Many, though not all, of the violations of segregation taboos in the period studied were also punishable through law enforcement, but in these instances, at least some members of either or both racial populations were unable to accept the institutions normally used for handling such offenses. Instead a riot occurred, involving, by definition, a generalized response directed at a collectivity rather than the offender—indeed, the actual offender was often untouched.

Although the immediate precipitants were highly inflammatory, we may still ask why a riot occurred rather than the normal processes of arrest, trial, and punishment, for inter-racial friction occurs far more often than the small number of occasions that erupted into race riots indicates. Why did violence break out where it did rather than at other places where similar incidents occurred? Or to put it another way, the types of violation described earlier probably occur almost daily, yet in most instances they do not lead to collective violence. Are there special circumstances that increase or decrease the chances of a riot ensuing?

One possible interpretation of the location and timing of riots is simply that riots are randomly distributed. Any precipitating incident of this type increase the chances of a riot, but there is no systematic reason why riots occur when and where they do, other than possible differences among cities in the frequency of precipitating incidents. A second approach is based on the notion that certain social conditions in the community increase the probability that a precipitating incident will lead to a riot. From this perspective, we can ask whether cities experiencing riots differ from other cities with

[17]Emile Durkheim, *The Division of Labor in Society*, Glencoe, Ill.: Free Press, 1933, p. 105.

266

regard to the institutional conditions suggested as increasing the chances of a riot.

Poisson distribution

To evaluate the first interpretation, that is, whether riots are randomly distributed in time and place, we used the Poisson distribution, which the low frequency of race riots (1.5 per year between 1913 and 1963) makes appropriate for comparing the actual frequency of riots with what would be expected in a random distribution.[18] Columns 2 and 3 of Table 2 show, respectively, the actual and expected number of riots per year in the 51 years from 1913 through 1963. Inspection indicates that the Poisson distribution yields a poor fit. For example, in 26 of the years no riot was reported though the theoretical distribution would lead us to expect only 11 such years. Applying the appropriate chi-square test for goodness of fit, we conclude that we cannot accept the assumption that the probability of riots is equal each year.[19]

In similar fashion, we can consider the concentration of riots in cities. Restricting ourselves to the 333 cities with 50,000 or more population in 1960, we have compared the actual and expected frequencies of cities experiencing a specified number of riots. There are more cities without any riots, and more with several, than would be expected on the basis of the Poisson distribution (columns 5 and 6): riots occurred in only 33 of these cities. The goodness-of-fit test confirms our impression that the theoretical distribution does not fit the actual distribution of riots in cities.

Two types of sampling bias may have influenced these results. First, newspapers probably fluctuate in their propensity to report riots, so that the frequency of riots at a given point in time increases the probability that riots occurring shortly afterwards will be reported. This is analogous to the tendency of newspapers to make the frequency of rapes or other events into a crime wave when in fact the major variable is the frequency of reporting such events.[20] A second possible bias arises from the fact that our primary

[18]For discussions of the application of the Poisson distribution, see G. Udny Yule and M. G. Kendall, *An Introduction to the Theory of Statistics*, London: Charles Griffin, 1950, pp. 189–94; M. J. Moroney, *Facts From Figures*, Harmondsworth, Middlesex: Penguin Books, 1951, Ch. 8.

[19]Our computation of chi-square is based on the adjustments suggested in Helen M. Walker and Joseph Lev, *Statistical Inference*, New York: Henry Holt, 1953, pp. 105–7.

[20]See, for example, Nahum Z. Medalia and Otto N. Larsen, "Diffusion and Belief in a Collective Delusion: The Seattle Windshield Pitting Epidemic", *American Sociological Review*, **23** (1958), pp. 180–6.

TABLE 2. RACE RIOTS: ACTUAL AND EXPECTED FREQUENCIES

By year			By city		
Riots per year (1)	Observed frequency (2)	Poisson frequency (3)	Riots per year (4)	Observed frequency (5)	Poisson frequency (6)
0	26	11.4	0	300	281.2
1	10	17.1	1	25	47.2
2	7	12.8	2	3	4.3
3	2	6.4	3	3	0.3
4	1	2.4	4	1	0.0
5	0	0.7	5–14	1	0.0
6	0	0.2			
7	2	0.0			
8	1	0.0			
9	1	0.0			
10	0	0.0			
11	1	0.0			
Total years	51	51.0	Total cities	333	333.0

source is the *New York Times*. Milder forms of racial violence in metropolitan New York and the mid-Atlantic area are more likely to be covered than riots of equivalent severity elsewhere. This would lead to a distribution of repeated riots different from that expected on the basis of the Poisson formula. Also, note that our test refers only to riots, not to precipitating incidents *per se*. Therefore we can reach no conclusions with respect to the distribution of precipitants by time or place. These difficulties notwithstanding, the results give us no reason to think riots are random with respect to time and place.

A COMPARATIVE ANALYSIS

Since the type of event that precipitates riots is far more common than actual riots, we ask whether this form of collective violence is due to underlying conditions that keep at least one segment of the population from accepting the normal institutional response to a provocative incident. From this perspective, precipitants are a necessary but not sufficient cause of riots.

A rather wide-ranging array of interpretations have been advanced after the occurrence of riots in particular communities. Such factors as rapidly expanding Negro population, economic hardships, police brutality, job ceilings, Negro competition with whites, slums, unsympathetic city officials, contagion, communist elements, agitators, warm weather, unruly elements, and others have figured in popular and semi-popular interpretations of race riots. Although case studies of race riots are extremely valuable where they provide an accurate description of events before and during riot, obviously it is impossible to determine which factors are critical on the basis of one city's experience.

When we move from the presentation of *plausible* reasons to a systematic empirical test of the actual importance of various attributes in increasing the chances of riots, we encounter serious difficulties. Not only do we have a plethora of independent variables, but their actual significance is very difficult to test. Quantitative data on many of these characteristics are scarce, and in any case it is difficult to know how much causal significance to attribute anyway. For example, a riot may occur in a city containing a Negro slum area. The cruel truth is that housing conditions for Negroes are inferior in virtually every city in the U.S. To infer a causal link, one must determine not whether Negro slums exist in the riot city, but whether that city is worse in this respect than others where no riots occurred. Similarly, in any large city unemployed whites and Negroes might respond to an opportunity for a racial riot. Again the question is whether an unusually large number of such people live in one community compared with another.

Our requirements for quantitative data covering at least part of a 50-year span limit the causal hypotheses we can test. For the most part we have relied on U.S. censuses of the past six decades for data bearing on some of the propositions encountered in case studies and popular interpretations of race riots. This part of our study, therefore, necessarily has a certain *ad hoc* quality.

Method

To examine the influence of variables others have suggested as under-lying causes of race riots, we used a paired-comparison analysis. Each city experiencing a riot compared with a city as similar as possible in size and region which had no riot in the ten years preceding or following the riot date.[21] Preference was given to the city in the same state closest in population

[21]For the most recent riots we could not apply the ten-year limit into the future in selecting control cities, but such cities were included in our analysis.

size, with the provision that it has at least half but no more than twice the population of the riot city. Where no such city existed we selected the city closest in size in the same subregion or region.[22] We compared the very largest cities, such as New York, Chicago, and Los Angeles, with other leading centers in the nation closest in population, regardless of region.

Using the nonparametric sign test, we evaluated the extent to which riot cities differ from their control cities in the direction hypothesized. When a given city experienced more than one riot, it was included as many times as the number of riots. Because census data by size of place and decade were not always available, our "N" in most cases is considerably less than the 76 riots discussed earlier. For convenience in presentation, we have divided the hypotheses into four major categories: population growth and composition; work situation; housing; and government.

DEMOGRAPHIC FACTORS

The rapid influx of Negroes and sometimes whites into cities is certainly one of the most frequently cited reasons for the occurrence of race riots. Although large-scale migration is not usually viewed as a sufficient cause for a riot, it is commonly considered important because rapid influx disrupts the on-going social order and creates various problems in the Negro community. For 66 riots we could determine the growth of the Negro and white populations between the census years preceding and following the race riot, for each riot city and for a comparable community selected at the beginning of the decade. We thus have data for 66 pairs of cities, each pair consisting of a riot city and a control city.

In about half the cases, percentage increases in both total and white population were smaller in the riot cities than in the non-riot cities. Moreover, in 56 per cent of the comparisons the control cities experienced greater percentage increases in Negro population than the riot cities did. Our results clearly fail to support the contention that rapid population change accompanies riots. For the years between 1917 and 1921—a period marked by both Negro migration and numerous riots—we found no sizeable difference between riot and control cities in their percentage gains in Negro population during the decades. Also contrary to expectation are the differences in racial

[22]See U.S. Bureau of the Census, *U.S. Census of Population: 1960. Selected Area Reports, Standard Metropolitan Statistical Areas.* Washington, D.C.: U.S. Government Printing Office, 1963, pp. xvi–xvii.

composition of riot and control cities. Again for 66 pairs, we find that in exactly half the comparisons, the proportion of Negroes is smaller in the riot city than in its control city.

Since this comparative approach is used with succeeding hypotheses, we should consider briefly the implications of these findings. First, we draw no conclusions about whether Negro population growth in riot cities differs from its growth elsewhere in the U.S. Riot cities have experienced more rapid growth than the remainder of the nation simply because Negro population movement has been largely from rural to urban areas. Similarly, since our method is designed to compare riot cities only with other cities similar in size and region, we make no inferences about differences between riot cities and all other U.S. cities. What we do conclude is that riot cities do not differ from non-riot cities of the same size and region in their rates of population increase, and therefore that increases in population fail to explain the occurrence of outbreaks in one city rather than another.[23]

WORK SITUATION

Traditional occupations

The occupational world of Negroes is far more restricted than that of whites. In particular, certain occupational pursuits have been more or less "traditional" for urban Negroes. These are generally lower in both status and income. Accordingly, wherever possible we determined the proportion of Negro men in the labor force who are employed either as laborers or in domestic and service occupations. Needless to say, we were forced to use some rather crude measures as well as broad categories which undoubtedly include some occupations outside the "traditional" rubric. A serious difficulty is created by contradictory hypotheses that depend on which group appears to be the aggressor. On the one hand, we might expect greater antagonism on the part of Negroes in cities where they are relatively restricted in occupational opportunities, i.e. where most Negroes are in traditional pursuits. On the other hand, we might well expect that where Negroes fare relatively

[23]See Robin Williams, Jr., in collaboration with John P. Dean and Edward A. Suchman, *Strangers Next Door*, Englewood Cliffs, N.J.: Prentice-Hall, 1964, pp. 135-7. In a study based on a nationwide sample of cities, they find the general level of race conflict and tension no higher in cities with rapid population growth and high mobility than in those with relatively stable populations. In short, our method gets at the question of why riots occur in the particular cities they do, rather than in comparable urban centers.

271

well in their efforts to break through the job restrictions, whites' hostility might be greater and hence riots more likely to ensue.

For 43 riots we were able to determine the Negro occupational distribution in both the riot and control city during the closest census period. In 65 per cent of these paired comparisons ($N=28$), the percentage of Negro men holding traditional occupations is lower in the riot city.[24] This suggests that riots are due to the realtive threat to whites where Negroes are less concentrated in their traditional pursuits. If such were the case, then we might expect the white and Negro percentages in these occupations to be more alike in the riot city than in the control city. This is precisely what we find: in 30 of the 43 paired comparisons, the *difference* between whites and Negroes, in proportions engaged in laboring, domestic, and service occupations, is smaller in the riot city.[25] The encroachment of Negroes in the white occupational world evidently tends to increase the chances of a riot, although we must also consider the possibility that Negro militancy increases as Negroes move out of their traditional niche.

Store owners

A more specific occupational factor sometimes associated with riots— particularly ghetto riots—is the low frequency of store ownership in Negro areas and the consequent resentment of white store owners in these areas. We are unable to get at these data directly. If we assume, however, that virtually all Negro store owners are located in the ghetto, then we can simply examine the percentage of employed Negro men who are self-employed in various facets of retail trade, such as store, restaurant, or tavern owners. Although differences between riot and control cities tend to be slight, nevertheless in 24 of 39 riots, the percentage of Negroes who are store owners is larger in the nonriot city.[26] Results might be even stronger had it been possible to subcategorize riots. For instance, the absence of Negro store owners would presumably contribute to Negroes' rioting but would contribute relatively little to white assaults.

Unemployment

As was the case for traditional occupations, unemployment presents contradictory possibilities, so that we might well expect riots when either

[24]Using a two-tailed test, $p=.0672$.
[25]$p=.0073$, single-tailed test.
[26]These differences are significant at the .10 level.

Negroes or whites have relatively high unemployment rates. Our analysis is even cruder here, since unemployment is far more volatile from year to year, and we are able to use data only for the closest census year.[27] First, the white unemployment rate appears to have no influence on the likelihood of a riot. In 12 comparisons white unemployment rates were higher in the city experiencing the riot, and in 13 cases, higher in the control city. For Negro unemployment, results tend to run counter to what we might expect. Negro unemployment is higher in the control than in the riot city in 15 out of 25 comparisons. And Negro–white *differences* are lower in the riot than in the control city in 15 out of 25 comparisons.[28]

These results do not confirm our expectations: high white unemployment apparently does not increase the chances of a riot, nor is high Negro unemployment associated with riots in the direction expected. On an aggregate basis, the number of riots during the Great Depression of the thirties was not unusually large. In view of the weakness of the data—particularly the fact that we do not have unemployment rates for the specific year in which the riots take place—all we can conclude is that we have failed to confirm the hypothesis, not that we have disproved it.

Income

Since the influence of income on riots may reflect either group's position, our problem is similar to that discussed in connection with Negro occupational composition. Median income data are available for only 12 riots and their controls. In six comparisons Negro income is higher in the control city and in the other six it is higher in the riot city. In 11 of the 12 cases, however, white income in the riot city is lower than in the control.[29] The *difference* between Negro and white income was larger in the city without a riot in 10 of the 12 cases.[30] The small number precludes analysis of these findings in greater detail, but we can observe that riots tend to occur in cities where white income is lower than that of whites in comparable areas. The lower white income also means that Negro–white differences tend to be smaller in these cities than in the control areas. Thus, the results, though extremely limited in time and place, do not support the notion that race riots are a

---

[27]Although data are available for other years, to our knowledge none can be obtained by race for specific cities.

[28]$p = .212$, single-tailed test.

[29]$p < .01$, single-tailed test.

[30]$p = .038$, two-tailed test.

consequence either of low Negro income or of relatively large Negro–white discrepancies in income.

HOUSING

Ghetto riots in particular are often attributed to the poor housing conditions of Negroes, but our data fail to disclose any tendency whatsoever for housing to be of lower quality in cities that have experienced riots. For 20 paired comparisons we could determine which city had a larger percentage of Negro families in sub-standard housing (using the census categories of "dilapidated" in 1950 and 1960 and "needing major repairs" in 1940). In ten cases the non-riot city had poorer Negro housing than the riot city. Although obviously not all riots could be considered ghetto riots, surely we should find some tendency for Negroes in cities experiencing riots to have poorer dwellings than they do in cities without riots, if it were true that poorer housing quality increases the likelihood of a race riot. Very likely, Negro housing is poor in so many locales that it cannot distinguish cities experiencing riots from those that do not.

GOVERNMENT

Police

Local government is one of the most important institutions to consider in an analysis of race riots. Municipal policies, particularly with respect to police, can greatly influence the chances of a race riot. Earlier, we observed that many of the precipitating incidents involve white police behavior toward Negroes, and adequate police training and tactics often prevent incipient riots from developing.[31] Moreover, police activities reflect the policies, sympathies, and attitudes of the local municipal government.

One often-cited factor in race riots is the lack of Negro policemen. First, one major complaint on the part of Negroes is that of white police brutality. So far as the police are Negroes, actual brutality will probably not arouse strong racial feelings. Second, police in some riots have encouraged or tolerated white violence toward Negroes, so that we might expect stronger police control where the force is mixed, as well as greater confidence in police protection among Negroes. Finally, since the number of Negro

[31]Joseph D. Lohman, *The Police and Minority Groups*, Chicago: Chicago Park District, 1947, pp. 80–93; Smelser, *op. cit.*, pp. 261–8.

policemen is for the most part controlled by the city administration, the representation of Negroes is an indicator of city policies toward race relations in general.

Data are hard to obtain and for 1950 and 1960 we have been obliged to use census reports for entire metropolitan areas. Also, for some decades policemen are not reported separately from closely related occupations such as sheriffs and marshalls. Nevertheless, of 38 pairs of cities, in 24 the city without the riot had more Negro policemen per thousand Negroes than did the matched city that experienced a riot.[32] Although differences between riot and control cities are rather slight, these results do suggest that police force composition influences the likelihood of a riot.

City council

We hypothesize that the manner in which councilmen are elected and the relative size of the city council will influence the occurrence of riots. Our reasoning is based on several assumptions. The election of councilmen at large gives numerically smaller groups a greater handicap in expressing their interests than they encounter in communities where councilmen are elected directly from spatial districts.[33] In cities where the average size of a councilman's constituency is small, we assume that representatives are more responsive to the wishes of the population and therefore that members of the community have a more adequate mechanism for transmitting their interests and concerns. This implies that more diverse interests will be expressed in the city's governing body.

Our hypothesis is that the more direct the relation between voter and government, the less likely are riots to occur. A more responsive government makes riots less likely because it provides regular institutional channels for expressing grievances. Small districts provide more responsive government than large districts, and large districts, more than elections at large. In comparisons between a city with a city-wide election system and one where councilmen are elected both at large and by district, we classified the latter situation as the less likely to lead to riots. Where both cities have the same form of election, we computed the mean population per councilman. (Comparisons involving Deep South cities were based on the white population only.) Thus, we gave form of election priority over size of constituency in our causal hypothesis.

[32] $p = .07$, single-tailed test.
[33] James Q. Wilson, *Negro Politics*, Glencoe, Ill.: Free Press, 1960, pp. 25–33.

In 14 of 22 pairs, population per councilman was larger in the city experiencing the riot than in the control city, or elections at large were used in the riot city and direct election of representatives in the control city.[34] Considering our inability to take into account the degree of gerrymandering in cities with direct representation, these results offer an encouraging degree of support for our hypothesis.

DISCUSSION

Our analysis of the precipitating and underlying conditions of race riots suggests several generalizations about their evolution. First, precipitating incidents often involve highly charged offenses committed by members of one group against the other, such as attacks on women, police brutality and interference, murder, and assault. In recent years, violation of segregation taboos by Negroes as well as white resistance have been increasingly frequent precipitants. Riots are generalized responses in which there is categorical assault on persons and property by virtue of their racial membership. Such violence is not restricted and may even exclude the specific antagonists responsible for the precipitating event.

The diffuse response generated by the precipitating event, as well as the fact that often the alleged offenses are of the sort normally dealt with by appropriate communal institutions, suggests that additional factors channel the inflammatory act into a riot. Since there are usually a number of factors that could have contributed to a riot in any given community, we used a comparative approach to determine why riots occur in some cities and not in others of comparable size and location.

Going beyond our data and trying to place our findings in a broad framework, we suggest that riots are more likely to occur when social institutions function inadequately, or when grievances are not resolved, or cannot be resolved under the existing institutional arrangements. Populations are predisposed or prone to riot; they are not simply neutral aggregates transformed into a violent mob by the agitation or charisma of individuals. Indeed, the immediate precipitant simply ignites prior community tensions revolving about basic institutional difficulties. The failure of functionaries to perform the roles expected by one or both of the racial groups, cross-pressures, or the absence of an institution capable of handling a community problem involving

[34]Though p is not significant (.143), the relationship is in the predicted direction.

276

inter-racial relations will create the conditions under which riots are most likely. Many riots are precipitated by offenses that arouse considerable interest and concern. When members of the victimized race are dubious about the intention or capacity of relevant functionaries to achieve justice or a "fair" solution, then the normal social controls are greatly weakened by the lack of faith in the community's institutions.

Our evidence supports the proposition that the functioning of local community government is important in determining whether a riot will follow a precipitating incident. Prompt police action can prevent riots from developing; their inaction or actual encouragment can increase the chances of a race riot. Riot cities not only employ fewer Negro policemen, but they are also communities whose electoral systems tend to be less sensitive to the demands of the electorate. Local government illustrates the possibility that riots occur when a community institution is malfunctioning, from the perspective of one or both racial segments.

Our finding that Negroes are less likely to be store owners in riot cities illustrates the problem arising when no social institution exists for handling the difficulties faced by a racial group. Small merchants require credit, skill and sophistication in operating and locating their stores, ability to obtain leases, and so on. To our knowledge no widely operating social institution is designed to achieve these goals for the disadvantaged Negro. Similarly, our finding that riots are more likely where Negroes are closer to whites in their proportions in "traditional" Negro occupations, and where Negro–white income differences are smaller, suggests that a conflict of interests between the races is inherent in the economic world.

Our use of significance tests requires further comment. Many of the relationships are in the direction predicted but fail to meet the normal standards for significance. Several extenuating circumstances help account for this. First, many of our hypotheses refer to specific types of riots: for example, some riots are clearly "white riots"; others, equally clearly, are Negro; and many are both, in the sense that extensive attacks are directed at both groups. Were the data in an ideal form, we could separate the ghetto riots, the white assaults, and the interracial warfare into separate categories, and then apply our hypotheses to specific subsets of riots. Because our sample is small and the accounts of many riots are very scanty, we are prepared to accept these weaker associations as at least consistent with our approach to the underlying conditions of race riots.

Several implications of our results are relevant to riots elsewhere. Racial and ethnic incidents in other parts of the world are also frequently precipitated by physical violence. Dahlke's description of the Kishinew pogrom in Russia ascribes considerable importance as a precipitant to the widespread legend that Jews annually kill Christian children, as a part of their religious rites.[35] The extensive riots in Ceylon in 1958 included a number of highly provocative rumors of inter-ethnic violations. For example, "a Sinhalese baby had been snatched from its mother's arms and immersed in a barrel of boiling tar".[36] The Durban riots of 1949 were precipitated by an incident in which an African youth was knocked over by an Indian trader.[37]

A number of other riots, however, are precipitated by violations of symbols rather than persons or taboos. The burning of an American flag by Negroes triggered a race riot in the United States. Our impression is that this type of precipitant is more common in some other parts of the world. Riots in Kashmir, West Bengal, and East Pakistan in late 1963 and early 1964, for example, were precipitated by the theft of a hair of the prophet Mohammed from a Mosque in Kashmir.[38] One of the precipitants of the Chinese–Thai riots of 1945, the Yaorawat Incident, was the Chinese tendency to fly Chinese flags without also flying the Thai flag of the nation.[39] Jews tore down the czar's crown from the town hall and damaged portraits of various rulers prior to Kiev's pogrom in 1905.[40]

Our results also suggest that race riots are frequently misunderstood. We have encountered a number of accounts in the popular literature attributing riots to communist influence, hoodlums, or rabble-rousers. Although lower-class youths and young adults are undoubtedly active during riots, potential participants of this type are probably available in almost any community. What interests us is the community failure to see the riot in terms of institutional malfunctioning or a racial difficulty which is not met—

[35]H. Otto Dahlke ,"Race and Minority Riots—A Study in the Typology of Violence", *Social Forces*, **30** (1952), p. 421.

[36]Tarzie Vittachi, *Emergency '58: The Story of the Ceylon Race Riots*, London: Andre Deutsch, 1958, p. 48.

[37]Anthony H. Richmond, *The Colour Problem* (rev. ed.), Harmondsworth, Middlesex: Pelican Books, 1961, p. 123.

[38]*New York Times*, January 16, 1964, p. 17; January 19, p. 6; January 20, p. 6; January 24, p. 2; January 26, p. 15.

[39]G. William Skinner, *Chinese Society in Thailand: An Analytical History*, Ithaca, N.Y.: Cornell University Press, 1957, p. 279.

[40]From the diary of Shulgin, in *Source Book for History 2.1*, Vol. 2, "History of Western Civilization", Brooklyn, N.Y.: Brooklyn College, Department of History, 1949, Ch. 31.

and perhaps cannot be—by existing social institutions. Many riots in other parts of the world revolve about national political institutions such that a disadvantaged segment is unable to obtain recognition of its interests and concerns through normal political channels. While this type of riot is not common in the U.S., the same basic conditions exist when either whites or Negroes are unable to use existing institutions to satisfy their needs and interests.

The Politics of the Police

Seymour Martin Lipset

Ortega y Gasset predicted in his book, *The Revolt of the Masses*, published in 1930, that free societies would come to fear their police. He argued that those who rely on the police to maintain order are foolish if they imagine that the police "are always going to be content to preserve . . . order (as defined by government). . . . Inevitably they (the police) will end by themselves defining and deciding on the order they are going to impose—which, naturally, will be that which suits them best." In some cities in the United States, leaders of police organizations have openly threatened that the police will disobey orders to be permissive with black or student demonstrators. The head of the Patrolmen's Association in Boston has stated that the police there will enforce the law, no matter what politicians say. The president of the New York Patrolmen's Benevolent Association has also announced that his members "will enforce the law 100 per cent", even when ordered not to do so. Why is this happening? What shapes the attitudes of the police?

This "rebellion of the police" is a response both to increased crime rates and to their being faced with "confrontation tactics" by student and black radical militants, who seek deliberately to inflame the police into engaging in various forms of brutality.

Thus, Stokeley Carmichael has declared that a demonstration which does not result in police action against the participants is a failure. The events at Chicago during the Democratic convention constitute the best recent example of the way in which a major police force can completely lose its head when faced by a confrontationist demonstration. (Ironically, the Chicago police force has been one of the few major ones which had made real efforts to adjust to changing conditions. According to William Turner's book, *The Police Establishment*, close to 25 per cent of the force is Negro, a proportion far above New York and Los Angeles.) Some black and white New Radicals openly declare that the killing of police in the ghetto is not

280

murder, that it is an inherent form of self defence. Police have been shot at and occasionally killed in ambush.

The current tensions between the police and New Left student and black nationalist radicals probably involve the most extreme example of deliberate provocation which the police have ever faced. The tactics of the campus-based opposition rouse the most deep-seated feelings of class resentment. Most policemen are conservative, conventional, upwardly mobile working-class supporters of the American Way, who aspire for a better life for their families. To find the scions of the upper middle class in the best universities denouncing them as "pigs", hurling insults which involve use of the most aggressive sexual language, such as "Up against the wall, mother fucker", throwing bricks and bags of faeces at them, is much more difficult to accept than the normal problems of crime and vice, or violence stemming from minority ghettos.

The deliberate efforts by contemporary New Left radicals to bait and provoke the police is new in the history of leftist movements. The American Socialist Party in its early history actually pointed to the police department as a good example of the way the government could provide needed services efficiently. Allen Benson, the party's candidate for President in 1916, cited the police department, together with the post office, and municipal railways, as socialist institutions, in his book, *Socialism Made Plain*, published in 1904.

The European left still remembers that the police come from proletarian origins. During the May 1968 student demonstrations and strikes in Italy, a leading communist intellectual, Pier Paolo Pasolini, told the New Left students that in a conflict between them and the police, he stood with the police: "Your faces are those of sons of good families, and I hate you as I hate your fathers. The good breeding comes through. . . . Yesterday when you had your battle in the Valle Giulia with the police, my sympathies were with the police because they are the sons of the poor. . . ."

Given the interest shown in the welfare of the police by sections of the European left, it is not surprising that the political behaviour of European police has been more ambivalent than that of the American police. On various occasions, segments of the police in Europe have shown sympathy for left and working-class forces, particularly where they have been serving under left governments for some time.

This was true in Social Democratic Berlin and Prussia generally before 1932, in Vienna before 1934, and in parts of Republican Spain before 1936. The ambivalent attitudes of the police have shown up most recently in

281

France, where a number of police unions issued statements after the May 1968 events, denying responsibility for use of force against student demonstrators. The police organizations wanted it known that the government, not the police, was responsible for the vigour of the actions taken. The Cohn-Bendit brothers, in their recent book, *Obsolete Communism*, stress the lowly origins of the police as reducing their political reliability for the Gaullist regime.

It is unlikely, however, that the American New Left students will come to see the police in a sympathetic light, as exploited, insecure, alienated members of the underprivileged classes. To a large extent, the provocative efforts of the students reflect their privileged social position, the biases of the educated upper middle class.

They are thus prepared to alienate the police, as well as conventional working-class opinion, in order to provoke police brutality which will enable them both to prove their manhood, and validate their total rejection of all social institutions. Hence, we may expect a continuation of the vicious circle of confrontation and police terror tactics.

Liberal moderates properly react to this situation by demanding that the police act toward deviant behaviour much as all other professionals do, that they have no more right to react aggressively towards provocative acts than psychiatrists faced by maniacal and dangerous patients, that no matter what extremists do, the police should not lose their self-control. Such a policy is easy to advocate, but difficult to carry out.

To urge that the police should react to provocations and deviant behaviour like other trained professionals ignores the fact that most of them are "working-class" professionals, not the products of postgraduate education. Society treats their job like a semi-skilled position which requires, at best, a few weeks' training. Norman Kassoff of the research staff of the International Association of Police Chiefs has compared the legal minimum training requirements for various occupations in the different American states. Calculated in terms of hours, the average minimum is 11,000 hours for physicians, 5000 for embalmers, 4000 for barbers, 1200 for beauticians, and less than 200 for policemen. The vast majority of policemen begin carrying guns and enforcing the law with less than five weeks' training of any kind.

Indications from a number of cities across the country suggest that the police will continue to be a source of support for the more extreme right wing and conservative groups. They have been an effective force in mobilizing opposition to urban social reform proposals pressed by liberal mayors. Police anger at restrictions on their use of force in black communities has dramatically raised the issue of civilian control over police policies. In a situation where the extremists of the left seek police violence, the right wing predisposition of many patrolmen may increase the process of political polarisation.

But at the same time new tensions have increased the old conflict between the police and the liberals. For it must be said that liberals are prejudiced against police, much as many white police are biased against Negroes. Most liberals are ready to assume that all charges of police brutality are true. They tend to refuse to give the police the benefit of any doubt. They rarely denounce the extreme black groups and left radicals for their confrontationist efforts. They do not face up to the need for tactics to deal with deliberate incitement to mob violence. If the liberal and intellectual communities are to have any impact on the police, if they are to play any role in reducing the growing political alienation of many police, they must show as some recognition that the police force is also composed of human beings, seeking to earn a living. They must be willing to engage in a dialogue with the police concerning their problems. Few liberals or intellectuals have shown any readiness to do so. Adam Yarmolinsky is one of the rare liberal leaders to take up the economic cause of the police in the public press, arguing for the need sharply to increase salaries, as well as death benefits for police killed in the line of duty.

An increasing body of evidence suggests an affinity between police work and support for radical right politics, particularly when linked to racial unrest. During the 1968 Presidential campaign, many journalists reported on the widespread public expressions of sympathy for George Wallace by patrolmen voiced directly to the candicate, or to reporters accompanying him. Wallace was unmistakably a hero to many policemen. John Harrington, the president of the Fraternal Order of Police, the largest such organisation in America, with over 130,000 members and affiliates in over 900 communities, publicly endorsed him. A poll of police opinion in Colorado revealed heavy backing for him.

Similar reports concerning police support for right wing or conservative candidates, who have campaigned against civil rights and integration proposals, have appeared frequently in the press. Thus, in 1967 Boston journalists commented on the general support for Louise Day Hicks among the police of that city. Mrs Hicks had won her political spurs in the fight

283

which she waged as chairman of the Boston School Committee against school integration. And when she ran for mayor, she seemingly found the police among her most enthusiastic backers. In New York, police have stood out among the supporters of the Conservative Party, an organization which also has opposed public efforts to enforce school integration. The New York Conservative Party was the one political group in the city to fight the setting up of a civilian public review board for the police.

A study by Jerome Skolnick (of the University of Chicago) of the Oakland, California, police in 1964, based on interviews with many of them, concluded that "a Goldwater type of conservatism was the dominant political and emotional persuasion of the police". In Los Angeles, an official order had to be issued in 1964 telling the police that they could not have bumper stickers or other campaign materials on their police cars, because of the large number who had publicly so indicated their support for Goldwater.

In 1964, John Rousselot, then National Director of the John Birch Society, claimed that "substantial numbers" of the members were policemen. All the available evidence confirms his contention. Thus a study of the national membership of the society by Fred Grupp, a political scientist at Louisiana State University, who sent out a questionnaire to a random sample of the Birch membership with the help of the society, found that over 3 per cent of those who reported their occupation were policemen, a figure which is over four times the police proportion of the national labour force. A number of journalistic reports on the activities of the Birch Society in different parts of the country have commented on the relatively high police membership. In New York City, in July 1965, a reporter judged that the majority of the audience at a large rally in the Town Hall sponsored by the Birch Society's speakers bureau wore Police Benevolent Association badges. The society itself "estimates that it has 500 members in the New York City Police Department". In Philadelphia, the mayor placed a number of police on limited duty for membership in the society.

Some indication of the fact that peace officers in high places are sympathetic to the society may be seen in the fact that former Sheriff James Clark of Selma, Alabama, who not only played a major role in suppressing civil rights demonstrations in his city, but has been a frequent featured speaker for the Birch Society, was elected president of the national organization of sheriffs. While serving as chief of the Los Angeles Police Department, William H. Parker took part in the Manion Forum, a right wing radio discussion programme run by Clarence Manion, a leader of the Birch Society.

All this is no new development. During the 1930s, police were reported as heavily involved in the Black Legion and in Father Coughlin's Christian Front, two neo-fascist groups. And Gunnar Myrdal, in his classic study of the race problem in America, *An American Dilemma*, conducted in the late 1930s and early 1940s, asserted that one of the principal sources of Ku Klux Klan activity in the south at that time came from law-enforcement officers. Studies of the Klan at the height of its power in all sections of the United States in the early 1920s indicate a considerable police presence. Typical of Klan propaganda which attracted police support was the plank in the programme of the Chicago Klan which called for "supporting officials in all phases of law enforcement", a slogan close to the "Support your local police" campaign waged by the Birch Society and George Wallace four decades later.

It is astonishing to discover when we move back to the main predecessor of the Klan among powerful exponents of religious bigotry—the anti-Catholic nativist American Protective Association (APA), which flourished in the early 1890s—that it also appears to have been the recipient of police support. My own researches on this movement indicate that the police were considerably over-represented among APA members. Thus, in Minneapolis 6.5 per cent were policemen, in Sacramento 8 per cent, and in San Jose 7 per cent.

In citing some of the evidence which links the police over time to these movements, I do not want to suggest that most police have been right wing radicals. In fact, as a group, the police have typically been involved in conventional two-party politics. Although there is a general understanding that they should be politically neutral, their role as public employees has involved them in local politics. Prior to the emergence of civil service examinations, appointment to the force was a political plum in most cities. And, once hired, chances for promotion often depended on having access to the local office-holders. In many communities, the police were often part of the machine organization. The widespread pattern of toleration of corruption and the rackets which characterized urban political life until the 1940s usually depended on the cooperation, if not direct participation, of the police.

Although machine and racketeer domination of local government is largely a thing of the past in most cities, the police are necessarily still deeply

285

interested in local politics. High-level appointments are almost invariably made by elected officials. Police chiefs and others who hold high places in the departments must remain in the good graces of the politicians. Those who control city hall determine police pay and working conditions. Hence, the police as individuals and as a body must be actively concerned with access to the political power structure.

Such assumptions would lead us to anticipate that police would avoid any contact with radical groups, with those who seek to change the existing structure of political power. Thus the evidence that significant minorities of police join or openly back right wing and bigoted movements is particularly impressive. (This comment, of course, does not apply to those communities dominated by extremist movements.)

Much of police political behaviour reflects the fact that they are not much different in their social outlook from others in the lower middle class or working class. A recent study of the New York City police by Arthur Niederhoffer, a former member of the department, reports that "for the past 15 years, during a cycle of prosperity, the bulk of police candidates have been upper lower class with a sprinkling of lower middle class; about 95 per cent had no college training". In a survey of the occupations of the fathers of 12,000 recruits who graduated from the New York police academy, he found that over three-quarters were manual or service workers.

Once employed as policemen, their job experiences press them in a conservative direction, reinforcing whatever authoritarian traits they bring to the job from their social background. In general, the policeman's job requires him to be suspicious of people, to value conventional behaviour and toughness. As Niederhoffer points out: "He needs the intuitive ability to sense plots and conspiracies on the basis of embryonic evidence." The political counterpart of such an outlook simplifies political conflict into a black and white fight, and is ready to accept a conspiratorial view of the sources of evil. This basically describes the outlook of extremist groups, whether of the left or right.

The propensity of police to support a radical political posture is also related to their sense of being a low-status out-group in American society. Studies of police opinion have indicated that some police conceal their occupation from their neighbours, finding that many people do not like to associate with policemen.

If policemen judge their social worth by their incomes, they are right in rating it low. A recent article reports that their "pay in major cities now averages about $7500—33 per cent less than is needed to sustain a family of four in moderate circumstances in a large city, according to the US Bureau of Labor Statistics". As a result, many are forced to moonlight to earn a living. Fletcher Knebel cites an expert estimate that from a third to half of all the patrolmen in the country have a second job.

The relative socio-economic status of the police has worsened over time. Richard Wade, an urban historian at the University of Chicago, points out that the situation has changed considerably from 50 years ago when "policemen had an income higher than other trades and there were more applicants than there were jobs." The relative decline in their economic position has heightened their resentment.

Further evidence that such changes in morale have occurred may be found in Albert J. Reiss's surveys of police opinion in Chicago, Boston, and Washington D.C. He reports that 59 per cent believe that the prestige of police work is lower than it was 20 years ago. Lower police morale is not simply a function of a relative decline in income or in perceived status. The police believe their conditions of work have also worsened. Thus 80 per cent state that "police work (is) more hazardous today than five years ago". Sixty per cent believe that the way the public behaves towards the police has changed for the worse since they joined the force.

This view was given eloquent voice in 1965 by the then New York City Police Commissioner, Michael J. Murphy: "The police officer, too, belongs to a minority group—a highly visible minority group, and is also subject to stereotyping and mass attack. Yet he, like every member of every minority, is entitled to be judged as an individual and on the basis of his individual acts, not as a group." Clearly, the police appear to be a status-deprived group, one which feels deep resentment about the public's lack of appreciation for the risks it takes for the community's safety. These risks are not negligible in the United States. In 1967, for example, one out of every eight policemen was assaulted, while 100 of the 350,000 were killed. These rates are considerably higher than in any other developed democratic country.

The policeman's role is particularly subject to fostering feelings of resentment against society, which flow from a typical source of radical politics, "status discrepancies." This term describes the position of individuals or groups who are ranked relatively high on one status attribute and low on another. The fact of having a claim to some prestige is presumed to make people indignantly resent evidence that they are held in low regard by other standards. The police are given considerable authority by society to enforce

287

its laws and are expected to risk their lives if necessary; on the other hand, they feel they receive little prestige and they get a relatively low salary.

The police find few segments of the body politic who appreciate their contribution to society and the risks they take, and if they do, they find this appreciation among conservatives, and particularly the extreme right. It is the Ku Klux Klan, the Birch Society and George Wallace who call for support of the police. The Birch Society has even established awards for police heroism, and has set up funds which provide financial assistance to the families of police killed in the line of duty.

The radical left, in contrast, has almost invariably been hostile. Liberals and leftists have tried to limit the power of the police to deal with suspects. Efforts to enhance the rights of defendants, to guarantee them legal representation, to prevent the authorities from unduly pressuring those taken into police custody, have largely been made by liberals. To many policemen, the liberal side of the political spectrum appears engaged in a constant struggle to make their job more difficult, to increase the physical danger to which they are subject. Many are convinced that dangerous criminals or revolutionists are freely walking the streets because of the efforts of soft-hearted liberals.

To the police, who are constantly exposed to the seamy side of life, who view many deviants and law-breakers as outside the protection of the law, the constant concern for the civil rights of such people makes little sense, unless it reflects moral weakness on the part of the liberals, or more dangerously is an aspect of a plot to undermine legitimate authority. And the fact that the Supreme Court has sided with the civil libertarian interpretations of individual rights in recent years on issues concerning police tactics in securing confessions, the use of wiretaps, and the like, constitutes evidence of how far moral corruption has reached into high places in American society. Reiss's survey of police opinion found that 90 per cent of the police interviewed felt that the Supreme Court "has gone too far in making rules favouring and protecting criminal offenders". The liberal world, then, is perceived as an enemy, an enemy which may attack directly as in the form of demonstrations or riots, or indirectly through its pressure on the courts.

The willingness of police to join or back groups which have been antagonistic to religious (Catholics in the 19th century, Jews in the 20th) and racial minorities, may be partly a function of their job experience. Ethnic slums have often been centres of crime, violence, and vice. Most immigrant groups living in urban America in the past, as well as more recent Negro migrants, have contributed disproportionately to the ranks of criminals and racketeers.

Such groups have often demonstrated a high degree of ethnic solidarity which has led them to refuse to cooperate with police seeking to find and arrest law violators among them. The ethnic slum has been an enemy stronghold, a place of considerable insecurity. Right-wing political groups, which define the minorities or the leftist radicals as conspiratorial corrupters of American morality, have strongly appealed to the morally outraged police.

In evaluating the disposition of the police to participate in the radical right, it is important to reiterate that only a minority of the police in most communities are so involved. Most police, though relatively conservative and conventional, are normally more concerned with the politics of collective bargaining, with getting more for themselves, than with the politics of right-wing extremism. The Patrolmen's Benevolent Association is basically a trade union, which seeks alliances with other labour unions, particularly those within the civil service, and with powerful leaders in the dominant political parties. Police have struck for higher wages on occasion, much as other groups of workers have done. There have been occasions in which police have shown sympathy for striking workers on the picket line, particularly when the workers and the police have belonged to the same ethnic groups. One of the main attractions of police work to new recruits is the lifelong economic security and early pensions which it gives. In this sense, the policeman, like others from low-income backgrounds, is concerned for the expansion of the welfare state.

Like all others, the police are interested in upgrading the public image of their job. They do not like being attacked as thugs, as authoritarians, as lusting for power. Many cities have successfully sought to increase the educational level of those they recruit to the force, and to have a continuing education programme for their police. The academic quality of the courses given at police academies and colleges in various communities has been improving. All of these trends may help upgrade the self-conception of the police as protectors of the peace. It is unlikely, however, that they will have any appreciable impact on the sense of alienation and consequent right-wing radicalism of many police during the current political cycle.

Immigrant Involvement in British and Australian Politics

JAMES JUPP

BRITAIN, the United States, Canada, Australia and New Zealand all have a common heritage of basically "British" stock, English language, Protestantism and liberal democratic institutions. All have also experienced considerable immigration which has introduced important elements from other political cultures, while Canada and the United States have major long-resident minorities—in one case linguistically in the other racially—distinct from the general population. Where Britain has differed from the others is in being primarily an emigrant country, in fact, with Ireland included, the largest single source of immigrants for the other four during the past century. But over the past twenty years the gain from immigration into Britain has offset the loss of two million Britons who have left mainly for Australia and Canada. The overseas-born element in the populations of the five is now: Australia 17 per cent, Canada 15.6 per cent, New Zealand 14 per cent, United States 5 per cent and Britain 5 per cent (counting Eire as a separate country). Thus Britain is still at the bottom of the league and has shown its determination to stay there by passing the restrictive Commonwealth Immigrants Acts of 1962 and 1968. Entry into the Common Market could bring a revival of immigration, although from Europe and not the Commonwealth.

Although Britain has such a relatively small overseas-born element, and has very little in the way of an adult second generation, it is still reasonable to suppose that immigrants will have some influence on its politics as participants, rather than merely as objects to be deplored and voted against. The great majority of adult immigrants to Britain, whether Irish or Commonwealth, are eligible to vote and stand for office at all elected levels. As in all immigrant countries, Britain's new arrivals have concentrated in certain

290

areas and thus maximized their statistically insignificant voting influence. There is no reason to suppose that immigrants have common political loyalties or feelings of solidarity, however. On the contrary, many immigrants are hostile towards each other and try to relate themselves to the host majority rather than to their polyglot neighbours. Immigrants in Britain and Australia have generally tended to settle in "immigrant areas" rather than in "ethnic areas", producing a variety of origins within a single neighbourhood. Despite this variety it would not be unreasonable, on American experience, to expect growing immigrant and second-generation involvement in local politics and the emergence of ward bosses and voting blocs.

It would, however, be absurd to use the American example exclusively as a guide to likely developments in Britain or Australia. While most analytical work on immigration has come from the United States and must, perforce, be used in all theoretical discussion, in terms of political impact the U.S.A. is a misleading case. Firstly, the sheer bulk of immigration to the U.S.A. has not been experienced by Britain or Australia. For seventy years, between 1860 and 1930, one-eighth of the American population was recorded as overseas-born. This level has only been maintained in Australia since 1951 and has never been reached in Britain. Moreover one-half of immigrants to Australia have been British. Thus we can roughly estimate the "British and Irish" composition of America to be 55 per cent, of Canada to be 45 per cent, while for Australia it is perhaps 87 per cent and for Britain still about 95 per cent. The numerical possibility of "ethnic" politics in Canada and the U.S.A. is thus much greater. Secondly, the party and electoral systems of Britain and Australia are very close while for America and Canada they are quite distinctive. Class-based voting is almost absent in Canada, while the American parties are much more loosely structured than those in Britain and Australia. Both Britain and Australia have major Labour parties based on trade union affiliations. As the bulk of immigrants are manual workers this is an important factor in assessing their likely political impact and the points at which it will be exercised. Again, in the United States far more positions are open to election or party patronage than is the case in Britain and Australia. Thus not only are there more "ethnic" voters but there are more jobs to offer them.

For these reasons I would suggest that Australia may offer a better guide in this field than does America. The actual numbers of overseas-born are almost equal in Britain and Australia at about two million in each. Of these nearly one-half are British in Australia, while nearly one-third are Irish in

Britain. In both countries four-fifths are entitled to vote if old enough. In both countries there is considerable variety of origins. Thus in Britain in 1966 there were overseas-born groups of 30,000 or more from sixteen different countries. In Australia there were twelve such national groups in 1961. The great difference is, of course, that Australia excludes all non-European immigrants except for a tiny handful who are mostly Chinese. This does make it possible to distinguish between situations and attitudes which are "racial" and those which apply to immigrants regardless of race. The large Greek, Lebanese, Yugoslav and, to some extent, southern Italian communities in Australia seem to share some of the attributes of non-European immigrants in Britain. The greatest differences will emerge in the second generation, although there is little doubt that British Commonwealth immigrants suffer far more discrimination in the United Kingdom than do Southern Europeans in Australia.

SETTLEMENT AND OCCUPATION

In both Britain and Australia immigrants have gravitated towards the most prosperous areas, avoiding those districts in which fellow-countrymen may previously have settled if they are no longer economically buoyant. The picture of immigrants settling near the pierhead, which may have held for New York, Liverpool or Sydney in the past, is no longer appropriate. Immigrants are found in the greatest numbers and concentrations in those areas with the lowest unemployment, the highest wages and the greatest economic expansion. Thus the largest absolute numbers of Irish in Britain are now in north and west London, while there are higher proportions in Birmingham, Coventry and Luton than in the "historic" areas of Liverpool or Glasgow.[11]* Similarly in Australia the State of Queensland, once a strong magnet for immigrants, has attracted very few in recent years and has consistently had the highest unemployment and the lowest wage level of any state.

The typical areas of immigrant concentration in both countries are of three major kinds. Firstly, and embracing the largest numbers, are some of the inner areas of the most expansive of the major cities.[1] These are not just "the slums". For example, there is only limited immigrant settlement in most of

*References in brackets refer to bibliography at end of this article.

[1]This means in practice, in North and West London, North and West Birmingham, North and West Melbourne, Western Adelaide and central Sydney and Perth.

east and south-east London and only recent movement into waterfront areas of Melbourne. The particular "twilight areas" to which immigrants gravitate are those left free of rent control or major low-cost public rehousing. They have a shifting though generally declining population, a high proportion of rented rooms and divided houses and a tradition of housing transients. These areas are often without a highly developed community spirit or a consistent political tradition, as they have only a small, declining and elderly long-resident population. As immigrants become settled they often buy houses in adjoining but more stable suburbs further from the city centre.

The second type of area is in the outer suburbs of the same large cities, in newer housing close to engineering works and particularly to the motor industry. Political traditions are more consistently Labour, based usually on strong trade unions and large public authority housing estates.[2] Thirdly are a number of new and expanding towns, again often associated with the motor or other recently established industries. In this latter category the picture of immigrant settlement is often quite pleasant as housing is new and fairly good. Many of the native residents are also new arrivals from other parts of the country. Political traditions are relatively unformed and swings in voting allegiance are common.[3]

Apart from these three comparable classes of area, there are some settlement patterns peculiar to one country. The large British settlement in newly built Australian outer suburbs has no counterpart in England. This type of area is not so important in the overall British housing situation and there is no counterpart for the assisted British families who are officially encouraged to come to Australia. In Britain there is a large middle-class settlement of European and "white" Commonwealth origin in areas like Chelsea, South Kensington and Hampstead which have no important Australian equivalents. In both countries there is a large Jewish middle-class settlement of European origin in middle-distance suburbs.[4] However, these settlers do not look upon themselves as "immigrants" and are not normally so regarded by their

[2]These include Southall and Acton in London, Sunshine, Broadmeadows and Dandenong in Melbourne, Liverpool in Sydney and Hindmarsh in Adelaide. Increasingly, as studies in Southall and Batley have shown, immigrants are becoming owner-occupiers and show only limited interest in council housing.

[3]These include Bedford, Coventry, Luton, Slough and High Wycombe in England, and Geelong, the Latrobe Valley, Elizabeth and Wollongong in Australia.

[4]For example, Hendon and Finchley in London or St. Kilda and Caulfield in Melbourne.

neighbours. Apart from these exceptions to the three major types of settlement, both countries produce pockets of a particular nationality clustered around a particular industry far away from the general areas of immigrant settlement. These include the Pakistanis in the Yorkshire woollen industry or the Finns around the ore mines of Mt. Isa in Queensland. Nor is there any major city in either country which does not contain some immigrants although usually too few to have much political importance.

The settlement characteristics of immigrants are obviously important in any system based on geographical representation. So are the occupational characteristics in any system where class loyalty is the basis of voting and of party support in general. Immigrants can be broadly divided into two major classes. There is a very large foreign population in London who are in upper-middle class and professional jobs associated with embassies, education, tourism and international commerce. In Australia there is a high professional component amongst British immigrants. Where these have any interest in local politics, it is not surprising that many favour the conservatism of their neighbours and co-workers. This confuses the political picture for areas like Kensington and Hampstead where this type of "immigrant" lives close to the poorer Commonwealth and Irish immigrants. However, the majority of Commonwealth and Irish immigrants in Britain, and of European immigrants in Australia are employed in closely corresponding occupations. The main occupations of such immigrants are: building and construction, public transport, factory labouring, clothing and textiles, food and catering, domestic and menial.[2] These are all the lowest paid, most insecure and most unpleasant jobs—within these areas. Within them immigrants also gravitate towards the least pleasant sectors. They are in the foundry rather than the machine shop, are conductors rather than drivers, assistants rather than operators. The craft unions often sustain this by their barriers to promotion without apprenticeship or length of service. This tendency for immigrants to be concentrated in jobs which natives do not want is also central to the economies of European countries, especially Switzerland, West Germany, France and Holland. Thus it is a truly immigrant, rather than a specifically racial phenomenon. Some immigrant groups, particularly Greeks in Australia and Indians in England, quickly create business and professional classes which may at once provide political leaders for, and be more conservative than, the general communities.

The political consequences of this geographical and occupational concentration are by no means clear cut. Immigrants bring the beginnings of a political culture with them and are not simply objects determined by the working or living environment of their new country. Thus although most East European immigrants in Australia live in Labour-controlled working-class districts and belong to Labour-dominated trade unions, there is some evidence that they vote for the Liberal or Democratic Labor Parties and not for the Australian Labor Party.[5] This reflects their strong anti-Leftism based on experience as refugees from Communism. In both countries there is the opposite feature of middle-class Jews living in Conservative areas and belonging to Conservative occupations, yet voting Left, in part because of their pre-war persecution by right-wing movements.[3] Thus when an immigrant brings attitudes with him which were formed by political persecution it is often irrelevant where he lives or what he works at.[4]

However, recent immigrants in both countries rarely have such back-grounds. It is reasonable to suppose that occupational and residential influences will move them to support the Labour parties, although not always with much enthusiasm. Of fifteen British parliamentary seats in which one-quarter or more of the population were born overseas, nine were Labour in 1964 and ten in 1966. In Australia, where Labour support was lower than in Britain, the picture was slightly clearer. Of sixteen seats with over one-quarter immigrant population, twelve were Labour in 1963 and ten in 1966. The difference between the two countries is largely explained by the quite large immigrant populations in central and north London upper-middle class suburbs like Chelsea or St. Marylebone.

For such a cross-cultural comparison to be valid certain assumptions have to be made. I take it as almost self-evident that despite its American-inspired constitution, Australian political institutions approximate closely to those of Britain. State governments, although composed of professional politicians, deal largely with matters such as education and housing and may be compared with top-tier local authorities in Britain. Like those authorities they are concerned in a whole range of functions which affect immigrants very closely, including employment in public transport, construction and other fields towards which immigrants tend to move. The two sets of major

[5]The Liberal Party and the Australian Labor Party correspond very closely to the British Conservative and Labour Parties in terms of electoral support. The Democratic Labor Party broke away from the Australian Labor Party between 1955 and 1957, is predominantly Catholic, strongly anti-Communist and pro-American. It has four members in the Australian Senate, two from Victoria and two from Queensland. Three are of Irish Catholic descent.

295

urban parties are also very similar in social composition, voting support and philosophical outlooks.[5] Political terminology is the same. There are differences in attitude which may be important. In particular, Australian anxieties about social class are less acute than in Britain. If, as seems possible, regional differences in racialism in Britain are related to regional differences in class attitudes,[6] then Australia can be treated as yet another regional variant. There does exist a white to black scale of values in Australia which grades Southern Europeans in a lowly place and, where actual contact exists, causes discrimination against aborigines.

Apart from these many similarities, one must also accept that we are still dealing primarily with an *immigrant* and not a *racial* situation. Sheila Patterson, for example, does argue this. She writes: "The situation can more usefully be seen, not in black and white, but in terms of socio-economic class affiliations, of cultural contacts and conflicts, of rural and urban differences, of adaption and acceptance between migrants or a minority group and the receiving society."[7] This led her to treat all immigrant groups together as capable of classification in a way which does not centre on colour. For comparisons between Britain and Australia to be valid this approach is obviously vital. I believe that it is applicable to the "immigrant situation", but am very sceptical of Mrs. Patterson's optimism about the second and later generations. Here the barrier of physical assimilability cannot be so easily broken down as the socio-economic barriers facing the initial immigrants. The P.E.P. Report[8] and subsequent correspondence in *The Times* suggest that coloured people will continue to face discrimination for the foreseeable future whether immigrants or not. In acute situations, for example in Northern Ireland, discrimination may continue against minorities who are neither immigrants nor physically distinguishable. Such has been the case, where Catholics are concerned, in some Australian institutions like the Liberal Party. However, in the cool, affluent style of politics which exists in Britain and Australia, it is reasonable to regard immigrants as potentially assimilable provided they do not *appear* markedly different from the norm. Then it is the behaviour of the hosts, not the immigrants, which is determined by colour, producing anti-immigrant political movements and "colour-based" counter-movements.

The phenomenon of Powellism, for which there is no Australian equivalent, cuts across consensual politics and is only tenuously related to the economic issues regarded as central by conventional politicians. Powell himself publicly claims that by moving off at a tangent in this way he has swum from the backwaters of formal politics into the mainstream of public opinion. Many of his complaints against coloured immigrants are very closely related to those made against white immigrants in Australia in the early 1950s. An optimist might note that the conventional parties won the battle for a consensual approach to immigration against the extremists and were moving by the 1960s towards acceptance of the modification of the "White Australian Policy" under pressure from a very small minority of liberal churchmen and intellectuals. However, this was against a background of increasing affluence and economic expansion in Australia, much of it clearly created by immigrant labour.

VOTING AND ELECTIONS

On Australian and American experience one would expect immigrants to have an effect on politics at a number of points. I would estimate that, as voters, they are unlikely to have an important influence until their proportion in an area reaches more than about one-quarter, although there is no reason why individual immigrants may not "accidentally" secure election in non-immigrant areas on their individual merits.[6] However, it seems probable that as distinctive immigrant communities grow, the chances of "accidental" selection outside areas of concentration may fall rather than rise. Thus the "ethnic" candidate will be found almost entirely in areas of concentration, which in England means almost exclusively in Greater London as in Australia it means very largely in Melbourne and Adelaide. The "ethnic vote" will be limited in its impact by a number of factors. In areas of concentration there is normally a great deal of mixing of origins. The "one-nation" area is very exceptional and rarely reaches the level which seems crucial for effective influence on the choice of candidate. There is little feeling of immigrant solidarity, only of ethnic solidarity, and even that varies a great deal. The ethnic vote is further limited in impact by the characteristics of immigrants. Even where they are naturalized, as nearly 80 per cent are in both countries, they tend to mobility, to a lack of interest in host country politics and to an

[6]For example D. Naoroji (Liberal M.P. for Finsbury Central, 1892–5), S. Saklatvala (Communist M.P. for Battersea North 1922–3 and 1924–9) and Krishna Menon, a St. Pancras borough councillor, were not noticeably helped or hindered by their Indian origin nor, with the possible exception of Menon, did they have many Indian constituents.

identification with the homeland or with intra-community affairs. In Australia, with compulsory voting the effect of this may simply be to lessen the solidarity of ethnic groups, because of indifference about the electoral result. In Britain, with voluntary voting and laxer registration, it may lead to massive abstention and failure to register. This can only be remedied by organized efforts by fellow nationals. Where these work through established parties this may facilitate the capture of an ethnic vote for the party concerned. However, until the ethnic vote is an appreciable part of the total, it seems unlikely that most local parties will try to organize it at all.

At the level of candidate selection the Australian experience suggests the unlikelihood of anything approaching the American case of the "ethnic" ticket. Candidates are normally chosen at all levels from single-member areas and there is nothing like the range of elected offices found in the U.S.A. and requiring multi-candidature. In the rare cases where multi-candidature is required, for example in the Australian Senate or on the Greater London Council, there has been slightly more chance of an immigrant being nominated. Immigrants suffer serious disadvantages in selection. Unlike most elected representatives they come largely from the unskilled and semi-skilled working classes. These have always been very under-represented even where, as in both countries, there are powerful Labour parties. Even more importantly, immigrants are outsiders and seem less likely to join parties or to be settled long enough or to have established enough local interests and associations to fit the normal requirements of candidates. The fear that an immigrant candidate will lose votes is a very realistic one, given that there are no constituencies or municipalities and scarcely any wards in either country in which immigrants form a majority.

This leads inescapably to the finding that immigrants and possibly their descendants too, will be grossly "under-represented" in all elected assemblies. This is even true for the United States. Those immigrants who do secure nomination will almost invariably be long-established middle-class community leaders. Even these will normally only win at the municipal level. It seems that in both countries only a courageous act of faith is likely to secure the nomination of an immigrant for a national elective office by the major parties. Such acts are so rare as to constitute almost unique cases so far if one excludes British immigrants in Australia or Irish immigrants in Britain.

The selection of successful candidates in the urban areas of both countries rests entirely in the hands of the two major parties. This applies almost as much to municipal as to national or regional elections. Thus the degree to which immigrants participate in the parties is crucial. It is quite possible for a minority group to maximize its representation through a party, as Irish descended Catholics did in the Australian Labor Party between 1916 and 1955 or as Jews have done in the Democratic Party in the U.S.A. or the Labour Party in Britain. So far the newer immigrants have failed to achieve this in either country. There is of course a handful of British-born parliamentarians in Australia, most of them quite indistinguishable from Australians, and an even smaller proportion of "white" Commonwealth and European Members of Parliament in Britain who are equally close to the norm. In local government the stake of the overseas-born is only slightly greater. In the Melbourne metropolitan area, with 12 per cent of its people born in Europe, less than 3 per cent of councillors are of European origin. In Greater London, with 12 per cent born outside the United Kingdom, there is one West Indian on the Council of one hundred. Immigrants have been as unsuccessful on the Kensington, Camden, Brent and Islington councils as on their Melbourne and Adelaide counterparts. But in May 1968 both the Conservative and Labour Parties nominated one Sikh candidate in their list of three for a ward in the London Borough of Ealing. The Labour Sikh won, with more votes than his two fellow-Labour candidates. [10] The creation of Greater London, submerging the immigrant communities in larger London boroughs, diminished the possibility of maintaining a big enough "ethnic vote" to secure the election of immigrants.[7] Nor has the situation in the few provincial cities with heavy concentrations of immigrants been any different.

This suggests that apart from being inadequate at registering and voting, immigrants are also reluctant to join parties and do not make much progress even when they do. In both countries immigrants have stood for office as independents because they either do not understand the grip of the two parties on the voters or they have failed to secure party endorsement and have taken the desperate alternative of running alone. [11] Even where, as in some Australian states, the parties have set up immigrant committees, these have either been ineffectual as pressure groups or as ladders to leadership or have actually been disbanded by the party. In Britain this situation has not

[7]The 1961 Census shows twenty-one boroughs in Greater London where over 10 per cent of the population were Irish, Commonwealth and foreign-born. In 1966, after five further years of immigration, there were only twelve of the new London boroughs with this proportion (Barnet, Brent, Camden, Ealing, Hackney, Islington, Kensington, Lambeth, Southwark, Tower Hamlets, Wandsworth and Westminster).

arisen. The relationship between the Labour Party and groups like the Indian Workers' Association has many of the features found in the links between the Australian Labor Party and the various ethnic groups which sympathize with it. Immigrants are seen as votes and as vote gatherers. But they are not seen as candidates or officials.

THE LABOUR MOVEMENT

Immigrants tend towards the party which ostensibly appeals to the working classes and has a radical tradition which attracts middle-class liberals. This is not to say that the two Labour Parties can rely on immigrant support indefinitely without giving something in return. There is substantial support for the Liberal and Democratic Labor Parties among immigrants to Australia and in Victoria this may well exceed the support given to the Australian Labor Party.[12] The most prosperous areas are those to which immigrants have moved in both countries and these have swung from party to party fairly freely over the past twenty years. In Australia the appeal of the radical working-class party has been lessened by proletarian ethnocentrism which is also found, of course, in some local Labour Parties in Britain. British Labour has a much stronger "liberal" element, especially in London where half of all immigrants are concentrated. Nevertheless it is worth noting the discontent with Labour which the tightening of the Commonwealth Immigrants Acts has brought. In contrast to Australia, the immigrant has nowhere much to go. He rightly assesses that the Conservative Party is even less sympathetic to him and much less likely to encourage him to join or to become a candidate. The immigrant's road to political influence still lies through the Labour movement in both countries, however many gates the Labour Parties may erect across the road. This will mean that the Labour Parties must make themselves more amenable to immigrant pressure and more willing to endorse immigrant candidates. Otherwise immigrants will move to the Right, as in Australia or remain abstainers as in Britain.

The other segment of the Labour movement which may give immigrants some access to political influence is that of the trade unions. On the whole unions have appeared to immigrants as protectors of established interest.[13] In turn, immigrants by their drive to rapid accumulation of money are more likely to engage in contract work, in sweated trades or in other ways unpalatable to the restrictionist approach of craft unionism in both countries.

The problem of communication between officials and members is probably more acute in Australia because of the number of Europeans involved. The protection of conditions is more acute in Britain with its lower level of unionization and the absence of legal enforcement of conditions and official encouragement of the closed shop. In both countries some large unions have officially encouraged immigrants. These include the Ironworkers in Australia and the Transport and General Workers in Britain. In both cases there were ideological reasons for this encouragement. But many unions in the unskilled trades are barely efficient, have little idealism and have such a high turnover of members that they are scarcely democratic either. The only immigrant groups having much impact on the unions are those like the Greeks in Australia or the Sikhs in Britain who have a high level of social cohesion already and who transmit this to the industrial field. Some trades like building labouring have seen their radical traditions (or bad labour relations) sustained by immigrants. Others like public transport seem to have had a different experience. Unionists have been reluctant to encourage the development of immigrants' skills and it cannot be said that the craft unions have looked after their new members any better than the labouring ones. In both countries there have been attempts to set up unions based exclusively on immigrants and this has only worsened relations with the Labour movement.

PRESSURE GROUPS

The obvious avenues open to immigrants seem so narrow that it is hardly surprising that they have not had much impact on the formal aspects of representative politics. But it cannot be assumed because they are mainly in the ineffectual unskilled and semi-skilled working classes, because they are still interested in their own affairs rather than those of the hosts, that immigrants do not need or want methods for influencing public policy. Because immigrants feel no common sense of solidarity it must not be assumed that they do not have some common interests. The increasingly harsh application of British immigration laws in the past five years is now affecting such previously welcome guests as Australians. While they would be the last to feel solidarity with West Indians, they are caught in a common dilemma requiring a political answer. Similarly in Australia, while there is no communication at all between British and European immigrants, the former are now organizing against hostel conditions just as the latter did in 1961. Immigrants need political pressure points because they are affected by

301

immigration laws and their administration, because they are relatively at a disadvantage in the labour market and in housing and education, and because they need to ensure protection for themselves and their children in an environment which may become hostile at any time.

Having said that immigrants are relatively ineffectual in the formal democratic process, it must be added that they are not very successful at pressure groups activities either. The conscription of aliens in Australia in 1966 and the new Commonwealth Immigrants Act in Britain in 1968 were both campaigned against by immigrant pressure groups but with very little outcome and with only a modest response from the established politicians. This weakness in organizing applies particularly to those who, like the Irish in Britain or the British in Australia, do not see themselves as a distinctive group with common interests but have made some impact on formal politics as acceptable individuals. Those groups with high social solidarity, with religiously sanctioned endogamy, with historic experience of isolation or persecution, with distinctive languages and cultures, are the most likely to form effective pressures just as they are the most likely to resist assimilation, to vote as a bloc or to play a concerted rather than an atomized part in organization. Such groups have included the Germans and Irish of the nineteenth century but not of the twentieth, the Jews, Greeks, Baltic peoples, Sikhs and Pakistanis. Within these groups there is, of course, a very high level of controversy and even dissension with shadings of regional or local loyalty. Towards the outside world they present a far more united front than do West Indians or Italians for example. For an ethnic pressure group to succeed it must have the discipline to overcome its alien character and small numbers. Only the tightly-knit communities are likely to achieve this. But it cannot be assumed that previously disunited groups may not coalesce in the face of adversity or persecution. The second generation of West Indians may feel more solidarity than the first.

Pressure groups involving immigrants may be divided between those arising out of an immigrant community itself and those encouraged by non-immigrants.[14] In neither Britain nor Australia are there many successful immigrant pressure groups embracing several communities. These may arise from the "externally encouraged" category, even from government-sponsored bodies like the Race Relations Board or the National Committee for Commonwealth Immigrants. In Australia the official Good Neighbour Council is currently incapable of, and was never intended to adopt, pressure group tactics. The strength of assimilationist attitudes in official Australian circles inhibits such a body from seeing itself as acting for immigrants. In Britain, paradoxically, the greater opposition to immigrants and the controversies which have arisen created several bodies in which British liberals work for and with immigrants and attempt to protect them. Immigrant organizations which arise from particular communities, like the various Indian, Pakistani and Caribbean groups, thus have a ready made avenue for pressure which is largely absent in Australia. But the split in the Campaign Against Racial Discrimination shows how difficult it is for such multinational groups to retain their cohesion.

Pressure groups based on one community may be formed specifically for political purposes or may have other aspects. They may, like the Jewish Boards of Deputies, attempt to represent the whole community or, like the Connolly Association, only speak for a very small minority. Their greatest disadvantage is that they can be isolated as an alien force. Some groups, particularly emigré political parties, may indeed consciously try to isolate themselves from the host country. Others try very hard to be accepted within a pluralist frame. All that the more representative groups have to offer politicians is the prospect of electoral support for one party or another or the provision of useful assistance and information for public agencies. The former promise is not usually very important. However, both the Greeks in Melbourne and the Sikhs in London have been able to assemble rallies of five thousand people in the past year, which is more than the major parties could do themselves. This "old-fashioned" kind of activity may impress politicians but probably does not. The more subtle approach of dealing directly with public agencies is gradually coming to be understood in both countries. Immigrant pressure groups may be able to use embassies and High Commissions as a channel for approaching the host government. They may also, as with the Australian Greeks and the British Pakistanis during the past year, storm their own embassies in protest. Immigrant leaders also try to establish links with the Home Office or Australian Immigration Department. This may be difficult if their group is also engaged in public criticism as it often must be to retain its following.

There are only a relative handful of effectively functioning pressure groups on an ethnic base in both countries, despite a great proliferation of ephemeral associations. Most of these are also social, cultural, religious or political bodies and derive much of their support from these activities. Some pressure groups, such as the Yugoslav Settlers Association in Australia or the Indian Workers' Association in Britain, have attached themselves to the Labour Parties as the most effective method of working. Some East European political groups in Australia have attached themselves to the Liberals or the Democratic Labor Party. In Britain some Poles have recently founded an Anglo-Polish Conservative Association under the patronage of Mr. Selwyn Lloyd. Clearly all these acknowledge the difficulty of exerting pressure from a purely "alien" base. Yet it is the very fact that their followers are so alien that gives them their solidarity. Without the feeling of being different the main cementing factor disappears. The more assimilated groups and their children become, the less powerful are their pressure groups likely to be. Only if they are denied the right to assimilate, as some Jews believe they are and as most coloured immigrants certainly will be, are communities likely to support such pressure groups indefinitely.

ALIENATION

Relative indifference or even hostility towards the politics of the host district is not confined to overseas immigrants alone. It has been noted that in America, Britain and Australia, internal migrants are also fairly indifferent to the politics of the areas into which they have moved. In the United States the combination of massive internal and external migration has given rise to speculative theories about the alienated and potentially totalitarian characteristics of uprooted people in a modern urban environment. It seems clear from the "black power riots" that the political institutions of America are incapable of satisfying the Negro population and that some of them have turned against the entire system and the concept of a multi-national American state. Second-generation immigrants have often shown non-political symptoms of anti-social behaviour which psychologists explain in terms of rejection of parental norms as a way of gaining acceptance in the host society. On the analysis of American writers like Kornhauser and Smelser one would expect dissatisfied immigrants to be ready material for violent and anomic political movements and to be especially susceptible to totalitarian or millenial appeals. There was widespread fear in Australia in the early 1950s that East European and later German immigrants would bring such movements with them and plant them on local soil. In Britain the indefatigable Duncan Sandys drew similar inferences from the visit of Stokely Carmichael in mid-1967: "We read of race riots in America with detached sympathy. We do not seem to realise that the same will happen here unless we do something quickly about coloured immigration. . . . The breeding of millions of half-caste children would merely produce a generation of misfits and create increased tensions."[15]

On the current evidence of Britain and Australia there is little to support these views. The classic American picture is of immigrants tending towards radicalism or reaction but in either case rejecting calm middle-of-the-road pragmatic politics.[16] It is certainly true that Irish immigrants and descendants played a major role in the Australian Labor Party, the Industrial Workers of the World and the Australian Communist Party. In both countries Jewish influence on the Labour parties has been noticeable, and under the influence of Hitler some of this was redirected towards the communist parties. In Britain today there is some Irish militancy in the building trade and some Sikh radicalism through the Indian Workers' Association. The attraction of Greeks towards communism and militant unionism is also noticeable in Australia. These trends are easily explicable in terms of the native traditions and work situations of the particular groups concerned. It is certainly not true that immigrants as a whole are "available" for anomic or totalitarian movements. Where is manifest the political alienation of most British, Dutch, German, Maltese or Italian immigrants in Australia or of most West Indians, Pakistanis, Polish or Cypriot workers in Britain? If there is a radical potential it is very latent at present. The typical immigrant response to politics is one of apathy rather than militancy.

Analyses of the proposition that immigrants may tend towards the politics of alienation are very hard to validate. In the first place many adult immigrants import political traditions with them. Thus Greeks or Finns may already be Communist before the Australian industrial situation calls up their militant reaction. Many West Indians are already affiliated to messianic sects before arriving in England. Many East Europeans are believed already to have been fascists or reactionaries before becoming refugees. Secondly, immigrants often tend towards industries like mining, transport or the metal trades in which local militant traditions are expected of union members. Some of these are industries which Kornhauser has typified as "socially isolated" and thus susceptible to extremism whether the labour force is immigrant or not. Thus militancy has continued amongst Australian watersiders, who have not accepted many immigrant members, but has not grown markedly among immigrant-dominated trades like hospital work, clothing and textiles.

Theories of susceptibility to extremism are only weakly sustained in the current British and Australian contexts. They have been based on past

305

American experience. Immigration was predominantly from poor and backward areas with authoritarian politics. Absorption was into a *laissez-faire* society where entry was uncontrolled and politics based on spoils and patronage. American politics were dominated by men with rural interests who opposed welfare programmes, employment policies or any public expenditure likely to assist the cities or to tax business. A racial schism already existed and there were substantial areas of native poverty, not only in the South but also in the eastern seaboard cities. None of these factors are present in Britain and Australia today, except in a very mild and modified form. Unemployment has been virtually absent since 1945, particularly in those areas most favoured by immigrants. Thus the severe strains existing in America were not applied. Such strains as there are have been dealt with by means other than anomic political outbursts. Entry into Britain was quickly restricted. In Australia economic strains have simply led to reversed migration rather than to any political complaints of a serious nature.

Where there have been protests these have often reflected frustration of the kind of structural and organizational limits to immigrant influence outlined above. Thus British immigrants protesting about Australian hostel conditions had exhausted constitutional channels and took to rent strikes in 1966. Sikhs in the Midlands inadequately protected against hooliganism and unable to influence the police through political channels, formed their own defence corps. Herein lies the danger in both situations. For if aggrieved immigrants cannot use the many channels open to citizens they are likely to find unconstitutional methods attractive. This applies especially to first- and second-generation immigrants in Britain denied normal rights such as equal consideration for employment and housing. In Australia by contrast immigrant protests are often acceded to. The recent extension of social services to aliens is but one example of the greater ease of achieving political objectives in a society which actively encourages immigration. Provided that all constitutional channels are kept open and that discrimination is progressively reduced by legislation and example, there is little reason to suppose that Britain or Australia will produce a militant radical generation of immigrant origin. In the British case, however, there are very big provisos.

CONCLUSIONS

The British and Australian situations begin to diverge at the point where substantial numbers of second-generation children enter the labour force and the electoral rolls. In Australia as in America, this generation is anxious to assimilate and to reject the position of its parents. It is not particularly political but when it is it tends towards conservatism and conformity. But in Britain the position may be quite different and the parallel is with the young Negroes of America. When colour alone is a bar to acceptance then political groupings grow on quite a different basis from those ethnic foundations surveyed above. While "New Australians" feel little solidarity, "black Englishmen" may do so. The recent split in the Campaign Against Racial Discrimination is an excellent example of two tendencies at work. On the one hand is the normal fissiparousness of immigrant multi-national organizations. On the other is a new-found solidarity based on colour and directed against white liberals, a response similar to that now current in militant Negro movements in America, but completely unknown in any "white" immigrant group in Australia. As Sir Edward Boyle has argued, "Britain today is in transition from an *immigrant* situation to a *colour* situation."[17] This suggests that in contrast to Australia where ethnic groups are sustained by the immigrant generation and are centred on community problems, the British face an expansion of alienated and possibly violent "racial" movements. While these may not become any more important than the marginal racialist groups sustained by the general population, they will prove even more difficult to integrate into the established political system than are existing ethnic pressure groups.

Neither in Britain nor in Australia have immigrants yet exercised the influence on politics which they have in America. This is partly because of their recent settlement which has not allowed an immigrant élite to become established and recognized, and partly because the rigid party systems and the limited number of elective positions do not encourage the approach to immigrants which proved so fruitful in the United States. The parties have been very cautious in their approach, perhaps because they fear the effect on their vote of seeming to sympathize with the newcomers. The immigrants themselves have been very reluctant to get into politics. In Australia assimilationist attitudes and in Britain mildly racialist attitudes, have emanated from the government itself. This has probably alienated immigrants from the political process to a greater degree than if a more permissive approach had been adopted. Immigrants in both countries have been disappointed in both the major parties. They have had less impact on policy making than most other indigenous groups.

REFERENCES

1. The 1966 Sample Census (on which all British figures in this article are based) showed 403,450 Irish-born in the Greater London Council area and 57,000 in the West Midlands conurbation, against only 20,200 in the Merseyside and 22,990 in the Clydeside conurbations. Only the South-east Lancashire conurbation (52,370) are still attracting Irish immigrants to a "historic" Irish area. Of course these figures exclude "second generation Irish" who are likely to be more politically influential. *10 per cent Sample Census of England and Wales, 1966* (London, H.M.S.O., 1967).
2. See *1961 Census of England and Wales: Commonwealth Immigrants in the Conurbations* (London, H.M.S.O., 1965), and J. Zubrzycki, *Immigrants in Australia* (Melbourne, Melbourne University Press, 1960).
3. See P. Y. MEDDING, *From Assimilation to Group Survival* (Melbourne, Cheshire, 1967), for Melbourne Jewry, and J. GOULD and S. ESH, *Jewish Life in Modern Britain* (London, Routledge and Kegan Paul, 1964).
4. For a brief reference to the political views of Polish and other East European post-war settlers in Britain see *London—Aspects of Change* (London, McGibbon and Kee, 1964), p. 325.
5. For comparisons of the voting support of British, Australian, American and Canadian parties see R. R. ALFORD, *Party and Society* (London, Murray, 1964). For party programmes and organisation in Australia see J. JUPP, *Australian Party Politics* (Melbourne, Melbourne University Press, 1964).
6. See W. G. RUNCIMAN, *Relative Deprivation and Social Justice* (California, University of California Press, 1966), pp. 165–6, suggesting that self-perception of manual workers as "middle-class" is most pronounced in the Midlands.
7. SHEILA PATTERSON, *Dark Strangers* (Harmondsworth, Penguin, 1965), p. 19.
8. P.E.P., *Racial Discrimination* (London, P.E.P. 1967).
9. For a discussion of attempts to organize immigrant voters in Australia see J. JUPP, *Arrivals and Departures* (Melbourne, Cheshire-Lansdowne, 1966), Chapter Five. See also N. DEAKIN (ed.), *Colour and the British Electorate 1964* (London, Pall Mall Press, 1965).
10. GRAHAM THOMAS, 'The Council Election in Southall—May 1968' in Institute of Race Relations *News Letter* (July 1968).
11. In the 1965 and 1967 municipal elections in the Melbourne city of Fitzroy, where over 40 per cent of the population were born outside Australia, Greek independents were returned against official Labor nominees. There seems to be no British, nor other Australian, parallel. For attempts by immigrants to secure municipal election in Bradford see *Colour and the British Electorate 1964* (Chapter Seven) by Maurice Spiers, pp. 120–56.
12. For an attempt to correlate voting patterns with immigrant concentration in Melbourne see CHARLES A. McCOY, 'Australian Democratic Labor Party Support' in *Journal of Commonwealth Political Studies*, Vol. III, no. 3 (November 1965), pp. 199–208.
13. The failure of the Wolverhampton bus branch of the Transport and General Workers' Union to support the campaign of its Sikh members for retention of their

turbans, is the latest in a long line of similar failures by unions to stand up for their immigrant members. See also P.E.P., *op. cit.*, pp.132–40.

14. For an outline of the current position see 'Who's Who in Race' in *Observer* (3 March 1968).
15. *Guardian* (25 July 1967).
16. See especially W. KORNHAUSER, *The Politics of Mass Society* (London, Routledge and Kegan Paul, 1960); N. J. SMELSER, *Theory of Collective Behaviour* (London, Routledge and Kegan Paul, 1962); and W. RECORD, *Race and Radicalism* (Cornell University Press, 1964).
17. *Race*, Vol. IX, no. 3 (January 1968), p. 291.

Economic Insecurity and the Political Attitudes of Cuban Workers*

MAURICE ZEITLIN

NUMEROUS students of working-class politics have noted and studied the relationship between economic insecurity and political radicalism. For example, Karl Marx argued that a major consequence of recurrent unemployment would be the workers' formation of organizations "in order to destroy or to weaken the ruinous effects of this natural law of capitalist production in their class".[1] Karl Kautsky believed that economic insecurity would become so "intolerable for the masses of the population" that they would be "forced to seek a way out of the general misery, . . . (finding) it only in socialism".[2] More recently, some social scientists have interpreted left voting as a consequence, *inter alia*, of the fact that certain central "needs" are not being met, the "need for security of income" being foremost among them.[3] A good deal of comparative research has found that the workers

*Parts of this article appeared in "Political Attitudes of Cuban Workers", a paper delivered at the Annual Meetings of the American Sociological Association 1963, and in the writer's unpublished doctoral dissertation, *Working Class Politics in Cuba: A Study in Political Sociology*, University of California, Berkeley, 1964. I am indebted to Robert Alford, Seymour Martin Lipset, Gerald Marwell, and Martin Trow for their helpful comments on various drafts of this article; to Frederick Stephan for designing the sample for this study; to the center of International Studies, Princeton University, for a grant which made this study possible; and to its director, Klaus Knorr, for his encouragement.

[1]Karl Marx, *Capital: A Critique of Political Economy*, New York: Modern Library, 1936, p. 702.

[2]Karl Kautsky, "Krisentheorien", *Die Neue Zeit*, **20** (1901–2), p. 140.

[3]Seymour Martin Lipset, *Political Man: The Social Bases of Politics*, Garden City, New York: Doubleday, 1959, p. 232. The original article in which this formulation appeared was by Lipset, Paul Lazarsfeld, Allen Barton, and Juan Linz, "The Psychology of Voting: Analysis of Political Behavior", in Gardner Lindzey, ed., *Handbook of Social Psychology*, Vol. 2, Cambridge: Addison-Wesley, 1954, pp. 1124–75.

experiencing the most recurrent unemployment and underemployment are the ones most likely to be discontented with the existing order, to conceive of themselves as its "exploited victims", to be "class conscious", and to support the political left in their country.[4] Particularly apt to our own study is the conclusion by Zawadski and Lazarsfeld in their study of unemployed Polish workers during the depression of the thirties, that "the experiences of unemployment are a preliminary step for the revolutionary mood, but . . . they do not lead by themselves to a readiness for mass action. Metaphorically speaking, these experiences only fertilize the ground for revolution, but do not generate it."[5]

Less than a decade before the Revolutionary Government, headed by Fidel Castro, came to power in Cuba, the International Bank for Reconstruction and Development noted that "the insecurities which result from chronic unemployment and from the instability and seasonal fluctuations of

[4]See Richard Centers, *The Psychology of Social Classes*, Princeton: Princeton University Press, 1949, pp. 177–9; Herbert G. Nicholas, *The British General Election of 1950*, London: Macmillan, 1951, pp. 297–8. Lipset, *op. cit.*, pp. 113–4, 232–7, contains an excellent summary of the literature and findings on the political effects of unemployment. For the earlier literature, see Philip Eisenberg and Paul Lazarsfeld, "The Psychological Effects of Unemployment", *Psychological Bulletin*, **35** (June, 1938), pp. 358–90. O. Milton Hall, "Attitudes and Unemployment: A Comparison of the Opinions and Attitudes of Employed and Unemployed Men", *Archives of Psychology*, **165** (March 1954), is a monograph on the effects of unemployment on the attitudes of professional engineers during the depression of the '30's. Also see John C. Leggett, "Economic Insecurity and Working Class Consciousness", *American Sociological Review*, **29** (April 1964), pp. 226–34, and Richard F. Hamilton, "The Social Bases of French Working Class Politics", unpublished doctoral dissertation, Columbia University, 1963. General economic insecurity in any form—whether because of the fear and presence of unemployment, or being in an economically vulnerable position—apparently conduces to support of radical politics. Thus, Lipset noted in *Agrarian Socialism*, Berkeley and Los Angeles: University of California Press, 1950, pp. 10–18, that: "It was the economically and climatically *vulnerable* wheat belt that formed the backbone of all protest movements from the independent parties of the 1870's down to the contemporary C.C.F. in Canada. . . . It is highly significant that the first electorally successful Socialist Party in the United States or Canada should have developed in the same Great Plains wheat belt that earlier produced the Greenbackers, the Populists, the Non-Partisans, and other agrarian upheavals." Evidence has also been adduced to show that the general insecurity of small businessmen in a large-scale corporate capitalism results in their support of *right-wing* "radicalism"; see Martin Trow, "Small Businessmen, Political Tolerance, and Support for McCarthy", *American Journal of Sociology*, **64** (November, 1958), pp. 270–81.

[5]Bohan Zawadski and Paul E. Lazarsfeld, "The Psychological Consequences of Unemployment", *Journal of Social Psychology*, **6** (May, 1935), p. 249.

311

the Cuban economy, continue to keep the worker in a state of anxiety".[6] That the recurrent unemployment and underemployment and the consequent "state of anxiety" of the Cuban workers in pre-revolutionary Cuba later became a significant determinant of their support for the revolution and its leadership is the thesis of this article.

Cuba, prior to the 1959 revolution, was both misdeveloped and underdeveloped. Her economy was subject to the vagaries of export demand for sugar, and this created a "boom and bust" psychology affecting all strata of the population, not merely the working class, and inhibiting general economic growth. Chronic economic stagnation, a fluctuating, perhaps decreasing, *per capita* income,[7] and widespread unemployment and underemployment, both seasonal and structural, characterized the pre-revolutionary economy.

As early as the first decade of this century, Charles Magoon, Provisional Governor of Cuba during the United States occupation, reported that "practically all the sugar cane cutters are unemployed during six months of the year and by August find themselves without money and without means of maintaining themselves and their families".[8] A half century later this situation persisted without substantial change, and an authority of the United States Bureau of Commerce quipped that a Cuban worker might find it "easier to find a new wife than to find a new job".[9]

How correct this remark was, and how strategic an experience in the life of Cuban workers their ability to get work and keep it must have been, can be indicated by the circumstance that in the two years preceding the establishment of the Revolutionary Government, *known* average unemployment and underemployment in the labor force averaged about 20 per cent.[10] This

[6]*Report on Cuba*, Baltimore, Md.: Johns Hopkins Press, 1951, p. 359.

[7]Real *per capita* income in 1903–6 averaged $203; in 1923–6, $212; in 1943–6, $211; and in 1956–8 about $200. Data for first three periods are from Julian Alienes y Urosa, *Caracteristicas fundamentales de la economia cubana*, Havana: Banco Nacional de Cuba, 1950, p. 52. He deflated his income series by means of the old United States wholesale price index, since there was no Cuban index. Money income figures for 1956–8 were adjusted by the writer, using the same set of prices.

[8]As cited in Alberto Arredondo, *Cuba: tierra indefensa*, Havana, 1945, p. 176.

[9]*Investment in Cuba: Basic Information for United States Businessmen*, Washington, D.C.: U.S. Government Printing Office, 1956, p. 21, fn.

[10]The 1953 Cuban census estimated 8.4 per cent of the labor force was unemployed during the year's period of *fullest* employment, namely, at the height of the *zafra* (Oficina Nacional de los Censos Demografico y Electoral, *Censos de poblacion, viviendas y electoral*, Havana: Republica de Cuba, 1953). Systematic data on unemployment and

figure for the labor force as a whole *underestimates* the extent of unemployment and underemployment *in the working class alone.* Although there are no industry-by-industry data, we do know that in the major industry of the island, sugar, the vast majority of the workers, including perhaps two-thirds of the mill workers, were unemployed most of the year. In the sugar industry, "most of the workers were employed only during the zafra", which averaged about 100 days a year.[11] The labor force estimates probably are themselves underestimates, then, since *just counting the workers in the sugar industry* (who comprised 23 per cent of the labor force, and about three-quarters of whom worked no more than five months a year) approximately 18 per cent of the labor force was unemployed seven months of the year.[12]

underemployment were not collected in Cuba until 1957. In 1957, 10.8 per cent of the labor force was estimated as unemployed, on the average, during the *zafra*, with a high during the dead season of 15.1 per cent. In 1958, the average unemployment in the *zafra* and dead season was an estimated 8.4 per cent and 18 per cent respectively. Annual averages were 12.6 per cent in 1957, and 11.8 per cent in 1958. Estimated *underemployment* averaged 7.6 per cent in 1957, and 7.2 per cent in 1958, making a combined total of known average underemployment and unemployment of 20.2 per cent in 1957, and 19.0 per cent in 1958. These figures are calculated from data in the following: *Anuario de estadisticas del trabajo, 1959*, Geneva: Oficina Internacional de Trabajo, 1959, Table 10, p. 186; Oficina Nacional de los Censos Demografico y Electoral, Departamento de Econometria, "Cantidades y Indices de Empleo y Desempleo", *Empleo y desempleo en la fuerza trabajadora*, Havana: Consejo de Economia, June 3, 1958, mimeographed; *Encuesta sobre empleo, desempleo, y subempleo*, Havana, 1961 (unpublished data made available to the author). A table showing unemployment and underemployment in the Cuban labor force 1957–8, by month, appears in the author's dissertation, *Working Class Politics in Cuba*, p. 121. "Underemployment" was defined by the Department of Economic Statistics of the Cuban Government to include "persons who work less than thirty hours a week for pay, or 'on their own account' (self-employed) and those who work without pay for a relative". Departamento de Econometria, "Informe Tecnico No. 7", *Empleo y desempleo en la fuerza trabajadora*, Julio, 1959, Havana: Consejo Nacional de Economia, October 5, 1959, p. 12, mimeographed.

[11]*Investment in Cuba*, p. 24. "Only one-third of the millworkers and one-twentieth of the field workers are kept fully employed during the dead season." *Cuba: Economic and Commercial Conditions*, London: Her Majesty's Stationery Office, 1954, p. 39.

[12]Cuba Economica y Financiera, *Anuario Azucarea de Cuba, 1954*, Havana, 1954; *Investment in Cuba*, p. 23. If the 1953 census categories, "Craftsmen, foremen, operatives, and kindred workers", "Laborers, except farm" and "Laborers, farm", are taken to constitute the working class, that class numbered 1,111,743 in 1952, or 56.3 per cent of the "economically active population". There were an estimated 474,053 sugar workers; thus they constituted about 42 per cent of the manual working class, excluding private household workers, service workers, and unclassified occupations, the latter of which

313

Since the volume and value of the sugar crop profoundly affected unemployment not only in sugar but throughout the island's industries, 20 per cent is an absolute minimum estimate of pre-revolutionary average unemployment.

It scarcely seems problematic, therefore, that the severe and recurrent fluctuations of the entire economy, and the consequent widespread unemployment and underemployment in the population, were of major significance in the formation of the workers' political consciousness—especially given the significant influence that revoluntionary socialists (first anarcho-syndicalists and then Communists) had always exerted in the Cuban working class.[13]

That Fidel Castro believed unemployment politically significant is clear. For example, in his speech at his trial for leading the abortive attack on Fort Moncada on July 26, 1953, he said that the revolutionaries had based "their chances for success on the social order, because we were assured of the people's support . . ." Among "the people we count on in our struggle", he said, "are the seven hundred thousand unemployed Cubans, who want to earn their daily bread honorably without having to leave their country in search of sustenance; and the five hundred thousand rural workers who live in miserable *bohios* (huts), work four months of the year and spend the rest of it in hunger, sharing their misery with their children. . . ."[14]

Repeatedly in his speeches since coming to power, Castro has referred to the problem of unemployment, linking it with the meaning and the destiny of the revolution:

> A people which produces below its capacities, and, further, where an appreciable portion of what it produces is carried off by others, is not a people enjoying the economic and social conditions propitious to progress and to resolving its problems.

---

totalled about 10 per cent of the economically active population. Since most workers in the sugar industry were employed only during the *zafra*, this means that between one-third and two-fifths of the working class in Cuba must have been unemployed and underemployed most of the year before the establishment of the Revolutionary Government.

[13]"It must be remembered that nearly all the popular education of working people on how an economic system worked and what might be done to improve it came first from the anarcho-syndicalists, and most recently—and most effectively—from the Communists", *Report on Cuba*, p. 366. On the political history of the Cuban working class, see the author's dissertation, *Working Class Politics in Cuba*, Chapters 1 and 2, and the references cited therein.

[14]*Pensamiento politico, economico, y social de Fidel Castro*, Havana: Editorial Lex, 1959, p. 38.

That is why our country suffered that problem of permanent unemployment; . . . that is why there was chronic unemployment in our country extending to several hundred thousand idle citizens; that is why the fields were worked only three or four months a year. That is the reason for the ills of the Republic, which could never have been overcome if the Republic had not adopted forms of social organization and production putting human effort in harmony with the interest of the people in progress and greater production. . . . The issue became one of the revolution having to resolve the unemployment problem and, even more difficult, to resolve it under conditions of economic aggression, embargo on spare parts, raw materials and machinery, and complete suppression of the sugar quota.[15]

That such speeches as these would appeal to the workers, and especially to the ones who had borne the brunt of unemployment and underemployment before the revolution, seems clear. In fact, whatever their own political persuasion, most serious observers of the revolution have argued that this vast reservoir of unemployed and underemployed workers inherited by the Revolutionary Government has been a major source of its popular support, although they were not the initiators of the struggle against the old regime.[16] Once the Revolutionary Government came to power, however, its social base was formed, in the words of Boris Goldenberg, by the "enormous and heterogeneous mass of the economically 'rootless', . . . the unemployed (and) underemployed . . ." throughout the population.[17]

The major hypothesis of the present article, then, is that the revolution's

[15]Speech to the workers' delegates to the Council of Technical Advisers, *El Mundo*, Havana, February 12, 1961.

[16]It should be noted, however, that the rebels emphasized that workers were well represented among them. A youthful unidentified leader of the 26th of July Movement's Labor Front told an interviewer in February, 1958, that he "was eager to dispel the notion . . . that the 26th of July Movement headed by Señor Castro was predominantly a middle class affair. He said that, although Cuban labor leaders were 'on Batista's payroll,' the rank and file sympathized with Señor Castro." (*New York Times*, February 3, 1958, p. 7.) More to the point, Javier Pazos (son of Felipe Pazos, the former head of the Cuban National Bank), who was active in the anti-Batista urban underground, but who is now in exile from Cuba, wrote recently that "of the militants in the action groups, some were students, others were *workers* who were either *unemployed* or sick of a corrupt trade union in league with Batista". *Cambridge Opinion*, No. 32, p. 21, as cited in Robin Blackburn, "Sociology of the Cuban Revolution", *New Left Review*, 21 (October, 1963), p. 80. (Italics mine.)

[17]Boris Goldenberg, "El desenvolvimiento de la revolucion cubana", *Cuadernos*, 46 (January–February, 1961), Paris, p. 35. Theodore Draper cites Goldenberg's views with approval in *Castro's Revolution: Myths and Realities*, New York: Frederick Praeger, 1962, p. 53.

program and policies differentially appealed to the workers in accordance with their relative economic security before the revolution—the greater their pre-revolutionary experience of unemployment, the greater the likelihood of their support for the revolution. The correctness of this hypothesis will be examined following a description of the methods employed to obtain the data for this study.

METHODS

The data for this study are drawn from the writer's interviews with industrial workers in Cuba in the summer of 1962. What was significant about that period as far as this particular study is concerned was that the Revolutionary Government had by then clearly consolidated its power (the Bay of Pigs invasion being a year in the past); the original relatively undifferentiated popular euphoria had by then been long replaced by relatively clear lines of social cleavage generated in response to actions taken by the Revolutionary Government; it was then more than a year since Fidel Castro had declared the revolution to be "socialist", and, therefore, a study of the differential appeals of the ideology and social content of the revolution to Cuban workers could be meaningful and valuable.[18]

Our interviews were carried out with a randomly selected sample of 210 industrial workers employed in twenty-one work centers widely scattered throughout the island's six provinces. The writer chose the work centers from a list of all mines, mills, factories and plants functioning in Cuba under the direction of the Ministry of Industries. There were approximately 200,000 industrial workers employed in the industrial work-places under the direction of the Ministry of Industries. Excluded from representation in the sample were the approximately 120,000 industrial workers employed in some 250 industrial work-places under the direction of the Department of Industrialization of the National Institute of Agrarian Reform (JNRA). Thus, 62 per cent of Cuba's industrial workers constituted the population from which the sample of workers interviewed for this study was drawn.

The work-places were selected by means of a self-weighting random sample in which the probability of a work-place being chosen was directly proportional to the number of workers employed in it. This sampling

[18]See the writer's "Labor in Cuba", *The Nation*, **195** (October 20, 1962), pp. 238–41, and "Castro and Cuba's Communists", *Ibid.* **195** (November 3, 1962), pp. 284–7.

method tended to exclude the smaller industrial work-places (known in Cuba as "chinchales") which abounded there.[19]

In each work-place, the ten workers were selected by one of three methods:

(a) by visiting each department personally and selecting from a list of the jobs in that department (used in fifteen work-places);

(b) by selecting from a list of all workers employed in the work-place on the shift or shifts during which the interviewing was done (in five work-places);

[19]In detail, the technique utilized was the following:

(a) Using a list of all industrial work-places and the number of workers employed in each, as compiled by the Ministry of Industries, the number of industrial workers was added cumulatively and the sub-totals noted.

(b) Twenty-one six-digit random numbers were drawn from a table of random numbers, and twenty-one factories were then selected whose cumulative sub-totals were at least as large as or larger than each of the random numbers.

In each of the work-places a predetermined fixed number of workers (because of time and resources available, ten workers per work-place) was selected at random to be interviewed. In each work-place, the probability that a worker would be selected was inversely proportional to the number of workers employed in it.

The sample consisted, then, of 210 industrial workers selected at random from a population in which each worker had a known equal probability of being selected for the sample. Eight workers refused to be interviewed, and were not replaced by others; this gave a total of 202 actual interviews as the basis of this study. As a check, the refusals were tabulated for the appropriate classification in which the refusals themselves could be construed as significant answers, viz. 'hostile' to the revolution, and in all instances the relationships persisted or were strengthened. We obtained the age, sex, race, average months worked before and since the revolution, and place of work of each "refusal".

The above method of sampling may be expressed in the following formula:

$$P = m(s/N) \cdot (k/s) - km/N$$

where

m equals the number of industrial work-places selected to be in the sample,

s equals the number of workers employed in a given work-place for the sample,

k equals the fixed number of workers randomly selected to be interviewed in each work-place,

N equals the total number of workers employed in all work-places from which the sample was drawn,

P equals the probability that a worker in the population would be selected to be interviewed.

The method of sampling was employed to assure the inclusion in the sample of workers actually involved in industrial production using machine power and machine methods of production, rather than handicrafts methods of manufacture. In general, the larger the factory, the more likely that it was actually an industrial center. This was done for the theoretical reason that a major focus of the larger study, of which the findings

317

(c) by selecting among the homes in the industrial community in which the workers employed in the work-place live (in one work-place).[20]

The advantage of employing method (a) for selecting the workers to be interviewed is that the writer was able to see the workers' reactions within the work-places visited—the reactions of the workers chosen to be interviewed as well as of the other workers present at that moment in the various departments. Observation of the general reactions of the workers—of reserve or suspicion, curiosity or friendliness—was an important aspect of this study. Moreover, so as to be certain that the worker selected was, indeed, the worker interviewed, this method of selection was preferable. Perhaps if Cuba had not been the center of controversy and the focus of American hostility during the period in which the study was done, this method would not have been necessary. This precautionary measure was also beneficial to the writer's research since it did provide the opportunity for direct observation of the interaction among the industrial workers themselves and between them and administrative personnel.

The interviews were carried out in Spanish by the writer and his wife, each separately interviewing five workers per work-place. All interviewing was carried out in complete privacy, in a location provided within the work-place, such as a class-room or storage room or office. Each worker inter-

---

reported here are a part, was to be the revolution's impact on the workers' estrangement from their work. It was, therefore, particularly necessary to interview "industrial" rather than handicraft workers. It need hardly be pointed out that this method of sampling the working class does not affect the explanatory purposes of our study. "Representativeness", as Hans Zetterberg points out, "should not be confused with randomization. Randomization can be used to obtain representativeness. However, it is also used as a method of controlling irrelevant factors when testing a working hypothesis." (*On Theory and Verification in Sociology*, New York: Tressler Press, 1954, p. 57).

[20]This last method was employed only in the mining town of Matahambre in Pinar del Rio. The selection was not demonstrably random. It was impossible to pull men out of the mines during their work. The attempt was made to select names from the list of workers not working during that shift, go to their homes, and interview them there. However, this proved to be impossible because there are no addresses and fewer street names in Matahambre. It was necessary, therefore, to go to neighborhoods in the community in which a high concentration of miners lived, choose a house, and inquire whether or not a miner lived there. If a miner did live there and was home, then, with the miner's consent, he was interviewed. Obviously, this is not the most reliable method of assuring a random sample, yet there is no evident bias. The inadequacy here consists in our inability to know what degree of confidence to place in the randomness of the Matahambre sample.

viewed, as well as anyone else concerned, was specifically told before the interviewing, in a variant of the following words, that the writer was

> . . . a correspondent for a liberal objective American news-weekly called *The Nation*, that is published in New York city. We have permission from the Ministry of Industries, your administrator, and the union delegate to interview ten workers here. We have chosen you to be interviewed by selecting at random from a list of the jobs in this department (or all workers in this work-place). That means we do not care to know your name or to be able to identify you personally in any way. These questions are simple and do not require special knowledge. We just want your opinions about some things in your work and in Cuba in general. All your answers are between ourselves and are completely anonymous. We would very much appreciate your permission to interview you.

Every precaution was taken in the interviewing to discover and to prevent dissimulation. Dissimulation, as well as unconscious distortion, must be taken into account in the evaluation of all interview data, in whatever type of study. Internal checks for consistency as well as external checks on reliability must be built into any interview schedule, wherever possible; this was done in our study. The interviews were carried out according to a formal set of questions on a mimeographed interview schedule prepared by the writer. It was quite clear to the worker that he was being formally interviewed in accordance with pre-determined questions, and that notes on his answers were being taken throughout the interview.

Stylized probes were also employed in these interviews to make it especially difficult for the workers interviewed to give answers they did not actually feel to be true. For example, if a worker were asked: "Do you think that your children have the same opportunities, better opportunities, or worse opportunities than others to live comfortably and happily?" and he answered: "All children are equal now", he would then be asked some variant of "How is it possible for all children to be equal? Please explain what you mean." Such probes were freely used throughout the interview.

Because there were obviously some workers who were suspicious or even frightened of the purposes of the interview, every effort was made to establish rapport quickly and to put the respondent at his ease by stressing that the interview was voluntary and completely anonymous, and that the interviews were very important because they would provide the basis for information about working conditions in Cuba to Americans and other non-Cubans throughout the world. Occasionally a respondent would ask that his words not be recorded until the interview had terminated; we complied readily. The interviews ranged in length from forty-five minutes to three-and-a-half

319

hours, averaging about one hour and a quarter, in privacy; a great effort of will would be required in that situation consistently to give answers thought to be suitable to the government and the interviewer. It would require a certain level of dramatic skill to feign enthusiasm or to manifest feelings where these did not exist. Moreover, the refusal rate was very low (8 of 210 respondents, or less than 4 per cent); in only a few instances did opponents of the regime evidence either hesitancy or fear in speaking their minds freely. Cubans are highly voluble, volatile and loquacious, irrespective of their political views.

The interview schedule was organized in such a way as to begin the interview with questions which were, on the surface, far removed from political questions of any kind—such as length of residence in a particular place, or length of time working in the work-place. The interviews were carried out in accordance with established canons of sociological interviewing, with especial emphasis on anonymity, on the establishment of rapport, and on special probing to ascertain the truthfulness of a response.[21]

In order to get at the workers' attitudes towards the revolution, several questions were asked of them during the interview which are believed to be more or less indicative, taken in concert, of how they viewed the revolution. Of the five chosen for combination into an index of these attitudes, two were "open-ended" questions to which the variety of responses possible was limited only by the workers' own imagination. The first of these was:

[21]The assistance of the Ministry of Industries was enlisted in the realization of this study. The theoretical and historical purposes of this study were explained to the Minister of Industries, Major Ernesto "Che" Guevara. It was his approval which made this study possible. There were no conditions attached to the writer's work and no restrictions whatsoever placed on his travel or on the kinds of question he might ask. The writer explained the purposes of his research, submitted a copy of the mimeographed interview schedule, clarified the purposes (but did not change the wording of a number of questions which appeared to the Minister to be "loaded"), and received permission to enter any mine, mill, factory or plant he wished, and to have workers taken from their work for as long as was necessary for the interviews. The writer was given credentials by the Ministry to identify him to administrators and labor union officials at the work-places visited, and was, after that, left to carry out the research at his own convenience. There was no predetermined schedule of when the writer was to arrive at any work-place, nor, it was evident, had any administrators been informed to expect the writer's visit. On several occasions, administrators or personnel chiefs telephoned to the Ministry of Industries in Havana to check the writer's credentials and his insistence that he had permission—which was apparently unbelievable to administrators trying to raise production levels—to take ten workers from their work for as long as was necessary.

(a) "Speaking in general, what are the things in Cuba that you are most proud of as a Cuban?" One hundred and fifteen workers replied to this question in terms clearly favorable to the revolution. Only such responses as could be regarded as clearly indicating or explicitly stating support of the revolution, such as mention of the revolution itself, of the "socialist government", of specific economic and social reforms of the Revolutionary Government, or of increased work security since the revolution, were counted as "favorable". All others, whether more or less "neutral" responses or "clearly hostile" ones, were classified as "not clearly favorable".

The workers could be especially blunt in their opposition, as was a young worker at a paper milling plant in Cardenas, whose answer was simply, "O nothing, *chico* . . . I don't like Communism", or as a West Indian worker (with two teenage daughters in the militia) at the nationalized Portland Cement plant in Mariel explained (in English): "I stay only because I have two daughters who will not leave—otherwise I'd go away . . . . No one bothers me, I just do not like it. Why? I can't say why. I guess I just prefer the old Cuba. . . ."

In contrast to such clearly hostile remarks were such noncommittal replies as a shoemaker's "Of our movies and our athletes", or a brewery worker's equivocal, "I am a peaceful worker. I have no passionate interest in anything. After my work, I pass my time in my house in Manaca with my little one and my wife", or a cigar-maker's witty but equally noncommittal, "Our women and our cigars".

Occasionally a revolutionary worker would wax poetic, as did a copper miner in Matahambre: "Cuba is a cup of gold to me. It is the only country in the world that is now moving forward. . . ." A sugar worker's simple statement was more typical, however: "I earn good money now. I lack nothing. . . . All of the workers are with the revolution." A Havana brewery worker said: "I am content with the revolution in general. . . . For the first time one can do what one wants without fear."

The second of these open-ended questions was (b) "What sort (*clase*) of people govern this country now?"

One hundred and twenty-five workers replied to this question in terms clearly favorable to the revolution.

Given the double meaning in Spanish of the word *clase*, which can mean "type", "sort" or "kind", as well as "class", the workers could, of course, choose to interpret the question's meaning in a number of ways. As with the preceding question, only replies which could be regarded as clearly favorable to the revolution were counted as such: "the people", "the humble", "hardworking", "good", "sincere", "moral", "honest", "defenders of the poor and humble", "the working class". Responses such as "socialists" or "revolutionaries" which did not clearly commit the worker were not regarded as favorable; neither were such equivocal replies as "Cubans", "Fidel", "Communists", nor replies which were likely meant to be hostile such as "Russians", or "Soviets", or which were undoubtedly meant to be hostile such as "shameless", or "traitors".

"To me," an opponent of the revolution working at the nationalized Texaco oil refinery in Santiago said, "they are completely Communists. All of their accomplishments have been through the work of others—including how they think. I have a sister-in-law and a brother-in-law in prison for speaking against the government—(sentenced to) seven years. . . ." Another worker opposed to the revolution said: "Socialists they say. The kids say Communists. I don't know. Listen, if somebody comes and takes that pen of yours, and you bought it, what are you going to think?"

"Well, I've never been 'political'," a cigarette-machine operator said. "For me, they are all right." A brewery worker's reply was equally equivocal: "My experience so far is good. I don't worry about such things—neither before the revolution nor now." A skilled electrician in Santiago committed himself only so far as to say that the men in the government are "persons with socialist ideas, who though they have good intentions have committed many serious administrative errors".

"The truth is", a carpenter in a sugar central said, "that *now* those who govern here are Cubans. They are honest and hard-working men." A 67-year-old maintenance man at the Nicaro nickel plant who had been an agricultural worker until recently said: "Look, before I couldn't look a boss in the eye—I looked at my feet. Not now; now we have liberty and walk where we wish, and nothing is prohibited to us. It is a great joy to be alive now. These men (who govern us) are 100 per cent better than before. I have known governments from (Mario Garcia) Menocal (Cuban President, 1913–21) until Batista left three years ago, and I have never seen any like this government." Equally articulate in his support of the revolution was a twenty-year-old bootmaker in a newly established factory in Guanajay "*We* are the government, *we* run things. Go to a factory or *consolidado* anywhere, *chico*, and see: those who work govern, those who govern work, not like the capitalists who lived without working before the revolution triumphed. Now, the power of the workers and peasants has emerged."

The workers were also asked the following two questions with fixed alternatives:

(c) "Do you believe that the country ought to have elections soon?"

Answer	(N)
No	136
Yes	52
No opinion	22

(d) "Do you think the workers have more, the same, or less influence on (en) the government now than before the revolution?"

Answer	(N)
More influence	170
The same	17
Less	16 (includes 8 refusals)
No opinion	7

In addition, this question was included in the index as an "action criterion":

(e) "Do you belong to the militia?"

Answer	(N)
Yes	110
No	100 (includes 8 refusals)

As is clear, the likelihood that a question would elicit a response clearly favorable to the revolution was directly related to the case with which such a response could be given.[22] Favorable responses were distributed as follows:

Question	(N)
e.	110
a.	115
b.	125
c.	136
d.	170

[22]Item analysis of the workers' answers to the five questions indicates that the latter form an acceptable Guttman scale, 88 per cent of the workers giving answers exactly (67 per cent) or consistently (21 per cent) in conformity with a Guttman model of ideal classification of respondents. The coefficient of reproducibility equals 0.95. See Samuel Stouffer, *et al.*, *Measurement and Prediction*, Princeton: Princeton University Press, 1950, p. 117.

The index of attitude toward the revolution was constructed from answers to all five questions by coding all favorable responses (militia membership included) as $+1$, and all others as 0 (zero):

Index

Points	Definition	(N)
3–5	Favorable (4–5, very favorable, $N = 100$; 3, moderately favorable, $N = 42$)	142
2	Indecisive	24
0–1	Hostile	36

TOTAL: 202

FINDINGS

Using this index to gauge the differential appeals of the revolution to the workers we interviewed, our expectation that the relative security of their employment *before* the revolution would have a significant bearing on their attitudes toward the revolution *now*, is borne out by our findings, as presented in Table 1. There is a clear relationship between the average number of months the workers worked during the year before the revolution and the probability of their support for the revolution. The workers with the least

TABLE 1. PRE-REVOLUTIONARY EMPLOYMENT STATUS AND ATTITUDE
TOWARD THE REVOLUTION[1]
(per cent)

Months worked per year before revolution	Favorable[2]	Indecisive	Hostile	(N)
6 or less	86	9	5	(63)
7–9	74	10	16	(19)
10 plus	62	13	25	(105)

[1]This and the following tables do not include workers who had not yet entered the labor force before the revolution.

[2]Among the workers who were employed six months or less and also among those employed 7–9 months before the revolution, 63 per cent were "very favorable" to the revolution; among those who worked 10 months or more, only 40 per cent were "very favorable".

pre-revolutionary economic security are the ones who are most likely to support the revolution.

If their relative economic security before the revolution has been of significant consequence for the workers' responses to the revolution, then it should be expected that their pre-revolutionary situation significantly affected their pre-revolutionary political orientations as well. We know, for example, that a major social base of the Communists in the labor movement was among the workers in the sugar industry, i.e. in the industry which was itself most economically unstable and whose workers suffered perhaps the greatest burden of the seasonal unemployment cycle. We should, therefore, expect on both historical and comparative sociological grounds, that the workers who experienced the most unemployment and underemployment before the revolution were the ones who were most likely to support the Communists.

A simple structured question was asked of all the workers in our sample in order to gauge their pre-revolutionary orientation toward the Communists:

"How would you describe your attitude toward the Communists before the revolution: hostile, indifferent, friendly, or supporter?"[23]

Answer	(N)
Hostile	57
Indifferent	83
Friendly	49
Supporter (*partidario*)	10
Don't know	3
Refusal	8

When we compare the workers' pre-revolutionary views of the Communists with their pre-revolutionary security of employment, the evidence indicates that the workers who experienced the most unemployment before

[23]It is relevant to note here that, according to this crude measure of their attitude toward the Communists before the revolution, 28 per cent of the workers in our sample classified themselves as pre-revolutionary friends or supporters of the Communists; and according to the International Bank for Reconstruction and Development *Report*, written after the Communists had been officially purged from the labor movement, the Communists still had "a strong underground influence in some unions, and some authorities estimate that perhaps 25 per cent of all Cuban workers are secretly sympathetic to them". *Report on Cuba*, p. 365.

the revolution were the ones most likely to be sympathetic to the Communists.[24]

This relationship is strengthened when we view it among only those workers in our sample who were also workers before the revolution. There has been a sizeable influx of formerly salaried or self-employed persons, as well as agricultural laborers and peasants, into the working class since the

TABLE 2. PRE-REVOLUTIONARY EMPLOYMENT STATUS AND PRE-REVOLUTIONARY
ATTITUDE TOWARD THE COMMUNISTS
(per cent)

Months worked per year before revolution	Friendly or supporter	Indifferent[1]	Hostile	(N)
6 or less	35	36	29	(63)
7–9	32	52	16	(19)
10 plus	26	45	29	(105)

[1]Includes three "don't knows".

TABLE 2a. PRE-REVOLUTIONARY EMPLOYMENT STATUS AND PRE-REVOLUTIONARY
ATTITUDE TOWARD THE COMMUNISTS, AMONG WORKERS BEFORE THE
REVOLUTION ONLY
(per cent)

Months worked per year before revolution	Friendly or supporter	Indifferent	Hostile	(N)
9 or less	40	32	29	(63)
10 plus	27	46	27	(89)

[24]It may be objected that this relationship between pre-revolutionary unemployment and pro-Communism is an artifact of the circumstance that revolutionary workers are likely to "recall" a favorable attitude toward the Communists, because of their present support for the revolution. The fact that the proportion favoring the revolution exceeds the proportion who favored the Communists before the revolution by more than twice casts doubt on the validity of this objection. Moreover, when we view the relationship between pre-revolutionary employment status and pro-Communist attitudes *among revolutionary workers only*, the same relationship holds: 44 per cent of the recurrently unemployed (N=68) supported the Communists before the revolution, compared to 35 per cent of the regularly employed (N=65).

revolution—and this is reflected in our sample; these non-workers were less likely to support the Communists before the revolution than the workers. When we exclude those who were not workers before the revolution, we find that the gap between the proportions pro-Communist among the pre-revolutionary unemployed and among the employed workers becomes larger (Table 2a). There is also a slight strengthening of the relationship between pre-revolutionary employment insecurity and support for the revolution when viewed among only those who were workers before the revolution (Table 2b).

TABLE 2b. PRE-REVOLUTIONARY EMPLOYMENT STATUS AND ATTITUDE TOWARD
THE REVOLUTION, AMONG WORKERS BEFORE THE REVOLUTION ONLY
(per cent)

Months worked per year before revolution	Favorable	Indecisive	Hostile	(N)
9 or less	87	6	6	(63)
10 plus	62	13	25	(89)

To this point we have only referred to the workers' pre-revolutionary economic security, yet there has been a significant change in the economic security of many workers since the establishment of the Revolutionary Government. Among our respondents, for example, more than three-quarters (79 per cent) of those who had worked six months or less before the revolution, reported that they were working ten months or more on the average since the revolution, and 19 per cent said they now worked between seven and nine months a year. Thus, 98 per cent of the previously most under-employed workers said they were working more regularly than they had been before the Revolutionary Government came to power. It would seem quite likely that these changes have had consequences for their response to the revolution. In order to test the proposition that the workers whose economic security has been most enhanced since the revolution would be the most likely to support it, we would have to look simultaneously at their pre-revolutionary and present employment status.

The optimum test of the hypothesis concerning the relationship between change in employment status since the revolution and attitude toward it

327

would require relating *decreased* economic security, as well as maintenance of *the same level* of security, to the workers' attitudes. However, as is obvious from inspection of Table 3, not all the necessary types of change in employment status are represented among the workers in our sample. We can, nevertheless, make some useful inferences concerning the consequences of relative change in economic security on the workers' attitudes by comparing the available groups of workers.

As can be seen from Table 3, our expectation is confirmed that those workers whose economic security is greater than it was in pre-revolutionary years are more likely than other workers to support the revolution—in this case, than those workers who were employed regularly before and have continued to be since the revolution.

TABLE 3. THE RELATIONSHIP BETWEEN EMPLOYMENT STATUS BEFORE THE REVOLUTION, EMPLOYMENT STATUS SINCE THE REVOLUTION, AND ATTITUDE TOWARD THE REVOLUTION

| Months worked per year before revolution | Per cent favorable | | |
| | Months worked per year since the revolution | | |
	10+	7–9	6 or less
10+	62 (101)	(4)	(0)
7–9	78 (18)★	(1)	(0)
6 or less	86 (50)★	82 (11)★	(1)

★Of these seventy-nine workers whose economic security is greater since the revolution, 83 per cent support the revolution.

RACIAL GROUP MEMBERSHIP

If it is correct, as our evidence seems to indicate, that economic insecurity conduces to revolutionary politics, then it should follow from this that a racial or ethnic group whose position is comparatively less secure economically than that of the racial or ethnic majority should also be more responsive to the revolution than the latter is. From what we know about pre-revolutionary Cuba, it is probably correct to say that Negroes and Mestizos were in general subject to greater economic insecurity than whites. (In our sample, for instance, 49 per cent of the Negroes and Mestizos reported that they were employed nine months or less before the revolution, compared to 39 per cent of the white workers.) While Negroes were distributed throughout the occupational structure, they were disproportionately concentrated in the poorest income groups and the most menial jobs—they were, as Lowry Nelson put it, "predominantly the 'hewers of wood and drawers of water' ".[25] Apparently, there was also a tendency for Negroes working at the same jobs as whites to receive less pay,[26] although this was primarily true of the workers in the weakest unions and least organized industries. Further, in the urban slums, or *solares*, Negroes predominated; the better rooms were commonly rented only to whites. Insofar as their economic position was particularly insecure, then, it might be expected that Negro workers would be more likely to be revolutionary than white workers.

In fact, some of the most prominent left-wing leaders in Cuba were Negroes; among leaders of the Communist Party, as well as of the non-Communist labor unions, Negroes were well represented. During the revolution of the thirties, *Realengo 18*, the "soviet" of workers and peasants which withstood the military forces of Batista the longest, right into the early months of 1934, was led by a Negro Communist, Leon Alvarez. Perhaps the most revered labor leader was the martyred Jesus Menendez, the Negro head of the sugar workers' union, who was murdered in 1947 by cohorts of the notorious Eusebio Mujal. Furthermore, Oriente Province, the province with the highest concentration of Negroes in the population—perhaps twice the proportion of other provinces—was the rebel stronghold[27] during the guerrilla struggle against Batista; and Santiago, the province's capital, was the one major city in which the otherwise abortive general strike of April, 1958, was fully supported by the workers, and the entire city shut down.

However, it must also be emphasized that the social status of the Negro in pre-revolutionary Cuba differed markedly from the status of the Negro in the United States. Largely as a result of social processes characteristic of

[25]Lowry Nelson, *Rural Cuba*, Minneapolis, Minnesota: University of Minnesota Press, 1950, pp. 157 ff. Cf. also Direccion General de Censo, *Censo de 1943*, Havana: Republica de Cuba, 1945; and *Censos de poblacion, vivienda y electoral,* Havana: Republica de Cuba, 1953.

[26]Nelson, *op. cit.*, p. 156.

[27]*Investment in Cuba*, p. 179. Forty per cent of the population of Oriente was estimated to be Negro or Mestizo, compared to 20 per cent or less in the other five provinces.

Negro slavery, and of the slaves' emancipation in Cuba—in contrast to slavery in the United States—the barriers to social intercourse between Negroes and whites, well before the revolution, were not as formidable as those in the United States. While these early developments are too complex to explore here,[28] it is important to emphasize that "Jim Crow" laws comparable to those in America have never existed in Cuba, nor were there other legal, political, and social buttresses to Negro exploitation after emancipation from slavery of the type in force in the United States. Compared to the United States, at least, the social history of Cuba involved a relatively high degree of racial integration and inter-marriage, especially in the working class. Nevertheless, racial discrimination was socially and politically enforced to a certain extent. "Before 1959, Negroes were excluded from most of the better hotels, beaches, and places of entertainment patronized by Americans and upper class Cubans."[29] While not a common practice, in some cities the public squares and parks in which Cubans congregate in the evenings had a promenade plaza reserved for whites which was a step higher than the one reserved for Negroes. As the Cuba survey of the Human Relations Area Files states: "Opponents of Castro maintain that he invented the racial issue. It is, however, an old problem which has always become more serious in times of political crisis. . . . Many wry Negro proverbs commenting on the relations between Negroes and whites refer unmistakably to home grown attitudes of long standing: 'The black fought the war, the white enjoys the peace'; 'If you see a black and a white together, either the white man needs the black, or else the black has won a lottery.' "[30] That many Negroes recognized their social status as a problem is indicated by the fact that a Negro national federation was organized against racial discrimination.

One further element of importance in the formation of the Negroes' attitude towards the revolution is the fact that they had a history of experience with broken promises before the revolution and, for that reason, were not likely to take too seriously mere assertions by the Revolutionary Government that it would eliminate discrimination. "Before 1959", as the HRAF survey notes, "various political leaders gained electoral support by promising

[28]See Frank Tannenbaum, *Slave and Citizen*, New York: Alfred Knopf, 1948; and Stanley Elkins, *Slavery*, *Chicago*: University of Chicago Press, 1959.

[29]Wyatt MacGaffey and Clifford R. Barnett, *Cuba: Its People, Its Society, Its Culture*, New Haven: Human Relations Area Files Press, 1962, p. 32. Cf. also Nelson, *op. cit.*, pp. 158–9.

[30]MacGaffey and Barnett, *op. cit.*, pp. 32–3.

to uphold Negro rights but subsequently failed to carry out these promises. The legislative initiative gradually fell to the Communists and to the Frente Civico contra la Discrimination Racial, sponsored by the CTC (Confederation of Cuban Workers) and incorporated in Batista's patronage system. Many Negroes resented left wing efforts to capitalize on the issue, and pointed to progress made by the United States in racial matters as a commendable example. Others saw signs of a deliberate imperialist effort to weaken Cuba by depriving it of part of the resources of its population."[31]

Given this complex mix of relative Negro economic insecurity, a rebel tradition, the presence of discriminatory practices despite a relatively high level of social integration, and the probability of disillusionment with political programs, prediction of the differential response to the revolution

TABLE 4. RACIAL GROUP MEMBERSHIP AND PRE-REVOLUTIONARY
ATTITUDE TOWARD THE COMMUNISTS
(per cent)

	Friendly or supporter	Indifferent	Hostile	(N)
Negroes	28	36	36	(50)
Whites	29	45	26	(152)

of Negro and white workers is not without difficulty—although one would probably surmise that Negroes would be more likely than whites to support the revolution. It is particularly interesting, therefore, as Table 4 shows, that, taken as a whole, the Negro workers in our sample were no more likely than white workers to sympathize with *the Communists in Pre-Revolutionary Cuba*, and more likely to be hostile to them. We shall take a closer look at this relationship after discussing the differential response of Negro and white workers to the revolution.

Since the revolution, the Revolutionary Government has not only conducted a propaganda campaign on behalf of racial equality, but has also opened all hotels, beaches, and resorts (previously almost entirely privately owned and closed to the public) to all Cubans, regardless of color. "In the larger cities conspicuous desegregation was accomplished although the

[31]*Ibid.*, p. 282.

familiar patterns were to be observed in provincial towns in 1961."[32] Fidel Castro has sprinkled his speeches with allusions to the past exploitation and revolutionary traditions of the Negro, a typical example of which comes from a speech the writer attended at the 26th of July anniverary celebration in 1962 in Santiago: "In the past when voices were raised in favor of liberation for the slaves, the bourgeoisie would say 'impossible, it will ruin the country' and to instill fear, they spoke of the 'black terror'. Today they speak of the 'red terror'. In other words, in their fight against liberty they spread fear of the Negro; today they spread fear of socialism and communism."

It seems likely that the social barriers between members of the races were least among workers; consequently, the impact on them of non-discriminatory policies alone should be least, although not necessarily insignificant. Most beaches, resorts and hotels were closed to the *poor* of Cuba—white and black alike—and not just to the Negro. Thus, the Negro worker may have felt the impact of *class* more than of *racial* membership. It is unclear whether or not economic policies of the regime have benefitted Negro workers more than white workers. While it is probable that Negroes have felt that their status has improved, the complexity of events since the revolution makes the Negro workers' responses difficult to predict. Our data indicate that the Negro workers in our sample are more likely than their white fellows to support the revolution.

In the preceding discussion both economic and status variables were relevant in predicting the differential appeals of the revolution to Negro and white workers. Perhaps our finding that Negro workers are more likely than white workers to support the revolution indicates only the relatively less secure position of Negro workers as a group before the revolution, i.e. that control for pre-revolutionary employment status would eliminate the Negro–white difference. However, this reasoning is not supported by our evidence. As Table 6 indicates, both among the workers who were recurrently unemployed before the revolution and among those who were regularly employed, Negroes are more likely to support the revolution than whites. The table also shows that the original relationship between pre-revolutionary employment status and attitude toward the revolution holds among both Negro and white workers. The inference is clear that, given the persistence of the differences between Negro and white workers—even with pre-revolutionary economic security controlled—the fact of membership

[32]*Ibid.*

TABLE 5. RACIAL GROUP MEMBERSHIP AND ATTITUDE TOWARD THE REVOLUTION
(per cent)

	Favorable*	Indecisive	Hostile	(N)
Negroes	80	8	12	(50)
Whites	67	13	20	(152)

*Among Negro workers the proportion "very favorable" to the revolution is 58 per cent; among white workers the proportion "very favorable" is 47 per cent.

TABLE 6. THE RELATIONSHIP BETWEEN RACIAL GROUP MEMBERSHIP, PRE-REVOLUTIONARY EMPLOYMENT STATUS, AND ATTITUDE TOWARD THE REVOLUTION

	Per cent favorable	
	Months worked per year before revolution	
	9 or less	10 plus
Negroes	91 (22)	73 (22)
Whites	80 (60)	59 (83)

in the Negro racial group is in itself significant. Indeed, if we look at the effect on Negro and white workers of change in employment status since the revolution, the results are essentially the same as for pre-revolutionary employment status alone (Table 7). Both among the workers whose employment status is higher and those whose employment status is at the same level since the revolution, Negroes are more likely than whites to favor the revolution. Although employment security is not the only aspect of economic security, it is certainly among the most significant; we might infer that the social status of the Negro racial group accounts for the Negro–white differences.

Although the Negro unemployed are more likely to support the revolution than regularly employed Negro workers, the parallel result does not hold for *pre-revolutionary attitudes toward the Communists* (Table 8). This finding is especially interesting in the light of some recent research to be

TABLE 7. The Relationship Between Racial Group Membership, Change in Employment Status, and Attitude Toward the Revolution

	Per cent favorable	
	Change in employment status	
	Same high level	Higher
Negroes	71 (21)	90 (21)
Whites	60 (80)	81 (58)

discussed below. Among white workers we observe the expected relationship that the workers who experienced the most pre-revolutionary unemployment were the most likely to support the Communists. Among Negro workers, on the other hand, there is no significant difference between the unemployed and the regularly employed in their pre-revolutionary attitudes toward the Communists.

INTERPRETATION

There are two fundamental questions about our findings:

1. Why are the pre-revolutionary unemployed and underemployed workers more likely than the regularly employed to favor the revolution, and to have had pro-Communist political orientations before the revolution? Indeed, the general theoretical question of the reasons for the increased probability of political radicalism among the more economically insecure workers is at issue.

2. Why are the Negro pre-revolutionary unemployed more likely to support the revolution than their regularly employed counterparts, despite the fact that they were no more likely to be pro-Communist before the revolution?

Radical politics and "leftist voting", as Lipset has noted, are "generally interpreted as an expression of discontent, an indication that needs are not

TABLE 8. THE RELATIONSHIP BETWEEN RACIAL GROUP
MEMBERSHIP, PRE-REVOLUTIONARY EMPLOYMENT STATUS,
AND PRE-REVOLUTIONARY ATTITUDE TOWARD THE
COMMUNISTS

	Per cent friendly or supporter	
	Months worked per year before revolution	
	9 or less	10 plus
Negroes	27 (22)	32 (22)
Whites	37 (60)	24 (83)

being met". He suggests, as noted above, that one such central "need" is "the need for security of income. This is quite closely related to the desire for higher income as such; however, the effect of periodic unemployment or a collapse of produce prices, for example, seems to be important in itself."[33] Positing such a "need" is not, however, a particularly fruitful formulation, especially as it stands. We know, for instance, that stable poverty, such as that of subsistence peasantry, tends to be a source of political conservatism rather than radicalism, yet their "need" for security of income is obviously not being met. One crucial factor, as Lipset himself indicates elsewhere, is whether or not individuals are exposed by their situation to possibilities for a life better than their present one.[34] In fact, of course, disemployed workers have had a better life and lost it.

The question remains, nonetheless, whether such an interpretation is sufficient to explain what makes unemployed workers likely to perceive a connection between their private troubles and the economic structure—and in class-conscious or politically radical terms—rather than simply to blame themselves and look inward for the source of their troubles. The answer, it is suggested, lies in the very fact of their observation that their troubles are not private but rather ones which *simultaneously affect many of their fellow workers.* Their radical response, that is, "is especially linked", in Max Weber's phrase, "to the *transparency* of the connections between the causes and the

[33]*Political Men*, p. 232.
[34]*Ibid.*, p. 63.

335

consequences" of their situation as unemployed workers. It is not only the contrast between their situation and that of employed workers, which makes them amenable to the appeals of radical politics, but also (perhaps primarily) the fact that they can so easily recognize the source of their problems to be in the "concrete economic order". "For however different life chances may be", as Weber put it, "this fact in itself, according to all experience, by no means gives birth to 'class action'. . . . *The fact of being conditioned and the results of the class situation must be distinctly recognizable. For only then the contrast of life chances can be felt not as an absolutely given fact to be accepted*, but as a resultant from either (1) the given distribution of property, or (2) the structure of the concrete economic order."[35] This reasoning, which Weber applied to "the class situation of the modern proletariat", is particularly appropriate to the situation of those who are unemployed and under-employed. Especially in Cuba was the connection transparent between the "concrete economic order" and the situation of the unemployed. For it was precisely from *recurrent disemployment* that the unemployed suffered. The relationship between the seasonal nature of their unemployment, and the misdevelopment of the economy was therefore "distinctly recognizable". It is understandable that they should be more likely than employed workers to want to alter radically an economic order which is perceived as the source of their collective troubles and, therefore, be more amenable to the appeals of Communist political agitation.

This same line of interpretation applies to our contrasting findings on the Negro unemployed and their political attitudes. Let us compare, first, what John Leggett reported recently concerning his research into sources of class consciousness of Negro and white workers in Detroit. Having found a general relationship between unemployment and class consciousness, he noted that it might be expected that "unemployed Negro workers should be more class conscious than their employed counterparts". His evidence, however, failed "to support this hypothesis. If anything, the Negro unem-ployed are slightly *less* class conscious than the employed, while the whites are distributed as expected. Clearly, unemployment, considered by itself, is not a source of class consciousness among Negroes."[36] He did find, however,

[35]Hans Gerth and C. Wright Mills, eds., *From Max Weber: Essays in Sociology*, New York: Oxford University Press, 1946, p. 184. Except for italicization of "transparency", italics are not in the original.

[36]John C. Leggett, "Economic Insecurity and Working Class Consciousness", *American Sociological Review*, **29** (April, 1964), 230.

that among *unionized* Negro workers unemployment is related to class consciousness as expected, and that unionized unemployed Negro workers are far more likely than their non-union counterparts to be militantly class conscious. His interpretation of the effects of union membership on Negro workers was, in brief, that the impact of unions is partly to make Negroes more likely "to develop and use a class frame of reference to appraise their circumstances", and "partly because of the behavior of these unions on class and race questions such as unemployment. . . ."[37]

Now, while it is true that class consciousness and left-wing political orientation are not precisely the same, they are certainly similar phenomena, and their determinants have consistently been found to be similar. There is, in fact, a parallel worth speculating about between Leggett's findings and the present ones. Leggett found that "the combination of unemployment and union membership clearly heightens class consciousness". Although on the basis of our data, it was not possible to gauge the effect of union membership on the worker's pre-revolutionary political orientations, we did find, as noted above, that the combination of unemployment and their experience since the revolution apparently heightened the probability of revolutionary political orientations among Negro workers who were unemployed before the revolution. We might speculate, then, that living through the revolution has been an experience for Negro unemployed workers equivalent in significant respects to that of union participation for unemployed Negro workers in Detroit. The revolution may have had an impact on the Negro unemployed in three relevant ways:

First, since the revolution they have been reached effectively by an ideology which stresses, as Leggett said regarding industrial unions, "a class frame of reference to appraise their circumstances".

Second, the Revolutionary Government's "behaviour on class and race questions" has emphasized racial equality both in propaganda and in deed.

Third, to the extent to which revolutionary propaganda and deed have, in fact, altered the social status of the Negro racial group and of the unemployed, the connection between the racial situation and the pre-revolutionary class structure and economic order which the revolution destroyed becomes distinctly recognizable. This process may also be likened to the impact of unionization on unemployed Negroes who may recognize that their unemployment cannot now be "explained" by (be attributed to) their

[37]*Ibid.*, pp. 233–4.

racial membership alone, but is also a condition affecting members of the working class regardless of race.

This third point may deserve amplification, especially since it relates to our earlier interpretation of the radicalizing effects of unemployment. Class consciousness and political radicalism may not be meaningful responses for unemployed, non-unionized Negroes, because the fact of *being Negroes* is the significant aspect of their lives, to which they probably attribute their situation as unemployed workers. They do not see the interests of organized workers as relevant to their lives because in a significant respect those interests are indeed *not* relevant to them, so long as their *racial group* does not necessarily benefit from the furthering of those interests. *Class* issues become relevant to Negro workers when, as members of the organized working class, *they* benefit as their *class* benefits. A class-conscious perspective or radical political orientation can then be meaningful to them.

The same reasoning may apply to the impact of the revolution on unemployed Negroes. Their response to the revolution may have its source in the transparency of the connections between the causes and the consequences of their pre-revolutionary situation and that of unemployed white workers. The connection between the pre-revolutionary racial situation, the pre-revolutionary class structure and economic order, and the new structure of social relations formed since the revolution, may now be recognizable. To Negroes who were unemployed before the revolution, however, the connection between their situation and that of white unemployed workers was not transparent. It is, we may surmise, the revolution which has made the fact of their having been conditioned by the pre-revolutionary economic order, as well as by membership in the Negro racial group, "distinctly recognizable" to Negro workers who were unemployed before the revolution.

Particularly apt in this connection are the remarks of a Negro worker at the Nicaro nickel refinery in Oriente, when asked what he was most proud of in Cuba. Implicit in his words is the recognition of a connection between the fate of Negroes who were unemployed before the revolution and the pre-revolutionary economic order, yet with emphasis on their racial membership as the significant reason for their situation:

> I am most proud of what the revolution has done for the workers and the *campesinos*—and not only at work. For example, Negroes could not go to a beach or to a good hotel, or be *jefes* in industry, or work on the railroads or in public transportation in Santiago. This was because of their color! They could not go to school

or be in political office, or have a good position in the economy either. They would wander in the streets without bread. They went out to look for work and could not get it. But now, no—all of us—we are equal: the white, the Negro, the *Mestizo*...."

SUMMARY AND CONCLUSION

Generally, sociological studies of political behavior and of the determinants of "class consciousness" and political radicalism have been made within (relatively) stable social and political contexts. Consequently, it is difficult on the basis of the findings of such studies, to place much confidence in predictions of political behavior in times of social crisis and especially of revolutionary social change. Therefore, one important aspect of our own findings, from a theoretical point of view, is precisely and paradoxically the fact of how *expectable* they were on the basis of prior research and theory. From knowledge of a significant fact of their lives before the revolution, namely, their relative economic security, it was possible to predict more or less accurately the workers' differential responses to the ideological and social content of the revolution.

The workers who had experienced the most unemployment during pre-revolutionary years were found to be the ones who were most likely to support the revolution. Pre-revolutionary unemployment was also found to be a significant determinant of pre-revolutionary pro-Communist orientation. Change in employment status since the revolution also proved to be significant; it was found that the workers whose economic security had been enhanced since the revolution were more likely to support it than were the workers who had retained their previously high level of economic security. Negro workers were more likely than whites to support the revolution; this relationship was found to hold even with pre-revolutionary employment status and change in employment status since the revolution controlled. Among Negro and white workers, the original relationships between (a) pre-revolutionary employment status and attitude toward the revolution, and (b) change in employment status and attitude toward the revolution, also were found to hold. In contrast, it was found that while unemployed white workers were more likely to support the Communists before the revolution than their regularly employed counterparts, this was not true among Negroes. In the latter racial group, unemployed workers were no more likely before the revolution than the regularly employed to favor the Communists.

339

Recurrent unemployment and underemployment led to revolutionary politics among the Cuban workers in part because of their exposure to the possibilities of a better life during periods of regular employment and in part because the connection between their situation and the concrete economic order was so transparent. To the Negro unemployed before the revolution, who very likely saw their racial membership as the prime cause of their situation, a class-conscious or pro-Communist political orientation likely appeared to be meaningless. The revolution apparently made distinctly recognizable the connection between their fate and that of white members of the working class, and the pre-revolutionary economic order. Thus, the combination of their racial membership and of their pre-revolutionary unemployment now reinforced each other, making them more likely than the white pre-revolutionary unemployed to support the revolution.